Environmental Protection and the Law of War

To Caroline

Environmental Protection and the Law of War:

A 'Fifth Geneva' Convention on the Protection of the Environment in Time of Armed Conflict

Glen Plant

244458

Belhaven Press
London and New York

First published in Great Britain in 1992 by
Belhaven Press (a division of Pinter Publishers Limited)
25 Floral Street, London WC2E 9DS

British Library Cataloguing in Publication Data

A CIP catalogue record for this book is available from the
British Library

ISBN 1 85293 234 1

For enquiries in North America please contact
PO Box 197, Irvington, NY 10533

Library of Congress Cataloging in Publication Data

Environmental Protection and the Law of War/edited by Glen Plant.
   p. cm.
   Includes bibliographical references (pp. 267–8) and index.
   ISBN 1–85293–234–1
   1. War (International law) – Environmental aspects.
2. Environmental law, International. 3. Persian Gulf War, 1991–2.
Environmental aspects. I. Plant, Glen, 1957– .
  JX5011.P76 1992
341.6′3–dc20

91–35125
CIP

Typeset by Mayhew Typesetting, Rhayader, Powys
Printed and bound in Great Britain by Biddles Ltd of Guildford and Kings Lynn

Contents

Part III: The Aftermath and Prospects for the Future

Appendices of Documents and of Written Responses

Table of Cases Cited

Corfu Channel Case, (United Kingdom v. Albania) (1949) ICJ Reps. 4.

The Hostages Trial of Wilhelm List and Others, US Military Tribunal, Nuremberg, Judgement No. 47, 8 July 1947–19 February 1948, US Government Printing Office, 11 Trials of War Criminals before the Nuremberg Military Tribunals under International Law, No. 10 (1947) at 1253.

Island of Palmas Arbitration, (1928) RIAA ii, 829; 22 AJIL (1928), 867, award of Max Huber.

Lac Lanoux Arbitration, RIAA xii, (1957), 281.

Case concerning Military and Paramilitary Activities in and against Nicaragua (Nicaragua v. United States of America), ICJ Reps. 1986, p. 14.

Nuclear Tests Cases, (Australia v. France; New Zealand v. France) (1973) ICJ Reps. 99 and (1974), ICJ Reps. 253.

Trail Smelter Arbitration, award dated 11 March 1940: 33 AJIL (1941) 182: 35 AJIL (1943), 684.

UN War Crimes Commission Case No. 7150 ('Polish Foresters') (UNWCC, 1948, at 496).

Table of Treaties

Notes on Contributors

The Organizing Committee of the London Conference was comprised as follows:

Michael Clarke (Centre for Defence Studies) is Executive Director of the Centre for Defence Studies, King's College, London. Previously he was Lecturer in International Politics at the University of Newcastle-upon-Tyne. He has also held posts as Lecturer and Researcher at the University of Manchester and the University College of Wales, Aberystwyth. He has been a Guest Fellow at the Brookings Institute and an Associate Fellow at the Royal Institute of International Affairs. He writes on international affairs, in particular on British foreign and defence policy, on NATO strategy and Western defence and on policy-making.

Dr Gerd Leipold (Greenpeace International) (also a round tabler) studied physics and physical oceanography at the University of Munich, the Max Planck Institute for Meteorology in Hamburg and the Scripps Institution for Oceanography, La Jolla, California. He worked on numerical and theoretical ocean modelling and climate research at the Max Planck Institute for Meteorology in Hamburg. He joined Greenpeace in Germany as a volunteer in 1981, becoming a full-time member of staff in 1983. He has protested against nuclear-weapons testing with a balloon flight over the Berlin wall in 1983 and a ship-based protest in Moruroa, French Polynesia, and has participated in and organized many other direct actions. As Trustee of Greenpeace Germany he represented that organization internationally from 1983 to 1990 and was Executive Director of Greenpeace Germany from 1983 to 1987. He is now a member of the Board of Greenpeace Germany. Since its inception in 1987, he has internationally coordinated the Nuclear Free Seas Campaign of Greenpeace, one of the biggest worldwide campaigns that Greenpeace is conducting. In the wake of the Gulf War he initiated a Greenpeace campaign for a Geneva Convention for the Environment.

Dr Glen Plant (London School of Economics) (Rapporteur) is Director of the LSE Centre for Environmental Law and Policy, a Lecturer at the LSE and a practising barrister. He holds degrees from Oxford and London Universities and the Fletcher School of Law and Diplomacy as well as the Hague Academy Diploma in International Law. He has previously held Lectureships in Law at London University, King's College and Durham University, has taught at the Fletcher School and served as a Legal Adviser at the UN (1984–5) and the Foreign and Commonwealth Office (1986–9).

The following round tablers participated in the London Conference around which the book centres:

Sir Crispin Tickell, KCMG, GCVO (Chairman, A.M.) is Warden of Green College, Oxford; President of the Royal Geographical Society; and Chairman of the Climate Institute of Washington, DC. He also holds other posts. Sir Crispin was formerly a member of the United Kingdom Diplomatic Service. He served *inter alia* as Chef de Cabinet to the President of the European Commission (1977–80), Ambassador to Mexico (1981–3), Permanent Secretary of the Overseas Development Administration (1984–7) and British Permanent Representative to the United Nations (1987–90). He is the author of *Climatic Change in World Affairs* (1977 and 1986) and has written and spoken widely on environmental matters.

Professor Rosalyn Higgins, QC, (Chairman, P.M.) has been Professor of International Law at the London School of Economics since 1981. Having graduated from Cambridge University and Yale Law School, she served an internship at the UN Office of Legal Affairs before becoming a Staff Specialist on International Law at the Royal Institute of International Affairs (1963–74). She then served as a Visiting Fellow at the LSE (1974–8) and was Professor of International Law at the University of Kent (1978–81). She became a Member of the UN Committee on Human Rights in 1985 and a Bencher of the Inner Temple in 1989. She also presented the General Course of Lectures at the Hague Academy of International Law in 1991.

Dr Jeremy Leggett (Speaker) was Greenpeace UK's Scientific Director in 1989 and 1990 and is now Director of Science in Greenpeace International's Atmosphere and Energy Campaign. He is author-editor of *Global Warming: the Greenpeace Report* (Oxford University Press, 1990) and was the first scientist to leave a University faculty to join Greenpeace. After obtaining a PhD from Oxford in 1978, he spent eleven years lecturing in earth sciences at the Imperial College of Science, Technology and Medicine, where he also served on the coordinating committee of the Centre for Remote Sensing. He was appointed a Reader of the University of London in 1987. He was Director of the Verification Technology Information Centre, researching the applications of science in verifying arms-control treaties from 1985 to 1989. He is the author of over fifty scientific papers and many more articles and the winner of two major awards for his research – including in 1980 the President's Prize of the Geological Society.

Professor Richard Falk (Speaker) graduated from the University of Pennsylvania and Yale and Harvard Law Schools. Following upon academic posts at Ohio State University and Harvard Law School, he became an Associate and, since 1965, a full Professor of International Law and Practice at Princeton University. He was Visiting Olof Palme Professor in Sweden, attached to Stockholm University, during the 1990–1 academic year. He has been an active member of several professional organizations, including the American Society of International Law, of which he was Vice President in 1969–71 and 1974–5, and has served on the Editorial Board of the American Journal of International Law since 1961. He has actively participated in many independent commissions and campaigns on international issues, including Panels of Jurors of the Permanent Peoples Tribunal. He has given expert testimony in a number of internationally significant cases and to a number of legislative committees on international legal issues. A prolific writer, he is sole or co-author or editor of some 35 books and many articles, some of which are cited in this book.

Ambassador Dr Helmut Türk (Speaker) having graduated from the University of Vienna and the College of Europe in Bruges, joined the Austrian Federal Ministry for Foreign Affairs. He has served in Hong Kong and Bonn as well as the International Law Department of the Ministry, of which he has been the Head since 1982, with the rank of Ambassador since 1984. Since March 1991 he has been Deputy Secretary-General for Foreign Affairs. He has served on or headed many Austrian delegations to international conferences, including the Third UN Conference on the Law of the Sea, several CSCE meetings and several negotiations on legal measures against terrorism, including the 1988 IMO Convention on the Suppression of Unlawful Acts against the Safety of Maritime Navigation, of which Austria was a co-sponsor. In 1988 he became a Member of the Permanent Court of Arbitration and in 1989 acted as Chairman of the Sixth (Legal) Committee of the UN.

Professor Adam Roberts, FBA (Speaker) has been Montague Burton Professor in International Relations at Oxford University and Fellow of Balliol College, Oxford, since 1986. From 1968 to 1981 he was Lecturer in International Relations at the London School of Economics. From 1981 to 1986 he was Alastair Buchan Reader in International Relations and Fellow of St Antony's College, Oxford. He has been a Member of the Council of the Royal Institute of International Affairs since 1985. His many publications include *Documents on the Laws of War*, 2nd edn., Oxford University Press, 1989.

Awn Al-Khasawneh (Special-Rapporteur) is Legal Adviser to Crown Prince Hassan of Jordan and a Member of the International Law Commission.

Professor Dr Michael Bothe (Special-Rapporteur) is Professor of International Law at the J. W. Goethe University, Frankfurt. He has degrees from the Universities of Hamburg, Geneva and Heidelberg. After an initial position with the Max Planck Institute for Foreign Public Law and International Law, he has held various university positions in Heidelberg, Hanover and Frankfurt. He served on the German delegation to the diplomatic Conference on Humanitarian Law which resulted in the adoption of the 1977 Additional Protocols to the Geneva Conventions, and wrote, together with Solf and Partsch, a leading Commentary on the Protocols. He is at present Executive Secretary of the German Association of International Law.

Ambassador Philippe Kirsch, QC, (Special-Rapporteur) has been Deputy Permanent Representative of Canada to the United Nations since 1988. During Canada's term on the Security Council in 1989–90, he was Deputy Representative to the Security Council, Vice-Chairman of the Security Council Committee on Sanctions against Iraq and Chairman of its subcommittee on states confronted with special economic problems as a result of sanctions. Ambassador Kirsch is also Chairman of the Working Group of the UN Special Committee on Peacekeeping Operations. He joined the Canadian Department of External Affairs in 1972 and has had postings to Lima (1973–5) and to the Canadian Mission to the United Nations (1977–81), in addition to various assignments in Ottawa. He has been a member of the Quebec Bar since 1970, obtained a Master's degree at the University of Montreal in 1972 and was appointed Queen's Counsel in 1988. Among other positions at External Affairs he was Director of the Legal Operations Division (1983–8) and Ambassador and Agent for Canada in an international arbitration on fisheries. He has represented Canada in many UN legal organs and conferences, including the Sixth (Legal) Committee of the UN General Assembly, of which he was elected Chairman in 1982. In 1988 he was President of the ICAO Conference for the Suppression of Unlawful Acts of Violence at Airports, and Chairman of the Committee of the Whole of the IMO Conference on the Suppression of Unlawful Acts against the Safety of Maritime Navigation.

Anthony Brenton studied at Queens' College, Cambridge before joining the Foreign and Commonwealth Office (FCO) in 1975. After an initial period of Arabic language training, he served in the following places until 1986: HM Embassy, Cairo (1978–81); European Community Department, FCO (1981–5); and UK Permanent Representation in Brussels (1985–6). Between 1986 and 1988 he was on loan to the European Commission in Brussels as Deputy Chef de Cabinet to Commissioner Clinton Davies. He then returned to head successively the United Nations Department of the FCO and Environment, Science and Energy Department of the FCO.

Professor Luigi Ferrari Bravo has been Head of the Legal Service of the Italian Ministry of Foreign Affairs since 1985. He graduated from the University of Naples and has held various academic posts there and at other university institutions in Naples, Bari and Rome since 1956. He has been Professor of Public International Law at the University of Rome since 1982. His services for the Italian Government have included acting as Legal Adviser to its Missions to the UN in New York (1981–4) and Geneva (1984–5) and as Agent before the European Court of Justice, European Court of Human Rights and International Court of Justice. He served on the Italian delegation to the Diplomatic Conference on Humanitarian Law between 1975 and 1977. In 1988 he was President of the IMO Conference on the Prevention of Unlawful Acts against the Safety of Maritime Navigation and in 1990 Secretary-General of the Siena Forum on the International Law of the Environment.

Professor Lucius Caflisch, received his Licence en Droit (1958) and Doctorate of Law (1968) from the Faculty of Law, University of Geneva and an MA from Columbia University (1962). Called to the Geneva bar in 1963, he became Professor of International Law at the Graduate Institute of International Studies, Geneva, in 1972 and later Director of that Institute (1984–90). He acts as Registrar of several international tribunals and was Counsel to the Government of Senegal in the arbitration relating to the *Determination of the Maritime Boundary: Senegal/Guinea-Bissau.* He became first an Associate Member (1979) and later a Member (1985) of the Institute of International Law and has been a Member of the Permanent Court of Arbitration since 1990. He is also Legal Adviser to the Swiss Department of Foreign Affairs.

John Edmonds CMG, CVO, served in the Royal Navy from 1939 to 1959. He was on the staff of the NATO Defence College in Paris from 1953 to 1955 and served as Commander on the staff of the Chief of Defence Staff, Ministry of Defence from 1958 to 1959. He joined the FCO in 1959 and served in London (twice), Tokyo, Ankara and Paris before becoming Head of the Arms Control and Disarmament Department (1974–7). He then served as British Ambassador to the Comprehensive Test Ban Negotiations in Geneva from 1978 to 1981. Since retiring in 1981, he has been a Visiting Fellow at Reading University and a member of the Council for Arms Control, of which he is currently Chairman. He was Chairman of the SDP-Liberal Alliance Joint Commission on Defence and Disarmament from 1984 to 1986.

Evgeny Prokhorov is a Head of Division in the Department of International Law, Ministry of Foreign Affairs of the USSR. He graduated from Moscow State Institute of International Relations (International Law Department) and joined the Soviet Diplomatic Service in 1975. He has worked at the Soviet diplomatic and consular missions in India (1975–7) and Nepal (1981–6) and in the Soviet Foreign Ministry in the Departments of South Asia (1977–81) and International Law (since 1988). From 1986 to 1988 he attended the Soviet Diplomatic Academy, Moscow. In his current post he deals with the laws and customs of war, humanitarian law and settlement of armed conflicts.

Alberto Szekely is a Mexican Attorney. Formerly Legal Adviser to the Mexican Ministry of Foreign Affairs, he now serves as a Legal Consultant to the Mexican Government.

Nicholas Rostow is Special Adviser to President Bush and Legal Adviser to the US National Security Council.

Professor Lawrence Freedman is Professor and Head of the Department of War Studies at King's College at the University of London. He holds degrees from the Universities of Manchester, York and Oxford. Formerly, he held research positions at Nuffield College, Oxford and at the International Institute for Strategic Studies before becoming Head of Policy

Studies at the Royal Institute of International Affairs. He was appointed to the Chair of War Studies in April 1982. In 1990 he also became Honorary Director of the University of London's Centre for Defence Studies.

Professor Harvey M. Sapolsky has been Professor of Political Science at Massachusetts Institute of Technology since 1977, having joined MIT in 1966 with degrees from Boston and Harvard Universities. He served as Chairman of the Faculty between 1981 and 1983. He has served on a number of Expert Panels and Commissions.

Christopher Greenwood is a Fellow, Tutor and former Dean of Magdalene College, Cambridge and a Lecturer in the Faculty of Law, University of Cambridge. He was educated at Wellingborough School and Magdalene College, Cambridge, where he obtained degrees in Law and International Law. He is currently teaching International Law, including a course on the Law of Armed Conflict and the Use of Force, at Cambridge. A practising barrister since 1985, he has appeared in a number of cases involving international law. He is co-editor of *The Kuwait Crisis: Basic Documents* (Grotius, 1991) and Joint Editor of the *International Law Reports*.

Françoise Hampson is Senior Lecturer in Law in the Department of Law and the Human Rights Centre at the University of Essex. She has: served as a 'stagiaire' with the European Commission of Human Rights and the International Committee of the Red Cross (ICRC); held a NATO Research Fellowship; been awarded a bursary to study certain aspects of the Israeli occupation of the West Bank territories; and held a British Academy Research Award and Nuffield Foundation Award for a project on humanitarian law. She has lectured on behalf of the ICRC at the Warsaw summer school and is on the British Red Cross Panel of Instruction. She has lectured at and taken part in courses on the law of war for US Marines and Canadian officers.

Judge Stephen Schwebel is a Judge of the International Court of Justice (ICJ), being first elected in 1981. He was educated at Harvard College, the University of Cambridge and Yale Law School. After an initial period in private practice, he taught at Harvard for two years before serving as an Assistant Legal Adviser and later Special Assistant to the Assistant Secretary of State for International Organization Affairs between 1961 and 1967. He subsequently became Consultant, then Counsellor on International Law and later Deputy Legal Adviser at the Department of State (1967–81). He served as a Representative of the USA in various UN Committees and as Agent in various ICJ cases. Between 1977 and 1981 he combined this service with Membership of the International Law Commission. At the same time, he was a Professor of International Law at Johns Hopkins University. He has also served as an Arbitrator in a number of cases and is a Member of the Institute of International Law.

Christopher Pinto is a Sri Lankan lawyer and Secretary-General of the Iran-US Claims Tribunal. He has a strong personal interest in dispute settlement and international environmental law.

Dr Hans-Peter Gasser is Legal Adviser to the Directorate of the International Committee of the Red Cross (ICRC).

Roy Lee is a Principal Legal Officer in the Office of the UN Legal Counsel, New York.

Dr Jíri Toman is Director of the Institut Henri Dunant, the research body of the Red Cross in Geneva. He is co-author of Schindler and Toman, *The Laws of Armed Conflict.*

Dr Abdul Rahman Al-Awadhi was the Kuwaiti Minister of State for Cabinet Affairs before the Iraqi invasion and is now Executive Secretary of the Regional Organization for the Protection of the Marine Environment (ROPME), Kuwait/Bahrain.

Dr Jozef Goldblat has university degrees in international relations, law, economics and linguistics. He has been involved in disarmament negotiations in Geneva and New York in different capacities, including service for the United Nations, as well as in international commissions verifying compliance with armistice agreements. In 1980 he assisted the UN Secretary-General to prepare a report on a comprehensive nuclear test ban. In 1984 he received the Pomerance Award in recognition of his scholarship in the field of disarmament and arms control. From 1969 to 1988 he directed the arms control and disarmament programme of studies at the Stockholm International Peace Research Institute (SIPRI). Since 1989 he has been a Senior Research Fellow of the Programme for Strategic and International Security Studies at the Graduate Institute of International Studies in Geneva. He is a Board Member of the Geneva International Peace Research Institute, as well as a member of the Core Group of the International Programme for Promoting Nuclear Non-Proliferation. He also acts as the Research Representative of the Oslo International Peace Research Institute and as a Consultant to UNIDIR.

William M. Arkin is a military analyst and Director of Military Research and Director of the Nuclear Information Unit of Greenpeace International. After service with the US Army and graduating from the University of Maryland and Georgetown University, he served as a Senior Staff Analyst at the Centre for Defence Information in Washington DC from 1979 to 1981. He then joined the Institute for Policy Studies as a Fellow and Director of its National Security Programme and Nuclear Weapons Research Project. He has also served as a consultant to the Natural Resources Defence Council, Washington DC, *Stern* Magazine and as a contributing editor to the *Bulletin of Atomic Scientists.*

Michael A. Meyer is Head of Legal and Committee Services at the British Red Cross. He is a graduate of Yale University and has degrees in international law and international relations from the University of Cambridge. He is an English barrister and has written articles on humanitarian matters related to armed conflict and disaster relief.

Raul Sohr is a member of the South American Peace Commission and an expert on internal armed conflict in Latin America.

Frank Barnaby formerly worked at the Stockholm International Peace Research Institute. He writes extensively on issues of international peace and security and is a well known expert in the field.

Matti Wuori has law degrees from the University of Helsinki. He is a barrister practising in Helsinki and also a university teacher, member of and adviser to various governmental, inter-governmental and non-governmental bodies and organizations on human rights and environmental affairs. A former Ombudsman and arbitrator, he is President of the Human Rights Committee of the Finnish Bar Association and a member of the Human Rights Committees of the International Bar Association and the Union Internationale des Avocats. He is Vice-President of the Finnish Section of the International Commission of Jurists.

Gerard Tanja served as a Lecturer in Law at the University of Leiden between 1982 and 1985 and as a Senior Lecturer between 1985 and 1990, before becoming an Assistant Legal Adviser at the Netherlands Ministry of Foreign Affairs.

Acknowledgements

I should like to acknowledge the assistance of all of those who helped in the arrangements for the London Conference around which this book centres and, in particular, besides the other members of the Organizing Committee, Gerd Leipold and Mike Clarke and their support staff, Professor Rosalyn Higgins, QC, of the LSE, Anthony Hallgarten, QC, my Head of Chambers at 3, Essex Court, Sir Arthur Watts, QC, Legal Adviser to the Foreign and Commonwealth Office and Lena Ag of Greenpeace Sweden. Thanks also go to Michael Meyer and the British Red Cross, who helped in various ways, including through the donation of copies of the Additional Protocols to the Geneva Conventions.

I should also like to thank all of those who attended the conference and their organizations or governments for either releasing them or sending them. Special thanks should be extended to the governments of Austria, Italy and Sweden for financing respectively the participation of Ambassador Türk, Professor Ferrari Bravo and Kaj Mannheimer and to the ICRC and the Institut Henri Dunant for doing the same for Hans-Peter Gasser, Antoine Bouvier and Jirí Toman. The cooperation of the UN, ICRC and IAEA is also warmly acknowledged in relation to the reproduction of materials in Appendix 2. Thanks also go to Commissioner Ripa di Meana.

I wish to acknowledge the helpful written responses and suggestions made by several participants following the conference, in particular Alfred Rubin, Françoise Hampson, Michael Meyer and David Tolbert.

Finally, I wish to thank Susan Hunt and Colleen Etheridge for their secretarial and other assistance in the preparation of this book, Lynne Jurgielewicz and Henry Krupa for their research assistance, Neil Gregory and Michael Oliver of LSE Research and Consultancies for managing the budget, travel and accommodation, the LSE and Greenpeace International Press Offices, and my fiancée, Caroline Tonkin, for her patience and support.

Glen Plant

Preface

This book seeks to introduce the reader to the international law relevant to environmental protection in time of armed conflict and to the short-term political choices facing the international community, in the wake of the recent Gulf conflict, concerning the development and effective implementation of that law. Accordingly, it is not a comprehensive analysis of the law nor an attempt to deal thoroughly with possible long-term political developments in the field. In particular, it is written against a very tight deadline in an effort to ensure that the book appears in time to aid the policy debates at the United Nations General Assembly in the autumn of 1991 and at the XXVIth International Conference of the Red Cross and Red Crescent to be held in Budapest in November and December 1991, which will have a tremendous impact upon short-term political responses.

It employs as its main vehicle the London Round Table Conference on 'A "Fifth Geneva" Convention on the Protection of the Environment in Time of Armed Conflict' of 3 June 1991, organized by the London School of Economics, Greenpeace and the Centre for Defence Studies, although a description is also given of the Ottawa Conference on the Use of the Environment as a Tool of Conventional Warfare of 10–12 July 1991 and subsequent developments.

A thorough analysis of the main legal issues and of long-term political choices will be made in a separate project, but it does not follow that this work is entirely descriptive. It aims to set before the reader the initial considered analyses of many of the greatest experts in the relevant fields, who were gathered at the London Conference, and to present the main options for change.

Glen Plant
London School of Economics
25 September 1991

Part I
The Issues

1 Introduction

Glen Plant

Environmental destruction in the Gulf War

On 21 January 1991, a few days after the launch of the Coalition air campaign against Iraq, the US military in Kuwait accused the Iraqis in occupation of Kuwait of opening valves at the Sea Island (Mina al-Ahamadi) oil terminal near Kuwait City and of pumping large quantities of crude oil into the Gulf. The slick moved southward and began to accumulate on the north coast of Saudi Arabia; only the precision bombing of the manifolds at the terminal by US bombers stemmed the flow of oil.[1] On 31 January it was reported that Iraq had begun pumping oil into the Gulf from its Mina al-Bakr terminal to the north-east of the Kuwaiti island of Bubiya, thus creating a second major slick.[2] Coalition aircraft also precision bombed this. A number of smaller slicks in the Gulf appear also to have been caused by damage to tankers and oil-storage facilities.

Iraqi soldiers set fire to many well-heads in occupied Kuwait before the Coalition land offensive was launched, and continued to do so during the short land conflict.[3] Over 700 were burned. Many other well-heads were damaged by explosive charges without actually being set alight and began to spill oil over the desert. In addition, the occupying Iraqi forces destroyed or severely damaged all Kuwait's oil refineries, oil gathering stations and power and water desalination plants, as well as other installations.[4]

Coalition bombing and missile attacks resulted in damage to a large number of facilities in Iraq, including nuclear and chemical installations and at least one installation claimed by the Coalition to be a biological weapons production plant (and by Iraq to be a baby-food factory).

---

1 John Salter, 'Environmental Legal Issues Arising from the Gulf Conflict' (1990) 10 OGLTR 348; Paul Fauteux, 'L'utilisation de l'environnement comme instrument de guerre au Koweït occupé', to be published in *Les cahiers du Centre de Droit International de Nanterre*, at pp. 3–4.
2 Ibid.
3 Salter, ibid.; Fauteux, ibid. at pp. 5–6.
4 Letter dated 12 July 1991 from the Chargé d'affaires a.i. of the Permanent Kuwaiti Mission to the United Nations addressed to the Secretary-General, 15 July 1991; UN Doc. A/45/1035, S/22787, at 2, reproduced in Appendix 8. In addition a number of oil tankers moored off Kuwait were damaged during the conflict. As late as 60 days after the end of the conflict, Jim Guthrie of Gulf Resources Limited, Calgary, reported to the Ottawa Conference on the Use of the Environment as a Tool of Conventional Warfare (*infra* p. 4) that three terminals and six tankers were still leaking oil into the Gulf.

I do not attempt to estimate the environmental impact of this war. I will not speculate upon the many factors involved: the scale and long-term effects of the marine pollution caused by the oil slicks; the air, surface and ground-water pollution and the contribution to global warming caused by the destruction of the well-heads, as well as the possibility of its disrupting the pattern of the seasonal Asian monsoons; the environmental degradation in Iraq caused by the Coalition air campaign; the disruption of the fragile land surface and desert ecology of large areas of northern Saudi Arabia, Kuwait and southern Iraq resulting from the sheer physical presence and movements of large armies; and the effects of those armies' consumption of water and other resources and their production of wastes. This has been the subject of much discussion and speculation elsewhere,[5] and I refer the reader to Jeremy Leggett's analysis in Chapter 4 for a fuller account.

Significant international meetings in 1991 on environmental protection and the law of war

Suffice it to say for the present that Iraq's acts in particular caused a worldwide sense of outrage and have led to governments and others reconsidering the adequacy of existing international law to protect the environment in times of armed conflict. This book is intended to contribute to the resulting debate.

To date there have been two particularly significant international meetings where the issues have been debated: the *London Conference on 'A "Fifth Geneva" Convention on the Protection of the Environment in Time of Armed Conflict'* of 3rd June 1991, which was organized by Dr Gerd Leipold of Greenpeace, Michael Clarke of the University of London's Centre for Defence Studies (CDS) and myself; and the *Ottawa Conference on 'The Use of the Environment as a Tool of Conventional Warfare'* of 10–12th July 1991, which was cosponsored by the Canadian Ministry of External Affairs and Trade and the United Nations (UN).[6]

---

5 For example, Salter, op. cit., *supra* n. 1, at pp. 348–50; Philip Elmer-Dewitt, 'A Man-Made Hell on Earth', *Time*, 18 March 1991, pp. 22–3; John Horgan, 'Up in Flames', *Scientific American*, May 1991, pp. 17, 20, 24; Neville Brown, 'The Blazing Oil Wells of Kuwait', *The World Today*, June 1991, p. 93; V. Mallet, 'Disaster Leaves Experts Guessing', *Financial Times*, 8 July 1991, p. XX; and the *Guardian*, Environment Page, 2 August 1991.

6 These meetings were significant in that they brought together in each instance experts from over 40 different countries, including government and other high-level experts. This is not to say that this subject, including the possibility of a new Geneva-style convention to protect the environment in wartime, was not discussed in inter-governmental fora before and since the London Conference of 3rd June. It appears to have been discussed to varying degrees in NATO, UN and OECD circles (for the latter see OECD, *Declaration of Environment Ministers on the Ecological Situation in the Gulf*, Communiqué SG/PRESS(91) 8, 30 January 1991). It has also been discussed within the European Communities in the context of a Dutch initiative in the context of European Political Cooperation in July 1991, and Commissioner Ripa di Meana first went on record as supporting such a convention in March 1991 following a meeting of governmental experts of OECD countries: see, for example, the *Guardian*, Environment Page, 22 March 1991. The Netherlands has,

Part II of this book concerns the London Conference and reproduces, with slight editing and editorial comment from myself and the addition of references, the verbatim record of it, with the one exception of Jeremy Leggett's paper (chapter 4), which is a rewritten version. Part III is made up of two chapters. Chapter 11 contains my initial reactions, as Rapporteur to the London Conference, to the Conference debate and to additional written responses from various participants, as well as a description of the Ottawa Conference. The Ottawa Conference was the first proper intergovernmental initiative in the field and was thus important in helping not

---

moreover, set up a task force of government and academic experts to examine the political and legal parameters of the issue. In addition, the German and Soviet Environment Ministers concluded an agreement at the beginning of June 1991 supporting the introduction of the topic of a fifth Geneva convention into the debates of the UN Conference on Environment and Development (UNCED), to be held in Rio di Janeiro in June 1992. This agreement is not reproduced in this book, as it is in Russian and German and in any event very brief in relevant part, but the letter in English of Soviet Environment Minister Vorontsov welcoming the London Conference is reproduced in Appendix 4 and the statement of Dr Ansgar Vogel of the German Environment Ministry describing it and its subsequent follow-up is reproduced in Appendix 8. Also in May, the Governing Council of the UN Environment Programme adopted a decision (UNEP/GC.16/L.53; Part B, 'Environmental Effects of Warfare', and see Türk, at p. 102, on the matter), which is reproduced in Appendix 3 and discussed further in chapter 12. Finally, the question of a possible new convention was discussed at the regional meeting of Latin American Red Cross Societies in Costa Rica in late July 1991 and a copy of the Executive Summary of the London Conference Report was discussed at the meeting of Council of Europe Foreign Office Legal Advisers in August 1991.

There has also been discussion at a number of academic conferences, including: the 'Gulf Conflict' Conference at the University of Dundee Centre for Petroleum and Mineral Law Studies, Dundee, 14 March 1991; a special panel of the annual meeting of the American Society of International Law (ASIL), Washington DC, 18 April 1991, *The Environment and the Gulf War*; the Sixth Biennial Conference of the International Bar Association (IBA), Montreal, 2–5 June 1991; the 'Colloque du Centre de Droit International de Nanterre sur les Aspects Juridiques de la Crise et de la "Guerre" de Golfe', Paris, 8 June 1991; and the San Remo Institute of International Humanitarian Law Expert Meeting on Naval Warfare meetings in September 1991. The 1992 Jessup Moot Court Competition of ASIL will involve a case based upon the Gulf War, which is likely to touch upon the environmental aspects.

Several excellent legal analyses of the environmental aspects of the Gulf War have emerged from these, including: John Salter's keynote speech at the IBA Conference and his article, 'Environmental Legal Issues Arising from the Gulf Conflict', loc. cit. *supra* n. 1; Paul Szasz, 'The Environment and the Gulf War: Overview of the Existing Law', to appear in 1991 ASIL Proceedings; and Paul Fauteux, 'L'utilisation de l'environnement comme instrument de guerre au Koweït occupé', loc. cit. *supra* n. 1, (shorter English version, 'Environmental Law and the Gulf War', IUCN Bulletin, July 1991).

In addition, a report entitled 'The Protection of the Environment in Time of Armed Conflict', EC Doc. SJ/110/85, was prepared in 1985 by a group of professors, Michael Bothe, Antonio Cassese, Frits Kalshoven, Alexandre Kiss and Kenneth Simmonds. This group was convened at the initiative of Karl-Heinz Jarjes, a Member of the Commission of the European Communities, in view of the Iran-Iraq War then being fought, in order to study the problems of prevention of and compensation for damage caused to the environment by acts of war. This report is unpublished, but, although it represents the opinion of the group and not necessarily that of the Commission, it is reportedly available upon request from the Commission's Directorate-General for the Environment, DG XI.

only further to clarify the issues but also to assess the reactions of a cross-section of Government experts and so the immediate prospects for future action at the international level. These prospects are the main subject of the closing chapter, Chapter 12, which describes the early government initiatives which have followed the Ottawa Conference, most notably that of Jordan[7] (reproduced in Appendix 8 *infra*), and which attempts to draw some conclusions.

This introductory chapter will concentrate on the London Conference, which was a high-level round-table conference,[8] because the main aim of this book is to record the views given there on the need or otherwise for new law to protect the environment in wartime and, in particular, on the prospects for a new overarching instrument specifically dealing with environmental protection in wartime, and also on the steps that ought to be taken in the short term in the wake of the Gulf War to improve the implementation of or adherence to the *existing* relevant legal instruments. This Conference was the first 'testing of the waters' in this matter, and the book is intended to act as a guide to policy-makers and other interested persons in determining their short-term reactions by laying the results of that testing before them and suggesting how the matter might be taken forward in both the short and long term.

The book is not intended to be a thorough analysis of the relevant international law or of everything that might be included in a reform of the law. These are matters that I shall be pursuing in a separate, longer term project at the LSE[9] and also in cooperation, I hope and expect, with the other sponsoring organizations of the London Conference and possibly other institutions or Governments.

Aims of the London Conference and composition of the round table

Three very different organizations were deliberately involved in organizing the London Conference out of a desire to bring together as diverse a range of expertise and opinion on the subject as possible. In many senses it was a unique occasion. The intention was to feed academic, non-governmental organization and other non-governmental opinion into the equation before the normal inter-governmental review and decision-making processes were fully under way. All three members of the Organizing Committee were

---

7 Note verbale dated 5 July 1991 from the Chargé d'affaires a.i. of the Permanent Mission of Jordan to the United Nations addressed to the Secretary-General, 8 July 1991; UN Doc. A/46/141.

8 The reader is referred to pp. x–xvii for the names and brief biographical details of the round tablers and to Appendix I for the names of the invited guests and observers.

9 The intention is to conduct a 'Harvard Research in International Law'-type project within the LSE Centre for Environmental Law and Policy, which will involve a thorough analysis of the relevant international law, the necessity for a definition of 'environment' or a list of environmental elements needing protection in this context and perhaps the preparation of draft articles or principles and commentaries upon them. In this respect it is hoped that cooperation with the Dutch Task Force mentioned above in note 6 will be possible.

determined to capture the moment while events were fresh in peoples' minds. Greenpeace, as a campaigning organization, was clearly anxious both to publicize the issues and to influence the decision-making process in certain directions, in particular towards the negotiation of a comprehensive new convention dealing with the environment and the laws of war; its basic aims are set at the end of Jeremy Leggett's opening speech reproduced in Chapter 4.[10] They are also discussed to some extent in a Greenpeace case-study of the Gulf War, referred to in this book as 'On Impact',[11] which was not an official Conference document, but the publication of which was timed to coincide with the holding of the Conference. The LSE and CDS on the other hand were concerned with exposing the issues to the maximum degree of intellectual examination at the highest possible levels.

The Organizing Committee did not consider it possible to achieve agreement within such a diverse round table on a common statement of views, and the subsequent experience of the Ottawa Conference bore this out. Such a common statement proved to be impossible at that Conference, and the Chairman of the Conference, Barry MaWhinney,[12] produced instead a set of 'Chairman's Conclusions', which was limited to an attempt to describe the main points of view expressed there.

The Organizing Committee of the London Conference also felt it unnecessary and too great an imposition upon such busy men to ask the Special-Rapporteurs to submit written reports. This book, however, should be treated as the Rapporteur's full report on the Conference; an executive summary has also been made available.

The London Conference round table was deliberately comprised of three main categories of expert to ensure the maximum possible range of experience and opinion (governmental, inter- and non-governmental and academic), although, unless they stated otherwise, all round tablers participated in their private capacities. All statements reproduced in this book should thus be read as statements made in the speaker's private capacity, subject to the same proviso.

The round table was also intended to reflect a broad geographical distribution, although sadly no African invitee was able to be present. A broad spectrum of political opinion was also sought, although it was decided not to invite elected politicians as such.[13] The governmental category of round tabler was intended to include a contingent of British serving military laws of war experts, but sadly in the end none of those invited was able to attend, and several round tablers remarked on this

---

10 At pp. 76–77.
11 William Arkin, Damian Durrant and Marianne Cherni, *On Impact: Modern Warfare and the Environment – A Case Study of the Gulf War*, Greenpeace, London, 3 June 1991.
12 Legal Adviser to the Canadian Ministry of External Affairs.
13 The Soviet Environment Minister, Professor N. Vorontsov, was invited but was unable to be present. His letter of regret, which strongly supported the idea of a new Convention, is reproduced in Appendix 4. Dr Abdul Rahman Al-Awadhi, a former Kuwaiti Minister, also attended in his capacity as Executive Secretary of the Regional Organization for the Protection of the Marine Environment, Kuwait/Bahrain (ROPME).

omission.[14] It is intended, therefore, to organize a further conference, to coincide with the publication of this book, where the comments of military experts will be sought.

Finally, a balance was sought, as far as the lawyers on the round-table were concerned, between those generally associated with greater expertise on the laws of war and those likewise associated with the laws of peace, including international environmental law. The enforced last-minute absences of Lloyd Cutler[15] and Professor Kenneth Simmonds,[16] upset the balance perhaps in favour of the former, and in particular there was less discussion of the meaning of 'environment' in this context than the organizers had hoped. One of the invited guests, David Tolbert,[17] was, however, prevailed upon to present a written contribution on the latter question after the conference, which is reproduced in Appendix 6, together with similar comments by Michael Meyer of the British Red Cross, a round-tabler.

The Organizing Committee were also concerned that discussion should not be restricted to an analysis of the legal environmental aspects of the Gulf War alone among wars, still less to one of Iraqi actions in that war. The Conference announcement was thus in the following terms in relevant part:

> The recent conflict in the Gulf has highlighted the manner in which natural resources may be used as 'weapons' or instruments of revenge in war with long lasting and serious environmental consequences. Other recent conflicts have seen the mass destruction by defoliation,[18] burning and cratering of forests and agricultural land,[19] the breaching of large dams[20] and extensive bombing of industrial targets,[21] each of which has frequently resulted in serious environmental as well as human damage. Quite apart even from the obvious adverse environmental effects of the use of weapons of mass destruction, many conventional weapons, if used indiscriminately, and many unrecovered persistent devices, like certain varieties of mine, may cause unnecessary damage to the environment.[22]
>
> There are some provisions in existing international instruments which purport to protect the environment. These include provisions in Protocol I (to the Geneva

---

14 See *infra* Rostow at p. 123 and Hampson at p. 131.
15 Partner of Wilmer, Cutler and Pickering, Washington DC.
16 Of Queen Mary and Westfield College, London.
17 Of the Law Faculty, Hull University.
18 See *infra* Ripa di Meana at p. 65 and Leggett at pp. 68–69. See also Richard Falk, 'Environmental Warfare and Ecocide' 4, *Bulletin of Peace Proposals* (1973), 1 at pp. 6–8.
19 Ibid.
20 See, for example, Margareta Bergström, 'The Release of Dangerous Forces from Hydrological Facilities', in Arthur Westing (ed.) *Environmental Hazards of War*, Sage Publications, London, New Delhi (1990), pp. 3–8 and especially pp. 40–3.
21 See, for example, Allan Krass, 'The Release of Dangerous Forces from Nuclear Facilities' and Jiri Matousek, 'The Release in War of Dangerous Forces from Chemical Facilities', ibid., at pp. 10–37.
22 See generally Arthur H. Westing (ed.), *Explosive Remnants of War: Mitigating the Environmental Effects* (1985) Taylor and Francis, London and Philadelphia.

Conventions)[23] on the Protection of Victims of International Armed Conflict of 1977 ('Protocol I'),[24] the Convention on the Prohibition of Military or any other Hostile Use of Environmental Modification Techniques ('ENMOD') of 1977[25] and Protocol III to the so-called Inhumane Weapons Convention of 1980.[26] But these are open in varying degree to some or all of the following criticisms: that they set the threshold at which environmental destruction is prohibited too high; they do not, in general, tie those prohibitions to the protection of the environment *per se*, but to their ultimate impact upon human welfare; they permit broad exceptions and the making of reservations; and they are often not adhered to by significant numbers of states, including major military Powers.[27]

Governments are now examining the adequacy of the existing instruments, and it is time also for them to consider the adoption of a new instrument specifically protecting the hitherto largely forgotten victim of armed conflict, the environment, in the same way as the existing four Geneva Conventions and their Protocols protect human victims of armed conflict.

Furthermore, it is generally agreed that a State's deliberately causing large-scale damage to the human environment results in that State's responsibility under customary international law towards other States whose rights and interests are affected. Nevertheless, those States' claims are confined to the *human* losses suffered as a result of the destruction. They may not extend to compensation for damage to wildlife or to the environment in general.

There is, moreover, very little evidence that such acts under present law are to be branded as international crimes for which individuals might be held responsible, as, for example, 'grave breaches' of certain of the provisions of the Geneva Conventions are branded by those Conventions (footnotes and parentheses added).[28]

---

23 Convention (I) for the Amelioration of the Condition of the Wounded and Sick in Armed Forces in the Field; Convention (II) for the Amelioration of the Condition of the Wounded, Sick and Shipwrecked Members of Armed Forces at Sea; Convention (III) Relative to the Treatment of Prisoners of War; and Convention (IV) Relative to the Protection of Civilian Persons in Time of War: done at Geneva, 12 August 1949: *Final Record of the Diplomatic Conference of Geneva of 1949*, Vol. I, Federal Political Department, Berne, at pp. 195–341; 75 UNTS 5–417.

24 Protocol I Additional to the Geneva Conventions, 1977, done at Berne, 10 June 1977: Off. Rec. of the Diplomatic Conference on the Reaffirmation and Development of International Humanitarian Law applicable in Armed Conflicts, Geneva (1974–7); 16 International Legal Materials (ILM) (1977), 1391–449.

25 Done at Geneva, 18 May 1977: UNGA Resolution 31/72, 10 December 1976, Annex, Off. Rec. 31S., Suppl. no. 39 (A/31/39); 1108 UNTS 151.

26 Convention on the Prohibition or Restrictions on the Use of Certain Conventional Weapons Which May be Deemed to be Excessively Injurious or to Have Indiscriminate Effects, done at New York, 10 April 1981: Final Report of the Conference to the General Assembly, UN Doc. A/CONF.95/15, 27 October 1980, Annex I; UKTS Misc. 23(1981); Cmnd. 8370.

27 There were 84 Parties to Protocol I, 57 to ENMOD and 28 to the Inhumane Weapons Convention by the end of 1989. Of the Permanent Members of the Security Council, China had not yet ratified ENMOD, France Protocol I and ENMOD, the UK Protocol I and the Inhumane Weapons Convention, the USA Protocol I and the USSR the Inhumane Weapons Convention. Protocol I now has 105 Parties.

28 This was sent to invitees in an explanatory document and also formed the basis of two newspaper articles announcing the conference in the British press: Michael Binyon, *Plan to Save the Environment*, The Times, 14 March 1991, p. 10; and G. Plant, untitled article in the *Guardian*, 22 March 1991, Environment Page.

The Organizing Committee's invitation to round tablers, therefore, was to reconsider the adequacy of existing law and to consider the merits of a new Convention. Hence the title of the conference, *'A Fifth Geneva' Convention, etc.* The intention was not to prejudge the issue of whether a new Convention should be adopted or not, nor were the LSE and CDS, unlike Greenpeace, necessarily associating themselves with a call for such a Convention.

The Organizing Committee's original intention, moreover, extended to following the London Conference with a meeting of a smaller working group. This was to draft a Draft Convention for consideration by governments as an aid to determining their policies concerning the possibility of adopting a new Convention in advance of the key debates upon the issue likely to take place in the UN General Assembly in the autumn of 1991. In view of the Canadian announcement of the Ottawa Conference, however, and taking into account the views expressed at the London Conference, it was felt wiser to postpone judgement on the need for such follow-up action until the course of developments at the inter-governmental level became clearer.

Title of the London Conference

It is significant that the words 'Fifth Geneva' in the title of the London Conference were placed between inverted commas. This was to indicate that the final outcome of the discussions initiated there was not necessarily expected to be a new Geneva Convention as such. The title merely suggested the possibility of a new 'Geneva'-style Convention somewhat along the lines of the existing Geneva Conventions of 1949. It was never pretended that the negotiation of such an instrument would be other than time-consuming and difficult. Nevertheless, the title chosen appeared to be the most imaginative and public eye-catching way in which to raise the issues needing discussion.

The word 'Fifth' in the title of the Conference, moreover, was intended merely to suggest that a new instrument should bear some relation to and be at least as important as the existing four Geneva Conventions; in particular, the issues seemed to be too important to be dealt with by a mere protocol, like a protocol to the existing Geneva Conventions, quite apart from the technical difficulties involved in defining such a protocol's relationship with the existing two additional protocols (see *infra* p. 31). The organizers, however, did not intend to suggest that the existing Geneva Conventions (let alone the additional protocols) and states' adherence to them be disturbed in any way. Unfortunately, these messages implicit in the title of the Conference were not readily apparent to all of the round tablers; this is reflected in certain passages in their interventions, which appear in Chapters 7 to 9.

London Conference documentation and organization and plan of this book

In order to allow round tablers to concentrate their discussion upon a single document, I was appointed Rapporteur of the Conference and asked to prepare an 'Elements of a Convention' document (hereinafter 'Elements' document) to form the basis of the round table's discussion. This is reproduced in its original form in Chapter 2, and its introduction[29] contains additional explanation of the reasoning behind the convening of the Conference as well as of the document itself. It was divided into an introduction (with a summary) and five parts, each containing an element, itself divided into a number of sub-elements each with a commentary. These were organized as follows: Part 1, 'General Principles'; Part 2, 'Geneva Law'; Part 3, 'Hague Law'; Part 4, 'Execution of the Convention'; and Part 5, 'Institutions'. I intended merely to suggest elements that *might* be included in a new Convention and did not necessarily regard the elements I chose to be either necessary or sufficient. I attempted to draft a balanced document which proceeded as far as possible from the 'internal logic' of the idea of a new Convention rather than from any particular political stance, trying nevertheless to take into account what I saw to be the most important political realities by, for example, excluding nuclear weapons from its scope.

The round table discussion of the document was preceded by four opening speeches, which were intended to set the scene for the participants and are reproduced in Chapters 3 to 6. Carlo Ripa di Meana, the European Environment Commissioner, was invited to give the opening speech, because he was perhaps the most important public figure to date to have gone on record as supporting the call for a new Convention,[30] and because he represented the Commission of the European Communities, which is a forum from which an initiative of some sort might emerge and is in any event an organization with some weight in the international debate. Dr Jeremy Leggett of Greenpeace spoke next to explain the scientific aspects of the environmental impact of war, including the Gulf War and Greenpeace's views on the call for a new Convention. Professor Richard Falk of Princeton University followed with an analysis of the existing law and his views on its inadequacy, and finally Ambassador Helmut Türk added to Professor Falk's account with some practical observations, derived from his experience as the Legal Adviser to the Austrian Federal Foreign Ministry, upon the realities of negotiating such a treaty.

The round table discussion itself was divided into three sessions, each led by a Special-Rapporteur charged with introducing and summing up the debate upon a different part or parts of the 'Elements' document. It proceeded as follows: Awn Al-Khasawneh, the Jordanian Member of the International Law Commission (ILC), led discussion of Parts 1 and 4, which involved, *inter alia*, issues of state responsibility and international criminal liability which the ILC has recently been studying; Professor

---

29 *Infra*, pp. 37–42.
30 See *supra* n. 6.

Michael Bothe of Frankfurt University, an acknowledged expert on the law of war, as well as international environmental law, followed with Part 2 on 'Geneva' law; and Ambassador Philippe Kirsch, QC, Deputy Permanent Representative of the Permanent Canadian Mission to the UN, a distinguished international lawyer and diplomat with great experience of international institutions, concluded with Parts 3 and 5 on 'Hague' law and institutions. The edited verbatim record of each session is reproduced in respectively Chapters 7, 8 and 9.

The Conference was chaired in the morning by Sir Crispin Tickell, Warden of Green College, Oxford, who combined his well-known environmental expertise with several years' experience as the Permanent Representative of the United Kingdom (UK) to the UN. In the afternoon Professor Rosalyn Higgins, QC, of the LSE, whose expertise in the fields, *inter alia*, of international institutions and the use of force by states is well known, took the chair after Sir Crispin's departure.

The record of the Conference is the unchanged verbatim record,[31] except for the addition of footnoted references and some editorial corrections and comments, the latter added by myself where I think the 'Elements' Document contradicts or even invalidates the round tabler's point or the matter needs further explanation. The reader should be able to read Parts II and III of the book in the order in which they are set out, needing only to refer forward to Chapter 2 and backward to Appendix 2 to consult respectively the original version of the 'Elements' document and relevant treaty texts.

Unfortunately, because of lack of time, it was impossible to have many comments from the Conference floor, but invited guests and observers were invited to submit their written comments after the conference, and some of these are reproduced in Appendices 6 and 7, which can be read in isolation from the main text of this book.

I produced a revised version of the 'Elements' document, which took into account the discussion at the London Conference and which I submitted to the Ottawa Conference. This is reproduced in part in Appendix 5. A final revised version prepared after the Ottawa Conference is reproduced, with further explanation, at the end of Chapter 12.

Only one change to the 'Elements' document needs to be explained in this introduction, because it refers to comments made by several round tablers. In the original version the titles to Parts 2 and 3, 'Geneva Law' and 'Hague Law', like the title of the conference itself, were chosen, in preference to the drier terms, respectively 'Targetry' and 'Weaponry' now used in the revised versions, with a view to reaching the imagination and understanding of a wider audience. The suggestion was that a new convention would be building upon established categories of law rather than a venture into the unknown. Unfortunately, this involved the deliberate adoption of a

---

31 With the exception, already noted, of chapter 4.

simplistic distinction between the two which was not readily accepted by several of the round tablers.[32]

Existing law: conservation or reform?

The 'Elements' document does not include an exhaustive analysis of the existing relevant law in any version, but the original version proceeded from my considered opinion that the law was inadequate. It would be beyond the scope of this book, and specifically of this introduction, for me to try to give a thorough analysis of the existing law. Chapter 5, which contains some of Professor Falk's ideas on the subject is, nevertheless, a useful introduction to it and to the kinds of concerns that many lawyers have. On the other hand, Professor Falk's represents only one approach, and it *is* within the scope of this introduction for me to attempt to describe the range of opinion, both conservative and reformist, on this subject. In doing so, I shall of necessity refer the reader to the 'Elements' Document in Chapter 2, to Part II and to Appendix 2, and shall try to set the main themes of the round table in context, without ascribing any particular position to any of the round tablers. In addition, I shall seek, within the constraints of available space, to emphasize dimensions of the topic which could not be adequately explored in the time available or were, at most, merely implicit at the Conference. Finally, I shall endeavour to present some of the main arguments for and against each position within the spectrum of opinions.

I shall leave detailed discussion of the options for pursuing whatever changes come to be agreed to be necessary, if any, and the various fora in which they might be pursued to Chapter 12.

Fundamental distinctions

I begin with three caveats concerning fundamental distinctions that must be kept in mind. The first is that between the *ius ad bellum* and the *ius in bello*: that is between on the one hand the law concerning the rights of states to engage in armed conflict (essentially the inherent right of self-defence preserved by Article 51 and Security Council enforcement actions

---

32 For example, Prokhorov, at p. 141. Historically and theoretically the distinction between Hague and Geneva law has been complicated (see Yves Sandoz and Jean-Jacques Surbeck, *The Hague Conventions*, unpublished paper, dated September 1984, available from Michael Meyer, British Red Cross, 9 Grosvenor Crescent, London SW1), but in practical terms the only category of Hague Conventions of significance to modern jurists is that which lays down elementary rules for the conduct of war: ibid., at p. 2. Most of the Conventions in this category in fact refer to prohibitions on the use of certain weapons (although, it is true, others refer to matters such as treachery in warfare). It is for this reason that I felt justified in using the term 'Hague Law' as synonymous with 'Weaponry' and identified 'Geneva Law' with 'Targetry', in contrast with the more general distinction drawn between them, which emphasizes the more humanitarian objectives of Geneva, as compared with Hague, law: see *infra* Falk at p. 83.

under Chapter VII of the UN Charter) and on the other the law governing how wars are to be fought (in terms of avoiding unnecessary destruction and suffering and the like) once they have started. This book concerns only the latter, although it is noteworthy that some round tablers suggested that the two should not be entirely separated.[33]

Secondly, in examining the *ius in bello*, it is important to distinguish the legal relationship between on the one hand two or more belligerents and on the other between a belligerent and a neutral state, although it is admitted that this distinction is not always clear-cut in practice.[34] As between belligerents it is generally agreed that the law of war applies as *lex specialis* and that their normal peacetime legal relationship is suspended, with the exception of only a few norms which continue to operate exceptionally, such as certain human rights norms. One point of debate is to what extent do and should norms of (peacetime) international environmental law continue to be applicable in wartime. A second matter to bear in mind is the extent to which the rules of the law of war which are relevant to environmental protection differ according to whether the belligerent causing the environmental damage in question is doing so in occupied territory or on the field of battle.[35] A third matter is the extent to which the requirements of the law of war in relation to the environment differ as between attackers and defenders.[36]

The relationship between a belligerent and a neutral state, on the other hand, is governed by the law of neutrality, which preserves the normal

---

33 Greenpeace appear to contemplate the possibility that strong regulation of the way in which wars can be fought is likely to contribute to an increasing perception that war itself is not an instrument by which disputes can be legitimately settled: see generally the paper given by Sebia Hawkins of Greenpeace USA to the ASIL Panel on *The Environment and the Gulf War*, loc. cit., *supra* n. 6. At the London Conference Helmut Türk considered *ius ad bellum* scenarios to be relevant in the context of *ius in bello* regulation of environmental protection (*infra* p. 128, *sed contra* Higgins, at p. 128). Roy Lee suggested that they should not be kept separate: *infra* p. 126; *sed contra* Bothe, who strongly resists such a link: *infra* p. 125.

34 See, for example, Fritz Grob, *The Relativity of War and Peace*, New Haven, (1949), esp. chapter 1.

35 The traditional rules concerning wanton destruction of property, for example, appear to apply with particular force in the case of property in occupied territory: see Richard Falk, *Revitalizing International Law*, Ames: Iowa State University Press, (1989), at pp. 171–2.

36 The so-called 'scorched earth' rule seems to be more liberal to the defender than the attacker in certain circumstances. The earth-scorching acts of a German commander in northern Norway during the Second World War were held to be justified only because they were carried out in order to facilitate defence and withdrawal in face of advancing Allied forces and he had no other alternative: see the *Case of Wilhelm List and Others*, US Military Tribunal at Nuremberg, 8 War Crimes Reports (1949) 66 at pp. 66–9; see also the *High Command Trial (Wilhelm Leeb and Others)*, 12 ibid. (1949) at p. 93 and Openheim *International Law*, vol. II, 7th ed. (1952) at pp. 416–7. Article 54 of Protocol I now places severe restrictions upon recourse by States Party to such methods, but paragraph (5) adds an exception in favour of states defending their national territory from invasion where such methods are required by imperative military necessity (for text see Appendix 2). This exception, however, does not apply to defenders of occupied territory: see Frits Kalshoven, *Constraints on the Waging of War*, ICRC, Martinus Nijhoff, (1987), Geneva and Leiden, at pp. 95–6.

peacetime legal relationship with certain exceptions, such as the right of belligerent blockade.

Most of the round table discussion centred upon the relationship between belligerents. Nevertheless, it can be said with some confidence that many round tablers would readily agree with the content of the 'Elements' Document to the extent that it relates to the law of neutrality, such as the principle set out in Element 1.E.[37] concerning responsibility for transboundary damage to neutral states or the global commons, although they would not all agree that this needs to be restated in a new instrument.

Thirdly, most discussion at the London Conference centred upon the *ius in bello* in the context of *international* armed conflict and conflict *on land*, because the Gulf War was very fresh in the round tablers' minds and was widely perceived as a model to proceed from in trying to predict what would be needed in terms of legal provision for the next major international conflict. There was the danger of over-concentration upon the destruction of oil fields, marine pollution by oil escaping from land-based sources and desert ecologies, although it is far from certain that the next war will involve any of these or will be quite as land-based. The additional, and more important, point was strongly made by Raul Sohr[38] and Eduardo Marino,[39] moreover, that future armed conflict was frequently likely to take the form of low intensity or internal armed conflict rather than international armed conflict along the lines of the Gulf War. It followed in their view that more attention needed to be paid to such conflicts and to the adequacy, for example, of Protocol II to the Geneva Conventions, which is applicable to such conflicts where it is accepted by the warring parties. It cannot be said, however, in view of the shortness of time, that the Conference was able to address these issues adequately. The Organizing Committee of the London Conference, therefore, intend to explore the possibility of an additional conference upon the law concerning low-intensity and internal armed conflict during the 1992–3 academic year.

Spectrum of views: four camps

The holders of the spectrum of views on the state of the law applicable to deliberate and collateral damage to the environment in the context of international armed conflict can, in my opinion and on the basis of publications in the field as well as interventions in the London Conference (and the Ottawa), be roughly characterized into four hypothetical 'Camps' as follows: *Camp 1*, those who consider the existing law relevant to environmental protection in wartime to be an amalgamation of principles established in the customary international law of war and a number of codifying provisions to be found in the Regulations attached to the Hague

---

37 *Infra*, pp. 44–5.
38 At pp. 114–15.
39 At pp. 107–9.

Conventions of 1899 (II) and 1907 (IV)[40] and in the Geneva Conventions of
1949 and that this law reflects environmental concerns and is adequate to cover
the worst environmental excesses of any foreseeable war; *Camp 2*, those who
accept this but consider Protocol I to the 1949 Conventions also to represent
customary law, including among several relevant provisions two directly and
expressly referring to environmental protection, Articles 33(5) and 55, and that
this law, together with other relevant instruments such as the ENMOD and the
Inhumane Weapons Conventions (where they apply), is adequate to protect
the environment in wartime, needing no further elaboration; *Camp 3*, those
who consider the existing law of war, whatever it may be, to be inadequate or
at least in need of restatement and who contemplate various means for
improving the standards of, adherence to or implementation of that law,
whether by using existing instruments and mechanisms or by developing new
ones, such as a new Geneva-style Convention; this Camp generally inclines in
favour of ensuring that developments in the international environmental law
of peacetime are fully reflected in the law of war, but considers that the matter
should be tackled essentially within the framework of the law of war; and
Camp 4, which considers the distinction between wartime and peacetime acts
in this context to be so vague, irrelevant or misleading that, if any new
development is to take place, it should be concerned with environmental
destruction in all scenarios, whether wartime or peacetime.

It will be noticed that Camps 1 and 3 are concerned only with the law
of war and that Camp 4 wishes to deal with the issue of environmental
protection more broadly.

My designation of these four Camps is not intended to serve as a sound
method of introduction of the law in this field, but rather as background
and an aid to the understanding both of the debate in the round table and
of the sorts of choices that face decision-makers. The arguments for and
against each Camp's position are given in outline only, and the reader is
referred to the bibliography in Appendix 9 for more thorough analyses of
the law. I emphasize that the Camps are hypothetical and I avoid ascribing
positions to any named individual; it will be rare that any individual will
fit neatly into any one Camp, and references to their statements below
should not be taken to place the speaker in question in any particular
Camp. Nevertheless, I believe that all the positions expressed at the round
table can be fitted roughly into one or the other for the purpose of
illustrating the main choices to be made in this area of law. My own views
can be constructed from the discussion of Camp 3 below (in relation to
short-term options), from the first part of Chapter 11 and from Chapter 12
(including the final versions of the 'Elements' document, in terms of what
I think should be considered in the longer term).

Common Ground

This can be found between each Camp concerning both the law of war and
international environmental law.

---

40 See *infra* p. 17 and pp. 21 and 26 for discussion.

The common ground on the law of war may be stated as follows:

1 The law of war has been concerned with environmental protection since ancient times at least in the sense of prohibiting wanton destruction of forests, orchards, fruit trees and vines and forbidding the poisoning of wells, springs and rivers.[41]

2 Deliberate and wanton destruction of the environment in circumstances where no legitimate military objective is served is contrary to international law.[42]

3 The principle of proportionality between means and methods employed in an attack and the military objective sought to be attained by it, the prohibition against military operations not directed against legitimate military targets, the prohibition against the destruction of enemy property not imperatively demanded by the necessities of war and other well established principles of customary international law have the indirect effect of protecting the environment in many wartime situations.[43]

4 The Martens Clause, as formulated in its most modern version in Protocol I, reads as follows:

> In cases not covered by this Protocol or by other international agreements, civilians and combatants remain under the protection and authority of the principles of international law derived from established custom, from the principles of humanity and from the dictates of public conscience.[44]

Thus the customary law of war, in reflecting the modern increase in concern for the environment as one of the dictates of public conscience in the sense understood in that Clause, now includes a requirement to avoid unjustifiable damage to the environment.

5 Violations of Article 23(g) of the Regulations attached to the Hague Convention of 1907 (IV) Respecting the Laws and Customs of War on Land,[45] or of Article 53 of the 1949 Geneva Convention (IV) Relative to the Protection of Civilian Persons in Time of War,[46] which prohibit destruction by an Occupying Power of enemy property not required by military necessity, give rise to civil liability.[47] Wanton destruction is considered a grave breach, for which individual criminal responsibility can be attributed by virtue of Article 147 of the latter Convention.

---

41 See *infra* Roberts at p. 153 and Plant at p. 165.

42 Françoise Hampson had no doubt about this at the London Conference (see *infra* p. 131), and several others suggested that the real problems were to be found with regulating collateral rather than deliberate damage: see *infra* Greenwood at pp. 123–24 and Arkin at p. 129.

43 For a description of these principles see *infra* Falk at p. 184.

44 This reformulation of the Clause appears in Article 1(2) of Protocol I. The Clause originally formed part of the preamble to the Hague Conventions on Land Warfare of 1899 (No. II) (done at The Hague, 29 July 1899: 1 *American Journal of International Law* (*AJIL*) (1907) Suppl. 129) and of 1907 (No. IV) (done at The Hague, 18 October 1907, UK Treaty Series No. 9 (1910).

45 Ibid.

46 Loc. cit., *supra*, n. 23.

47 For texts see Appendix 2.

6 States should ensure the wide dissemination and effective implementation of their existing obligations under the law of armed conflict as they may be relevant to the protection of the environment, as well as proper instruction of the military in their application. They should be adequately incorporated into military manuals and rules of engagement,[48] in particular, through instructions to military commanders on the planning and preparation of military activities.

As far as international environmental law is concerned, I suggest in the introduction to the 'Elements' document that the need to reflect major developments in that law applicable in peacetime since the 1970s in the law of war might be one reason for establishing a new instrument, and I briefly describe some of the principles of law that might be involved.[49] The common ground on this area of law is likely to be limited to the existence of two principles of customary international law applicable in peacetime and to the possibility of the emergence of additional principles and rules. It will be readily agreed that these principles continue, as I have explained, to apply *vis-à-vis* neutral states during an armed conflict, within the context of the law of neutrality.[50] On the other hand, it is unlikely to be accepted that they apply equally in wartime.

The first of these principles is that each state has the responsibility 'to ensure that activities under its jurisdiction or control do not cause damage to the environment of other states or of areas beyond national jurisdiction'.[51] As far as the global commons are concerned, widely supported

---

48 Bothe also stressed this at the London Conference, referring to 'rules of engagement', *infra* at pp. 118–19; and Lee did so too, referring to 'national law', at pp. 142–3.

49 *Infra* p. 187, in its final revised version.

50 During the Second World War, for example, all belligerents accepted responsibility for transfrontier damage caused to Switzerland. This included Allied acceptance of responsibility for damage caused by bombing aimed at Germany: Jaccard, 'Uber Neutralitätsverletetzungsschäden in der Schweiz während des zweiten Weltkrieges,' 87, *Revue de la Société des Juristes Bernois* (1951), pp. 225–51. It can be concluded from the description of the developments in the law below (text at pp. 18–20) that the sorts of damage now contemplated also include non-economic environmental damage.

51 Principle 21 of the Stockholm Declaration of Principles on the Human Environment 1972, Report of the Stockholm Conference on the Human Environment, Stockholm, 5–16 June 1972: UN Doc. A/CONF./48/14 (1972). This has been particularly strongly endorsed in UN General Assembly Resolution 2996 (1972). It is, therefore, reflected in Element 1.E of the 'Elements' Document (*infra* pp. 44–5). The principle is originally derived from a number of sources which were not primarily directed at non-economic environmental damage or protection of the global commons (such that the principle has been put through a transformation process as a result of and since the Stockholm Conference). These include: judicial decisions (for example, the *Trail Smelter Arbitration*, award dated 11 March 1940: 33 *AJIL* (1941) 182 35 *AJIL* (1943) 684; the *Corfu Channel Case*, (1949) ICJ Reps. 4. See also the *Nuclear Tests Cases*, (1973) ICJ Reps. 99 and (1974) ICJ Reps. 253; the *Island of Palmas Arbitration*, (1928) RIAA ii, 829; 22 *AJIL* (1928) 867, award of Max Huber); international conventions (for example, the Law of the Sea Convention, done at Montego Bay, 10 December 1982, UN Doc. A/CONF.62/122, especially Articles 192 and 194(2), and a number of UNEP Conventions established under its Regional Seas Programme (listed by Fauteux, loc. cit., *supra* n. 1, at footnote 50), and more particularly in the context of the Gulf War, the Regional Convention on Cooperation with a view to Protection of the Marine Environment against Pollution, done at Kuwait, 24 April 1978; and other instruments, such as the ILC Draft Articles on State Responsibility and the Charter on Economic Rights and Duties of States.

treaties have given effect to this principle in respect of the ozone layer, outer space, the high seas and Antarctica and point to the fact that states are no longer free to pollute or degrade these areas.[52]

The second customary principle is shortly put: it requires notification and consultation with other states in cases of transboundary risk of environmental damage to areas within their jurisdiction.[53]

This second principle appears to many, moreover, to have become extended into a new principle of 'risk avoidance' which applies equally to protect the global commons as areas within other states' jurisdiction. It has long been established that the principle of cooperation between states could extend to the protection of the global commons from risk of environmental harm, but this was only clearly the case in relation to the exploitation of the *natural resources* of those commons. But many believe that this principle can now be put more widely as follows: that states must cooperate with others where they are proposing to engage in activities which have the potential of causing harm to the global commons or where they become aware of hazards to the environment of the global commons.[54] UNEP Guidelines and growing evidence of state practice, moreover, suggest that monitoring and prior environmental impact assessment might also be required by this principle of 'risk avoidance'.[55] An even less well-established candidate for acceptance as a component of such a principle is, moreover, the precautionary principle.[56] None of the matters described in this paragraph, however, are by any means likely to be common ground among the round tablers.

In describing the development of the law, it is important to note that the ILC is engaged in attempting to codify and progressively develop relevant norms and is doing or has recently done so under a number of topic headings.[57] It has been stated above that Awn Al-Khasawneh, a serving member of the Commission, was invited to lead the discussion on the general principles and on the execution of a possible Convention (Elements 1 and 5 of the 'Elements' document) precisely in order to suggest what elements of the ILC's work might be extended into a law of war instrument concerning the environment.

Some consider that states' obligations go even further and extend to the protection of the environment in general, whatever the applicable legal

---

52 A.E. Boyle, 'State Responsibility for Breach of Obligations to Protect the Global Environment', in W.E. Butler (ed.) *Control over Compliance with International Law*, Martinus Nijhoff, Dordrecht, Boston, London (1991), 69 at p. 70 and endnote 12, which lists these treaties.

53 The *Corfu Channel Case*, op. cit., *supra* n. 51; the Convention on the Law of the Sea, Article 198, ibid.; the *Lac Lanoux Arbitration*, RIAA xii (1957) 281; and the Convention on Long-Range Transboundary Air Pollution, done at Geneva 1979, Articles 5 and 8: UKTS No. 57 (1983); Cmnd 9034.

54 Boyle, op. cit., *supra* n. 52, at p. 71.

55 Ibid.

56 Bothe suggests that the question of the applicability of the precautionary principle in relation to military activities should be considered, see p. 135.

57 These are briefly described by Awn Al-Khasawneh in his introduction to Session I of the round table discussion, *infra* pp. 105–6.

regime; in other words, that states have an obligation to protect the environment in areas subject to their own jurisdiction as well as elsewhere. Some support from this might be derived from certain treaty provisions, prohibiting, for example, marine and air pollution, as well as some state practice.[58] The majority view, however, is that this is not established in customary international law.[59]

Even where there is common ground, moreover, the efficacy of applying the two accepted customary principles as narrowly formulated above to the environmental impact of military activities of a belligerent upon areas within the jurisdiction of a neutral state or the global commons is seriously open to question in the absence of specific treaty obligations embodying the principles in concrete form and providing other means of enforcement in addition to the normal means of ascribing state responsibility. It is not clear whether the standard of conduct demanded of a state by the first two principles is only one of due diligence or whether strict or absolute liability applies.[60] If due diligence is the standard, which seems the more likely, neutral states must bear many or all of the costs of environmental harm in cases where this harm is unforeseeable or unavoidable. There are also serious problems of proof and, where the global commons is damaged, of standing to sue.[61]

If it were to be established that these principles of customary law were applicable in some shape or form as between belligerents, which seems doubtful, these problems would be encountered with equal force in concrete cases. It appears highly unlikely, however, that they do apply as the law stands, or will be applied to any real degree, as environmental destruction is to an extent a necessary concomitant of belligerent acts; the realistic question to ask is: 'to what degree should those acts be restrained by other means in order to help protect the environment?'

To sum up, the common ground between the four Camps is likely to be limited to the existence of the two major principles as narrowly formulated above. There is unlikely to be much common ground on the degree to which they have developed into broader principles since the 1970s, the degree to which norms of international environmental law do or should continue to apply as between two or more belligerents, and the degree to which the development of these norms argue for a restatement or restructuring of the relevant law. This is because major differences in philosophy are involved, best expressed by Michael Bothe when introducing the Second Session of the round table.[62]

---

58 See Fauteux, loc. cit., *supra* n. 1, at pp. 10–11.
59 Ibid.
60 Boyle, op. cit., *supra* n. 52, at p. 72.
61 Ibid., at pp. 72–4.
62 See *infra* p. 117.

The Four Camps Resumed

I now turn to the description of the four Camps.

Camp 1 The views of the first Camp, which are probably most prominently held in certain sections of the US Administration and military and their equivalents in certain other major Powers, in essence go no further than the common ground.

Holders of this view regard the existing customary principles of the law of war, such as the principles of proportionality, military necessity and avoidance of unnecessary suffering, together with the conventional law developed up to 1949, which codified or has come to represent customary law,[63] to be adequate to protect the environment, both in the context of the Gulf War and in any foreseeable future conflict. They do not consider a rearticulation of these principles and norms in a binding instrument to be necessary, although they are likely to accept that improvements in their implementation might be possible.

They are likely to place particular emphasis upon: Article 23(g) of the Regulations attached to Hague Convention IV of 1907 and Articles 53 and 147 of Geneva Convention IV (*supra*) concerning the wanton destruction of property by occupying Powers. They would emphasize that these provisions permit destruction of civilian property only where this is militarily *necessary* and not merely when it is convenient. They would consider this to provide protection to installations containing dangerous forces, albeit with more qualifications than are present in Article 56 of Protocol I (see *infra* p. 26). They might also consider that Article 15 of Geneva Convention IV provides, by way of permitting belligerents to agree to the establishment of neutralized zones to protect the civilian population, adequate means to protect the environment of ecologically important or vulnerable areas.[64] Finally, they would emphasize that the Martens Clause now extends by virtue of state practice to environmental protection (*supra* p. 17).

---

63 See also *supra* pp. 14–15.
64 For texts see Appendix 2. They might also refer to: the Declaration of St Petersburg (Renouncing the Use, in Time of War, of Explosive Projectiles Under 400 Grammes Weight, St Petersburg, 29 November/11 December 1868: Martens, NRGT, Ie série, Vol. XVIII at 474–5; translated in Parliamentary Papers (1869), vol. LXIV at 659); Principle 6b) of the Nuremberg Principles as formulated by the ILC (Yearbook of the ILC, vol. II, p. 194); and certain Nuremberg Judgements for example No. 47, *The Hostages Trial of Wilhelm List and Others*, US Military Tribunal, Nuremberg 8 July 1947 – 19 February 1948, US Government Printing Office, *11 Trials of War Criminals before the Nuremberg Military Tribunals under International Law*, No 10 (1947) at p. 1253.

They might in particular point to UN War Crimes Commission Case no. 7150 (UNWCC, 1948, at p. 496) in an effort to demonstrate that the prohibition on wanton destruction extends to the natural environment (albeit only when this is also private or public property in occupied territory). In that case nine among ten German civilian administrators of Polish forests were charged with war crimes, based upon their 'ruthless exploitation of Polish forestry' by way of wholesale cutting of timber to a degree that threatened the sustainability of the resources: see Falk *infra* at p. 86; also UN War Crimes Commission *History of the United Nations War Crimes Commission and the Development of the Laws of War*, HMSO, (1948), London, at p. 496.

The incorporation of these principles and norms in appropriate form in national military manuals is likely to be regarded by them as the most effective method to protect the environment, as this helps to ensure that environmental damage is taken into account by a military commander when he is considering military action against enemy forces or other targets. This emphasis upon the military and their manuals or rules of engagement is significant in that it seems to involve the preservation of great scope for subjective discretionary judgements by the military in the circumstances as they perceive them on the ground and also to rely upon their self-restraint in view of their supposed perception that attacking the environment is either abhorrent or self-defeating.

Members of this Camp might be concerned that the negotiation of a Fifth Geneva Convention on the environment would detract from the strength of adherence to the existing Geneva Conventions, to which there are almost as many Parties as there are even to the UN Charter.

They are unlikely to be persuaded that Protocol I, which has far fewer Parties and to which a number of major military Powers are not Party, (*infra* p. 25) represents customary law, and in particular Article 35(3), which prohibits the employment of 'methods or means of warfare which are intended, or may be expected, to cause widespread, long-term and severe damage to the natural environment' and Article 55, which requires care to 'be taken in warfare to protect the natural environment against widespread, long-term and severe damage'.[65] Indeed, they might even argue that the lack of an agreed definition of the term 'natural environment' and of the three criteria determining the threshold of prohibited environmental harm

---

65 The Reagan and Bush Administrations have both taken this position. Their most notable objection to Protocol I is the legal status it gives to national liberation movements: see Letter of Transmittal from President Reagan to the US Senate, dated 29 January 1987, reproduced in 81 (*AJIL*) *The American Journal of International Law* (1987), pp. 910–2; also Abraham Sofaer, 'Agora: the US Decision not to Ratify Protocol I to the Geneva Conventions on the Protection of War Victims,' 82 *AJIL* (1988), pp. 784–7. This aside, the objections have been largely limited to relatively unspecific assertions of military unacceptability. Sofaer, for example, alleges that the Protocol 'unreasonably restricts attacks against certain objects that have traditionally been legitimate targets; and . . . eliminates significant remedies in cases where an enemy violates [it]': ibid., at p. 785. It is, therefore, significant that the environmental protection provisions feature among those expressly singled out for criticism by American military and government commentators: see, for example, Michael Matheson, 'United States Position on the Relation of Customary International Law to the 1977 Protocols Additional to the 1949 Geneva Conventions', 2, *American University Journal of International Law and Policy* (1987) 425; Guy Roberts, 'The New Rules for Waging War: The Case Against Ratification of Protocol I', 26, *Va. J. Int'l L.* (1985), 109 at p. 148; and Burrus Carnahan, 'Additional Protocol I: A Military View', 19, *Akron L. Rev.* (1986), 543 at pp. 546–7. This does not necessarily indicate that the USA is more opposed to them than to other provisions, but it is a strong indication that it regards them to be far from representative of customary law.

('widespread', 'long-term' and 'severe')[66] is evidence that they could not have developed into precise norms of customary law. They are also likely to emphasize the fact that most NATO countries have recorded their views that Protocol I does not apply to the use of nuclear weapons, and to consider the exclusion of restrictions upon the use of such weapons in conventions relating to the law of war to be desirable.

Furthermore, they are likely to consider ENMOD and the Inhumane Weapons Convention to be adequate conventional (and not customary) law in their narrow fields of application and would not encourage the extension of their scope, except possibly on clear humanitarian, as opposed to environmental, grounds. They would point out that each has many potential environmental applications. Article 1(1) of ENMOD requires a State Party to undertake 'not to engage in military or any other hostile use of environmental modification techniques having widespread, long-lasting or severe effects as the means of destruction, damage or injury to any other State Party'. Article II defines these techniques as 'any technique for changing – through the deliberate manipulation of natural processes – the dynamics, composition or structure of the earth, including its biota, lithosphere, hydrosphere and atmosphere, or of outer space'.[67] Its scope is thus limited to the manipulation of such forces as earthquakes, tidal waves, ocean currents, the ozone layer and climate; it probably also extends to the massive use of herbicides, as the US Government has acknowledged.[68] Most would agree, however, that it would not have covered the destruction

---

66 No agreed definitions were reached by the diplomatic conference which resulted in the Protocol, although it was clear that the criteria were not to be read as necessarily having the same meaning as the similar criteria in ENMOD and, indeed, that they were intended to be read as imposing a much higher threshold. See: 'Elements' Document *infra* at pp. 47–8; George Aldrich, 'Progressive Development of the Laws of War: A Reply to Criticisms of the 1977 Geneva Protocol I,' 26, *Va. J. Int'l L.* (1986), 693 at p. 711; Michael Bothe, Karl Josef Partsch and Waldemar Solf (eds), *New Rules for Victims of Armed Conflicts*, Martinus Nijhoff, (1982), Boston, The Hague, London, at pp. 347–8; and Yves Sandoz et al. (eds), *ICRC Commentary on the Additional Protocols of 8 June 1977 to the Geneva Conventions of 12 August 1949* ('ICRC Commentary'), Martinus Nijhoff, (1987), Geneva, at pp. 419–22.

67 It thus adopts a wide definition of 'environment' for its purposes; see *infra* Meyer in Appendix 6.

68 According to Goldblat, who testified before the US Senate Committee on Foreign Relations Hearings on Ratification on ENMOD in the autumn of 1978, a US Government spokesman stated that the Convention prohibits the use of herbicides to cause destruction, damage or injury if the effects are widespread, long-lasting or severe: 'The Laws of Armed Conflict: An Overview of the Restrictions and Limitations on the Methods and Means of Warfare,' 13, *Bulletin of Peace Proposals* (1982), 127 at p. 129. The USA has also unilaterally denounced the use of herbicides in warfare except for minor applications: Executive Office of the President, Executive Order No. 11850, 'Renunciation of Certain Uses in War of Chemical Herbicides and Riot Control Agents', 8 April 1975.

of the Kuwaiti oil wells, even if Iraq were a Party.[69] By the end of 1989, moreover, there were only 57 Parties to this treaty, including among the major Powers only the UK, the USA and the USSR. It is unlikely to represent customary law.

Several provisions of Protocols II and III to the Inhumane Weapons Convention are relevant to the environment, but the most significant are the restrictions upon the use of remotely delivered mines in Protocol II and Article 2(4) of Protocol III concerning incendiary weapons. The latter, for example, prohibits the making of 'forests or other kinds of plant cover the object of attack by incendiary weapons,' but adds the following significant exception, 'except when such natural elements are used to cover, conceal or camouflage combatants or other military objectives, or are themselves military objectives'. Incendiary weapons are narrowly defined, moreover, to exclude illuminants, tracers, smoke and signalling systems and, more significantly, armour-piercing projectiles, fragmentation shells, fuel-air explosives and similar combined-effect weapons designed primarily to set fire to vehicles, military installations and the like, rather than to cause burn injury to persons.[70] This treaty had a mere 28 Parties by the end of 1989, including among the major Powers China, France and the USSR, most of which have accepted all three Protocols (although their strict obligation upon adherence is merely to select two). It is very unlikely to represent customary law.

In particular in relation to these two Conventions, members of this Camp would not accept that the existence of a lower threshold of environmental harm in the ENMOD Convention than that in Protocol I[71] serves in any way as a precedent for adopting a lower threshold in that Protocol or any new instrument on the environment. If the same or a similar lower threshold were so adopted, they would argue that it would unacceptably

---

69 The one exception appears to be Goldblat, who argues that this involved manipulation of the natural pressures present in underground oil reservoirs (*infra* at p. 133). With respect, this argument is not convincing. The direct cause of the environmental destruction was the detonation of explosives on the well-heads, and the fact that those well-heads have been constantly supplied with inflammable oil to feed the fire triggered by those explosions by virtue of the pressures in the strata below them is a secondary, not a causative, matter. Explosives, not oil pressure were 'manipulated'. It is equivalent to calling the explosion of gunpowder a manipulation of the natural forces involved in bringing together its component parts and igniting them. See also Goldblat, 'The Prohibition of Environmental Warfare,' 4, *Ambio* (1975), 186 at pp. 186–7.

70 Jozef Goldblat, 'The Mitigation of Environmental Destruction by War: Legal Approaches' in A. H. Westing (ed.), loc. cit., *supra* n. 20, 48 at pp. 54.

71 Or rather of the Conference of the Committee on Disarmament's Understanding attached to the draft ENMOD Convention concerning the threshold: UN Doc. CCD/520, 3 September 1976, Annex A; reprinted in UN Doc. A/31/27, loc. cit., *supra* n. 25, and set out in part *infra* at p. 47. On the point that the thresholds differ, see: ICRC *Commentary*, loc. cit., *supra* n. 66, at pp. 414–8; it is clearly stated in the Understanding that it is for the purpose of ENMOD alone. It is also interesting to note the interpretation of the USA, the co-sponsor of the draft ENMOD treaty together with the USSR: UN Doc. CCD/PV/691, 692, 698 and 703, August 1976. The threshold is lower in ENMOD, as the 'Elements' document explains *infra* at pp. 47–48, both because the three criteria are alternative and not cumulative and because they were understood to be less rigorous.

prohibit or restrict all or most military activities, as they would arguably all be 'long-lasting' in the understood sense of lasting about a season.

Camp 2 The International Committee of the Red Cross (ICRC) is, perhaps, the organization most likely to adopt the position characteristic of Camp 2, which accepts many of the views of Camp 1 but insists that Protocol I also represents customary law.[72] There are now 105 Parties, including China, the USSR and most NATO countries.[73] The absence of ratifications by a number of important states, in particular the USA, France and the UK, casts some doubt upon this claim. As the co-guarantor of the Protocols with the States Party, therefore, it is strongly interested in encouraging as many states as possible, including the three just mentioned, to adhere to them and in ensuring that they are implemented. There is increasing scepticism concerning the degree to which the States Party have implemented them effectively.[74] It follows that many, and the ICRC in particular, are concerned that a new instrument to protect the environment in time of war might overlap with Protocol I and detract from this process.

The cause of Camp 2 and of Protocol I is thus best served if it can be shown that the Protocol, together with other relevant instruments such as the ENMOD and the Inhumane Weapons Conventions (where they apply), deals more or less comprehensively with the protection of the environment in wartime. This Camp is, therefore, likely to stress that Protocol I is unique among existing instruments in establishing an explicit general prohibition on means and methods of warfare likely to cause environmental destruction above an established threshold (in Articles 35(3) and 55) and that this removes to a large degree the subjective discretion of the military complained of above in relation to Camp 1 (*supra* p. 22). It is also likely to rely upon the advice in the ICRC *Commentary*[75] that the term 'natural environment' in those provisions should, although undefined, be understood in the widest sense to cover not merely objects indispensable to the survival of the human population, such as foodstuffs, drinking water and livestock (which are mentioned in Article 54), but also forests and other vegetation mentioned in Protocol III to the Inhumane Weapons Convention (*supra* p. 24), 'as well as flora, fauna and other biological and climatic elements'. Whatever the initial intention of the Parties in 1977, they would say, the term 'natural environment' should now be read broadly in the light of the development of the public conscience in favour of protecting the environment.

---

72 Hans-Peter Gasser of the ICRC supports the view that Protocol I represents customary law; *infra* at p. 111.

73 The USA and France have decided not to ratify; and the UK is still to decide. Portugal has also not ratified and Germany ratified only recently.

74 See, for example, Rostow *infra* at p. 123.

75 Loc. cit., *supra* n. 66, at p. 662.

As far as the Article 35(3) threshold is concerned, this Camp is likely to take the view that, if it is felt to be too high in the light of experience, it is open to States Party to modify it through their practice or by reaching an Understanding concerning its interpretation. This is not, however, likely to involve an adoption of a threshold as low as the ENMOD one.

They would insist that only limited reliance can be placed upon Hague Convention IV of 1907 and Geneva Convention IV in respect of environmental protection, as they refer, unlike Article 35(3) of Protocol I, to damage to property (and property in occupied territory only) rather than to the environment itself. In other words, in the context of the Gulf War, they refer to the destruction of well-heads as objects rather than to the burning of the oil fields as an environmental phenomenon.

On the other hand, this Camp is not content to rely upon the above-mentioned provisions alone. They are likely to stress that a number of other provisions of the Protocol are relevant, in particular many of those in Chapter III, entitled 'Civilian Objects'. They might suggest, for example, that the narrow concept of 'military objectives' established by Articles 50 and 52 and the broad definition of 'attacks' in Article 49[76] tend to maximize environmental protection when combined with the other provisions.

Notable among the specific relevant provisions in this Chapter of Protocol I in terms of its environmental relevance is Article 56, which protects works or installations containing dangerous forces, where their attack 'may cause the release of dangerous forces and consequent severe losses among the civilian population'. These are expressly limited, however, to nuclear electrical generating stations and dams and dykes, although Article 56(6) does urge the States Party to conclude further agreements to provide additional protection for objects containing dangerous forces. Their protection is subject to a number of exceptions set out in paragraph (2) of the Article.[77]

The protection of ecologically sensitive areas, they would suggest, is already achievable through Articles 59 or 60 of Protocol I, which respectively permit a Party to declare a non-defended locality, which an adverse belligerent may then occupy, and belligerent Parties to agree to confer the status of a demilitarized zone upon an area, which cannot then be the site of military operations. These provisions, they would argue, can both be employed to protect an area because of its ecological sensitivity, whereas Article 15 of the IV Geneva Convention is properly restricted to the protection of the civilian population and so can only incidentally (and coincidentally) be employed to protect the environment.

---

76 See, for example, G. I. A. D. Draper, 'Humanitarianism in the Modern Law of Armed Conflicts,' in Michael Meyer (ed.) *Armed Conflict and the New Law: Aspects of the 1977 Geneva Protocols and the 1981 Weapons Convention*, British Institute of International and Comparative Law, (1989), London, 3 at p. 16.

77 For the effect of these see Aldrich, 'Prospects for United States Ratification of Additional Protocol I to the 1949 Geneva Conventions,' 85, *AJIL* (1991) 1 at pp. 12–14.

This Camp is likely to emphasize the prohibition upon reprisals against the natural environment in Article 55(2) of Protocol I and to accept the political reality that the use of nuclear weapons is excluded from the scope of its application.

Finally, this Camp might well argue that the best means of execution of the law of war is through a fact-finding commission, and that such a commission has recently been established under the provisions of Article 90 and is entirely capable of investigating complaints about environmental destruction.[78]

Camp 3 This Camp is comprised of those who consider the existing law of war to be in need of improvement and who contemplate various means for improving the standards of, adherence to or implementation of that law, whether by using existing instruments and mechanisms or by developing new ones, such as a new Geneva-style Convention. It might also be taken to include those who desire only a clear restatement in a single instrument of the existing law, with added emphasis on its environmental applications.[79] No government has associated itself with the sorts of views held by this Camp to date, except perhaps Jordan[80] and Kuwait,[81] although a number of important individuals, including Commissioner Ripa di Meana, have called for a new Convention.[82]

This Camp, therefore, takes improvement upon Protocol I as its starting point, as it contains the only general express provisions for the protection of the environment, and, to a lesser extent, improvement upon ENMOD and the Inhumane Weapons Convention. Six or seven minimum improvements, or core areas, can be identified with this Camp. They are broadly as follows:

1 Both deliberate and collateral damage must be regulated, and most attention should be paid to the more difficult of the two, collateral damage.[83]
2 A lower threshold of environmental harm than that in Protocol I is desirable, and this threshold must be particularly apposite to collateral damage.[84] A number of possible formulations of a substantially lowered threshold, taking into account the ENMOD threshold, were set out in Element 2.A of the 'Elements' document,[85] and round tablers at the

---

78 See *infra* Gasser at p. 111; Caflisch at p. 140; Pinto at p. 113; and Prokhorov at p. 142. Al-Khasawneh is more sceptical at pp. 106–7; and Ferrari Bravo does not believe such commissions to be useful in rapid escalation situations: at p. 143.
79 As to what this might contain, see *infra* Bothe at pp. 117–18 and 134.
80 In its letter to the UN dated 5 July 1991, loc. cit., *supra* n. 7, reproduced in Appendix 8 and discussed in Chapter 12.
81 In its letter to the UN dated 12 July 1991, loc. cit., *supra* n. 4, welcoming Jordan's initiative. It also appears that Syria has welcomed the initiative.
82 See *supra* n. 6 and *infra* at pp. 65–67.
83 See *infra* Greenwood at pp. 123–24 and Hampson at p. 131.
84 Greenwood, ibid.
85 *Infra* at p. 46.

Conference suggested a variety of alternative approaches ranging from limited adjustments to take into account regional differences in ecologies to radical diminution of legitimate military targets or of the principles of proportionality and military necessity;[86] indeed, Professor Falk and Ambassador Türk might add the latter possibility as a separate core area.[87]

3 The law should be adequate to protect the natural environment *per se*, as opposed to protecting it indirectly by protecting property or to protecting it only in so far as the environmental damage involved causes a direct and immediate, or soon-emerging, impact upon living human beings. If not actually treating the environment or wildlife as values in themselves, it should at least take a precautionary approach to the impact of military activities upon ecosystems and the ecology in general;[88] it might even adopt a mechanism to help take into account impacts upon future generations. This approach should include the protection of particularly sensitive areas, and this Camp is likely to be doubtful that either Article 59 or Article 60 of Protocol I can afford adequate environmental protection for such areas. This is because Article 59 does not prevent the occupation of non-defended areas by military forces, and because in practice few Article 60 agreements capable of ensuring demilitarization of environmentally vulnerable areas are likely to be made by warring belligerents. It seems to follow that provision should be made for the demilitarization of zones on environmental grounds in a manner which does not require an *ad hoc* agreement to be made by the belligerents. The most obvious course is to ensure the preparation of a list on a multilateral basis and in advance of any conflict, which would enable the interests of all states in the area in question to be taken into account.[89] It is necessary, moreover, to adopt a broad approach to the concept of the

---

86 See generally the debate in round table Session II (chapter 8 *infra*). Al-Khasawneh suggested a number of possible measures, based upon his experiences in the ILC, *infra* at pp. 105–6; Bothe felt that the ENMOD example was misleading, as in his view it was based upon the example of the Vietnam jungle (a view with which many American commentators would disagree) and that any threshold needed to be flexible in order to take into account the differences in the ecology of different areas (*infra* at p. 118), as well as the precautionary principle *infra* at p. 135); Leipold suggested the reversal of the presumption in favour of the existence of targeting 'rights' (at p. 120) (see also Al-Khasawneh at p. 120 and Bothe at p. 121); Arkin suggested that the Gulf War be used as a model to predict the collateral effects of attacks in any foreseeable conflict in order to set a new set of standards (at pp. 130–31); and Hampson (at p. 131) and Sapolsky (at pp. 144–45), among others, contemplated the possibility of prohibiting attacks which were not militarily necessary.

87 *Infra* Falk at p. 93 and Türk at p. 98, although they acknowledge that it would be difficult to obtain agreement on this; see also Goldblat at p. 110.

88 Bothe asks whether the (emerging) precautionary principle needs to be applied: *infra* at p. 135.

89 In the 'Elements' Document (*infra* at p. 51) I suggest that this could be based on a modification of the existing UNESCO Convention for the Protection of the World Cultural and Natural Heritage ('World Heritage Convention'), done at Paris, 23 November 1972: 11 ILM 1358; TIAS No. 8226; 27 UST 37.

environment, which might also include the cultural environment,[90] but opinions differ as to whether a definition of 'environment' is achievable or even desirable.[91] It may be that only a list of environmental elements to be protected can be achieved. What is clear is that the threshold of environmental protection can only be determined when the concept of the 'environment' for these purposes is clarified.

4 This Camp generally inclines in favour of ensuring that developments in the international environmental law of peacetime are as fully reflected as possible in the law of war, but considers that the matter should be tackled essentially within the framework of the law of war.

5 Like the other Camps, it is anxious to ensure adequate adherence to and implementation of the law.

To this list different adherents to the Camp might wish to add one or more non-core elements. These include the following:

1 The provision of additional protection for objects containing dangerous forces. The obvious candidate for reconsideration following the Gulf War is oil fields which were expressly considered and excluded from its scope in 1977;[92] others might include nuclear reactors and facilities containing nuclear material other than nuclear electrical generating plants (which are already protected), nuclear material in transit to such plants and installations containing harmful chemicals or biological substances. This can be achieved either by adopting an agreement of the sort called for by Article 56(6) of Protocol I,[93] or directly in a new Geneva-style Convention. The removal of certain exceptions to the protection of those installations already listed might also be considered. The exception permitting attacks (where they are a last resort) upon nuclear electrical generating plants when they are operating in direct support of the military arguably reduces the prohibition to an absurdity, as such plants will invariably feed into a national grid, from which the military will frequently extract electric power.[94]

---

90 See 'Elements' Document, *infra* at p. 42. It appears that Article 53 of Protocol I does not remove the exception, based on military necessity, to the prohibition of attacks against such objects established in the Hague Convention for the Protection of Cultural Property in the Event of Armed Conflict, done at The Hague, 14 May 1954 (249 UNTS 216), since it is expressed to be without prejudice to its provisions. Indeed, Italy and The Netherlands made declarations upon ratification of the protocol to this effect: Gasser, 'Some Legal Issues Concerning Ratification of the 1977 Geneva Protocols,' in Meyer (ed.), loc. cit., *supra* n. 76, 81 at p. 89.

91 Falk suggests that only a list of core areas is possible, *infra* chapter 5; and Meyer questions the value of a definition: see Appendix 6. My own view, as stated above, is that we should take the ICRC *Commentary* definition of 'natural environment' as it is used in Protocol I as a starting point and build upon it, drawing, for example, upon the considerations mentioned by David Tolbert in Appendix 6.

92 See *infra* Bothe at p. 126 and Hampson at p. 132.

93 This approach is advocated by Goldblat, *infra* at pp. 110–11. The extension to further nuclear installations would be entirely consistent with the trend established in the series of IAEA resolutions concerning attacks upon such facilities, which are set out in Appendix 2.

94 See Aldrich, loc. cit., *supra* n. 66, at pp. 12–13.

2 The addition of specific prohibitions against or restrictions upon the use of environmentally harmful weapons, going beyond those already established in the Inhumane Weapons Convention (in so far as this does not reproduce the effect of the restrictions upon methods and means of warfare resulting from a reduction in the threshold of the prohibition of environmental damage).[95] These could be achieved in either of two ways: by a modification of this Convention, following invocation of its review procedures, either to remove some of the exceptions applicable under Protocols II and III in respect of mines and incendiary weapons or to add new protocols dealing with new weapons systems; or by their inclusion in a new Geneva-style Convention.

3 The prohibition of attacks against specific areas of land;[96] this would be in addition to the prohibition against scorched-earth tactics discussed above (at n.36).

4 The creation of a new category of 'international crimes against (nature or) the environment' or, at least, the strengthening of international criminal law-enforcement procedures relative to those found in existing law of war instruments,[97] including the possible addition of provision for a new international criminal tribunal with competence in this area.[98]

5 The adoption of other procedures facilitating the observance of a new Convention, such as verification procedures,[99] or a panel procedure to permit the translation of general principles of the law of war into practical operational criteria.[100]

6 The establishment of a new organization,[101] possibly called the Green Cross/Crescent, or the extension of the functions of an existing organization or organizations,[102] to have parallel functions in the environmental

---

95 Goldblat states, *infra* at p. 110, that this is a particularly important problem.

96 Upon ratification of Protocol I The Netherlands made a declaration to the effect that a specific area of land could be attacked as a military objective if (among other criteria) 'its total or partial destruction, capture or neutralization in the circumstances ruling at the time, offers a definite military advantage: *International Review of the Red Cross* (1987) at pp. 425–6. Italy made a virtually identical declaration upon ratification (Gasser in Michael Meyer (ed.), loc. cit., *supra* n. 90, 81 at p. 87), as did the UK (upon signature) (ibid.) and New Zealand (US Department of the Navy, *Annotated Supplement to the Commander's Handbook on the Law of Naval Operations*, NWP 9 (Rev. A), (1989), at paras 8.2–8.3).

97 See, for example, *infra* the 'Elements' Document at pp. 55–56, Falk at pp. 93–94 and 122 and Türk at p. 99.

98 See *infra* Ripa di Meana at p. 66; Türk at p. 99 and Goldblat at p. 110. *Sed contra* Greenwood, who regards international criminal procedures as the least effective means of enforcing the law of war, at p. 124; and Caflisch at pp. 140–41. Greenwood's view appears to be borne out by the way in which various round tablers disagreed as to Saddam Hussein's possible defences were he to be tried for environmental war crimes: see Arkin at p. 130, Goldblat at p. 133 and Hampson at p. 132.

99 See, for example, *infra* Türk at p. 99.

100 See, for example, *infra* Bothe at p. 119.

101 Szekely thinks that the adoption of a new organization is desirable, but unlikely: at p. 148.

102 Caflisch at p. 140 and Sapolsky at p. 145 regard this option as preferable.

field to those of the Red Cross in the humanitarian field.[103]

Three questions of philosophy need to be examined by any adherent to this Camp. First, should differences in the weapons technologies of opposing belligerents, or in their abilities to use comparable technologies in an equally sophisticated way, be reflected in the law of environmental protection in wartime? The round tablers expressed divergent opinions upon this difficult question, which is also one which could be put to Camps 1 and 2 concerning the application of existing customary and conventional law.[104] Second, should certain acts on the fringes of warfare in the sense that they are committed in time of war but without any real military objectives, such as Iraq's setting fire to Kuwaiti oil-wells, be treated separately, for example, by prohibiting or criminalizing them as general crimes against the environment?[105] Third, should an attempt be made to regulate the use or first use of nuclear weapons, as well as other weapons of mass destruction, in any Convention to protect the environment in wartime? Opinions differ on the political feasibility of their exclusion.[106]

It is apparent from the discussion above that a number of methods and procedures can be employed in reforming the law concerning environmental protection in wartime. The most ambitious is the adoption by a diplomatic conference of a Fifth Geneva Convention. This would be a major task, involving perhaps years of negotiations and a further period of years pending the achievement of sufficient numbers of ratifications for it to come into force.[107] It is thus necessarily seen as a long-term option, even if negotiations begin immediately.

A third Protocol to the Geneva Conventions is a possible alternative. This might have the advantage of limiting the number of substantive provisions which might be partly repetitive of existing treaty provisions that would have to appear in a full-blown Convention.[108] On the other hand, the choice of protocol form might be taken to suggest that protection of the environment is only of secondary importance.[109] The fact that the existing Protocols to the Geneva Conventions, and notably Protocol I, already contain general provisions concerning environmental protection might also cause complications.[110]

---

103 See 'Elements' document, *infra* at pp. 57–61. For some reactions to this see *infra* Kirsch at pp. 138–39, Bothe at p. 119 and Lee at p. 143.

104 See, for example, *infra* Bothe at pp. 124–25, Falk at p. 122, Rostow at pp. 122–23, Pinto at pp. 126–27, Türk at p. 128, Higgins at p. 128, Arkin at pp. 129–30 and Sapolsky at pp. 144–45. See also Greenwood at p. 124.

105 See, for example, Falk at p. 122.

106 Goldblat argues that agreement on a new Convention could not be achieved unless nuclear weapons were included (*infra* at p. 110). I argue the opposite in the 'Elements' document (at p. 40).

107 See, for example, Türk at pp. 101–2.

108 Ibid., at p. 101.

109 *Sed contra* Prokhorov, at p. 141, who regards a protocol as good as a convention.

110 This would not necessarily involve adopting a protocol to protocols, although the relationship of a new protocol to the existing Protocols would have to be made clear.

Either of the above options would run the risk of seeming to diminish the value of the existing less controversial Geneva Conventions and Protocols. A third alternative, therefore, is to adopt a Convention which is not a Geneva Convention as such but is sufficiently closely related to it to be counted, nevertheless, as a law of war instrument, perhaps along the lines of the 1954 Hague Convention on the Protection of Cultural Property.[111] This might have the additional political advantage that a diplomatic conference to negotiate such a treaty could be convened under the auspices of one of a number of organizations, perhaps most notably UNEP, the political backing of which might be valuable.[112] Again this process would take some years to reach fruition.

An alternative set of approaches involves the use of interpretative understandings and established procedures under existing instruments. The strongest advocate for these is Dr Jozef Goldblat, of the Geneva International Peace Research Institute, who believes that they should be employed immediately, while giving thought in the longer term to the possibility of adopting a new Convention.[113] They include: broadening the understanding of States Party to Protocol I of the meaning of the term 'natural environment' and of the level of environmental degradation falling below the threshold in its Article 35(3);[114] making further agreements, in the spirit of Article 56(6) of Protocol I, to protect additional installations containing dangerous forces (and possibly removing existing exceptions to the protection of those already listed in Article 56); convening a consultative meeting of the Parties to ENMOD in order to modify the accepted Understanding concerning the threshold of environmental degradation established and/or the environmental modification techniques covered by it;[115] and agreeing new Protocols under the Inhumane Weapons Convention.

Finally, a number of measures falling short of imposing new legal obligations upon states might be employed, either as short-term political indications of a desire for reform or as a means to avoid such reform. The prominent possibilities include: a UN General Assembly (and/or Security Council)[116] Resolution; a Red Cross/Crescent Resolution; a Resolution or Declaration of UNCED;[117] and the drafting of a Code of Conduct for

---

111 Loc. cit., *supra* n. 90. See, for example, Gasser at p. 112.

112 It was most unfortunate that Mostafa Tolba, Executive Director of UNEP, was unable to attend the London Conference.

113 See pp. 110–11 and 133. See also Gasser at pp. 112 and 146.

114 It must be remembered, however, that there is not yet any official interpretative understanding relating to Protocol I.

115 It must be remembered, however, that the status of this Understanding is not a strong one, as it did not go to the UN General Assembly for approval: see Fauteux, loc. cit., *supra* n. 1, at p. 15.

116 See *infra* pp. 34–35.

117 The question whether or not the topic should be added to the agenda of UNCED was controversial: see *infra* Marino at p. 109, Szekely at p. 114, Prokhorov at p. 142 and Gasser at p. 146. See now Appendix 8.

Governments and their Military in any of these fora. I shall discuss the prospects for these in Chapter 12.

Many of Camp 3's arguments appear persuasive, at least on a theoretical level. The single greatest weakness of Camp 3's approach, however, is precisely that it assumes on purely theoretical grounds that Camp 2 is wrong. Since neither Iraq nor the vast majority of the Coalition members were Parties to Protocol I during the Gulf War, (only Canada and Kuwait were Parties) the application of the provisions of that instrument relevant to environmental protection was not tested. If the provisions had been applied and tested, they might possibly have been found to be sufficient in practice. The analysis of many scholars, however,[118] and the need to take into account fresh scenarios in future wars, gives some grounds for argument against this. At the very least, the theoretical arguments for reform should be thoroughly examined.

The other difficult problem for Camp 3 is to ensure that its proposals preserve a large measure of realism. Its task as a reformist group will be to test the limits of public tolerance of reform, while ensuring that the new standards are not pitched so high that the law of war is likely to be disregarded and brought into disrepute.[119]

Camp 4 This Camp would add an additional criticism to those just expressed about Camp 3. It would allege it did not take sufficient account of the vagueness or, indeed, irrelevance of the distinction between wartime and peacetime in the context of acts of environmental destruction.[120] Members of this Camp are, like those of Camp 3, likely to be reformist in approach, albeit that many will regard the prospect of a new instrument to be a matter of long-term aspiration rather than an immediate need. What they have in common is simply the view that, if and when such an instrument is negotiated, it should seek to tackle the question of environmental destruction whenever it occurs, whether in peacetime, in time of international armed conflict or in time of internal armed conflict.[121] This is to be distinguished from the notion of merely excluding a category of acts done in wartime without any military objective from the scope of a possible new law of war Convention discussed above at p. 31.

Little can be said at this stage about this approach, except that, while it has the merit of avoiding distinctions between wartime and peacetime which are frequently artificial, it appears to be very ambitious. It has proved possible to negotiate a good many global treaties concerning the environment in peacetime, but these vary in their degree of effectiveness and are frequently ineffective. It is an ambitious task to seek to negotiate a general

---

118 In particular, the writings of Goldblat and Falk cited above.
119 See, for example, Hampson at p. 131 and Bothe at p. 135.
120 See, for example, Ferrari Bravo *infra* at p. 144, who sees this as an argument against negotiating a new Convention, and Sohr at pp. 114–15.
121 See, for example, *infra* Falk at p. 94, Goldblat at p. 110, Sohr at p. 115 and Gasser at pp. 112 and 146.

treaty on environmental protection which takes into account both wartime and peacetime environmental destruction. There will be severe difficulties, for example, in delineating between acts of deliberate and collateral environmental destruction which are properly covered by such a Convention and more general and gradual environmental degradation which is likely to need separate treatment. Perhaps its best chances of success, therefore, are through the development of the concept of crimes against humanity, as suggested by Adam Roberts (*infra* at p. 156), or a new category of 'crimes against nature' (*infra* Falk at p. 94 and Türk at p. 99), but this might be to rely too heavily upon criminal law mechanisms.

Other proposals

A number of other proposals for change were made at the Conference which are not necessarily associated with any particular one of the hypothetical Camps described above. They include the following:

1 Extending the Security Council's powers to deal with environmental emergencies which threaten international peace and security. Sir Crispin Tickell's appeal in favour of this[122] did not receive support from the round table.[123]
2 Adopting a device or devices by which to enable clarification in concrete situations of precise applications of general principles and norms concerning permissible military activity and compensation for environmental damage occurring in wartime. Ideas on how to effect this ranged from organizing special meetings of States Party to the relevant treaties,[124] to establishing expert panels,[125] to seeking a Security Council Resolution. The latter suggestion arose from the precedent set by Resolution 687.[126] By paragraph 16 of that Resolution, the Security Council reaffirmed that Iraq:

> is liable under international law for any direct loss, damage, *including environmental damage* and the depletion of natural resources, or injury to foreign Governments, nationals and corporations, as a result of Iraq's unlawful invasion and occupation of Kuwait (emphasis added).

Under paragraph 18 it decided to create a fund for the payment of such claims and to establish a commission to administer the fund. Under paragraph 19 of the Resolution a plan has been drawn up concerning the administration of Iraqi assets to ensure that a proportion of the proceeds of permitted export sales is fed into this fund.

---

122 See pp. 115–16. This has its origins in a UK proposal that the Security Council might 'take up environmental issues from time to time under Article 34 of the Charter': Statement of Sir Crispin Tickell before the UN Economic and Social Council, 9 May 1989.
123 See Kirsch at p. 150 and Roberts at p. 158.
124 See Lee at p. 142.
125 See Bothe at p. 119.
126 UN Doc. S/RES/687 (1991), 3 April 1991.

Part C of the same Resolution,[127] moreover, imposed extensive disarmament obligations upon Iraq in view of its aggression against Kuwait.

Several round tablers regard this Resolution as a unique precedent for both the establishment of principles of compensation in respect of, *inter alia*, environmental damage[128] and the imposition of disarmament obligations upon individual states.[129] Arguments are being made that the Security Council can thus be treated as a new source of law in the sense of having broad issues of compensation and even of the permissibility of proposed military actions put before it for decision in terms of environmental impacts in advance of or during the operations in question. Since, however, the Security Council is designed to be the Executive Organ of the UN primarily concerned with the preservation of international peace and security, it is difficult to see how it can be properly used as a body for laying down abstract statements or principles in this manner.

3 Some round tablers considered the demands of improved dispute-settlement mechanisms to take priority over legislative measures in the field of environmental protection in wartime.[130] It was noted that the International Court of Justice (ICJ) could and did deal with inter-state disputes in the field of the law of war.[131] Professor Ferrari Bravo also described two initiatives concerning dispute prevention and settlement placed before the UNCED Preparatory Committee by the Pentagonale Group and Poland.[132]

Definition of 'Environment'

I remain of the view, finally, that the question of the definition of 'environment' for these purposes is a difficult one requiring exhaustive study. My suggestion for the short term is that we should take the ICRC *Commentary*

---

127 Ibid., paragraphs 7 to 14.
128 See, for example, Prokhorov at pp. 141–42.
129 But see, for example, Pinto at p. 145.
130 See especially Pinto *infra* at p. 113 and Caflisch at pp. 141–42.
131 Schwebel *infra* at p. 115. At the Ottawa Conference it was even suggested that the ICJ could be used to give an Advisory Opinion on which putative targets it would be lawful to attack in advance of a proposed military action. With all due respect to the author of this idea, this appears to me to be a little unrealistic. Quite apart from the necessity of seeking the agreement of a UN organ or specialized agency to seek an Opinion, and from the time delay involved, even if an accelerated procedure is employed, there are significant questions of judicial competence and military secrecy to be considered.
132 Letter dated 19 March 1991 from the Head of the Delegation of Austria to the Preparatory Committee for UNCED at its second session addressed to the Secretary-General of UNCED, A/CONF.151/PC/L.29, 22 March 1991, and Annex entitled *Resolution on Prevention of International Disputes Concerning the Environment*; and letter of same title dated 26 March 1991, A/CONF.151/PC/WG.III/L.1, 27 March 1991, and attachment entitled *Elements for a Resolution on Settlement of International Disputes Concerning the Environment*. See *infra* discussion at pp. 143–44. The proposals are reproduced in Appendix 3.

definition of 'natural environment', as it is used in Protocol I and is described above at p. 25 and by Michael Meyer in Appendix 6, as a starting point and build upon it, drawing, for example, upon the considerations mentioned by David Tolbert in the same Appendix.

2 Elements of a 'Fifth Geneva' Convention on the Protection of the Environment in Time of Armed Conflict

Glen Plant

The reader is invited to refer to Appendix 2 for relevant treaty texts.

A Introduction

Summary

The document is divided into several parts, each consisting of an 'Element' and a commentary on that Element. It is designed to guide the participants but is not a comprehensive guide. In Appendix I the main relevant treaty provisions and details of the Parties to those treaties are set out. In Appendix II a short bibliography of texts referred to in the main document is set out.

The deliberate, massive environmental damage in the recent Gulf conflict calls for a distinct instrument on the laws of war and the environment.

It seems desirable to include in this clear statements on the relevant rules of customary law concerning, *inter alia*, state responsibility and international criminal law.

It seems desirable in this connection to bring the laws of war up to date to reflect major developments in international environmental law as it applies in time of peace.

It also seems desirable to improve existing Geneva and Hague law to afford greater protection to the environment. It is necessary to establish a specific threshold of protection.

This calls for a new Convention, rather than a Protocol to the existing Geneva Conventions, because it essentially marks a new departure within Geneva law.

It is appropriate at this initial juncture to await developments in disarmament fora and elsewhere before seeking to regulate in such a new instrument the use or first use of nuclear weapons and other weapons of mass destruction.

Consideration should be given to the possibility of the establishment of a rapid response body which could carry out in the environmental field functions similar to that of the Red Cross/Crescent in the humanitarian field, including acting as a Protecting Power for the Environment.

It will be difficult to define 'environment' for these purposes. The main problem is to distinguish attacks upon humans and their environment from attacks upon the environment as such, in so far as this is a meaningful distinction. Similarly it will be difficult to determine the degree of damage to the environment warranting regulation or prohibition.

Introduction

This document is prepared under severe time constraints arising from the author's sudden illness;[133] he apologizes for any errors. It is not intended to be an exhaustive introduction to the many issues to be discussed at the CDS/Greenpeace/LSE conference of 3rd June, a possible Geneva-style Convention on the Protection of the Environment in Time of Armed Conflict, nor to be necessarily comprehensive of all matters which might be included in such a convention. It is designed to serve merely as a basis for the round table discussions at the conference, which are to be led by the three Special-Rapporteurs, each of whom will concentrate on a different Part of the document. The document is divided into several Parts, each consisting of an 'Element' and a Commentary on that Element. In Appendix I are set out the main relevant treaty provisions and details of the Parties to those treaties. In Appendix II is set out a short bibliography of texts referred to in the main document. No attempt is made to draft specific texts of articles nor to suggest a particular form and ordering of a possible draft Convention, although it is assumed that its form will be conventional in the sense of having a preamble, substantive clauses and final clauses. It uses throughout the term the 'environment', although others might prefer 'natural environment' or another term.

The instant impetus behind the convocation of the conference is obviously the widespread concern about two matters arising during the recent conflict in the Gulf region: first, the deliberate harm to the environment wreaked by Iraq, which created a major oil-spill in the Gulf and set fire to large numbers of Kuwaiti oil-wells to little apparent military advantage; and second the occurrence of 'collateral' environmental damage as a result of the Coalition's military activities, in particular its intensive aerial campaign.

The outrage felt at Iraq's actions alone arguably makes it desirable for the international community to mark in a new instrument the concern that in future the need to give protection to the *environment* as such in time of armed conflict should be *explicitly* catered for, if only in relation to deliberate environmental damage. This is so even if it is agreed that Iraq's actions were already proscribed by customary or treaty norms, since the

---

133 I had an emergency appendectomy in April 1991.

existing relevant norms do not address themselves to the environmental impact of the destruction so much as to the indiscriminate and excessive nature of damage to enemy *property*. Most existing norms which might be construed to apply to environmental damage do not expressly mention the environment.

It is also arguably no longer sufficient to rely on the fact that the environment as such *is* expressly protected in the odd provision in one or two instruments, such as Article 35(3) of Additional Protocol I to the Geneva Conventions (Protocol I), especially when the efficacy of those provisions is seriously in doubt.

In addition, there is growing evidence that the prohibition of actions like those in question either is or is developing into a norm of international criminal law. It seems desirable to state this clearly in an international instrument.

This is not the first time that the environment has been blatantly abused in time of armed conflict, but it is perhaps the first time that the facts have been broadcast on such a wide scale. An unscrupulous leader, moreover, is more likely to have increasing destructive possibilities for causing such harm at his disposal as the world moves to more and more intensive exploitation of natural resources and energy sources.

As regards collateral damage to the environment, two matters might suggest the need, at the very least, to update existing Geneva and Hague law to improve the protection afforded to the environment, notwithstanding that many areas of this body of law were re-examined and improved upon during the decade commencing in 1970. Those improvements, after all, were made largely for humanitarian rather than environment-protection purposes. First, the 1980s and early 1990s have seen the development of new generations of weapons systems, which are available in varying degrees to military establishments worldwide; many of these pose an enhanced threat to the environment either by their very nature or in circumstances where they are used intensively or indiscriminately. Second, those years have also seen an environmentally significant diversification of military options in relation to possible targets, in two senses: that new weapons systems might be taken to make possible (and 'legitimize') precision (or other) attacks against targets which it would formerly have been impracticable, or even unlawful, to attack, in such a way as to increase the risk of damage to the environment; and that the number of targets, such as nuclear-power stations, chemical facilities and high dams, the destruction of which might result in environmental disaster, has grown greatly. The Chernobyl disaster is a sobering indication of the potential effects of a strike against the core of a nuclear reactor in time of armed conflict, when evacuation and other response measures will be even more difficult than they are in peacetime.

This document, therefore, suggests improvements mainly in the Geneva law, but also in the Hague law, which cannot be entirely separated from Geneva law, as is illustrated by Protocol I itself. It calls for a new Convention, rather than a Protocol to the existing Geneva Conventions because it essentially marks a new departure within Geneva law, rather than an improvement upon an existing corpus of law. The author is conscious of the many fora in which the laws of war are dealt with. If it is felt that this document contains too much Hague law, it is suggested that to that extent the regulation of weapons systems might be pursued with a view to environmental protection within the review processes set upon under the various relevant conventions.

It is a trite proposition, too, that both Geneva law and Hague law are in practice closely connected with the law of disarmament.[134] It is, for example, much easier to regulate attacks upon targets or the use of certain weapons in armed conflicts, if those weapons are not being developed, tested or stockpiled or have not already been used in practice by armed forces. Improvement of the Geneva law, moreover, is frequently the first step in movements towards disarmament measures. The author is aware that disarmament negotiations are proceeding in various fora on various types of weapon and does not wish the round table conference to prejudice those negotiations.

It follows that, while nuclear and other weapons of mass destruction, for example, should properly be regulated by any new Geneva law instrument concerning the environment, being obvious examples of weapons which, if used, seriously threaten the environment, it is, in the author's view, appropriate at this initial juncture to await developments elsewhere[135] before seeking to regulate or further regulate in such a new instrument the use or first use of such weapons. This is certainly true of nuclear weapons, which form part of the deterrent forces of a number of states and are stockpiled in vast numbers; disarmament measures are likely to be far more important than Geneva law measures in their case. However, it might be that participants will consider that a provision or provisions concerning chemical, biological and other toxin weapons, the stockpiling of which is much less acceptable among the vast majority of states, should be included in a new instrument.

In this context, too, it is recognized that over-strict attempts to regulate weaponry and targetry in an indirect attempt to induce disarmament raises the danger of bringing the law into disregard, given the capacities of modern weaponry, and to weaken its legal and moral force. It is, therefore, necessary to seek a realistic threshold of regulation. What is clear is that this threshold should be expressed in specific, and not general, terms; it must have a real impact, at least sufficient to cover the excesses in the Gulf conflict, and not merely seek to prohibit or regulate weaponry or targetry which in practical terms is unlikely to be used.

---

134 See, for example, Ove Bring, 'Regulating Conventional Weapons in the Future – Humanitarian Law or Arms Control?', 24, *Journal of Peace Research* (1987), pp. 275–85, esp. at p. 275.

135 I was conscious of parallel talks taking place upon the issues of nuclear, chemical and conventional weapons and of the recent Third Review Conference of the Convention on the Prohibition of the Development, Production and Stockpiling of Bacteriological (Biological) and Toxin Weapons and their Destruction, done at Geneva, 10 April 1972: UN Doc. A/2826: see Jozef Goldblat and Thomas Bernauer, *The Third Review of the Biological Weapons Convention: Issues and Proposals*, UNIDIR Research Paper No 9, April 1991.

A third reason for the consideration of a new instrument governing the laws of war and the environment is the desirability of updating the laws of war to reflect major developments in international environmental law as it applies in time of peace. Changes in state practice and the adoption of a large number of international environmental law instruments since the 1970s have reinforced the establishment or imminent emergence of a number of principles and norms of international law. Few of the international instruments refer expressly to their application in time of armed conflict, and the precise applicability of the norms and principles at such times is not clear. Nevertheless, a number, if not all, of them have potential applications at such time too. They include: the principle that states are responsible for ensuring that activities within their jurisdiction or control do not cause damage to the environment of other states or of areas beyond the limits of national jurisdiction; (possibly) a duty to carry out an environmental impact assessment prior to such activities; requirements of notification of such activities and (possibly) of consultation with affected states; (possibly) the application of the precautionary principle to such activities; and requirements to warn neighbouring states when an injurious transboundary escape in fact takes place. A new 'Geneva' convention could be used to clarify their application in wartime. Even taking into account the difficulties surrounding the practical application of several of these principles and norms in peacetime, their application in time of armed conflict might have useful consequences, especially upon the geographical limitation of the effects of such conflict.

A number of states, inter-governmental and non-governmental organizations have been involved in trying to put out the burning oil-wells and clean up the pollution in the Gulf region following the recent conflict. With all due respect to their valiant efforts and cooperation through existing coordinating structures,[136] the response has been both improvized and delayed by the absence of a neutral body with access to the war zone during the conflict. The possibility of establishing a rapid response body which could also be accepted as a sort of Protecting Power for the Environment and could perhaps carry out other functions parallel to those of the ICRC and/or League of the Red Cross and Red Crescent Societies in the humanitarian field, called perhaps the 'Green Cross/Crescent', ought to be considered.

Finally, the author makes no attempt to define the term 'environment'. Many have failed in this difficult venture. A definition is not, however, a unique problem in this context; it has not always been easy to find a workable distinction between civilians and combatants. A new 'Geneva' Convention would clearly be concerned with: damage to the marine environment as a whole and marine wildlife and habitats in particular; pollution of the atmosphere, destructive climate modification, enhanced global warming and degradation of the ozone layer; and the destruction or

---

136 UNEP prepared a three point plan of action: UN News Summary: UN Doc NS/6/91 dated 14 February 1991. The IMO and IAEA were also very actively involved. See UNEP DOC. GC. 16/4/Add. 1, 10 May 1991.

degradation of terrestrial fauna and flora and their habitats. It should take an ecosystems approach.

Difficulties will be encountered in defining what amounts to destruction or degradation and what degrees of destruction or degradation warrant regulation or prohibition under a new Convention. Particularly strict protection would be justified, for example, of areas of special vulnerability or importance in aesthetic, evolutionary (biodiversity) or other similar terms.

Perhaps the greatest difficulty, however, is posed by the fact that man and many of his works form part of the environment. It is accordingly very difficult to determine whether or not, for example, attacks on the means of survival of human populations themselves, such as attacks upon agricultural land or harvested forest or attacks which result in the spread of malnutrition or disease among humans as well as animals or plants, should always be considered also as attacks upon the environment. If all attacks which cause human suffering were treated as attacks upon the environment for these purposes, the result would be absurdity; a dividing line must be found.

Similar considerations might also be applied to attacks upon culturally important sites and monuments. No provision is included concerning these, because they are already protected by the Hague Convention for the Protection of Cultural Property in the Event of Armed Conflict 1954[137] and by provisions in Protocol I. If such a provision were added to a new Convention, it would only make sense if it were intended to remove the exception to the prohibition of attacks on such objects on grounds of military necessity.

---

137 Loc. cit., *supra* n. 90.

PART 1
GENERAL PRINCIPLES
ELEMENT 1

UNDER A CHAPTER HEADING: 'CHAPTER I: GENERAL PROVISIONS'

UNDER A SECTION HEADING: 'SECTION I: GENERAL PRINCIPLES AND SCOPE OF APPLICATION'

A.   A provision that, in cases not covered by the Convention, the environment remains under the protection of principles derived from established custom and the dictates of public conscience.

Commentary

This is derived from, *inter alios*, Article 1(2) of Protocol I. It recognizes that much of the law of war remains customary law, despite the many steps taken to codify and progressively develop it. In this context, the 'dictates of public conscience' relate in particular to concepts of humanitarian treatment of fauna, inter-generational equity and sustainable development.

*****

B.   A provision that the Convention applies to all situations of armed conflict, whereever occurring, and at all times, except where the context requires that it apply only during hostilities.

Commentary

This is derived from Protocols I and II. The period of application of obligations which need not be applied in time of peace as well as in wartime can be defined along the lines set out in Article 3 of Protocol I. The Convention should apply to all situations of armed conflict covered by *both* Geneva Protocols.

*****

C.   A restatement of the principles that the right of the Parties to a conflict to choose methods and means of warfare is not unlimited and that the only legitimate objective of states in time of armed conflict is to weaken the enemy forces.

Commentary

These are well-known principles stated, for example, in Article 22 of the Regulations attached to the Hague Convention (IV) of 1907 Concerning the Laws and Customs of War on Land and the Declaration of St Petersburg of 1868,[138] and restated *inter alios* in Article 35(1) Protocol I.

*****

D.   A provision that states shall be liable to pay compensation in respect of and shall bear responsibility for breaches of the Convention.

Commentary

This derives from equivalent provisions in Article 3 of the Hague Convention (IV) of 1907 and Article 91 of Protocol I, which represent the customary law of war. It might in addition or alternatively be placed in Element 4.

*****

E.   A provision that:

(a) a Party has the responsibility to ensure that its military activities under its jurisdiction or control do not cause damage to the environment of neutral states or of areas beyond national jurisdiction;

(b) a Party wishing to conduct such military activities should notify any neutral state the environment of which is likely to be damaged by them of its intention to carry them out and should consult and, where appropriate, cooperate with it in minimizing the danger and effects of such damage, at least to the extent that this does not compromise the security of the military operation in question;

(c) where applicable, the precautionary principle and environmental impact assessments should be applied; and

(d) if such damage in fact occurs, the Party conducting the military activities should fully inform the neutral states affected and/or, where damage to the global commons occurs, appropriate international organizations.

---

138 Loc. cit., *supra* n. 44 and 64.

Commentary

This provision reflects established and emerging principles of international law. They are reflected in various formulations in various places, such as: international judgements, for example the *Trail Smelter*, *Corfu Channel* and *Lac Lanoux* cases; Principle 21 of the Stockholm Declaration of Principles on the Human Environment of 1972;[139] the ILC's draft articles on *inter alia* Non-Navigational Uses of International Watercourses and International Liability for Transboundary Injurious Consequences Arising from Acts not Prohibited by International Law ('Injurious Consequences'); and in various international treaties.

*****

F.   A provision or provisions expressly stating that the principles of state necessity and military necessity do not automatically prevail over the principle of environmental protection.

Commentary

This provision might be regarded as unnecessary, as it can be readily implied from the Geneva law provisions below. No equivalent occurs in Protocol I. Nevertheless, the concept of state necessity has been discussed within the ILC since the 1970s (see, for example, 1982 Yearbook II (Pt. II), para. 28 *et seq.*), and participants might well consider a statement of general principle to be useful, at least on the subject of state necessity in view of recent perceptions that national sovereignty must have effective limits.

*****

UNDER A SECTION HEADING: 'SECTION II:
LEGAL STATUS OF THE PARTIES TO THE CONFLICT'

G.   A provision reproducing with minor amendment Article 4 of Protocol I, that the legal status of the Parties shall not be affected by the Convention.

*****

UNDER A SECTION HEADING: 'SECTION III: DEFINITIONS'

H.   A provision defining 'environment' for the purposes of the Convention and other matters which the working group will find it necessary to define.

---

139 Loc. cit., *supra* n. 51.

PART 2
GENEVA LAW
ELEMENT 2

UNDER A CHAPTER HEADING: 'CHAPTER I:
METHODS AND MEANS OF WARFARE'

UNDER A SECTION HEADING: 'SECTION I:
METHODS AND MEANS OF WARFARE'

A. A provision establishing the threshold at which methods and means of warfare are prohibited because of their intended or expected impact upon the environment. There appear to be approximately four options for change:

Option (a): prohibiting the employment of methods or means of warfare which are intended, or may be expected, to cause *any* (except *de minimis*) damage to the environment;

Option (b): prohibiting it at least where the damage is widespread, long-lasting *or* severe;

Option (c): prohibiting it as under alternative (b), but adding a fourth alternative criterion, 'significant (or 'appreciable') and irreversible'.

Option (d): choosing some midway position between alternative (b) and the existing excessively high threshold as it appears in Article 35(3) of Protocol I.

Commentary

If option (a) were chosen, this prohibition would include the propositions that: the environment itself or its manipulation or modification may not be used as a 'weapon'; that weapons the sole or predominant purpose of which is destruction of the environment may not be used; and that other weapons may not be used in such a way as to damage the environment.

This would also be true in a modified sense if options (b), (c) or (d) were chosen.

The prohibition would apply to protect the environment *in general* and not merely (as in the case of the ENMOD Convention) the environment of the enemy state or the global commons. Similarly, like Article 35(3) of Protocol I, it would be aimed to protect the environment *per se*, and not merely (like Article 55 of that Protocol) the environment because of the ultimate impact of the damage upon humans.

As a minimum, just as Article 35(3) of Protocol I was essentially intended in 1977 to respond to some of the worst environmental excesses of the Vietnam conflict, *this provision should be aimed at providing a specific prohibition of a repetition of the worst environmental excesses of the Gulf conflict*. Only options (a), (b) or (c) are likely to do this.

Option (a): some support for a total prohibition might be derived from state practice as reflected in unilateral statements, such as those made by certain states during the Vietnam conflict, that weapons damaging the environment, such as defoliants and herbicides, were unlawful and in such soft law instruments as the World Charter for Nature of 1972. Article V of the Charter provides, for example, that 'Nature shall be secured against degradation caused by warfare or other hostile activities' and Article XX 'Military activities damaging to nature shall be avoided'.[140]

On the other hand, the only negotiated response to the outcry raised over the Vietnam War which was supported by the majority of states was the very high threshold in Article 35(3) of Protocol I, and, while the Charter is drafted in treaty language, it is still a soft law instrument and of limited significance.

Option (b) is derived from Article I of the Convention on the Prohibition of Military or any Other Hostile Use of Environmental Modification Techniques of 1977 ('ENMOD Convention').[141] It is lower than that established by Article 35(3) of Protocol I in two senses. First the three criteria to be applied are *alternative* and not cumulative, as in Protocol I. Second, although no definition of any of these three criteria appears in the ENMOD Convention itself, the Conference of the Committee on Disarmament (CCD), which drafted the Convention, drafted an 'Understanding relating to Article I', which, while not forming part of the Convention, is generally taken to reflect the intention of its drafters, and this is clearly to establish a lower threshold than under Protocol I.[142] It is set out below:

> It is the understanding of the Committee that . . . the terms 'widespread', 'long-lasting' and 'severe' shall be interpreted as follows:
> (a) **widespread**: encompassing an area on the scale of several hundred square kilometres;
> (b) **long-lasting**: lasting for a period of months, or approximately a season;
> (c) **severe**: involving serious or significant disruption or harm to human life, natural and economic resources or other assets.

In contrast the criteria in Article 35(3) of Protocol I, 'widespread', 'long-*term*' and 'severe' seem to be 'primarily *directed to high-level policy decision-makers* and would affect such unconventional means of warfare as the *massive use of herbicides or chemical agents* which could produce widespread, long-term and severe damage to the natural environment' (Bothe, Partsch and Solf at p. 348 – emphasis added), and the 'Conference Reports indicate that collateral damage from conventional warfare, even very severe damage such as that which occurred in France in the First World War, was not intended to be covered and that *"long-term" should*

---

140 UN General Assembly Resolution 37/7, 28 October 1982. The USA alone voted against it.
141 Loc. cit., *supra* n. 25.
142 Loc. cit., *supra* n. 71.

be understood in terms of decades' (Aldrich at p. 711 – emphasis added).

This existing high threshold in Protocol I certainly does not encompass the deliberate creation of a major oil slick and the setting light to extensive oil fields. Indeed, it is difficult to think of many realistic situations in which it would apply (apart from the destruction of dams, dykes and nuclear electrical generating stations which are in any event given additional protection in the circumstances described in Article 56 of Protocol I – see *infra*). Perhaps one example is the bombing of a chemical tanker containing a very noxious and easily spread chemical or a LPG/LNG tanker near a coast.

The ENMOD Understanding is expressed to be for the purposes of the ENMOD Convention alone, and thus the threshold at present applies only to such matters as the artificial creation of earthquakes or tidal waves, the artificial depletion of the ozone layer and the artificial modification of ocean currents or climate. It is difficult to envisage the successful use of any of these techniques by a belligerent, and this ineluctably leads to the conclusion that the negotiators were aware of this in 1977. It might well be difficult, therefore, to achieve the extension of the lower threshold to more meaningful armed conflict scenarios. Nevertheless, the Understanding set out above might be usefully used as a guide in drafting a new Convention. *This lower threshold so applied would certainly encompass the deliberate creation of an oil slick and the setting light to extensive oil fields.*

Option (c): The same considerations apply as in the case of Option (b), except that the threshold is set still lower. The criterion of *'irreversibility'* relates primarily to the loss of ecosystems, species or genetic material or the diversity thereof in a given area, which can have a serious impact upon the ecology of a region or of the world as a whole, even if the damage in other terms is limited. The addition of this criterion thus recommends itself. Guidance as to the choice of the qualifying term, whether *'significant'* or *'appreciable'*, might be derived from the debates of the ILC on the topics of State Responsibility, Injurious Consequences and International Watercourses mentioned above in Part I.

Option (d): is the least desirable, because it is difficult to see how a threshold can be set below the ENMOD standard in such a way as to capture realistic scenarios.

*****

B.   A provision that a state is obliged, in the study, development, acquisition or adoption of a new weapon, means or method of warfare, to determine whether or not its employment would, in all the circumstances, be prohibited by the Convention.

Commentary

This is derived from Article 36 of Protocol I. It aims to discourage the development of weapons systems on the ground that, although their use would be prohibited by Element 2.A, they might nevertheless be employed in disregard of the prohibition, if they existed, in the heat of war.

UNDER A CHAPTER HEADING: 'CHAPTER II:
GENERAL PROTECTION AGAINST EFFECTS OF HOSTILITIES'

UNDER A SECTION HEADING: 'SECTION I:
BASIC RULE AND FIELD OF APPLICATION'

C. A provision or provisions reproducing Articles 48 and 49 of Protocol I substituting the term 'environment' or suitable variations for 'civilian' and its variants, where appropriate.

Commentary

This would preserve the narrow definition of military objectives and the broad definition of attack which are progressive elements of the Protocol.

*****

UNDER A SECTION HEADING:
'SECTION II: PROTECTION OF THE ENVIRONMENT'

D. A provision that, in case of doubt whether or not an object or area is part of the environment, that it is to be presumed that it is.

Commentary

This reflects Articles 50(1) and 52(3) of Protocol I, which are progressive elements of the Protocol.

*****

E. A provision reproducing the prohibition of acts against the environment by way of reprisal in Article 55(2) of Protocol I. This is to clearly comprehend all acts of reprisal and not merely those which result in ultimate loss or injury of humans.

Commentary

Article 55(2) of Protocol I, which this essentially reproduces, was adopted by consensus.

*****

F. A provision that attacks upon works and installations containing dangerous forces is prohibited in all circumstances which carry an appreciable or significant risk of the release of dangerous forces and consequent severe environmental damage (regardless of losses among the civilian population). It

might also prohibit all attacks upon nuclear electrical generating stations in all circumstances. It should reproduce, with necessary modifications, Article 56(3)–(7) of Protocol I.

Commentary

This provision would follow the spirit of Article 56(6) of Protocol I. It is particularly important to enhance the protection afforded to nuclear electrical generating plants, which at present have less protection under existing Geneva law in certain circumstances than dams or dykes, notwithstanding the fact that, with few exceptions, their destruction is likely to have far more harmful results for mankind and his environment than a dam- or dyke-burst. The consequences of a full-scale attack upon such a station is well illustrated by the Chernobyl disaster.

Article 56(2)(b), for example, has the effect that such a station may be attacked, even if it is being used for its normal purpose of generating electricity, if it is doing so in regular, significant and direct support of military operations and the attack is the only feasible way to terminate this support. This appears to include attacks merely because the station is supplying the national grid and the operating armed forces of the state are drawing power from the grid, when other means of cutting off the power, such as attacking power lines, are proving inefficacious.

The criterion of 'appreciable' or 'significant' risk of causing an escape of dangerous forces with a high risk of severe environmental damage is loosely derived from the work of the ILC on Injurious Consequences.

*****

UNDER A SECTION HEADING:
'SECTION III: PRECAUTIONARY MEASURES'

G.   A provision or provisions reproducing the relevant parts of Articles 57 and 58 of Protocol I, substituting the term 'environment' and variants thereon as appropriate.

Commentary

This would mean that Parties could not carry out an attack which would cause excessive damage to the environment; in view of the intricacy of the provision in question, the judgement whether or not an attack should be carried out should be made at as a high a level of command as possible and in the light of all the information which is available or should be available upon making reasonable inquiry (see Kalshoven at pp. 98–100).

*****

UNDER A SECTION HEADING:
'SECTION IV: LOCALITIES AND ZONES UNDER SPECIAL PROTECTION'

H.   A provision that localities and zones containing ecosystems, species or genetic material of vital international importance shall not be subject to attack and shall be demilitarized zones.

Commentary

Guidance as to the precise content of this provision can be derived from Articles 59 and 60 of Protocol I. The protection of the areas and localities will be absolute. The areas and localities in question will not be subject to identification by agreement between the warring parties, but should be *identified by general international agreement* on a continuing basis. The World Heritage Convention might be modified to provide a suitable forum for this. A new sign might be adopted for their identification and demarcation, notwithstanding the practical difficulties encountered in using such signs.

PART 3
HAGUE LAW
ELEMENT 3

UNDER A CHAPTER HEADING:
'CHAPTER I: PROHIBITIONS OR RESTRICTIONS ON THE USE OF
CERTAIN WEAPONS WHICH MAY BE CONSIDERED TO BE
EXCESSIVELY INJURIOUS TO THE ENVIRONMENT'

UNDER A SECTION HEADING:
'SECTION I: GENERAL PROVISIONS'

A. A provision that nothing in Part 3 of the Convention should be interpreted to detract from other provisions in the Convention, nor from obligations imposed upon Parties by international humanitarian law, nor from the Convention on Prohibitions or Restrictions on the Use of Certain Conventional Weapons which may be Deemed to be Excessively Injurious or to Have Indiscriminate Effects 1980 (the Inhumane Weapons Convention).[143]

*****

UNDER A SECTION HEADING:
'SECTION II: DEFOLIANTS, HERBICIDES, *DAISY CUTTER* BOMBS,
MASSIVE CONVENTIONAL BOMBING OR CRATERING AND
FOREST PLOWS'

B. A provision prohibiting the massive use of defoliants, herbicides, *daisy cutter* bombs, massive conventional bombing and cratering and large plows to remove forest and other kinds of plant cover, except on a small scale to assist in the preparation of air strips, harbours or military camps and of reasonable cleared perimeters around these and roads or tracks bordered by cover which can facilitate an ambush.

Commentary

State practice seems to support the view that the massive use of defoliants and herbicides is already prohibited. They may well be prohibited by both Article 35(3) of Protocol I and the ENMOD Convention. A US Government spokesman has accepted that this is true of the ENMOD Convention; see also *supra* commentary to Element 2.A, option (a).

It is far more difficult to argue that the other methods are unlawful

---

143 Loc. cit., *supra* n. 26.

under existing law. Objections to their use on environmental grounds can only truly be voiced where they are used intensively or indiscriminately. It will be very difficult in practice to set a threshold of acceptability.

Daisy cutter-type bombs are high-explosive devices which burst at a height designed to ensure clearance of a forest area of a size sufficient to clear an air strip.

Forest plows were used extensively in Vietnam after 1969 largely to replace the use of defoliants and herbicides; as they uproot fragile forest earth and root systems, they tend, if anything, to be even more destructive than defoliants and herbicides.

*****

UNDER A SECTION HEADING:
'SECTION III: MINES, BOOBY TRAPS AND OTHER DEVICES'

C. A provision or provisions that provide that:
(a) the direction of mines, booby traps and other devices (as defined in Article 1 of Protocol II to the Inhumane Weapons Convention 1980, with the addition of sea mines) against the environment is prohibited;
(b) all precautions which are practicable or practically possible, taking into account all of the circumstances, should be taken to protect the environment from pollution caused by or other injurious effects of these weapons;
(c) these weapons are to be designed so as to minimize damage to the environment;
(d) the location of minefields, mines, booby traps and other devices is to be recorded; and
(e) Parties are to cooperate to ensure their removal after their military purpose has been served.

Commentary

This provision builds upon the provisions of Protocol II to the Inhumane Weapons Convention.

Certain varieties of persistent mine can secrete noxious chemicals which might have significant environmental impact if the mines are present in large numbers. Anti-personnel land mines present in large numbers can endanger significant numbers of large animals.

*****

UNDER A SECTION HEADING:
'SECTION IV: INCENDIARY AND BLAST EFFECT WEAPONS'

D. A provision or provisions that provide that:
(a) it is prohibited to make the environment, including forests and other kinds of plant cover, the object of attack by incendiary or blast effect weapons, *even when* plant cover is used to cover, conceal or camouflage combatants or other military objectives *and* the incendiary or blast effect is not specifically designed to cause burn injury or blast injury, respectively, to persons, but to be used against military objectives, such as armoured vehicles, aircraft and installations or facilities. In so far as this prohibition conflicts with Article 2(4) of Protocol III to the Inhumane Weapons Convention 1980, this provision is to prevail;
(b) incendiary weapons may as an exception to this prohibition be used to set fire to military obstacles such as oil-filled ditches, where this does not cause widespread, long-lasting or severe damage to the environment; and
(c) Blast-effect weapons may as an exception to this prohibition be used to clear minefields.

Commentary

This provision builds upon the provisions of Protocol III to the Inhumane Weapons Convention. The definitions in Article 1 of that Protocol might be used, with suitable modifications, to include, for example, blast-effect weapons, which are excluded from its scope. It is necessary to overrule the exceptions in Article 2(4) of the Protocol, which make a mockery of that provision, since virtually the only time that plant cover is likely to be attacked is when it is being used as cover or camouflage (Kalshoven at p. 157).

Blast-effect weapons, which disperse and then ignite an explosive fuel/air mixture, were originally developed as anti-mine weapons. The USA has announced that it will restrict their use to this purpose. Second, third and fourth generations may, however, be being considered by some states for anti-personnel use. They kill everything within the range of the mixture, humans and animals with lungs by internal asphyxiation and bleeding caused by explosion and burning within their lungs. If used in large numbers, they are likely to seriously affect the stability of wildlife in the area.

PART 4
EXECUTION OF THE CONVENTION
ELEMENT 4

UNDER A CHAPTER HEADING
'CHAPTER I: EXECUTION OF THE CONVENTION'

UNDER A SECTION HEADING:
'SECTION I: GENERAL PROVISIONS'

A.   A provision reproducing with minor modifications Articles 80 and 82 to 84 of Protocol I.

*****

UNDER A SECTION HEADING:
'SECTION II: REPRESSION OF BREACHES OF
THE CONVENTION'

B.   A provision that a deliberate breach of the prohibition on causing environmental damage under Element 2.A, F or H is a 'grave breach' of the Convention, justifying criminal prosecution of responsible individuals.

Commentary

Article 85(3)(c) and (4)(d) of Protocol I already give some limited protection to the environment in this manner. To make such provision in the Convention would, moreover, reflect certain trends in the work of the ILC on state responsibility and international crimes. In Article 19(3) of its Provisional Draft Articles on State Responsibility (Report of 33rd Session of ILC, 1981, in 1982 Yearbook II (Pt. II)), for example, it provides:

> Subject to paragraph 2, and on the basis of the rules of international law in force, an international crime may result, *inter alia*, from . . .

> (d) a serious breach of an international obligation of essential importance for the safeguarding and preservation of the human environment, such as those prohibiting massive pollution of the atmosphere and of the seas.

Paragraph 2 provides that 'An internationally wrongful act which results from the breach by a State of an international obligation so essential for the protection of fundamental interests of the international community that its breach is recognized as a crime by that community as a whole, constitutes an international crime.' This contemplates the possibility of state, as well as individual, criminal liability.

More recently the ILC has added a provision concerning the protection of the environment *per se* to its draft Articles on Injurious Consequences.

*****

C.   A provision or provisions reproducing with minor amendments Articles 86, 87, 89 and 90 of Protocol I.

*****

D.   There are two possible options:

Option (a): **A provision that a Party in whose territory an offender or alleged offender under Element 2.A, F or H is present and which does not submit his case for possible prosecution to its own prosecuting authorities shall detain him at the request of a state requesting it to do so and deliver him up to that state for prosecution. This obligation should also extend to the making available of evidence in the requested state's possession and should not depend upon the existence of extradition arrangements between the states in question. It should also reproduce Article 88(3) Protocol I;**

Option (b): **A provision reproducing with minor amendments Article 88 of Protocol I.**

Commentary

The intention of Element 4.B above is to create universal jurisdiction in relation to the international crime in question, permitting any state to detain and prosecute an alleged offender. Nevertheless, one weakness of war crimes' provisions to which this principle applies has arguably been the absence of effective means to ensure that alleged offenders are brought to justice. This is because, unless he is captured by enemy forces, an alleged offender can only be brought to justice if he is present in a state which is willing to prosecute him or to (deport or) extradite him to a requesting state. But extradition is only possible where extradition arrangements are in place between the two countries. Option (a) would avoid this reliance upon existing bilateral arrangements. Guidance as to its precise drafting could be sought from any of the existing *aut dedere, aut iudicare* Conventions.[144]

*****

E.   A restatement of the general principle of state responsibility stated in Element 1.D.

---

144 These are all referred to in Glen Plant 'The Convention for the Suppression of Unlawful Acts against the Safety of Maritime Navigation', 39 *ICLQ* (1990), 27, et. seq., esp. at footnotes 7–9.

PART 5
INSTITUTIONS
ELEMENT 5

UNDER A CHAPTER HEADING:
'CHAPTER I: EXECUTION OF THE CONVENTION'

UNDER A SECTION HEADING:
'SECTION I: PROTECTING ORGANIZATION'

A. A provision:
(a) requiring Parties to a conflict to accept a new organization (to be called the 'Green Cross/Crescent/Lion/Star?) for the purpose of applying the Convention and safeguarding the environment;
(b) permitting a substitute organization which offers all guarantees of impartiality and efficacy in the environmental protection field to be appointed instead, but only with the consent of all Parties to the conflict, and following and taking into account the results of consultations between it and the Parties;
(c) permitting the organization to operate under a distinctive emblem, such as a Green Cross/Crescent, and making its personnel operating under it to be immune from attack;
(d) referring to an *Annex I* setting out the structure and functions of the new organization (see *infra* pp. 60–61).

B. A provision reproducing Article 81 of Protocol I, with necessary modifications, requiring Parties to provide the new organization with all necessary facilities within their power.

Commentary to 5.A and B

Further discussion of the organization appears in the Commentary to 5.C below. These provisions are derived from Articles 5(4) and 81 of Protocol I.

It is inappropriate to adopt a system of Protecting *Powers* in relation to the environment, as no one state is in a position to protect the environment, which is a concern of mankind in general and not merely one or other of the belligerent Parties; an impartial international organization is necessary. This organization could, like the ICRC in relation to existing Geneva law, be a co-guarantor of the treaty and could produce an annual report on the environmental impact of armed conflict.

*****

UNDER A SECTION HEADING:
'SECTION II: RELIEF IN FAVOUR OF THE ENVIRONMENT'

C. A provision:

(a) authorizing the new Organization to carry out actions which are impartial and remedial of environmental damage caused by a Party in breach of its obligations under the Convention and stipulating that these actions shall not be regarded as interference in the conflict nor as unfriendly acts; and

(b) reproducing, with necessary amendments, Articles 70(2)–(5) of Protocol I.

Commentary

If the Organization were given a Relief role, like the Red Cross/Crescent, it would need, besides immunity, guaranteed rights of access to and inspection of protected and damaged areas, the right to be informed of damage and the rights to give advice and to take urgent remedial measures. Like the Red Cross/Crescent, it would need a right of initiative and would not merely be a passive organ.

This provision echoes in most respects the Soviet call for a new 'Council for Emergency Environmental Assistance' 'to send international groups of experts without delay to areas with a badly deteriorating environment' and 'to organize international cooperation in critical environmental situations' on the basis of the experts' recommendations concerning the limitation and elimination of the consequences of the environmental disaster (statement of President Gorbachev before the UN General Assembly, 7 December 1988: UN Doc. A/43/PV.72, p. 19; and letter from Edvard Sheverdnadze, then Soviet Foreign Minister, to the UN Secretary-General, dated 30 April 1989: Annex to UN Doc. A/44/264 E/1989/73, 2 May 1989). Although they had in mind a peacetime disaster, Chernobyl, nothing in their proposal suggests that such an organization could not also operate in time of armed conflict.

The Soviet suggestion is, however, for the formation of such a Centre within the UN Secretariat, like UNDRO and UNEP. It is likely, however, that certain states will consider such a UN body to be insufficiently impartial to carry out the counterparts to the relief activities of the Red Cross/Crescent in the environmental field.

One existing *non-governmental* international organization commends itself at first sight as an ideal alternative: the International Union for the Conservation of Nature and Natural Resources (IUCN). Founded in 1948, this is the largest and perhaps most representative alliance of conservation agencies and interest groups, with over 500 member organizations and a permanent Secretariat, operating in three specialist Centres with the support of over 3,000 experts. Indeed, Professor Nicholas Robinson of Pace University, New York, who will participate in the 3rd June conference, has prepared for the IUCN's Commission on Environmental Law a set of Draft

Articles for Inclusion in a 'Convention Securing Nature from Warfare or Other Hostile Activities'. This would give the IUCN powers of inspection in zones protected in time of conflict for environmental purposes, the right to give advice and the right to be informed of damage to natural areas. It would also give (unidentified) 'environmental workers' rights of access to such zones to permit their 'maintenance and operation'.

The fatal drawback, however, is that the IUCN's membership includes governments and government agencies, so that it might not be perceived as sufficiently impartial.

A new organization, possessing many of the characteristics which guarantee the impartiality of the Red Cross/Crescent, thus appears to be necessary. This will need to liaise very closely with the Red Cross/Crescent, the UN Organization, UNEP and the IUCN. It might be organized along a number of lines (see Annex I).

*****

ELEMENT 5 continued
ANNEX 1
ORGANIZATION OF THE GREEN CROSS/CRESCENT

The most sensible model to follow for the organization of the new Organization is the Red Cross/Crescent model. An organizational chart which assumes a single internationally-oriented organization and is based on the ICRC since 1980 is set out below.

If the organization is to have both a Protecting and a Relief role, the choice of President will be crucial. As well as having expertise in environmental science and administration, he will need to be capable of filling a high-profile diplomatic role. He will need an efficient permanent Secretariat.

The Organization will need a properly financed regular budget, as well as an Extraordinary Budget. It might be wished to copy the dual structure of the Red Cross/Crescent, the ICRC and the League of (national) Red Cross and Red Crescent Societies. This might ensure the 'Green Cross' grass roots support and might result in the equivalent of the League contributing to the finances of the ICRC equivalent, as occurs with the Red Cross/Crescent. If such an Organization were established, however, it is likely that it will rely relatively little on government contributions and will need to rely less on any national societies' contributions. Environmentalist NGOs are likely to contribute a large proportion of the budget. It might follow that a single streamlined structure could be adopted.

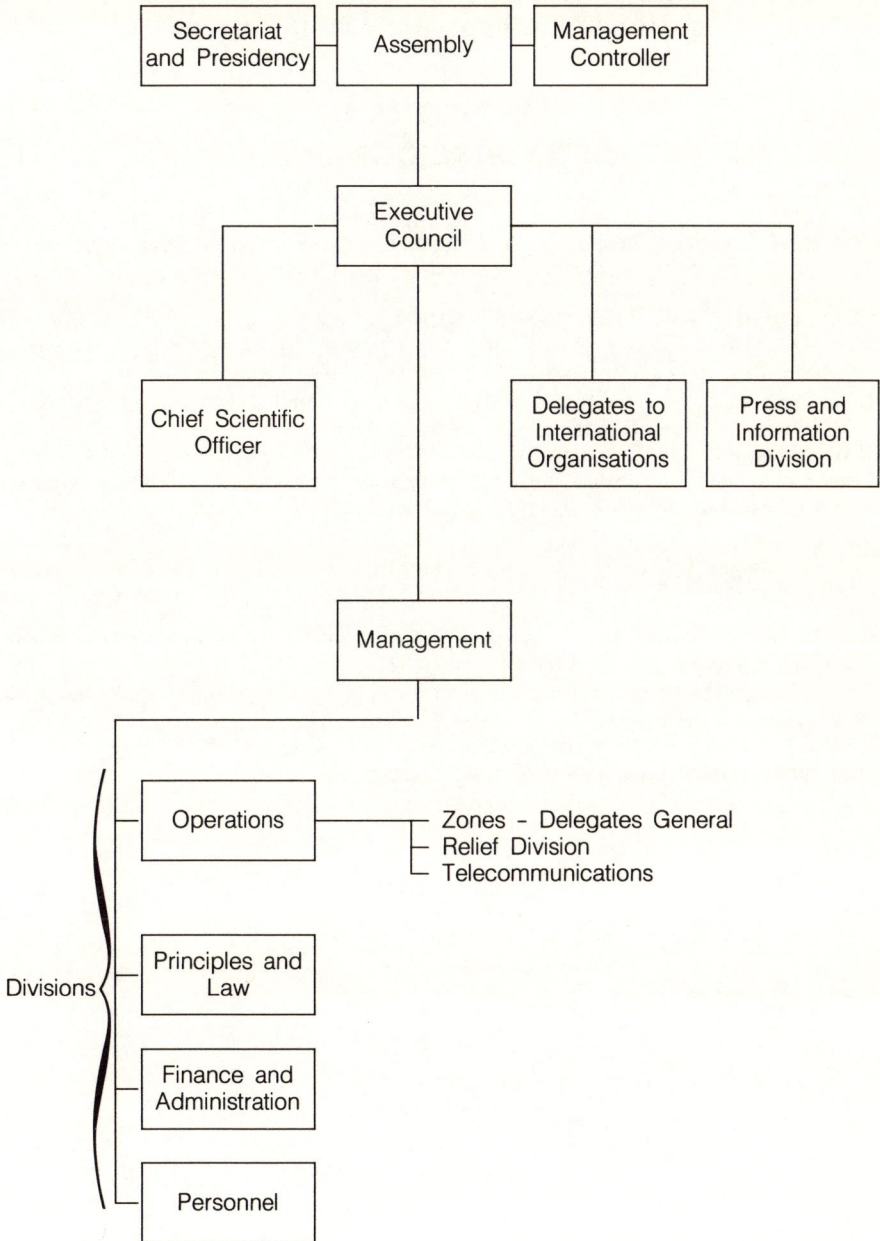

APPENDIX I
omitted (see Appendix 2 to this book)

APPENDIX II
BRIEF BIBLIOGRAPHY

George H. Aldrich, 'Progressive Development of the Laws of War: a Reply to
  Criticisms of the 1977 Geneva Protocol I', 26, *Virginia J. Int. L.* pp. 693–720,
  esp. at p. 711.
Michael Bothe, Karl Josef Partsch, Waldemar Solf, *New Rules for Victims of
  Armed Conflicts*, The Hague, Boston, London, Martinus Nijhoff, (1982) –
  Commentary to esp. Articles 35, 36 and 55 of Protocol I.
ILC Draft Articles on Injurious Consequences, State Responsibility and Non-
  Navigational Uses of International Watercourses.
ILC Yearbook of ILC II (Pt. II).
Frits Kalshoven, *Constraints on the Waging of War*, ICRC, Martinus Nijhoff,
  (1987), esp. at pp. 80–2, 96–104, 132–3 and 147–57.

Additional Reading

George Aldrich 'Prospects for US Ratification of Additional Protocol I to the 1949
  Geneva Conventions' 85 *AJIL* (1991) pp. 1–20.
On the ENMOD Convention, testimony of Dr Jozef Goldblat before the Committee
  on Foreign Relations of the US Senate, 95 Congress, 2nd. Session, 3.10.1978.
Enclosed chapter by Dr Jozef Goldblat (loc. cit., *supra* n. 70).
Draft articles by Professor Nicholas Robinson.

Part II
Proceedings of 3rd June Conference

A: PREPARED PAPERS

3 Introductory Speech

Carlo Ripa di Meana

Ladies and gentlemen, it is a great pleasure and honour for me to open the proceedings today and to be able to share some ideas with you.

It is sad that, even as the twentieth century draws to a close, it is still necessary for us to deal with the eventuality of war. Nor is the problem of trying to regulate war a new one. As you can see from Dr Plant's 'Elements' Document, inspiration is to be found in the 1868 Declaration of St Petersburg.[145]

Many years of supposed civilization have not brought us closer to a global peace. Of course the disarmament process, which I fully applaud, continues apace in the context of the emerging new World Order. At the same time, however, advances in technology mean that our weapons have become ever more sophisticated and the dangers and risks which face us and our environment have grown in proportion. I thus feel that this conference has special value.

Until now solutions for environmental destruction in time of war have been essentially reactive. Thus the international community moved to prohibit the use of herbicides, defoliants and *daisy-cutter* bombs after their use in Vietnam.

The public conscience is increasingly aware that our natural environment should no longer be seen as *res nullius*. On the contrary, future international law must be based on the concept of *res omnium*, that is that the environment is a common good of the whole of humanity.

It is vital that this conference is not seen as simply the start of the world's reaction to the environmental 'terrorism' of the Gulf War, but as a new start with a new approach. We should not base our deliberations only on the conviction that we must never let the events of the Gulf be repeated, although we must indeed avoid this. We should rather take as our starting point the same determination to protect the environment as we show in times of peace and we should build upon the basis of that determination a concrete and realistic international instrument which will ensure the protection of the environment in all future war situations.

---

145 Loc. cit., *supra* n. 64.

I am not a lawyer and, in the presence of such an eminent gathering, I would not presume to enter into detailed argument on fine legal points. I intend rather to put to you the essential elements which, it seems to me as EC Environmental Commissioner, any future instrument should contain.

First, there must be a clear definition of what constitutes unacceptable damage to the environment in time of war. That will be your first task in your discussions today. I appreciate that it is not an easy one, but without such a definition a new instrument is worthless. Despite the difficulties which we can all foresee, the definition must be a strict one. To settle for a less strict solution in the name of some sort of compromise will endanger the whole enterprise from the outset. Some actions are quite clearly beyond the pale. The deliberate release of oil into the Gulf and the setting on fire of the Kuwaiti oil-wells could only have served 'military objectives' in the twisted mind of Saddam Hussein. Instances of environmental damage incidental to legitimate military operations must be clearly distinguished from such obvious breaches. May I at this point interpose to say how pleased I am that there should be Kuwaiti participation today and extend a warm welcome to our Kuwaiti friend?[146]

Quite apart from the question of protecting the natural environment, I would hope that any definition should also seek to protect our cultural monuments, thus ensuring that incidents such as the deliberate bombing of Coventry and Dresden remain forever outlawed. It will also be necessary to deal with the situation where a protagonist forces his adversaries to attack such monuments by using them, for example, for military strategic purposes.

Second, the new instrument must make the infliction of unacceptable damage upon the environment a punishable war crime. To my mind this necessitates the establishment of an independent tribunal to decide on questions of interpretation, responsibility and punishment or reparation. It seems to me that the solution of allowing individual states either to try offenders or to extradite them to other states who will then try them has not worked, as the experience with airline hijackers has shown. There must be no safe haven for the new environmental criminals. I consider that this can only be achieved by a tribunal whose independence ensures that its jurisdiction and decisions can be accepted by all states. This solution has the additional advantage that the question of trying and extraditing environmental offenders does not become tied up in other unrelated arguments between states.

Third, the instrument should provide for a new force or a new body, the sole concern of which would be the protection of a threatened environment and saving or re-establishing it after a crisis. The instrument must ensure that such a force has a guaranteed independence which will ensure its acceptability. We have always in French talked of 'des casques verts' by way of analogy with the UN's 'casques bleues' or 'blue beret' force. I gather, however, that the term 'green berets' in English means something different!

---

146 Dr Abdul Rahman Al-Awadhi, one of the round tablers.

I have to say that the idea of a Green Cross or Crescent on an analogy with the Red Cross is an interesting one, and I would read your conclusions on this point with much interest.

These, it seems to me, must be the main pillars of a 'Fifth Geneva' Convention. Clearly, however, much flesh has still to be put on these bare bones, and today's conference will be a vital step in this process.

Let me conclude with two final remarks, and I ask you to forgive my frankness. The protection of the global environment is urgent. Do not give in to the lawyer's temptation to become involved in a sterile and arcane legal argument over inessential matters. The work in hand is too important for that, and I beg you to keep that point always in the front of your mind during your discussions. The importance and urgency of the obligations which we are seeking to impose far outweigh the need for absolute perfection.

Second, if the convention discussed today is to become a reality, governments must press for its adoption in the international forum with the broadest possible mandate; this I consider to be the United Nations Organization. I would urge all the government representatives here today to use their positions to encourage their authorities to pass from words to action.

For my part, I pledge that the European Community will do all in its power to ensure adoption of a fifth Geneva Convention. The adoption of one or more new protocols is not, in my opinion, sufficient to solve problems of the magnitude with which we are faced. Not only will the European Community encourage such a new convention, but, in my opinion, it has the competence to become a party to such a convention, whereas it cannot to the existing Geneva Conventions. Article 130r of the Treaty of Rome[147] permits action by the European Community in the environmental field to preserve, protect and improve the quality of the environment, to contribute towards protecting human health, and to ensure the prudent and rational utilization of natural resources. That competence is unaffected by the source of the threat to the environment. I believe, therefore, that it allows the European Community to become a party to a convention of the type which you are today discussing.

I wish you the very best in your deliberations today.

---

147 Treaty Establishing the European Economic Community, done at Rome, 1957 (UKTS No. 15 (1979); Cmnd. 7460), as amended by the Single European Act, done at Luxembourg, 17 February, and The Hague, 28 February 1986: European Communities No. 12; Cmnd. 9758.

4 The Environmental Impact of War: a Scientific Analysis and Greenpeace's Reaction

Jeremy Leggett

It is axiomatic that the natural environment suffers in time of war. Categorizing and cataloguing the extent of that suffering in past wars is clearly central to shaping any new instrument, in international law, designed to protect the environment in time of war.

Three broad categories of war-related environmental destruction can be recognized. The first involves destruction of the environment for 'active' military purposes. A major component of this class involves destruction of natural cover enjoyed by enemy forces (area-denial). Various forms of area-denial have been seen in recent warfare. Defoliation was a major feature of the Vietnam war. The scorched-earth policies that are pursued in so many low-intensity wars between governments and insurgents also fall into this category. Another active military rationale for environmental destruction arises when opportunities are taken to destroy enemy forces or civilians by directly exploiting powerful environmental forces, for example by deliberate destruction of dams.

The second category involves the destruction of the environment for economic purposes or 'passive' military purposes. Many destructive acts are often conducted with motives which are difficult to judge, in time of war, and hence this is a category which is of necessity loosely defined. Saddam Hussein's destruction of oil-wells in Kuwait, for example, may perhaps have numbered among its motivations both economics and the opportunity to attempt screening forces from infrared sensors. The main point is that there has been an increasing involvement of industrial and related infrastructures in wars of the mid- and late twentieth century. Oil-fires and oil-spills are a topical example in this category.

A third category, requiring even more loose definition, is the category of collateral damage.

In this essay, I shall describe aspects of each category. I shall restrict myself to conventional weapons: in particular, the scale of modern conventional weapons and the effects they can have on ecosystems.

Finally, I shall address the question of post-war responsibility and transparency of environmental information, an issue which would become vital in any legal Geneva Convention-type instrument designed to offer protection to the environment in time of war.

Area-denial

Area-denial reached its most extreme form during the war in Vietnam. Twenty million gallons of chemicals were poured over ten per cent of the surface area of Vietnam during that conflict. Half of this was Agent Orange, which has been found to be a particularly toxic substance. As a result of that activity, according to reports by American biologists, fifty-four per cent of the mangrove forests in South Vietnam were destroyed. Just a single application of Agent Orange on an area of mangrove would be enough to destroy an entire community. In the case of upland hardwood forests it would take four or more such applications to have the same effect.[148]

Mangrove forests are an ecosystem of incredible diversity, and of great importance to the economy of South Vietnam. They harbour many varieties of birds and fish-breeding grounds. A mangrove forest is also an ecosystem that recovers very slowly, because, once it has been denuded, herbivorous crabs pose a grave threat to any surviving seedlings.

Fourteen per cent of Vietnam's forests were destroyed by this chemical defoliation and the use of Rome ploughs, bulldozers and carpet bombing.[149] In Vietnam, 2.8 million tons of bombs were dropped, creating 250 million craters averaging 30 feet across, each one involving 88 cubic yards of earth thrown into the air. Many of these craters still exist, still only partly vegetated, and home to crater malaria.[150]

In another form of area-denial in Vietnam, fuel-air explosives were used to clear Vietcong tunnels, and landing areas for helicopters. Fuel-air explosives are a particularly destructive category of weapon.

In the category of area-denial also fall the various types of scorched-earth policy that have been pursued by governments. Such policies have been the mainstay of most counterinsurgency wars in the Third World in recent times. And that list is long: it includes Afghanistan, where the USSR chose to raze villages in areas used by the mujaheddin; the southern Sudan and Ethiopia, with particularly devastating impact on patterns of famine as a result of crops and vegetation destroyed in Tigray and Eritrea; El Salvador, where rebel-held areas have been napalmed extensively and hit with 500 and 750 pound bombs; and in Guatemala, East Timor, Myanmar and other countries.[151]

Dam-busting

The other category of active environmental warfare is a general class of acts involving the active use of water, which merits informal classification as

---

148 E. W. Pfeiffer, 'Degreening Vietnam', *Natural History*, 11, pp. 37–40, 1990.
149 B. Nietschmann, 'Battlefields of ashes and mud', *Natural History*, 11, pp. 35–7, 1990.
150 Op. cit., *supra* n. 148.
151 Op. cit., *supra* n. 149.

dam-busting. The history of warfare includes a number of examples, including the exploits of the Royal Air Force in the Second World War, and, more recently, the threat by Kurdish rebels to bomb the dams on the upper reaches of the Tigris, an act which would have had truly devastating effects downstream, particularly in Baghdad. During the Iran–Iraq conflict huge water defences were created east of Basra, which the Iranians in their turn attempted to destroy by engineering.

Involvement of industrial infrastructure in warfare

Throughout the twentieth century, the involvement of industrial infrastructure has increased with virtually every war we have seen. Many wars have also been partly or wholly fought over natural resources. Oil, for example, was a strategic component in the First World War, and the German advance upon Romanian oilfields saw British troops deliberately setting fire to oil-wells.[152] In the Second World War eighty per cent of the world's oil supplies were controlled by the USA, the UK and The Netherlands at the beginning of the conflict, and a further thirteen per cent by the Russians, so that the Germans obviously had a strategic problem. The German advance on the oilfields in the Caucasus was motivated by access to that infrastructure. The Japanese advance on Burma and the Dutch East Indies was similarly motivated. That, too, saw the deliberate destruction of oil refineries in Borneo, by Shell.[153] Hence, what the world has seen in the Arabian Gulf is not new; it has just reached a new level of intensity and horror with the 550 oil-wells which are now burning, putting – allegedly – six million barrels a day into the atmosphere.[154]

Oil-spills in wartime are also not new. To give just two examples, during the penultimate year of the First World War the Germans had particular success against US oil tankers in the Atlantic, so much so that the British were banned from driving on Sundays. In 1983 there was a less well-known oil-spill in Nowrouz in Iran, where three wells were ruptured and just under two million barrels were poured into the Gulf. The latest estimates for the composite spill as a result of the recent Gulf war are, according to Saudi officials, two and a half to three million barrels, so that this previous example was almost as big; many dolphins, manatees, fish and turtles were washed up dead along the coast of Saudi Arabia at that time.[155]

On the question of scale, the arithmetic of putting six million barrels of oil into the atmosphere per day merits consideration. This is four times the pre-war output of the Kuwaiti oilfields and over twice their production capacity.[156] The wells, at present, are taking five days on average to put

---

152 D. Yergin, *The Prize*, Simon and Schuster, 1991.

153 Ibid.

154 This is an estimate by Kuwaiti officials, quoted in *Scientific American*, May 1991, loc. cit., *supra* n. 5, at pp. 7–9.

155 G. Smith, 'The environmental impacts of the Gulf War', *Ecology Centre Newsletter*, XXI, no. 2, February 1991.

156 *Scientific American*, op. cit., *supra* n. 154.

out, either by detonating explosives above the wells to starve the fire of oxygen, or by inclined drilling and the use of electrical sensors to find the pipe, which is then plugged with concrete.[157] Either method is a formidable engineering task.

Thus, from initial estimates of about six months to put out all the fires,[158] even optimists are now telling us that it is going to be at least two years before they are all out. Pessimists are saying that it will be seven years before the last is extinguished.[159]

What are these fires putting into the atmosphere each day? A million tons of oil is being burnt. That translates into 50,000 tons of sulphur dioxide; 100,000 tons of sooty smoke; and most of the remainder is carbon dioxide.[160] Sulphur dioxide is the major component of acid rain. A report from the British Meteorological Office describes the black cloud as one that will remain visible for up to a few thousand kilometres, and smoke has been reported in the USSR and Pakistan. Episodes of what the Met. Office describes as 'severe acid rain and black snow and photochemical smog comparable with the highest concentrations around major industrial areas are likely to appear out to a distance of 1,000 kilometres or more downwind'.[161] This establishes the point that, while it appears on the balance of probabilities that the environmental impact of this war will be regional rather than global, nevertheless the regional effects are appalling. The 100,000 tons of sooty smoke has created all manner of problems in Kuwait. Visibility over much of the area around the oil-wells is often down to a few yards. Daytime temperatures have been reduced by up to 10 degrees C below normal within about 200 kilometres of the fires. A collage of health and environmental traumas is being suffered by the human and non-human inhabitants of Kuwait and southern Iran, ranging from bronchial asthma in previously healthy individuals to rife haemolytic anaemia in the bird population.

It is instructive to go through the track record of scientific opinion on this subject. In November 1990 at the Second World Climate Conference, King Hussein echoed the opinion of his scientific adviser, Abdullah Toukan, that there would be substantial global effects and a significant boost to global warming. But according to the British Meteorological Office and the Max Planck Institute in Germany, we are looking at about a one per cent addition to global warming.[162] This is either an important minority or a triviality according to your viewpoint. It is worth considering

---

157 C. Joyce and D. Charles, 'The battle to stop the Gulf from choking', *New Scientist*, 23 March 1991, pp. 20–1.

158 F. Pearce, 'Desert fires cast a shadow over Asia', *New Scientist*, 12 January 1991, pp. 30–1.

159 Loc. cit., *supra* n. 156.

160 Ibid.

161 K. A. Browning et al., 'Environmental effects from burning oil-wells in Kuwait', *Nature* 351, 1991, pp. 363–7.

162 S. Bakan et al., 'Climate response to smoke from the burning oil-wells in Kuwait', ibid. at pp. 367–71.

that more than 100 governments, at the negotiations for a Climate Convention, are currently deadlocked over the economic practicability or otherwise of achieving just such minuscule adjustments of the anthropogenic flux of CO_2 to the atmosphere.

Professor Paul Crutzen, world-class atmospheric chemist and originator of the nuclear winter concept, pointed out early in the debate that the 30 million tonnes of smoke per year which he estimated would be produced by the burning wells could engender a 'minor nuclear winter'.[163] Others professed that the fires could lead to disruption of the monsoon, with dire environmental and socioeconomic penalties.[164] Professors Sagan and Turco, also prominent advocates in the nuclear winter debate, worried about a 'self-lofting' process raising smoke to the stratosphere (where most harm would be done). But Dr MacCracken, an atmospheric scientist at the Lawrence Livermore National Laboratory, taking exception to the Sagan/Turco analysis, professed that the smoke problem would be 'about as severe as a bad day in LA'. Sir Frederick Warner came down in the middle ground, describing 'severe local pollution'.[165]

The point is that scientific opinion on the extent and magnitude of environmental damage in wartime – as in peacetime – is never likely to take the form of absolute consensus. This is a point that would number high among the difficulties of framing a Geneva Convention-type instrument.

The British Meteorological Office has flown 57 hours of monitoring flights in the Gulf with a Hercules P130. The results, at the time of writing, are about to be published. Modelling by the Met. Office shows that, fortunately, the smoke is being confined to the lower part of the troposphere, three kilometres above the earth's surface, and is not getting up to the stratosphere, where it could do major damage. The jury, however, may yet still be out on longer-term impacts on the monsoon: the area has been experiencing springtime conditions. Crutzen, among others, has argued that this spring has been unusually wet, taking the soot down out of the atmosphere, and that hot weather after May may have a self-lofting effect. Much also depends on the size of the particles. Crutzen calculates that, if one per cent of this smoke gets into the atmosphere, it could by the end of 1991 be enough to drop the average northern hemisphere temperatures by fully two degrees centigrade.[166]

The same concern applies to the impact of the oil-spill on the Gulf ecosystem, an ecosystem already close to natural tolerance limits. The water averages only 35 metres in depth and is nowhere more than 100 metres deep. The water-mass is well-mixed and is subject to extremes of temperature and salinity. When compared to the case of the Exxon Valdez, the scale of the clean-up task becomes clear. The Alaskan disaster was a smaller order of magnitude – 200,000 barrels as opposed to over two

---

163 Loc. cit., *supra* n. 156.
164 Loc. cit., *supra* n. 158.
165 Loc. cit., *supra* n. 156.
166 *New York Times*, 18 April 1991.

million. Exxon spent two billion dollars on that clean-up. They are still facing significant court costs. The Exxon Valdez clean-up involved 11,000 people and only 'cleared' 20 per cent of the beaches.[167]

The wildlife under threat in the Gulf comprises a diverse ecosystem, in which many of the creatures are close to their ecological tolerance limits. In the littoral zone, one recent ecological study showed that 400,000 organisms, comprising 127 species, inhabited just one square metre.[168] Such areas are in significant part blanketed by oil along the coast of Saudi Arabia. Many organisms depend ultimately on the algal mats in the inter-tidal zone. Many migratory birds – as many as two million, comprising 125 species – use the intertidal zone as biological feeding grounds, grazing on a rich natural fauna including crabs, shrimps, snails and worms. Coral reefs, themselves close to their tolerance limits, are home to many species of turtle, some of them endangered species. A particular problem involves the sea grasses which harbour many of the Gulf's animals. Biological studies have shown up to 369 species among the sea-grasses, living at densities of more than 36,000 per square metre.[169] Weathering oil will sink into the sea-grass beds in many places.

Collateral destruction of the environment

The petrochemical infrastructure of Kuwait and southern Iran, and the marginal zone with Saudi Arabia, is appreciable. As it was described in the *Energy Economist*, offensive military operations in such an area become 'rather like fighting the war inside what is in effect a gigantic fuel tank'. And if we look at the tonnage of bombs involved in modern 'hyperwar', the problem of collateral damage in an area like the Gulf becomes clear. In Korea, 22,000 tonnes were dropped per month (resulting in four dead per tonne). In Vietnam, 34,000 tonnes were dropped per month, resulting in 0.5 dead per tonne. In the 1991 Gulf War, bombing averaged out at 59,000 tonnes per month, with an unknown number of dead per tonne.[170]

Of the 88,500 tonnes dropped in total by the Coalition forces in the Gulf, only 6,520 (7.4 per cent) were precision-guided.[171] This is a remarkable statistic, which sits uncomfortably with Coalition claims of 'surgical strikes' in a theatre-of-war littered with a petrochemical infrastructure capable of unleashing serious environmental damage if destroyed.

The forms of weaponry are relevant. Cluster-bomb units (CBUs) were described as the most common 'workhorse' weapons in the war. A CBU-52/B can destroy everything within 1.3 million square feet (more than 22 football fields). A CBU-75 can carpet-bomb 157 football fields. A

---

167 *National Geographic*, January 1990.
168 M. McKinnon, *Arabia: sand, sea, sky*, BBC Books, 1990.
169 Ibid.
170 P. F. Walker and E. Stambler, *Bulletin of the Atomic Scientists*, May 1991, pp. 21–4.
171 Pentagon figures quoted ibid.

CBU-87/B bomb, described by US Air Force officials as 'the weapon of choice' in the Gulf, carries 202 individual bomblets, each capable of disabling aircraft 250 feet away from the site of its impact. A single B-52 bomber, carrying 40 CBU-87/Bs, can carpet-bomb 176 million square yards, or 27,500 football pitches. Twenty eight B-52s dropped 470 tonnes of these on 30 January 1991 alone: a quantity which could in principle have obliterated 1,600 square miles, an area one third the size of the state of Connecticut.[172]

These are not by any means the only instruments with which modern hyperwar is waged among the complex petrochemical infrastructure. Fuel-air explosives of the mass air delivery (MAD) type can cover 1,000 square feet with blast pressures equivalent to five times those from TNT, creating an explosion which can be compared with a small nuclear blast. The 'Big Blue 82', or *Daisy Cutter*, a 15,000 lb device, can disintegrate everything within hundreds of yards of impact. A 12-rocket volley from a multiple launch rocket system (MLRS) can spread two tonnes of explosives over six football fields. Several thousand such rockets were fired in the Gulf war.[173]

Other forms of collateral damage arise in a modern war like that which took place in the Gulf. The desert is a fragile ecosystem. Soils are held in place by an essentially living crust of algae, micro-organisms, ephemeral plants and non-organic particles. This is an environment where tank manoeuvres can result in unprecedented dust storms; where tank tracks can be seen several decades after they have been imprinted.[174]

Apart from the direct effect of weapons and vehicles, there is the direct effect of the infrastructure of the armies to consider. A city the size of Atlanta was transported to the Arabian continent from North America: not just its infrastructure but its half a million-plus inhabitants. Once there they consumed eight million gallons of water per day in an area where most of the water, notwithstanding the coastal desalination plants, is drawn from aquifers holding irreplaceable water 1,000 years old and more. One Saudi estimate holds that, on current rates of consumption, those aquifers might well run dry as soon as 2007. Six million 'ready meal' plastic bags were used each week. Together with the subsistence-related garbage, solvents, acids, lubricants and electrical waste – including PCBs – created a further waste-management problem. The Pentagon approach to this was that it was the responsibility of the country of origin. The outcome was rudimentary disposal in shallow burial sites in the desert. In time this vast waste repository will make its toxic effects felt in water contamination.[175]

There will also be problems with unexploded munitions. Some reports hold that the average modern war will leave between one and five per cent of these munitions lying unexploded, and they will include deliberately unexploded weapons like anti-personnel cluster munitions.[176]

---

172 Ibid.
173 Ibid.
174 Loc. cit., *supra* n. 155.
175 Ibid.
176 Ibid.

Information and transparency

We are living in a world where, however inadequate it is, the power of legal protection of the environment exists in peacetime. There is an emerging body of international law, and an emerging requirement is to provide transparency with regard to information.

This is far from the case in time of war. Let us consider the case history of the Gulf. Scientists face two key unknowns, for example where smoke from the burning oil-wells is concerned. In understanding the full extent of the regional environmental damage, much hinges on resolving these issues, as we have seen. The first involves unknowns over smoke-cloud behaviour in different atmospheric conditions. Computer-modelling studies are required, and remote sensing studies to study the behaviour of the smoke clouds over time. The second major unknown involves the particle size of the smoke clouds. On that, important information can be gathered by conducting monitoring flights and sampling of the kind that the British Meteorological Office has been pursuing.

The track record, in response to these apparent imperatives, is not encouraging. On 25th January 1991 the US Department of Energy (DOE) issued the following statements to its employees in government laboratories and institutes: 'DOE public affairs has requested that all DOE facilities and contractors immediately discontinue any further discussion of war-related research and issues with the media until further notice. The extent of what we are authorized to say about the environmental impact of fires/oil spills in the Middle East is as follows: "Most independent studies and experts suggest that the catastrophic predictions in some recent news reports are exaggerated. We are currently reviewing the matter but these provisions remain speculative. They do not warrant any further comment at this time."'

Officials in the US government's National Oceanic and Atmospheric Administration (NOAA) were ordered to withhold satellite images or other information of a kind normally on public sale in the Gulf after the war ended.[177] NOAA also found evidence of spikes of soot in the troposphere at a height of four kilometres over Hawaii. A press release about this information was suppressed. One US scientist told *Scientific American* that the first suspicious spike of soot arrived over Hawaii in early February, well before the Iraqis began their torching of Kuwaiti wells, suggesting that the soot may have resulted from Allied bombing of the Iraqi petroleum infrastructure.[178] NOAA weather satellite imagery received daily at Imperial College, London University, showed huge palls of smoke in southern Iraq during the Allied air offensive, leading a scientist studying the imagery to conclude, 'images revealed the allied objective to disable not simply Iraqi oil supplies near Kuwait, but all of Iraq's oil production capability. Images from 12th February 1991 showed smoke plumes in the

---

177 Loc. cit., *supra* n. 156.
178 *Scientific American*, July 1991, pp. 17–19.

northern Iraqi cities of Baiji and Kirkuk and the Al Zubayr oilfield in southern Iraq, both major oil-processing centres'.[179]

In early April 1991, a US Environmental Protection Agency (EPA) press release on smoke clouds in Kuwait professed that 'the preliminary data did not indicate levels of concern of sulphur dioxide'.[180] Meanwhile, the UK Met. Office described 'severe acid rain, comparable with the highest concentrations around major industrial areas', and likely to extend out to 1,000 kilometres.[181] The EPA press release went on to observe that 'susceptible sub-populations, such as individuals with asthma, may experience exacerbation of their symptoms'. Meanwhile, physicians in Armadi, Kuwait, were reporting increases in eczema, dermatitis, conjunctivitis and respiratory ailments even in healthy adults.[182]

The US attitude to information during and after the Gulf War is clearly not a position that sits comfortably with the imperative for adequate assessment of environmental damage which would be central to any regime in international law designed to offer environmental protection in time of war.

A Greenpeace perspective on environmental protection in time of war

Greenpeace supports the idea of a new Geneva Convention to protect the environment in time of war. This is not condoning war itself. Greenpeace would see such a legal instrument as a milestone towards the abolition of war. It would be a means of placing greater emphasis on conflict resolution and a means of raising the threshold for the use of force.

One of the motivations for a new convention is that international law-making, as it relates to the 'peacetime' environment, is growing and may well burgeon in the decade to come. The question arises of why governments should simply suspend that body of law when they delegate to their military commanders the right to go to war in an environment which is, even in the normal run of events, stressed in the extreme. Instead, the precautionary principle, obligatory environmental impact assessments and the polluter-pays principle should also apply in wartime.

Another motivation is the increased destructiveness of modern weaponry. Weapons such as the cluster munitions used in the Gulf are likely to be developed and evolved still further in the years to come, in the absence of international law-making offering disincentives. Yet we are living in a world where a tragedy on the scale of Bhopal can be caused essentially by a failure relating to one boiler. And just one bomblet in a cluster bomb is capable of destroying an aircraft 250 feet away from the point of its impact. Hence, profound questions arise where both direct and collateral damage are concerned.

---

179 V. Gupta, 'Weather-eye on the Gulf War', The *Guardian*, 15 March 1991.
180 US Environmental Protection Agency, Note to Correspondents, 2 April 1991.
181 Loc. cit., *supra* n. 161.
182 The *Guardian*, 11 April 1991.

Furthermore, there are the rights of neighbouring neutral states. Emerging international law obliges countries to limit long-range transboundary air pollution; Greenpeace believes that this must continue in time of war. Countries conducting a war are responsible for preventing environmental damage to neutral states.

Obviously it would be difficult to define what is meant by the 'environment' in this context. Greenpeace see human beings as an integral part of the environment. For the purpose of a new convention, however, the environment may have to be defined as the natural environment plus parts of the man-made environment. The existing Geneva Conventions already protect humanitarian values, albeit not effectively enough.

The principles Greenpeace advocates for a new Geneva Convention are as follows:

First, that the environment must not be used as a weapon. While the ENMOD Convention partially covers this point, a general prohibition is needed.

Second, weapons destroying the environment must be banned. Again the question of definition arises. But above the threshold, for example, should clearly come the use of herbicides on the environment. Without any doubt, nuclear, chemical and biological weapons should be banned for their effect on the environment alone.

Third, attacks on infrastructure that cause pollution must be banned. It is no use using precision-guided weapons if they are targeted on sanitation facilities, for example, and thus bring environmental devastation in their wake.

Fourth, attacks on installations causing the release of radioactivity or poisonous substances must be banned.

Fifth, nature reserves and areas of special ecological importance must be demilitarized zones. For example the Plain of Reeds in South Vietnam – a very marginal agricultural area west of Saigon which was attacked both from the air and by engineering means during the Vietnam war – would have been out-of-bounds under a meaningful Geneva Convention-type environmental-protection instrument.

Sixth, an agency for environmental protection in time of war, similar to that which exists for humanitarian purposes in time of war, would clearly be necessary.

5 The Environmental Law of War: an Introduction

Richard Falk

The purpose of this paper is to give an overview of international law in relation to environmental protection during wartime, and to identify deficiencies in existing law.

In an important respect, incidental and deliberate damage to the environment has been a part of warfare since ancient times, especially the burning of croplands and forests and the poisoning of wells. What has evolved in recent decades is a realization of the seriousness of environmentally detrimental behaviour and, alongside that, an increasing appreciation that there is a growing need for environmental protection in wartime and in relation to military activities. This is a consequence of the increasing destructiveness of military techniques and technology, as well as an expression of the developing consciousness of environmental values and of the human consequences of disregard of the environment. To a confusing, complicated and controversial extent these factors have led to an accelerated development of international law relevant to environmental protection during wartime, although, it should be stressed, the results are rather meagre, especially if measured against the need to ensure an effective environmental law of war.

Two wars have a particular importance in this regard. The first strong expression of concern about the environmental consequences of warfare arose during the latter stages of the Vietnam War. This coincided with the first wave of environmentalism on a global level that culminated in the 1972 Stockholm Conference on the Human Environment[183] and contributed to the drive to update and extend the humanitarian law of war (often called the 'Geneva' law) which led in turn, after long negotiations, to the two Geneva Protocols of 1977.

The Gulf War is the second of these wars and the extent of its influence is yet to be determined, but the rationale and reality of this Conference is itself an expression of the process of reacting constructively to the massive and deliberate efforts by Iraq to inflict punitive harm by way of environmental damage, sometimes characterized as 'environmental

---

183 Stockholm Declaration of the UN Conference on the Human Environment, loc. cit., *supra* n. 51.

terrorism', and, to a far lesser extent, to Coalition efforts to destroy from the air Iraqi facilities relating to weaponry of mass destruction. It is too early to assess these tactics and their effects or to describe the sort of precedent created by mounting such attacks under UN auspices in a war that was successfully waged against Iraq by a Coalition of countries in which the United States was pre-eminent.

Against this background, inquiry can be shaped more precisely: to what extent were the belligerent practices of these two wars that produced environmental damage in violation of the existing international law of war? What steps can be taken to reinforce and extend existing prohibitions in the light of past wartime experience and future prospects? What is needed and what is possible by way of innovation and through a multilateral law-making negotiation?

The problematic character of 'existing law'

In describing 'existing law' on this topic one is beset by complexity, which is itself part of the unsatisfactory character of the present international law of environmental protection in wartime. Briefly identifying the major areas of difficulty may help clarify the descriptive undertaking:

Degree of authoritativeness

The legal norms that exist are scattered, and are either very general and vague, as well as subject to 'military necessity' exceptions, or more specific and relevant, but not directed at prevailing belligerent practices of the sort most likely to generate environmental harm. Furthermore, the status and relevance of principles of customary international law are quite indefinite, as is the related matter of whether treaty norms reflect and embody customary norms. There is also the problem of evaluating the authoritativeness of norms contained in resolutions of the UN General Assembly or of specialized international agencies, such as the International Atomic Energy Agency,[184] or of the writings of international law experts (which are explicitly regarded as subsidiary sources of international law by Article 38(1)(d) of the Statute of the International Court of Justice). These issues of relative authoritativeness are of surprisingly great importance for the description and evaluation of existing international law; if general norms are treated as authoritative, then almost all environmentally harmful belligerent practices are illegal; if general norms are ignored, then almost nothing is prohibited.

Military necessity

The description of existing norms of the law of war is vitally affected by

---

184 For texts of some relevant IAEA Resolutions see *infra* Appendix 2.

the view taken of 'military necessity'. In practice, military necessity has been subjectively defined in wartime, and has prevailed over inconsistent norms of customary international law associated with the legal duty to restrict methods and means of combat by reference to the capacity to distinguish military and non-military targets ('Principle of Discrimination'), to confine military responses to an orbit of proportionality ('Principle of Proportionality'), and to avoid tactics that inflict superfluous and severe suffering ('Principle of Humanity'). Submarine warfare, aerial bombardment, and atomic/nuclear weaponry illustrate the breach of these customary constraints by subjective invocations of 'military necessity'.

It is agreed, even by defence establishments, that specific prohibitions (for instance, against bombing hospitals or using chemical or biological weapons), if authoritative, cannot be evaded by invocations of military necessity. Dominant states in international society, especially if they are participants in wars generating concerns about environmental practices, exert an extraordinary influence upon the shaping of this interplay between military necessity and the prohibitions of the law of war. Put briefly, what dominant states find militarily useful in war is unlikely to be prohibited, and, if it is, the prohibition is unlikely to be respected in the next war, unless ideas about the usefulness of the activity have shifted. The issues here are definitely entangled; nuclear weapons have not been introduced into warfare in recent decades mainly because of a widely accepted sense of the adverse implications of use that go far beyond any particular battlefield; our experience with chemical weapons illustrates both kinds of reactions: states refrained from their use during the Second World War but Iraq relied upon them in its war against Iran.

On the other hand, the practices of a defeated country, especially if they fall outside the conception of war held by the military commanders of the winning side, are likely to be condemned and are those most easily incorporated into the law of war, either by way of interpretation of existing law or through its extension by a variety of law-making procedures. The experience after the Second World War is especially illuminating, particularly the diplomatic moves that enabled the Nuremberg and Tokyo trials to be organized.[185]

Interpretation, implementation and enforcement

The law of war, being closely related to the dominant preoccupation of leaders of states with sovereign prerogatives in matters of security and survival, has been plagued to a greater extent than any other area of international law with a reluctance to confine governmental discretion within bounds. Hence, even where substantive standards can be established, their interpretation and implementation is left in the hands of governments adjudging their own conduct and complaining about the conduct of adversaries. There has been very little procedural development to augment the objectivity of the legal process, and there is virtually no capability for

---

185 R. Falk, Kolko and Lifton, (eds), *Crimes of War*, Random House, New York, 1971.

enforcement, except in the somewhat dubious circumstances of holding the losing side accountable for their deviations from the law of war.

Legislative moments

For the reasons suggested, the strengthening and developing of international law often occurs in the aftermath of a prominent war in which the victorious side was the victim of belligerent practices that fell outside its views of the canons of military necessity and exceeded permissible limits upon methods and means of warfare. Because the impact of such practices is exerted both upon the interpretative process pertaining to existing law and upon the reformative process that generates new law, it is sometimes difficult to distinguish the reinterpreted from the innovative when describing the content of the law of war.

One conclusion is clear from experience, however. Environmentally harmful practices of the victors have in the past proved almost impossible to stigmatize in any legally authoritative manner, that is by formal action that included the assent of leading governments. Experience with nuclear weapons is discouraging and illustrative. The USA and its main allies have blocked formal efforts to stigmatize past or prospective uses of such weaponry. The more impartial attempts at legal prohibition have included: the legal condemnation of the use of atomic bombs against Hiroshima and Nagasaki by a Japanese court in the *Shimoda* case;[186] various UN General Assembly Resolutions, including Resolution 1653 (XVI); writings by a wide array of international law specialists;[187] and some non-governmental organization (NGO) activity, especially on the part of the International Association of Lawyers Against Nuclear Arms (IALANA). These attempts have influenced the moral climate to some extent, but have not discernibly altered the dispositions of governments in the nuclear weapons states.

The Gulf War has, however, clearly generated a legislative moment with respect to the Iraqi practices causing environmental harm. These practices fell outside the general perception of actions justified by claims of military necessity and were performed by a belligerent condemned by the United Nations, opposed in the war by most leading states and badly beaten on the battlefield.

This legislative moment reaches backward in time via interpretation and forward via law-making, but it is far less likely also to cover the practices relied upon or favoured for possible future use by the victorious side. It may be possible to expand the legislative reach of this receptive time by energetic NGO activity and through the mobilization of public opinion; in this regard, the support given to this conference by Greenpeace is encouraging and the preparation of its report, *On Impact*, constitutes an invaluable

---

186 See R. Falk, 'The Shimoda Case: A Legal Appraisal of the Atomic Attacks upon Hiroshima and Nagasaki', 59, *AJIL* (1965) at pp. 759–93.
187 See, for example, Arthur Miller and Martin Feinrider, (eds), *Nuclear Weapons and Law*, Greenwood Press, Westport, CT, (1984).

resource in the struggle to make the response to the Gulf War more than in instance of 'victor's law' (an analogue to 'victor's justice', an influential line of criticism directed at the war-crimes trials conducted after the Second World War, especially those held in Japan).

A core issue of political feasibility is thus posed: should we approach the issue of feasibility by way of concentrating on Iraqi practices, thus enhancing the prospect of authoritative law but at the cost of overlooking or downplaying environmentally harmful practices by Coalition forces?

Describing existing law

It should be evident from the preceding discussion that the description of existing law is ambiguous in extremely important respects that need to be kept in mind. At the same time, clarification of what exists is a necessary part of deciding upon and advocating what needs to be done by way of strengthening environmental protection in wartime by way of international law. This paper builds upon the work of others, especially that of B. V. A. Roling,[188] Arthur H. Westing,[189] Jozef Goldblat[190] and now William Arkin, Damian Durrant and Marianne Cherni in *On Impact*. As with other aspects of this topic, the assured identification of existing legal norms is itself a matter that calls for reflection. Goldblat chooses a mixture of two approaches in his presentation of them, drawing a basic distinction between those norms that relate to targets and those that relate to weapons, and then extending this distinction to a chronological account of the main multilateral treaty instruments that address environmental questions. The Greenpeace Study, *On Impact* is more problem-oriented, discussing the legal status of environmentally harmful practices by both sides during the Gulf War, and including secondary legal materials such as resolutions of the UNGA and International Atomic Energy Agency (IAEA).

My own attempt is closer to Goldblat's, partly in order to enlarge the domain of our concern beyond the Gulf War experience, although I am somewhat more sceptical than he is about the utility of treaty norms and somewhat more affirmative in my attitude toward the role played by customary norms as part of the overall international picture.

What follows is an analytical survey of existing law on environmental protection in wartime, which draws heavily upon the enumeration of prescriptive norms set out in Appendix B to Greenpeace's report, *On Impact*,[191] and offers a judgement as to their current utility.

---

188 Roling, *The Law of War and Dubious Weapons*, SIPRI, Stockholm, 1976.
189 Westing, (ed.), *Cultural Norms, War, and the Environment*, Oxford University Press, Oxford, 1988.
190 Goldblat, loc. cit., *supra* n. 70, at pp. 48–60.
191 Loc. cit., *supra* n. 11, at pp. B–1 to B–23.

Normative foundations: historic treaty prescriptions

Nineteenth and early twentieth-century attempts to develop the law of war rested upon broad normative mandates that continue to inform the efforts of international law. The St Petersburg Declaration of 1868,[192] despite proclaiming itself as a declaration, has come to be regarded as a binding agreement by the leading states of Europe to renounce the use of explosive or expanding bullets in wartime because of their cruel effects. It represented the first formal inter-governmental attempt to limit the tactics and methods of warfare, explicitly adopting the view that there are 'technical limits at which the necessities of war ought to yield to the requirements of humanity' and that 'the only legitimate object which states should endeavour to accomplish during war is to weaken the military force of the enemy'. In the background to the St Petersburg Declaration is the central humanitarian objective of avoiding unnecessary suffering on the part of combatants and other war victims, and the importance of shaping choices about the development of and reliance upon weaponry in the light of such limiting considerations.

The St Petersburg Declaration retains its relevance to the subject at hand for two reasons. First, it subordinates and restricts claims of 'military necessity' by reference to a specific category of weaponry and through the coordinated action of the representatives of leading sovereign states; that is, from the outset of the modern law of war, absolute claims of 'military necessity' have been rejected. At the same time, *ad hoc* considerations of military necessity have been allowed to prevail in the absence of specified prohibitions on weapons or targets (for example, nuclear weaponry); hence the importance of having specific prohibitions in treaty form.

Second, the central notion that a mode of warfare must be relevant to a military purpose implies the 'illegality' of all modes of behaviour that involve punitive or vindictive destruction, including, by implication, deliberate damage to resources, infrastructure and the environment.

The Hague Conferences of 1899 and 1907 produced a series of international agreements on various modes of warfare, including that upon land and sea. These agreements, in many instances, continue to be the only codified formulation of restrictions on the generality of methods of warfare (often called the 'Hague' law to distinguish it from the mainly humanitarian objectives of the 'Geneva' law). Article 22 of the Hague Convention (IV) Respecting the Laws and Customs of War on Land (1907)[193] expresses a general normative sentiment that has often been invoked against military extremism: 'The right of belligerents to adopt means of injuring the enemy is not unlimited.' Such a general directive provides a legal foundation in certain settings for an authoritative condemnation of contested belligerent practices.

Of related, and reinforcing, significance is the 'Martens Clause' that was included in the preamble to the Hague Convention (IV) of 1907, which is

---

192 Loc. cit., *supra* n. 64.
193 Loc. cit., *supra* n. 44.

an insistence that states not adhering to the written laws of land warfare were nevertheless not liberated from legal restraint: 'the inhabitants and belligerents remain under the protection and the rule of the principles of the law of nations, as they result from the usages established among civilized peoples, from the laws of humanity, and the dictates of the public conscience'. Significantly, the Martens Clause is carried forward, although in more appropriate language, in Article 1(2) of Protocol I: 'In cases not covered by this Protocol or by other international agreements, civilians and combatants remain under the protection and authority of the principles of international law derived from established custom, from the principles of humanity and from the dictates of public conscience.'

The Martens Clause is important, because it confirms the persistence of customary international law in relation to belligerent practices not covered by treaty norms, and extends the law of war to states that have failed to accede to recent developments in treaty law. The true relevance of this purported applicability of customary norms depends on the existence of a forum or tribunal that can offer authoritative interpretations of contested practices.

Normative foundations: the principles of customary international law of war

There is no single accepted text that formulates the principles of customary international law of war, but there is a fairly wide consensus on the identity and purpose of these principles.[194] A summary follows of this consensus, organized around the four main principles and relying upon my own earlier formulations elsewhere, but with certain small changes in expression and content.[195]

(a) *Principles of Discrimination.* To be lawful, weapons and tactics must clearly discriminate between military and non-military targets, and be confined in their application to military targets. Indiscriminate warfare is illegal *per se*, although indirect damage to civilians and civilian targets is not necessarily illegal.

(b) *Principle of Proportionality.* To be lawful, weapons and tactics must be proportional to their military objective. Disproportionate weaponry and tactics are excessive, and as such, illegal.

(c) *Principles of Necessity.* To be lawful, weapons and tactics involving the use of force must be reasonably necessary to the attainment of their military objective. No superfluous or excessive application of force is lawful, even if the damage done is confined to the environment, thereby sparing people and property.

(d) *Principles of Humanity.* To be lawful, no weapon or tactic can be validly employed if it causes unnecessary suffering to its victims,

---

194 See Roling, op. cit., *supra* n. 188, at pp. 8–15.
195 For my earlier effort see, *The Bomb and the Law, A Summary Report of the London Nuclear Warfare Tribunal*, Stockholm, Myrdal Foundation 1989, pp. 1–5 and 1–6.

whether this is by way of prolonged or painful death or is in a form calculated to cause severe fright or terror. Accordingly, weapons and tactics that spread poison or disease or do genetic damage are generally illegal *per se*, as they inflict unacceptable forms of pain, damage, death and fear; all forms of deliberate ecological disruption would appear to fall within the sway of this overall prohibition.

In addition to these four cardinal principles, which are widely accepted in more or less the form I have expressed, two subsidiary principles seem to be well-grounded in authoritative custom and to have relevance to the array of special problems posed by deliberate and incidental environmental harm:

(e) *Principles of Neutrality*. To be lawful, no weapon or tactic can be relied upon if it seems likely that it will do harm to human beings, property, or the natural environment of neutral or non-participating countries. A country is neutral or non-participating if its government declares its neutrality and acts in a neutral manner, pursuing in relation to the armed conflict a policy that can be assessed to be impartial in view of its behaviour and situation.

(f) *Principle of Inter-generational Equity*. To be lawful, no weapon or tactic can be employed if it inflicts pain, risk of harm and damage, or if it can be reasonably apprehended to do so upon those unborn.

In my view these customary principles are of great importance in constructing the contours of existing international law pertaining to environmental harm arising out of warfare. Existing treaty law is, for various reasons, confined to the outer margins of these concerns and thus the only genuine basis for claiming violations of international law in relation to the sort of belligerent practices associated with recent war is based upon these customary principles.

It is instructive in this report to consider the reasoning of the International Court of Justice in the Nicaragua case,[196] which relied heavily upon the resources of customary international law to examine the contention that United States assistance to the Contras during the early 1980s was an illegal use of force that could not be justified as an instance of collective self-defence. The Court's somewhat controversial emphasis on customary law was compelled by a US reservation to its acceptance of compulsory jurisdiction which excluded the consideration by the Court of all multilateral treaties where all the affected parties were not before the Court; this thus precluded the Court from relying upon the UN Charter and other treaty instruments.

At the same time, however, there are extreme limitations associated with the need to rely upon these customary principles. Their formulation is

---

196 *Case concerning Military and Paramilitary Activities in and against Nicaragua* (Nicaragua v. United States of America), ICJ Reps (1986) p. 14.

general and abstract and their application to concrete circumstances susceptible to extreme subjectivity and selectivity. Because of these features, the
pedagogic and preventive functions of the law of war – that is, providing
clear guidance to political leaders and military commanders, orienting
public opinion and expert commentary – is not at all well-served. Indeed,
the history of modern warfare shows the subordination, if not abandon-
ment, of these customary principles in time of war, with postwar
assessments of 'illegality' confined generally to the practices of the losing
side.

This may be in the process of being changed through the growing impact
of NGO activity, which extends more impartially to all legally dubious
wartime practices. In future it may be less possible for the victorious side
to dominate the process of legal scrutiny. If Coalition bombing of facilities
associated with weaponry of mass destruction is legally assessed in relation
to the tactics of the Gulf War, it could well be indicative of a more objective process of postwar scrutiny. In the past it has been almost impossible
to obtain an impartial interpretation of these customary principles in relation to controversial belligerent practices, especially those associated with
the winning side.

Normative foundations: declaratory principles relevant to environmental protection

The evolution of the law of war proceeded against a background of virtual
environmental unconsciousness until some awareness was generated by
critics of belligerent practices harmful to the environment during the latter
stages of the Vietnam War.[197] In earlier wars, there were sporadic expres-
sions of concern, and even legal condemnations, associated with punitive
tactics toward a civilian population, such as the burning of croplands and
forests and the poisoning of wells. Several Germans were convicted of the
crime of 'pillage' at the secondary Nuremberg trials for their wanton
destruction of Polish forests.[198] Projections of nuclear-war scenarios often
rely on imagery of extreme environmental destruction to convey the full
sense of the horror of such weapons. Yet, until the early 1970s, when a
broader environmental concern took hold of the political imagination, no
focused attention was directed toward protecting the environment from the
ravages of war. Even at the 1972 Stockholm Conference on the Human
Environment the topic was intentionally kept off the formal agenda because
of the political sensitivity associated with implied criticism of US tactics in
the Vietnam War, although it was addressed at a so-called 'counter-
conference', held simultaneously in Stockholm, and received some media
attention. Beginning in 1972, normative attention began to be directed
toward environmental protection as a distinct public concern.

---

197 See A. H. Westing, *Ecological Consequences of the Second Indochina War*, Almquist
and Wiksell, Stockholm, (1976).
198 Loc. cit., *supra* n. 64.

Principles 21 and 26 of the Stockholm Declaration on the Human Environment adopted at the end of the Stockholm Conference are often referred to as foundational. Principle 21 confirms that states can 'exploit their own resources pursuant to their own environmental policies' but imposes 'responsibility to ensure that activities within their jurisdiction or control do not cause damage to the environment of other states or of areas beyond the limits of national jurisdiction'. This principle is not directly applicable to wartime, but it reinforces customary international law, particularly activities that cause transboundary pollution, climate change or release of radioactive, chemical and biological agents into the atmosphere. Principle 26, the very last provision in the Declaration, insists that 'Man and his environment must be spared the effects of nuclear and other means of mass destruction'; states are implored 'to reach prompt agreement . . . on the elimination and complete destruction of such weapons'. That is to say that war in general is not regarded as inherently destructive of the environment; only war fought with the weaponry of mass destruction is.

A decade later in 1982 the World Charter for Nature was adopted in the form of a General Assembly Resolution (No. 37/17) widely endorsed by leading states, but opposed in isolation by the USA; the vote on the Resolution was 111 in favour with 18 abstentions and only one vote against. In the section dealing with General Principles, paragraph 5 deals directly with war: 'Nature shall be secured against degradation caused by warfare or other hostile activities'. Paragraph 11, although expressed in general terms, insists that: 'Activities which might have an impact on nature shall be controlled, and the best available technologies that minimize significant risks to nature or other adverse effects shall be used.' Sub-sections detail duties to avoid activities that cause 'irreversible damage' and 'significant risk to nature'.

Several additional UN General Assembly resolutions deserve brief mention as building a normative climate: Resolutions 2849 (XXVI), 2994 (XXVII) and 3129 (XXVIII) affirmed and confirmed 'the responsibility of the international community to take action to preserve and enhance the environment'. On 14th December 1978 Resolution 3154 (XXVIII) deplored 'environmental pollution by ionizing radiation from the testing of nuclear weapons'. Passed on 9th December 1974, Resolution 3264 (XXIX) expressed the need 'to adopt through the conclusion of an appropriate international convention, effective measures to prohibit action to influence the environment and climate for military and other hostile purposes, which are incompatible with the maintenance of international security, human well-being and health'.

It should be stressed that these normative assertions are essentially aspirational, having as their most serious intention the encouragement of governments to take appropriate formal action. Such declaratory material, however, both shapes and reflects public opinion and is relevant to the activity of the NGO community. It builds support for strengthening international law through the adoption, if possible, of a comprehensive regulatory framework which is the outcome of a multilateral law-making process that engages the active participation of leading governments and is subsequently widely signed and ratified. In this regard, this declaratory material is evidence of a legislative impulse, but little more than this if taken on its own.

Prescriptive authority: core norms

Except in relation to some exceptional instances, such as Antarctica, endangered species, oil-spills and local pollution, there was no general environmental consciousness before 1970, and, to an even more marked extent, no evident sensitivity in international law about environmental harm incidental to warfare. It is true that the principles of the customary law of war could be convincingly extended, if the requisite political will and climate existed, to condemn many belligerent practices that produce environmental harm, but the various law-making efforts that have been undertaken to (at least to some extent) codify and develop the law of war had, until 1977, gone about their business with no sense that environmental harm was within their mandate. The closest approximation to concern, and this is not really very close, is to be found in Article 53 of Geneva Convention IV. This provision is directed against the destruction of real and personal property by an occupying Power, but it is only indirectly and tangentially concerned with the possibility that such acts of destruction might involve harming the environment.

By far the most direct and significant effort to extend the treaty norms of international law resulted in Protocol I. The negotiations of the Protocols I and II took place against the backdrop of the Vietnam War with its extensive reliance on pesticides and jungle- and river-bank-clearing as tactics justified by the US Government at the time as anti-guerrilla warfare, and subsequently by reference to military necessity. Furthermore, the early 1970s, as already suggested, was a period when governments first became actively engaged in environmental protection of a general character on a global level. Despite these considerations, the relevant provisions are oblique and far from satisfactory.

Article 35 of Protocol I is particularly relevant. Article 35(1) repeats Article 22 of the Hague Convention (IV) of 1907 to the effect that there are limits on the means that a belligerent may adopt to injure an enemy in war. Article 35(2) repeats the customary norm prohibiting methods and means of warfare that cause unnecessary suffering and superfluous injury. Article 35(3) is the innovative provision, being concerned explicitly with environmental harm: 'It is prohibited to employ methods or means of warfare which are intended, or may be expected, to cause widespread, long-term and severe damage to the natural environment.' This general directive is certainly welcome, but it is given no specification either in relation to controversial belligerent practices or as to the operational content of 'widespread, long-term and severe', beyond the dubious and uncertain guidance of the *travaux préparatoires*.

Article 55 of Protocol I is located in Chapter III, entitled 'Civilian Objects', under the section heading 'Protection of the Natural Environment'. Article 55(1) states: 'Care should be taken in warfare to protect the natural environment against widespread, long-term and severe damage. This protection includes a prohibition on the use of methods or means of warfare which are intended or may be expected to cause such damage to the natural environment and thereby to prejudice the health or survival of the population.' Article 55(2) adds: 'Attacks against the natural environment by way of reprisals are prohibited.' This latter provision has an apparently prophetic and manifest relevance to Iraqi tactics in the Gulf War, and this would have been especially so had Iraq invoked 'a right of reprisal' as a justification. It failed to do this, however, and it is doubtful that such environmental tactics could have been fitted convincingly within the legal right of reprisal, had it done so.

There are several other provisions in Protocol I that have some environmental bearing and are aimed at reducing the magnitude of legitimate warfare in general. Article 51(5) prohibits the merging of military targets in civilian areas, thereby sharpening the meaning of 'indiscriminate' in relation to bombardment or other means of attack; Article 54 prohibits methods and means of warfare designed to starve or displace civilians by attacking 'objects indispensable to the survival of the civilian population'; and Article 56 prohibits attacks upon dams, dykes and nuclear-power plants 'if such attack may cause the release of dangerous forces and consequent severe losses among the civilian population'. The latter prohibition is a qualified one, as Article 56(2) allows attack if the protected object is being devoted directly to the enemy's military effort.

Protocol I came into force in 1978, but had been ratified without qualification by only 59 countries and, with qualification, by another 19 by the end of 1990. The USA and many other leading countries are among the 37 countries that have signed Protocol I but not ratified it. Iraq, it appears, has neither signed nor ratified. It is uncertain whether an argument to the effect that Articles 35(3) or 55 are now part of customary international law, or of the still more jurisprudentially suspect category of 'general principles of international law', would succeed.

Protocol III to the 1980 Inhumane Weapons Convention[199] also qualifies as an attempt to generate core prescriptive constraints on military activity endangering the environment.[200] It is concerned with the indiscriminate use of incendiary weaponry, but explicitly extends its concern to forest and other types of natural cover. The Preamble recalls Article 35(3) of Protocol I to the Geneva Conventions, and Article 2(4) asserts that: 'It is prohibited to make forests or other kinds of plant cover the object of attack by incendiary weapons except when such natural elements are used to cover, conceal or camouflage combatants or other military objectives, or are themselves military objectives.' This provision is a fine illustration of the attempt to marry the drive toward environmental protection in wartime to the claims of military necessity. What results is a prohibition on frivolous, punitive and vindictive tactics, but no intrusion challenging the logic of warfare itself. What is more, the identification of what is or is not a military purpose is essentially left to the belligerent parties themselves.

Of some core relevance are certain specialized undertakings designed to address particular environmental concerns. For instance, the Partial Test

---

199 Loc. cit., *supra* n. 26.
200 See *On Impact*, loc. cit., *supra* n. 11, at pp. B–17 to B–18.

Ban Treaty of 1963[201] was directed at atmospheric and underwater nuclear weapons tests that were causing public alarm about their possible detrimental consequences for health and environmental damage. The demilitarization of Antarctica has been partially motivated by concern for its fragile ecologies and has been increasingly built into the Antarctica Treaty System grounded upon the Antarctic Treaty of 1959.[202] Treaty efforts to restrict the deployment and use of nuclear weapons are more modest, seeking to achieve denuclearization rather than comprehensive demilitarization. Prominent examples are the Treaty of Tlatelolco of 1967,[203] establishing a Latin American Nuclear Free Zone, and the Sea-bed Arms Control Treaty of 1971,[204] prohibiting sea-bed deployment of weapons of mass destruction.

A further type of core prescriptive attempt to constrain environmental harm arising from military activity is the Environmental Modification Convention of 1977.[205] Behind this law-making treaty were allegations of experimentation with rainmaking by the USA in its efforts to end the Vietnam War by disrupting traffic on the Ho Chi Minh Trail.[206] The basic undertaking of the treaty is specified in Article 1(1): 'Each State party to this Convention undertakes not to engage in military or any other hostile use of environmental techniques having widespread, long-lasting or severe effects as the means of destruction, damage, or injury to any other State Party.' Without my giving a detailed commentary, several general observations, nevertheless, seem to be relevant: this strengthening of the law of war occurred in the 'legislative' aftermath of the Vietnam War; its feasibility was undoubtedly helped by the apparent conclusions of the US Department of Defense that environmental modification was unpromising from a military point of view; the prohibition is not applicable to any state that is not a party to the treaty; in the absence of third-party procedures for interpretation, the central commitment to avoid 'widespread, long-lasting or severe effects' leaves a great deal of interpretative discretion to the governments involved; and the legal undertaking is carefully worded to avoid casting any legal doubt upon means and methods of warfare productive of environmental harm that appeared to be militarily useful during the Vietnam War.

Despite these cautionary comments, ENMOD is an important step forward. It addresses the problem of environmental harm in war as a distinct concern for the first time. It prohibits a wide range of potential techniques and may indirectly discourage research and development of the

---

201 Treaty Banning Nuclear Weapons Tests in the Atmosphere, in Outer Space and Under Water, done at Moscow, 1963, 480 UNTS 43.
202 Done at Washington, DC, 1959: 402 UNTS 71.
203 Treaty for the Prohibition of Nuclear Weapons in Latin America, done at Mexico (Federal District), 1967: 634 UNTS 281.
204 Treaty on the Prohibition of the Emplacement of Nuclear Weapons and other Weapons of Mass Destruction on the Sea-bed and Ocean Floor and in the Subsoil Thereof, done at London, Moscow and Washington, DC, 1971: TIAS No. 7337.
205 Loc. cit., *supra* n. 25.
206 See *On Impact*, p. 16.

technologies and skills supportive of environmental modification capabilities.

Prescriptive authority: weaker norms

There are prescriptive norms that touch upon core issues relevant to environmental harm in wartime, but do so in such a non-authoritative manner as to make their prescriptive status doubtful. Such doubt can arise from persistent deviant practices in wartime by leading states, as is the case in relation to the Hague Rules of Aerial Warfare adopted in The Hague in 1923.[207] The doubt is compounded, because these rules, although drafted in treaty form, were never embodied in a treaty and because the character of aerial warfare changed so fundamentally in subsequent decades. The burden of these rules is to extend the application of the principles of the customary law of war to the circumstances of aerial bombardment. With the advent of precision bombing, it may be feasible to reconcile discriminate bombing with considerations of military necessity. Such possibilities were exhibited in the Gulf War but should not be overstated. It was reported that 70 per cent of bombs dropped were not precision-guided, and more than 10 per cent of the precision-guided bombs missed their targets. Despite this promising turn as to the technical feasibility of bombardment and long-range missile and artillery attack, there is a political problem if the technologically sophisticated and wealthy countries alone can acquire weaponry that satisfies the normative criteria of the law of war.

Somewhat different problems are raised by the resolutions of the IAEA General Conference establishing a prohibition against attacks upon nuclear reactor facilities.[208] Manifestly, this prohibition bears on the legal character of Coalition attacks upon Iraqi nuclear facilities during the Gulf War. Even if these resolutions are not directly binding on states, their existence is at least some evidence that such attacks are legally problematic by reference to customary principles. Widely supported resolutions with a law-declaring intent may serve an important function in evolving new prescriptive norms, mediating between the generality of customary principles and the absence of specific prohibition in treaty form.

Prescriptive authority: peripheral norms

There is an additional series of prescriptive norms that have a peripheral bearing upon the existing law of war bearing on environmental protection. These norms are designated as 'peripheral' either: (a) because their true

---

207 Reproduced in Roberts and Guelff, *Documents on the Law of War*, Clarendon Press, Oxford, (2nd edn.) at pp. 123–35.
208 See IAEA General Conference Resolutions reproduced in Appendix 2, especially: 407 (XXVII), 14 October 1983; 426 (XXVIII), 28 September 1984; 444 (XXIX), 27 September 1985.

subject-matter does not directly encompass the environment, or (b) because, if any connection between them and war and military activity exists at all, this is purely tangential. It is possible, however, that under some set of unforeseen circumstances peripheral norms could become 'core' norms.

Examples of the first norms include the following: the Geneva Protocol on Poison Gas and Biological Weapons (1925) (the 1925 Geneva Protocol);[209] the Hague Convention on the Protection of Cultural Property in the Event of Armed Conflict (1954);[210] and the Biological Weapons Convention (1972).[211]

Examples of the second type include the following: the International Convention for the Protection of Birds (1950);[212] the Outer Space Treaty (1967);[213] the Convention on the Prevention of Marine Pollution by the Dumping of Wastes (1972);[214] the Convention Concerning the Protection of the World Cultural Heritage (1972);[215] and several arms-control agreements.

Deficiencies in existing law

It is now possible to identify the main deficiencies of the international law of war when it comes to environmental protection in war and in relation to military activities. Some of the underlying problems were touched upon in the introductory section to this paper. To an important extent, the weight of military necessity and of subjectivity is felt across the whole spectrum of issues addressed by the law of war. This condition is taken for granted. In this regard, the term 'deficiencies' is understood in a 'real world' sense, which is possible because of the persisting status of 'war' in international relations and the abiding influence of military expediency upon the definition of negotiable frameworks of legal constraint.

The image of a 'Fifth Geneva' Convention incorporates this understanding of 'feasibility' by implying the goal of doing for environmental protection what has been done previously in the four Geneva Conventions and supplemental agreements to protect the sick and wounded in the field, shipwrecked sailors, prisoners of war and civilians. Reliance upon a 'Geneva' law model has, however, the disadvantage of tying environmental protection to a legal project principally associated with humanitarian goals and is thus vulnerable to the criticism of treating environmental protection from an overly anthropocentric perspective and without sufficient appreciation of the autonomous status of environmental values.

---

209 Done at Geneva, 17 June 1925.
210 Loc. cit., *supra* n. 90.
211 Loc. cit., *supra* n. 135.
212 Done 10 October 1950: 638 UNTS 186.
213 Treaty on Principles governing the Activities of States in the Exploration and Use of Outer Space, Including the Moon and Other Celestial Bodies: UKTS No. 10 (1968); Cmnd 3519.
214 Done at London, 29 December 1972: UKTS No. 71 (1979).
215 Loc. cit., *supra* n. 89.

The main deficiencies of existing law are closely interlinked and overlap significantly. Despite this, it still seems useful to highlight, separate and enumerate deficiencies of the existing international law of environmental protection in wartime.

Authoritativeness

Compared to the humanitarian law of war, the environmental law of war is dependent on the application of customary principles and on the sweeping generalization of Article 35(3) of Geneva Protocol I. Such a dependency is a major deficiency, as considerations of military expediency are especially difficult to constrain in the absence of treaty norms, and even allegations about enemy conduct tend to sound propagandistic if based purely upon such general, vague, prescriptive principles. The US insistence that Iraq was guilty of 'ecological terrorism' partly reflected the absence of a more specific, focused and directly applicable set of prohibitions.

Incoherence

The treaty norms that exist, aside from the general injunctions in Articles 35(3) and 55 of Protocol I, do not address those belligerent practices that have been responsible for environmental harm in recent wars, nor are they likely to be very relevant to future wars. The conditional character of the general prohibitions is a further problem; it is rarely self-evident what constitutes 'widespread, long-term and severe' damage in a particular set of circumstances. The more specific norms address peripheral issues, and even then do so in a rather weak manner.

Lack of specification

Key terms are unspecified in existing treaty instruments, especially 'widespread, long-term and severe'.

Subjectivity

The more general and vague the legal imperatives, the more pronounced is the dependence of the law of war upon highly subjective modes of self-interpretation. To the extent possible in negotiations, it would be desirable to define the operational circumstances of legal prohibitions as clearly and concretely as possible and to designate procedures for third-party adjudication. As matters now stand, the existing legal framework relevant to wartime environmental harm is gravely compromised by the extent of its subjectivity.

Difficulty of implementation

There are virtually no avenues open for the implementation of existing environmental law of war. The Geneva Protocol I environmental prohibitions are not regarded as 'grave breaches' in Article 85(3), and hence do not necessarily count as 'war crimes' which would entail potential sanctions and individual responsibility on the part of responsible decision-makers. There is a closely related matter; unlike other categories of serious violations of the laws of war, violations of environmental prescriptions are not clearly or explicitly stigmatized as 'criminal'. The environmental law of war would be strengthened, if it were reinforced by a fourth category of war crime, namely a category designated as 'Crimes against Nature', and by an ecological offence analogous to genocide and embodied in an appropriate Convention, possibly entitled 'The Ecocide Convention'.[216] A strong argument has been made by Paul Fauteux that Iraq's acts of deliberately harming the environment can be treated as criminal within the meaning of Nuremberg Principle VI(b) (war crimes) as 'devastation not justified by military necessity'.[217]

Loopholes

The treaty norms that exist are subject to important qualifications and exceptions, as in the case of Article 2(4) of Protocol III to the Inhumane Weapons Convention and the ENMOD Convention.

Conclusions

Not surprisingly, on the basis of the analysis and interpretation presented, this paper concludes with a strong endorsement of the project to draft and codify in authoritative form, at the earliest possible time, a comprehensive convention on the environmental law of war to complement the Geneva Conventions and Protocols, whether embodied in a Fifth Geneva Convention, or made the subject of a treaty that is treated as distinct and possibly wider in scope than war itself. A name for such a convention could be 'Convention on Environmental Protection in Relation to Military Activities, Including War'.

The need seems clear from a recitation of the deficiencies of existing law. The time seems ripe, given the environmental harm inflicted by both sides in the Gulf War, but especially in the light of Iraq's retaliatory, punitive and massive environmental destruction in Kuwait, the full extent of which is likely not to be fully known for several years. There is now 'a legislative window of opportunity' for law-making in relation to environmental harm caused by war and military activities.

Despite my strong support for the extension of international law to this broad area of protection of the environment in relation to military

---

216 For an earlier proposal along these lines see Falk, 'Environmental Warfare and Ecocide', *Bulletin of Peace Proposals*, (1973), at pp. 1–17.
217 For careful formulation see Fauteux, loc. cit., *supra* n. 1 at pp. 31–34. *EDITOR'S NOTE*: In fact this argument was made by Mr Fauteux a few days later in Paris; Professor Falk felt it important, nevertheless, to include this point in the corrected version of his paper.

activities, it should be appreciated that the law of war has not been effectively observed in many instances. Creating an effective legal regime in relation to environmental protection will require more than a comprehensive international treaty, if successfully negotiated and widely ratified, but such a legislative step would contribute an indispensable element to the regime-building process.

6 The Negotiation of a New Geneva-style Convention: a Government Lawyer's Perspective

Helmut Türk

First of all, let me congratulate the organizers of this very important and topical round table conference for their timely initiative and thank them for inviting me to serve as one of the opening speakers. I feel very honoured indeed to have been given the opportunity to add some remarks to the brilliant interventions we have just heard from Dr Leggett and Professor Falk.

As we are all aware, international law constitutes the foundation of our present-day international community. The progressive development of international law and its codification are designed to bring us closer to the realization of the age-old dream of a peaceful world devoted to the welfare of mankind. Thus, international law-making must react to events in order to contribute to preventing their recurrence or at least to substantially mitigating their effects. The large-scale damage inflicted upon the environment in the recent Gulf conflict is a case in point which also underlines the importance of the international community's drawing the necessary lessons from these events by laying down appropriate legal rules. Scholars, international governmental and non-governmental organizations as well as legal advisers of ministries for foreign affairs are called upon to contribute to this task. The fact that the rule of law in international relations is not always respected by all the members of the international community, as experience even toward the end of this twentieth century, alas, shows time and again, should in no way discourage these efforts. On the contrary, in the long run these endeavours will not fail to contribute to an enhanced awareness by all governments of the fundamental importance of scrupulous respect for international law.

In the course of the Gulf conflict an incredulous world public was stunned by deliberate acts of environmental destruction with severe and long-term effects on the natural environment and ecosystems of a whole region. *These events have demonstrated that present international law is not sufficiently equipped to deal with such a situation*; there are no precise legal rules for assessing the damage done, for compensation for those who have suffered damage or for taking judicial steps against those responsible for such damage. Nevertheless, it could not rightly be claimed that international law in no way covers such a situation. On the contrary, apart from existing treaty law, in particular the specific provisions concerning environmental protection in the 1977 Additional Protocols to the Geneva Conventions and applicable norms of customary law, damage inflicted upon the environment may be considered a classic case for the application of the famous Marten's Clause already mentioned by Professor Falk (*supra* pp. 83–84). The principles of humanity and the dictates of public conscience indeed call for the most far-reaching protection of the environment in time of armed conflict. No one can deny the intimate linkage between humanity and environmental protection!

There can be no doubt that the relevant rules of international law require further expansion and precision. The process of brainstorming for which we have gathered here today in order to discuss the elaboration of a possible 'Fifth Geneva' Convention on the Protection of the Environment in Time of Armed Conflict thus seems all the more necessary. *A new and effective instrument in this field could also contribute to worldwide efforts aimed at a more effective protection of the environment against adverse effects of human activities of any kind, particularly against deliberate interference and damage in time of armed conflict.* The fifth general principle of the World Charter for Nature, UN General Assembly Resolution 37/7, just referred to by Professor Falk, already provides that 'Nature shall be secured against degradation caused by warfare or other hostile activities.'

According to the programme of this Conference I am to present some thoughts on the problems and difficulties that are likely to arise for government policy-makers and legal advisers contemplating and preparing a draft convention on the protection of the environment in time of armed conflict. This is by no means an easy task, particularly as work on the actual wording of such a new instrument has not yet begun.

We have taken note with great appreciation of the 'Elements' Document prepared by Dr Plant, but in my opening speech I shall refrain from commenting on these various Elements. I shall try instead to outline some reflections of my own.

Let me set out by sketching *possible scenarios* which would have to be considered when drafting a convention of this kind. Subsequently, I shall try to present some *basic principles* and *minimum elements* of a future new legal instrument. A further part of my presentation will be dealing with *procedural considerations*, in particular the most efficient forum to consider this matter, the possible format of such an instrument and the potential role of public opinion in the decision-making process. All of these issues have to be borne in mind when assessing the difficulties of elaborating a new international legal instrument.

As regards the *possible scenarios* of environmental warfare – apart from the recent sad example of the setting afire of oil-wells – let me point to: the artificial modification of climate; the alteration of precipitation through methods such as cloud seeding; the artificial causation of earthquakes and tidal waves; the deviation of tornadic storms; and the modification of lightning. Moreover, there have been instances, to which Dr Leggett has already referred, of the defoliation of forests and other vegetation and of flooding by the destruction of dykes and dams. According to the interpretative understanding of the Conference on Disarmament which adopted the ENMOD Convention, the following phenomena, amongst others, could be caused by the use of environmental modification techniques: earthquakes and seawaves; the upsetting of the biological balance of a region; severe changes in weather patterns regarding clouds, precipitation, tornadoes and cyclones; changes in climate patterns and ocean currents; and changes in the state of the ionosphere.

A *future legal instrument* would have to improve and expand upon the existing rules of international treaty law as well as customary law. In particular, the following points should be considered for inclusion in such an instrument:

(a) *Damage*, whether *deliberately or incidentally* inflicted on the environment or on ecosystems during a war or an armed conflict should be avoided not just in cases in which it could cause harm to human health, *but without any further requirements.*

(b) The cases in which the *principle of proportionality* between the military necessity of an action and the possible detrimental effects thereof on the environment may be invoked should at least be reduced, if not altogether abolished.

(c) Sufficient safeguards should be created in order to ensure that *collateral damage resulting from actions not prohibited in other circumstances* is avoided or at least reasonably remedied.

(d) *Criteria which permit the infliction of damage which is not 'widespread, long-lasting (or 'long-term') and/or severe'* – to use the terminology of the ENMOD Convention and Protocol I – *ought to be abolished completely, since they can in no way meet the concerns of environmental protection.*

What might be the *issues* to be dealt with by a future legal instrument? Should there be a prohibition of weapons, methods of warfare and certain interferences with and modifications of the environment and/or ecosystems? Should the convention also define protected areas, sites, objects, natural phenomena, natural processes etc.? There should, most likely, be a combination of these, and perhaps some other elements too. There is no need to emphasize the magnitude of such a task. In any case, *clear and unambiguous language* will have to be found.

Several international legal instruments which have already been mentioned today contain a clear and express reference to different *types of weapons* such as Atomic, Biological and Chemical (ABC) weapons or conventional weapons which may be deemed to be excessively injurious or to have indiscriminate effects. It might cause confusion if the new convention were to introduce new definitions of weapons and warfare not in line with the existing ones. In the existing legal instruments, the emphasis concerning these types of extremely noxious and, therefore, prohibited weapons is placed on the development, production and stockpiling of these weapons, as for instance in the Biological Weapons Convention.[218] As I have already stated, a new convention would have to supplement these

---

218 Loc. cit., *supra* n. 135.

prohibitions and concentrate on the *use of* these *weapons* and the methods of warfare in order to come to grips with the effects on the environment. This has to be seen above all in the light of collateral damage caused by such weapons and warfare. A very important task of a new legal instrument would also be to *provide for means of verification* of the implementation of the respective provisions. *The lack of verification arrangements is one of the major shortcomings of existing instruments.*

Another question to be answered regarding the possible approach when elaborating a new international legal instrument is whether only *deliberate actions* leading to environmental damage should be incriminated or whether the provisions should also cover *negligence*. Moreover, should the concept of environmental warfare also encompass methods which are not generally included in the concept of armed conflict, such as, the introduction of a potentially lethal virus which may lead to the elimination of a whole species of animal or plant into a foreign country, where no other acts of hostility take place? Should that be considered environmental warfare as well?

A further difficulty would be the definition of protected areas, sites, objects, natural phenomena and natural processes. In this respect, different approaches would seem possible, such as drafting a *list* of properties which form part of the natural heritage and are to be protected by a new convention. Such an approach has been adopted by the World Heritage Convention, which provides for a 'World Heritage List'.[219] Another possibility would be to agree a far more *general definition of objects to be protected*, containing an exhaustive enumeration of all the relevant criteria. Both approaches would raise problems: the first could prove to be too restrictive and difficult to keep up-to-date; the second could lack transparency and certainty.

In order to establish an effective regime for the protection of the environment in time of armed conflict, *violations of the respective legal norms should be defined as 'international crimes against the environment'*. This concept of international crime should be coupled with the principle of universal jurisdiction exercised by national courts. In that connection, the great differences of legal standards governing criminal prosecution and procedural guarantees in various countries would also have to be taken into account. One way to overcome such differences would consist in providing for a *standard of procedural guarantees and rights of the defendant in accordance with the relevant international human rights instruments*. Furthermore, the problems connected with possible *concurrent jurisdiction* of several national courts and the question of *extradition* would have to be given very close scrutiny. Finally, the establishment of an *international tribunal* for the prosecution of such crimes might be contemplated, as was suggested by Commissioner Ripa di Meana in his opening speech *supra* p. 66). Many states would certainly be very reluctant, to say the least, to agree to such an institution. However, this does not mean that endeavours in that direction should not be undertaken.

---

219 Loc. cit., *supra* n. 89.

I am afraid that in this later part of my intervention I have raised more questions than I have given answers, but I just wanted to illustrate the various difficult questions to be addressed by policy-makers and legal advisers.

Let me now turn to the important *procedural aspects* of international policy-making which seem to be relevant to the preparation of a new legal instrument.

The first aspect is of a general nature and concerns the body to be entrusted with the task of elaborating new international legal provisions. When trying to achieve the aim of *consolidating and progressively developing the body of universal international law, it is indispensable to take into account the different views held within the international community, for only those legal norms which have been elaborated with the consent of all segments of the international community will gain universal acceptance.* This is undoubtedly also true of a new international instrument for the protection of the environment in time of armed conflict. If such a new international instrument were adopted by consensus, it could certainly be more readily expected that states would adhere to it and respect the obligations enshrined in it.

It is thus of the utmost importance to consider carefully in which *forum* inter-governmental deliberations and decision-making on the present subject should take place. One of the possibilities would be to place the matter on the agenda of the *International Law Commission.* Experience, however, has shown that it usually takes quite a long time until draft articles prepared by the ILC are ready for submission to a diplomatic conference for consideration and adoption. Therefore, in my view, this would not seem to be the best way to proceed if one wishes to obtain results in the near future.

Another way of proceeding would be the *convening of a diplomatic conference by the Depositary Government of the Geneva Conventions,* following the example of the elaboration of the 1977 Additional Protocols. A further method yet would be to follow the *example of the preparation of the Rome Convention for the Suppression of Unlawful Acts against the Safety of Maritime Navigation of 1988.*[220] In that case, a group of like-minded countries elaborated a basic draft which was refined in several rounds of informal consultations. This draft was later submitted to the International Maritime Organization (IMO), which set up an *ad hoc* committee to study the draft before convening a diplomatic conference. This way of proceeding has, as you may be aware, proved to be very efficient in developing a legal instrument relating to international terrorism, certainly a very controversial issue. In particular, the opportunity to coordinate a great variety of conflicting views in the course of informal consultations prior to the diplomatic conference would seem to be the great advantage of this 'IMO'-model.

Previous efforts to establish a regime relating to the protection of the civilian population in time of armed conflict as well as to the prohibition

---

220 Loc. cit., *supra* n. 144.

or restriction of certain types of weapons have shown that such negotiations were extremely difficult and that some states have been reluctant to accept these instruments or certain provisions thereof. One of the reasons for the unwillingness to assume the relevant legal obligations has been the fear that the use of certain types of weapon might be unduly restricted from a military point of view, despite provisos written into these instruments which safeguard the primacy of the doctrine of *'military necessity'* over the prohibition of (certain) military actions. *In view of these considerations it may be doubted whether there would be a general willingness to accept strict and conditional prohibitions of certain weapons, methods of warfare and other possible actions with potentially detrimental effects on the environment*, that is prohibitions not modified by the restriction that they may be waived in cases of urgent military necessity.

That opposition would most likely be voiced by military authorities during the domestic discussions on the advantages and drawbacks of a new legal instrument. But the *sensitivity of public opinion* regarding the disastrous effects of armed conflict not only on the civilian population, but also on the environment, should not be underestimated. Therefore, one of the major tasks of national policy-makers during the law-making process regarding a future instrument would be to assure themselves of broad support in public opinion.

A precedent for a fundamental change in the attitude of the international community is the protection of *Antarctica*. This change was brought about by the unflinching commitment of certain persons, originally only a few – inspired by Greenpeace in particular – to the establishment of a natural reserve and the prohibiting of any mining activities for commercial purposes. This had a sort of snowball-effect on more and more sectors of public opinion in many of the countries concerned and finally determined their governments' policies. As the terrifying effects of the Gulf conflict on the environment are still fresh in everyone's minds, this should provide sufficient public support for the idea of a law-making initiative in this field.

The title of this Conference suggests that a new instrument should be called a *'Fifth Geneva' Convention*. Let me, however, reflect on *other possible approaches as to the legal form* in which the envisaged provisions could be enshrined. Would a *third Additional Protocol to the Geneva Conventions* not be as suitable as a new convention, or perhaps even more appropriate? The following practical and political reasons might be invoked in support of an additional protocol:

First, a new instrument would inevitably comprise only a *limited number of substantive provisions* as compared to the four Geneva Conventions. Critics might therefore argue that there would be a certain disproportion between the form of presentation and the number of substantive articles. Arguments of that kind, concentrating on mere formal aspects, could diminish the unquestionable political weight of the endeavour and should, therefore, be countered from the very beginning. Second, it should be recalled that the *negotiating process* preceding the adoption of the Geneva Conventions was very *protracted and time-consuming*. Also, in the case of an initiative of the present nature, *lack of political will* to accept certain provisions or a certain form of instrument might cause considerable loss, both of time and substance. *Perhaps a protocol supplementing and strengthening a set of already existing legal rules might thus be preferable in order to avoid creating the impression that a totally new approach is being taken to which resistance by certain governments might be much stronger.* I do not wish to discourage those who favour a convention, I just wanted to point out the difficulties of such an endeavour.

The UN General Assembly has declared the 1990s to be the '*United Nations Decade of International Law*'. This decade provides a unique opportunity to promote and strengthen the supremacy of the rule of law in international relations. As to the programme of the Decade, I believe that the development of international norms relating to environment protection in general and in time of armed conflict in particular would be a most suitable subject to be dealt with.[221]

I should, therefore, like to make the following suggestion. The present and very promising efforts of this Conference in London might serve as the basis for a more concrete formulation of general aims and draft articles of a new instrument. These results might be introduced into the UN Decade of International Law as a subject for further consideration. *I should like to announce now that Austria might be prepared to sponsor such an initiative within the United Nations or any other appropriate forum.*

In this context I also wish to mention the joint initiative of Austria, Finland, Italy, Sweden and Switzerland at the Sixteenth Session of the Governing Council of the UN Environment Programme (UNEP) in Nairobi last week, on the environmental effects of warfare. The Governing Council adopted a Decision, UNEP/GC.16/L.53; part B 'Environmental Effects of Warfare', on the basis of that proposal. In it, the Governing Council 'recommends that governments consider identifying weapons, hostile devices and ways of using such techniques that would cause particularly serious effects on the environment and consider efforts in appropriate forums to strengthen international law prohibiting such weapons, hostile devices and ways of using such techniques' (see further Appendix 3).

I have been informed that it proved quite difficult to reach agreement on such a text within UNEP, and this may be a foreboding of future problems when the negotiators of a new Convention get down to details. We may in the end have to settle for a less than perfect instrument, but the most important thing is that such an instrument be genuinely accepted by states. *What we need is an effective legal regime*, as Professor Falk stresses.

Despite the considerable obstacles regarding the adoption by general agreement of a new international legal instrument for the protection of the environment in time of armed conflict, I am convinced that we are on the right track and that this Conference will provide an impetus for

---

221 *Editor's note*. In fact the People's Republic of China has taken up the theme of inter-
national environmental law as its contribution to the UN Decade. It hosted a Ministerial
Meeting of 41 countries in Beijing in June 1991 and the Symposium on International
Environmental Law and Developing Countries in August 1991.

endeavours to speedily lay down the necessary legal rules in the interest of mankind as a whole. In any event, we should remain undaunted by the difficulties ahead and be determined to overcome them.

B: ROUND TABLE SESSIONS

7 Round-Table Session I: General Principles and Methods for Executing a New Convention

Awn Al-Khasawneh

Tickell (Chairman): The first thing I ought to say is that unfortunately the Soviet Minister of the Environment, Mr Vorontsov, cannot be with us and has sent me a message of regret. We are all sorry. I am going to introduce Awn Al-Khasawneh to make a few opening remarks. We will then have a round table discussion, the structure of which he will explain. Mr Al-Khasawneh is the Jordanian member of the International Law Commission and Legal Adviser to Crown Prince Hassan of Jordan. I think that he is thus uniquely well-placed to introduce the first round-table session today.

Al-Khasawneh (Special-Rapporteur): It is not my intention to turn this into a monologue; I will be mercifully brief. It is my intention, with your permission, to point out a number of the issues and parameters likely to be encountered by anyone who enquires into the protection of the environment through existing law.

Definition of 'Environment'. I think the best starting point is to recall that there are very few express references to the environment in the existing law of war. To be sure, of course, there are the two references in Protocol I, in Articles 35(3) and 55, and there is the ENMOD Treaty, and the assertion has been made that humanitarian law already protects the environment, directly or indirectly. Indeed, these are the very words with which an article that many of you have by Dr Jozef Goldblat starts.[222] It is with an accent on the indirect protection of the environment that I should like to commence my comments. These, as you know, take three forms: prohibition against excessive or indiscriminate attacks; prohibitions against attacking certain targets, mainly the 'Geneva' law; and prohibitions against the use of weapons that are inhumane, for example, the Inhumane Weapons Convention.

The second of these poses the question of the relationship between man

---

222 Loc. cit., *supra* n. 70. This article was distributed in advance to the round tablers.

and his environment, because those instruments try to protect the environment indirectly through protecting man, and this introduces the very difficult concept of defining what the environment is. I do not pretend that I have an answer to that particular problem, but I think that the environment has to be broadly understood and interpreted to include such indirect protection. But how broadly? That is the question. Because, if we always conceive of attacks against man as being attacks against the environment, then we are simply saying that humanitarian law is environmental law. A dividing line has to be found. In his very interesting and conceptual statement Professor Falk talked of core areas, and that is a possible approach.

Thresholds. The second matter that I think should be borne in mind is the question of thresholds. This raises problems related to the fact that humanitarian law instruments and instruments relating to the protection of the human environment have aimed at different objectives in the past. In its deliberations upon the topic, 'The Law of Non-navigational Uses of International Watercourses,' the ILC now favours the adjective 'appreciable' to describe thresholds; under other topics, it prefers the term, 'significant'. In Draft Article 19 on State Responsibility, adopted by the International Law Commission,[223] the threshold was set at the level of 'massive pollution of the atmosphere or of the seas'. There has to be, I think, an attempt at achieving a single threshold and at establishing responsibility commensurate with that threshold. I can think immediately of four possible approaches to this.

The first approach is the **'liability for injurious consequences'** approach, which has been and is being elaborated by the International Law Commission under the topic, 'Liability for Injurious Consequences Arising Out Of Acts Not Prohibited By International Law'. The suggestion that liability in relation to acts not prohibited by international law and the implications of paying compensation should find their way into the humanitarian law of war may look no more than a wild flight of fancy, given the fact that it is the intention in armed conflict to inflict damage, but one may recall here an article by Michael Akehurst in *The Netherlands Yearbook of International Law*[224] devoted to this particular International Law Commission topic, in which he suggested that cases of humanitarian law were amenable to treatment under this topic. He cited the right of reprisal and Articles 54–56 of the Regulations attached to Hague Convention (IV) of 1907 in support. I consider liability in this sense to be important in this context, because the forces of nature do not respect the division of the world into competing and often warring political sovereignties. If only in relation to the damage that is experienced in the environment of neighbouring states, if not also to damage to states that are not very close to where armed conflicts take place, I feel that we have to keep in the mind the possibility of an approach along the lines of 'Liability for Injurious Consequences'.

223 See *supra* p. 55.
224 M. B. Akehurst, 'International Liability for Injurious Consequences, Arising out of Acts not Prohibited by International Law,' XVI *Netherlands Yearbook of International Law* (1985) 3 at p. 11.

Recent developments are not, however, very encouraging. A study by a group within UNEP relating to the Protocol on Liability and Compensation for Damage Resulting from Transboundary Movements of Hazardous and other Wastes,[225] for example, contains an express exoneration in the case of armed conflicts from the application of a regime of strict liability. Nevertheless, in my view, this is one of the avenues that we can follow.

The second approach would be the 'state responsibility approach': that is responsibility for wrongfulness. I think that here the strengthening of the protection of the environment can best be achieved by introducing greater specificity into existing rules and by removing some of the reservations that are included or incorporated into existing instruments, such as those in Article 56 of Protocol I, where the protection of targets that may release dangerous forces if attacked is made conditional upon those targets not being used in direct support of military operations. The introduction of more prohibitions can be achieved by eliminating those reservations and by introducing greater specificity into general rules.

The third approach is that of the **personal criminalization of offenders** against the environment in wartime, and here I must confess that there is not very much in existing law. There is a case involving the prosecution of Nazi officials who were guilty of excessive deforestation of occupied Poland during the Second World War,[226] but that is probably best seen as a case relating more to the excessive and wanton destruction of enemy *property* than to the protection of the environment as such. A very encouraging development, however, is the adoption by the International Law Commission under the topic of the 'Code of Offences against the Security and Peace of Mankind', of a draft article which makes attacks against targets where the attack is expected or may lead to the release of dangerous forces into the atmosphere a grave breach of the Code.

The fourth approach, and this is one that I am a little hesitant about, is the **criminal responsibility of states** approach. This would build upon Article 19 on State Responsibility adopted by the International Law Commission. I am hesitant to suggest this, because the Commission has not yet had the opportunity to study in depth the consequences of the concept of international crimes committed by states, because the new Special-Rapporteur on the topic, Professor Arangio Ruiz, intends to review his predecessor's approach and has not yet had time.

Each of these four approaches has drawbacks, and I would be very interested to see round tablers' reactions to them.

Execution. Turning thirdly to the question of execution, it can be said that the relevant provisions in law of war instruments are very rudimentary. If one compared, for example, the very specific mechanisms that have been devised to deal with those offenders in anti-terrorism conventions[227] with

---

225 To the Basel Convention on Transboundary Movements of Hazardous Waste, done at Basel, 22 March 1989.
226 Loc. cit., *supra* n. 64.
227 Loc. cit., *supra* n. 144.

Article 91 of Protocol I, concerning the Fact-Finding Commission, one would have to come to the conclusion that there is much to improve in the Protocol. It is very important, for example, to look at the possibility of concurrent conflicting jurisdictional claims, that is not to confine the basis of jurisdiction to the state where the crime took place, but also to include at least the victim state and the state the nationals of which suffered as a result of the environmental harm. Possible modalities are, of course, available in precedents and can be studied.

I would like to mention one last point: that, once harm to the environment occurs, especially if it crosses the threshold of 'appreciable' or 'significant' harm, it becomes well-nigh impossible to repair. Some of the traditional remedies applied when an internationally wrongful act takes place may not be as effective in the area of environmental destruction in wartime. This, of course, argues for strengthening the *preventive* regime in any future instrument.

These, Mr Chairman, are the remarks that I would like to make. I make them in a haphazard way, simply to point out the possible difficulties, or very probable difficulties, that we are likely to encounter in this enquiry.

Tickell: Before we go to the next stage, are there any representatives of governments who want to say something on behalf of their governments? No. Then I come to the next category which is those of non-governmental organizations.

Eduardo Marino: The European Commissioner, Carlo Ripa di Meana, recalled the bombings of Coventry and Dresden during the Second World War as acts of war which should not happen again. I think that, similarly, acts of war such as the bombing of Hiroshima and Nagasaki ought not to happen again. In fact, for the purposes of this conference the experiences of Hiroshima and Nagasaki and their effects on doctrines of war, strategies and tactics are most apposite. There will be no credible and effective instrument of international law to protect the natural environment in times of war as long as there is no ban on *all* weapons of mass destruction, whether genocidal or ecocidal.

I have not yet taken a position for or against a 'new' instrument to protect the natural environment in time of armed conflict. The idea of negotiating a new Convention is appealing, because it is bold and spectacular and might provide environmental and green campaigners with an all-inclusive campaigning framework enjoying no less than the force of international law. Above all, it could prove useful to well-intentioned governments, armies or guerrilla groups as a comprehensive set of rules to follow when making and carrying out their defence and war plans. One of the problems with the idea, however, is that to many the taking of such an initiative will suggest that there is no existing law to protect the natural environment in time of war and, worse still, that the environmental destruction of modern wars is part and parcel of 'normal' war on a par with the killing of combatants, the taking of prisoners and the destruction of military targets.

All of us meeting here today know that there *are* clear rules in the

existing law of war which aim to protect the natural environment in addition
to innocent human life. The Rapporteur's 'Elements' Document itself has
reminded this Conference of the existing pertinent rules. The immediate
problem, as the Red Cross/Crescent and others often explain, is the
ignorance and defiance of the existing law by governments, armies and guerrilla groups in many parts of the world. Many would ask whether it does
not make sense to campaign for the acceptance (ratification) and enforcement of current law before thinking of making new law. One can see that
a good number of people are going to advocate this at this round table.

From the basic principle set out in the Regulations attached to The
Hague Convention (II) of 1899 that the right of belligerents to adopt means
of injuring the enemy is not unlimited to the more elaborate rules of recent
years, the obvious question is what remains to be done to secure the
compliance of government, armies and guerrillas.[228]

The 'Elements' document reminds us that this Conference takes place in
the aftermath of the Gulf War. The Organizers are to be praised for
convening this discussion precisely – yet not exclusively – to take stock of
the major questions raised by the appearance of the 'apocalypse' the world
has just witnessed in the Gulf and in the Arabian Desert. At the same time,
a serious review of the international law of war and the environment should
not ignore or take for granted other, and very different, theatres of war
today, in some cases decades-old scenarios of armed conflict. I am thinking
about both the genuine and the so-called 'non-international armed
conflicts', the field of application of Protocol II, whereas this conference
has in mind mainly conventional 'international armed conflicts', the field of
application of Protocol I.

The question of internal armed conflicts should be added to the agenda
for future debate. In this respect, the troubling questions may be put
succinctly as follows:

(1) The protection of the natural environment in time of war is one of the
    concerns of the law regulating the *means and methods of warfare*. Most
    experts agree that Protocol I has addressed that concern well regarding
    international armed conflicts, including wars of national liberation,
    apart from its deliberate silence on weapons of mass destruction.
(2) Regarding 'non-international armed conflicts', however, except for the
    Protocol II provisions prohibiting starvation of civilians and attacks
    upon installations containing dangerous forces,[229] there is virtually no
    law on means and methods of warfare and thus, except to the same
    extent, no law protecting the natural environment in the course of *inter-
    nal* armed conflict.
(3) It can be argued that the protection of *its own* natural environment

---

228 Article 22 of the Regulations, loc. cit., *supra* n. 44. This basic principle has been
    developed in Protocol I (*Editor's note*: Article 35(1)), and used in Protocol II (*Editor's
    note*: though not expressly) and in the Weapons Convention of 1980 (*Editor's note*: Third
    Preambular Paragraph).
229 In Part IV.

should be left to each sovereign country even in times of internal war. However, beyond a certain point, the destruction of any one country's environment becomes an environmental concern of other countries too and as such a matter for international law. Beyond a certain point of destructiveness regarding the natural environment, therefore, the distinction between 'non-international' and 'international' armed conflicts makes no material sense.

(4) When countries undergoing internal war obtain their weapons from other countries, the distinction between 'non-international' and 'international' armed conflicts may remain valid in a territorial and sociological sense but is false regarding means of warfare. Under the principle of co-responsibility stated by common Article 1 of the Geneva Conventions and Protocols,[230] therefore, states supplying weapons to parties of any armed conflict, including 'non-international armed conflicts' under Protocol II, become co-responsible for violations of the law on means of warfare under Protocol I, including attacks on the natural environment. By far the bulk of the environmental destruction caused by war over the last few decades has taken place in the course of 'non-international' armed conflicts in Africa, Asia and Latin America, where the warring parties have been supplied and resupplied internationally.

For the sake, therefore, of the defence of the natural environment, as well as of human life: all weapons of mass destruction should be banned; existing law on means and methods of warfare should be supported and tested to its limits before embarking on the preparation of a new law; and the distinction under international law between 'non-international' and 'international' armed conflicts should be dispensed with in all cases in so far as protection of the natural environment is concerned. Weapon suppliers should be deemed to be co-responsible with weapons users in cases of attacks on the natural environment.

In closing, I want to express agreement with those here who wish all these matters to be put on the agenda of the UN Conference on Environment and Development (UNCED), to be held in Brazil in June 1992. We are simply echoing and interpreting here the calls of millions of people in territories devastated by war or waging war to defend their territories.

Dr Rosalind Reeve, Environmental Investigation Agency (from the floor). We should consider including in any Convention which may be drafted a clause referring to endangered species in the area of armed conflict. Take, for example, the Dugong in the Gulf War. The Dugong is restricted to very few areas in the world, and no one knows what impact the oil-spill has had on them. One could emphasize the protection of the breeding grounds and

---

230 Article 1 common to all Geneva Conventions and Protocols: 'The High Contracting Parties undertake to respect and to ensure respect for the present Convention in all circumstances.'

take into account the fact that endangered species are not necessarily restricted to nature reserves.

Tickell: I will now turn to Dr Goldblat to say a word. We have all seen his admirable paper and I imagine that he wants to go beyond that.

Goldblat: I congratulate the organizers on their timely initiative in convening this meeting.

It would seem desirable, in my view, to have a document covering the protection of the environment against the effects of military activities not only in time of war but also in time of peace.

There may be difficulties in achieving such a document. There is the problem of procedure: how to convene a conference and how to negotiate a draft treaty?

I am afraid, however, that we might have problems with substance too. We have heard, for instance, complaints about the ambiguous terminology used in the existing instruments. Shall we rid ourselves of these ambiguities in a new document? Some people may insist, in particular, that we should rid ourselves of the notion of 'military necessity'. Even assuming that we find a way to do so, what do we do with another important problem, that concerning the use of certain specific weapons? I think that it would be impossible, under the present circumstances, to reach a comprehensive document, acceptable to the majority of states, that would not prohibit the use of nuclear weapons. At the time of negotiating Protocol I, in the 1970s, restricting the negotiations to conventional weapons was found to be very difficult. It is, of course, unlikely that questions relating to nuclear strategy would be solved at a conference convened to discuss the 'humanitarian' law of war. The question of legality of the use of nuclear weapons must be settled elsewhere. But we must also bear in mind that the environmental damage which could be done with nuclear weapons would be considerably greater than that of any combination of conventional weapons.

Another problem is the question of tribunals. It is desirable to have an effective tribunal, but people could ask, 'Why do you want to set up a tribunal only for environmental matters? What about the whole panoply of the laws of war?' One is bound to enlarge the area of discussion.

I believe that we may need a new document, but it would certainly take a long time and a great effort to achieve one. My suggestion is that we do not try to get it right away but take advantage, as far as possible, of existing treaties. We should deploy efforts to attract more adherents to these treaties and also enlarge their scope by using certain of their clauses which permit us to do this.

We are worried, for instance, about the release of dangerous forces from the installations enumerated in Article 56 of Protocol I. The prohibitions against attacking these installations are so hedged about with conditions that they have practically no practical value. A state can always say that it has to bomb a nuclear electrical generating station out of military necessity. The Article in question goes on to say, however, that the Parties are urged to conclude 'further' agreements in order to ensure 'additional' protection for objects containing dangerous forces. That means that one could convene an international conference to discuss the strengthening of the mentioned prohibitions. This would be much easier than convening a conference to redraft the existing instruments.

Furthermore, we have the ENMOD Convention; this contains a threshold of 'widespread, long-lasting or severe' damage, the effect of which is to reduce considerably the value of the Convention. Let me point out, however, that the definition of these terms is not contained in the body of the treaty. It is included in a separate 'Understanding'. That means that we could, at the next review conference held in accordance with the Treaty, give a different interpretation to this Understanding, and reduce the threshold to a minimum, if not to zero.

Another relevant Treaty is the Inhumane Weapons Convention and its three Protocols regarding the use of mines, incendiary weapons and certain other devices. This is an ingenious instrument. It is an umbrella Convention to which one can add further protocols on additional weapons. Thus, new norms prohibiting the use of new weapons could be introduced without the need to renegotiate the Convention as a whole.

These could, perhaps, be the first steps to improve existing laws.

Gasser: I do not speak on behalf of the International Committee of the Red Cross (ICRC), but as I work within its administration, some of my ideas might be rather close to opinion in Geneva. As you all know, the ICRC has been contributing to the process of law-making in the field of international humanitarian law, the law of war, for 127 years. Much of what is now called 'law of war' has come about through initiatives of the ICRC, and the ICRC has also, indeed, been instrumental in creating international law applicable in armed conflict for the protection of the *environment*. It seems to me, therefore, that there will be great sympathy within the ICRC for stronger protection of the environment in times of armed conflict.

Perhaps the ICRC does not look so much at the environment as such but more at the environment in the context of and around human beings. As you know the Geneva Conventions are geared essentially to the protection and safeguarding of human beings in times of armed conflict. Nevertheless, this apparent difference in approach and subject-matter seems to be rather academic. The environment as such is part and parcel of what has to be protected in armed conflict. Among existing relevant law we mention in particular Articles 35(3) and 55 of Protocol I. However, other provisions deal also with questions of concern for the environment. We find them mostly in the chapter on the protection of civilian objects against the effects of warfare (Chapter III); they include: Article 52 ('General Protection of Civilian Objects'); Article 54 ('Protection of Objects Indispensable to the Survival of the Civilian Population'); and very important indeed, and very important to the concern of those who want to protect the environment, Article 56 ('Protection of Works and Installations Containing Dangerous Forces'). These prohibitions protect the environment for *human beings* – when both civilians and combatants are affected. But do not most of the serious attacks on the environment inevitably affect mankind? Last but not least there is also a verification procedure in Protocol I: the Fact-Finding Commission provided for in Article 90 is going to be established within the next few weeks.

I am just back from a one month stay in the Gulf and I have seen what is going on there with the fires burning and the oil spilling around in the desert. It is an absolutely incredible sight. One conclusion I draw from what I have seen there is that the destruction of the wells was not an act of warfare. Militarily speaking it was nonsense. It was absolutely out of proportion to any military end. In addition, the wells were set on fire when the war was almost over. Thus the firing of the oil-wells was not in my view an act of warfare, although it happened in the context of a war.

This brings me to the question whether it is really the laws of war which we have to revise. This act was something which could equally have happened in other contexts too. I wonder whether a new instrument should not also cover the case of an ousted dictator in a given country who, on his way to exile, burns the oil refineries in his own country before he goes. That would not be armed conflict, but a purely internal situation. If there is going to be a new instrument, should it not adopt a comprehensive approach? In this respect I share the views of my neighbour, Dr Goldblat, who stressed the importance of the effects of weaponry upon the environment in peacetime too. The plane from Riyadh to Kuwait flies over the desert where the armada of Coalition forces prepared itself for battle. That desert is completely changed. Everywhere there are tracks and holes, and it is full of the residue of an army. Although this destruction was not an act of warfare – it resulted from preparation in a friendly country – why, should we not also deal with such types of problem?

Having said that the ICRC is looking with sympathy at the present debate, I do not think that it would look with sympathy if we were to go on with the idea under the heading of 'Fifth Geneva' Convention. The 1954 Convention on the Protection of Cultural Objects might serve as a better model. Although that treaty deals with an issue in the law of armed conflict (the protection of cultural objects), it has a different name and it does not refer to the Red Cross, no doubt because its primary concern is rather different from the purpose of international humanitarian law.

I wonder whether we should confine ourselves to discussing the 'Elements' document, which is geared to the idea of a new convention, or whether we shouldn't take some time to discuss different alternative approaches to achieve the same ends. These approaches could include, for example, the constructive development of interpretation of Article 56 of Protocol I, as Dr Goldblat says, and the working out of proposals to be put forward at next year's United Nations Conference on the Environment and Development (UNCED) in Brazil.

Edmonds: Speaking as a private individual, I think my interest is in the points made by several distinguished speakers about the unwillingness of many governments, when they get down to negotiating this sort of thing, to actually contemplate the kind of prohibitions we have already discussed. I am really asking a question. In certain fields, notably arms control, I have learned to identify the nay-sayers, those who are against any ban on nuclear tests, reduction in nuclear weapons or whatever it may be. I wonder, is it possible to identify the nay-sayers for the kind of prohibitions we are discussing today? It is easy to say 'the military'. My own experience is that sometimes the military are not the greatest opponents of this kind of improvement in humanity. I am really posing the question: Where is the enemy?

Pinto: I have a general comment and a comment about the execution of the Convention. I have difficulty in deciding whether we are discussing more the environment or more the laws of war, but I take the approach that we are discussing more the laws of war in relation to the environment than vice versa. The environment exists for people rather than people for the environment. I am saying this because we must not forget that wars are usually fought in circumstances of desperation. Countries' leaders feel that war should be avoided up to this point of desperation. That being the case, the question whether damage caused to the environment is proportional to what is sought to be achieved by these desperate measures, must be considered in the light of the proportionality of the action in question to the danger perceived by the politicians and by the people themselves in the events leading up to war. The question of how to interpret a particular situation necessarily places much more emphasis on the need for dispute-settlement mechanisms than is provided for under the 'Elements' document: namely an investigative commission on fact-finding.[231]

As Professor Falk wisely observed, we are at a very critical moment. It seems to me that we ought to seize that moment and pay attention to the regulation of dispute-settlement following a war. Fortunately, in this war we seem to be able to identify those who have clearly 'won' and those who have 'lost'. This is the right time to enforce the law, it seems to me and the time, perhaps, to consolidate what we have always wanted to consolidate, namely the right to bring our complaints before an international tribunal which could resolve the dispute.

This is a long way, even if we were to start along that road at all, from deciding that the International Court of Justice could serve as a criminal court in such cases, but the Court is there if we want it to do so. There is also the Permanent Court of Arbitration and numerous other dispute-settlement mechanisms which could be used.

It seems to be the right time now to emphasize arrangements for dispute-settlement. Whether or not these arrangements should be contained in a Protocol or a Convention or, indeed, in some other subsidiary document can be decided later. When the Protocols were drafted in 1977, no one could foresee the radical changes that would occur in dispute-settlement procedures, the Soviet Union agreeing, for example, to various dispute-settlement mechanisms, or the extensive and binding dispute-settlement provisions adopted in Part XV of the 1982 Law of the Sea Convention.[232] The critical moment ought to be seized in terms of dispute-settlement.

Szekely: We are hearing lots of notes of caution here, especially from Dr

---

231 *Editor's note*: In fact the Document does make provision for this in Element 4.C.
232 Done at Montego Bay, 10 December 1982.

Goldblat. They have more or less echoed the concerns of some of us that, at the same time that one can say that this is a very timely and opportune moment to devote efforts towards something as inspiring as a 'Fifth Geneva' Convention, we must nevertheless recognize that, precisely *because* of the freshness of the latest armed conflict in the Gulf, it may in another sense be also the *worst* moment for attempting something too far-reaching.

One reason for this is that it has been shown, especially in documents such as the 'Elements' Document, which is an extraordinary contribution to the debate, that it is not only the repetition of the acts of those who started burning oil-fields but also that of those of the other participants in that armed struggle which, according to the rules that we may eventually incorporate into a 'Fifth Geneva' Convention, might be rendered illegal in the future. We could expect, therefore, that, if we took the course of developing such a Convention, several participants in that recent conflict would resist and seek to exclude from the Convention any passage implying that anything they did in the Gulf was illegal, even though this would be in a Convention adopted *after* the conflict is over. This is an extra note of caution.

Our other problem is that we are finding that our mechanisms for international law-making are facing a crisis. I think it is morally lamentable that, for example, Ambassador Türk could realistically dismiss out of hand the possibility of sending this initiative to the main UN organ in charge of codification and progressive development of international law, the International Law Commission. The fact that it has proved to be an ineffective mechanism for these purposes shows that we have a crisis in the mechanisms that we have available for international law-making.

Pulling these two points together, therefore, I think that we should not restrict the alternatives before us to just one avenue, such as the 'Fifth Geneva' Convention, but should also keep an open mind to calls like the one made by Dr Goldblat in the sense that we may have to capitalize on what we have, despite its present vagueness, to improve on the existing norms and eventually to codify them all. There are many possible fora for this available to the international community where we could expect less resistance, especially from the more powerful countries, than we would if we tried to negotiate a new treaty. We could introduce, for instance, a draft resolution at the UNCED Conference in Brazil next year; we could introduce it as an important item in the United Nations Decade for International Law; or we could introduce it into the International Law Commission or other international fora. I think that we should keep our options open.

Sohr: I want to congratulate the organizers for this very important event. I would like to say that, even if the environment is a loose concept, armed conflict is equally loose. Since the Second World War, most countries have had, in one form or another, an internal conflict, albeit that it is often difficult to classify conflicts as international or internal. There was, for example, no formal declaration of war by the United States against Vietnam, and the policy of rollback carried out in Angola and in Mozambique was part of President Reagan's policy in Africa, so that these were arguably internal conflicts with the involvement of a state as a third party. I, therefore, take Professor Goldblat's view that we should deal with the use of arms in peace and with military tactics in both peace and war and not exclusively with armed conflict among states.

If we look at the world today, because of the East–West *détente*, we can probably expect more of a North–South conflict. We see already some very good examples, including the narcotics trade, which is becoming an important North–South issue. Some people in developed states have suggested that, in order to combat the growth of narcotics in certain Southern forest areas, aircraft should be sent to spray them with defoliants. The Pentagon has coined the term 'low intensity conflict' for this kind of situation. Many such examples might be excluded from the scope of a new instrument primarily concerned with international armed conflict. These situations are not always clear-cut, however. How does one deal, for example, with a situation where a host government agrees to large chunks of its country being defoliated, although the environment would suffer? Situations of insurgency, such as the scorched-earth policy being carried out in Guatemala and El Salvador by local military governments, might also not be covered by a new Geneva-style convention or similar instrument. We should address these extremely important issues.

Schwebel: There have been references to an international tribunal, and Christopher Pinto referred to the International Court of Justice. I would simply observe that there is no barrier to the Court's judging the responsibility of states on a state to state basis for violations of the law of war or for environmental breaches. Individuals may not be parties to the Court's contentious cases, but the Court certainly can deal with violations of the law of war, and, indeed, it has.

Tickell: I am going to abuse my position as chairman, because I want to inject one thought, which does not fall at all within the lines of thinking that have been explored so far. Until September I was the UK's Permanent Representative on the Security Council. I was then and remain now much aware of the fact that the words in the UN Charter on the prime responsibility of the Security Council – 'the maintenance of international peace and security' – covers a great many potentialities and possibilities. At one time I tried to bring the question of narcotics and narcotic traffic within the realm of the Security Council. Certain Governments didn't like it, because they thought that it was carrying the remit of the Security Council too far, but all of you can see clearly enough that narcotics traffic could indeed endanger international law and security.

This is equally true of the environment. We have all heard several references to the need for a new instrument to govern what happens in peacetime as well as in wartime. In fact the Security Council is capable of dealing with any threats to the peace, anything which endangers international peace and security, either in times of peace or in times of war. What I would add to your deliberations is the thought that there are occasions when actions by a state could endanger international peace and security because they put at risk the environment in one country in a fashion which affected the environment in another. Please don't neglect this possibility. The Security Council is a flexible institution, and it can deal with almost anything it wants to deal with, provided that it can use the language of the Charter, which is widely drawn. Thus I regard this as a potentially useful instrument for dealing with future environmental problems, provided, of course, that member governments are ready to use it.

Mr Al-Khasawneh summed up.

8 Round-Table Session II: Targetry

Michael Bothe

Higgins assumed the chair and introduced Professor Bothe.

Bothe (Special-Rapporteur): I will try to stick to the 'Elements' Document which was submitted to you by the organizers, and elaborate on the part which has been assigned to me – the one entitled 'Geneva Law'. Now what Dr Plant, the author of that document, did was really to put a green coat on those provisions of Protocol I Additional to the Geneva Conventions which deal with the protection of the civilian population (in particular Articles 48 to 60), and I think it is a very good idea to proceed in this way. It reflects a change of attitude which has occurred since these provisions were drafted in 1974–7. It was at the time a very anthropocentric approach, and international law generally and international environmental law in particular since then has, I would not say adopted a new ecocentric approach – that would be to go too far – but taken up a number of eco-centric approaches or elements.

There are two ways to approach the question of environmental warfare or the protection of the environment against acts of warfare. The traditional question to be asked would be: 'How could it be that I could not defend my country for the sake of the survival of some birds?' The other way of putting the question is: 'Why should the survival of the earth be put into jeopardy just because two or more states have this silly idea of shooting at each other?' The way in which you put the question of course to a certain extent predetermines your answers.

Going a little further into the details of the exercise of putting that green coat around the provisions of Protocol I, I think there are a number of elements where it is really appropriate to do this. Of course one can argue that the environment has always been protected, being 'civilian' in nature. It is protected as part of the civilian world – 'civilian' being the converse of 'military', military objectives alone being open to attack. Now to the extent that this is true, it might be a good thing to make this more explicit. We might thus wish to say that the environment as such is not a military objective and may thus not be the object of attacks. This is, I think, important and relevant for the definition of 'military objective', of which one finds some discussion in the 'Elements' document.

What is also important I think is to make it explicit that environmental damage counts in the 'proportionality' calculation which has to be made once one comes to the evaluation of possible collateral damage. According to the relevant rules of both customary and treaty law, incidental civilian damage caused by attack against military objectives is permissible only if it is not disproportionate, or 'excessive in relation to the military advantage to be gained'. Here again, one can say that the environment is already covered, but I think that it is very important to make it explicit that the environment is a serious concern which has to be taken into account in solving the proportionality equation. It is a difficult calculation anyway.

The final example which I shall give you is the protection of objects containing dangerous forces: dams, dykes and nuclear electrical generating stations. Again, as it is formulated in Article 56 of Protocol I, the end is to protect the civilian population. Here again it should be made explicit that damage to the environment comes into play.

Now, having said that we should extend the protection of the environment, or should make explicit the protection of the environment in existing law, the difficult questions, of course, arise when one comes to a commander's decision – 'Do I or do I not shoot?'; or 'Do I programme my little computer for this target?'; or 'Do I avoid this target?' A general guideline along the lines of 'You should respect the environment', or 'You should take into account the environment in an equation you have to solve', or 'You should not damage the cultural and natural heritage of mankind', cannot be given to such a programming officer. He will be in trouble, to say the least. Worse still, he will laugh at you, because that is not the language he (and nowadays she) might understand.

So how can you make this general rule operational? The question of thresholds was mentioned this morning and rightly so. How can we establish more precise terminology? If we have learned anything about international law and the correct formulation of acceptable thresholds over the last 20 years, it is another very general principle – it all depends on the specific context, on the particular circumstances. What we did in 1974–7 when the relevant rules of Protocol I were formulated, was in a way to refight the Vietnam War. As to the specific provisions protecting the environment, they prohibit causing 'long-term', 'severe' and 'widespread' damage. Looking at the suggested definitions of these terms in the 'travaux préparatoires', and at the similar provision in ENMOD, what do they envisage? The Vietnamese jungle, because that was the example that was in everyone's minds at the time. Now we are talking about oil-spills. Do the indications and numbers of square kilometres which figure in the Understanding relating to the ENMOD Convention[233] apply to oil-spills in the desert as they apply to them in the Vietnamese jungle? Their application would not make any sense. As all of us know, an oil-spill in the Gulf is not the same, for example, as an oil-spill in Antarctic waters. The environmental impact of an oil-spill of the same size is different from one location to another.

It is, thus, necessary to translate these general principles and clauses into concrete military orders. The Anglo-Saxon military tradition is familiar with

---

233 Loc. cit., *supra* n. 71 and p. 47.

a good device for doing this: the 'rules of engagement'. Those rules of engagement are written for particular conflicts and during the conflict they are secret, because one does not tell his enemy how he is going to behave. In this context what is necessary really is to find ways and means to translate these general principles which we are discussing, and which we want to reconfirm, into rules of engagement. This procedure is very effective, because lawyers are involved in writing rules of engagement. There are other military traditions where one does not have these rules of engagement – one relies rather upon more general instructions, and thus the commanding officer is stuck with general principles which are difficult to apply. If something reasonable is to come out of a development of the law, a procedure should be established which might give a precise and concrete content to those general rules. It should probably not be an obligatory procedure, because that might not be acceptable to states jealous of their freedom of military planning. It should, instead, involve experts being engaged in the examination of very concrete case-studies of possible environmental harm caused through wartime activities, and in the giving of their opinions upon them. These opinions, it can be hoped, will have a serious impact through national implementation processes, making the general principles more capable of practical operation by soldiers, as they have to be.

This brings me to my last point, which relates to institutions. The problem here is that one is faced with two different regulatory worlds. One has on the one hand international environmental law, which has its own institutions and should be (I'm afraid it isn't so far, but it should be) a coherent whole; and one has the law of armed conflict, which also has its own institutions and also should be and, because it is a smaller field of law, is to a certain extent, a coherent whole. When it comes to institutions, what one needs is expertise. The ICRC so far does not really have a great deal of experience with the environment, and I think that there will be few people at their office in Geneva with expert knowledge on oil-wells, albeit perhaps they will obtain this if they have to. They may have to, because where they *do* have expertise is in dealing with parties to a conflict and government officials, hard-headed military officers or prison directors, as the case may be, whom they have to talk into letting them or somebody else do something like visit prisoners, or into letting people out of detention or into agreeing to a ceasefire enabling the evacuation of the wounded or of other victims. That is certainly an expertise that the environmental institutions do not have but which will be necessary where appropriate conditions to permit environmental clean-up missions or the like are to be created.

So, if there is to be an institutional approach, different kinds of expertise have their importance. There are several possible models, and I have some ideas of my own, but I won't develop them now, because I am most curious to hear what other people think about it.

Higgins: Well, thank you very much for that introduction. You touched on several themes. Could I suggest that for the purposes of orderly discussion we hold over the institutional questions on which already some interest was shown this morning for its proper location later in the afternoon. It ties into everything we say on substance and procedure. In the meantime the issues for this session, particularly the Geneva law, is now very much open for the Round Table.

Leipold: It is, of course, extremely difficult not only for environmentalists but also for lawyers to define what is acceptable damage to the environment. It is a moral question as much as it is a question of definition. I wonder whether one could not come around this question and, at least as a useful exercise, shift the burden of proof. I would find it very interesting to have military people indicating which targets they would want to hit and which weapons they would want to use and to confront them by saying: 'You can't hit this and you can't use that.' The situation at the moment is that we have a longer and longer list, both the experts' and the public's, of what it is not acceptable to do, but the underlying assumption of the discussion is that war as such is very acceptable. I think, however, that the general trend in international relations is developing into something where environmental protection and humanitarian values enjoy much greater value, and thus they should be at the centre of consideration. I very much feel that it would be useful to have the military say: 'This is our wish list: tell us what you think is acceptable.'

Sapolsky: There are some limitations upon the military's freedom to act. If you compare the recent war in the Gulf with the Second World War, you will see tremendous differences. Even if the limitations are not codified in the law, they are still very effective. Today the American military doesn't bomb civilian populations if this can be avoided and it goes to great lengths to avoid doing so. The military also tries very much to reduce its own casualties. And you can see what impact these limitations have on warfare. They place constraints upon the kinds of targets that are going to be hit. The targets that are hit are going to be hit very hard, but the result is to limit the kinds of targets that are legitimate. I think that there are tremendous constraints upon warfare, and these shape both the way that wars are fought and the environmental effects of warfare.

Al-Khasawneh: May I ask a question, Madam Chairman? Dr Bothe in his famous book,[234] which you rightly referred to as being a standard book on this subject, mentions the case of a debate in the Third Committee of the diplomatic conference which adopted Protocol I, where one of the Representatives refused to admit the fact that attacks against the environment could be grouped among grave breaches. His reasoning, cited in the book,[235] is that the environment is not an object. There is a tendency in 'Geneva' law to concentrate on targetry. With our increase in concern for the environment, is not that approach in the 'Geneva' law a hindrance to the development of a law which is free from the concept of targetry?

---

234 Loc. cit., *supra* n. 66.
235 Ibid.

Higgins: That in a sense echoes the point that was put earlier by Professor Falk, although it was suggested elsewhere that targetry had served some useful purposes. I wonder if I could turn to Professor Bothe and ask him to answer Mr Al-Khasawneh's question.

Bothe: I can try, but I am not sure that I will succeed.

The Geneva Protocols belong to a period of development of international law which did not take into account the recent great concern for the environment. If one looks at parallel development, in national criminal law as an example, specific provisions for the punishment of environmental crimes at the national level are a development of the 1970s.[236] The International Association of Criminal Law took up the matter only as recently as 1979, when that development at the national level was taking shape.[237] Thus it is no wonder that the development of environmental law had not yet reached the international level, and certainly had not reached the law of war by 1977. It takes a while until these changes of attitude make their way from acceptance at the national level to acceptance at the international level. If the diplomatic conference which adopted the Geneva Protocols were to have met today, instead of in the 1970s, I am quite sure that the discussion would go the other way.

Having said that, I think that targetry is important. You may not like the idea if you are the target chosen, because you happen to be a part of the military, or you happen to work in an ammunition factory, or you happen to drive trains across bridges. In all these cases, it is just too bad for you; you are a military target. In addition, it is, I think a salutary development only in terms of embracing the lesser evil to have replaced area bombing by accurate targeting, but it is still an improvement in the 'civilization', so to speak, of war, and perhaps a step towards abolishing war by making it so complicated that it is no longer possible. Perhaps that is cheating the world out of war, but we will not get there otherwise. For the time being I think the careful choosing of targets is a way to spare as many potential victims as possible; it is better than nothing, and it is better than much of what we have had in the past.

Higgins: Passing to Professor Falk, I would like to say that I do not see for a moment that one has to choose between targetry, which, it seems to me, has served very valuable purposes, and moving more widely to the prohibition of actions for different contemporary community purposes. I do not see it as an 'either/or' choice, and I certainly do not think that one need become locked into it through a doctrinal debate about whether the environment is an 'object', any more than I think that our prescriptions should get locked into the sterile debate about which international actors on

---

236 Germany, for example, introduced provisions on environmental crimes into its Criminal Code in 1980.
237 XIIth International Congress of Criminal Law, Hamburg, 16 to 22 September 1979. See the report in 92, *Zeitschrift für die Gesamte Stratrechts Wissenschaft*, (1980) at p. 1047.

the scene are or are not subjects of international law. I think that they are equally dead paths and I hope we will not go down them today.

Falk: I want first to reinforce what Professor Higgins has just said and to add a small *caveat* in relation to what Professor Bothe said about the advance he associates with the modern emphasis on precise targeting. I think that, if one takes his point in isolation, it is quite correct, but, if one looks at it in the context of a world of very uneven technologies, there is the serious political danger that he is unwittingly restructuring the law of war on behalf of the technologically most sophisticated and advanced countries. I do not think that this issue should be evaded in a conference of this sort, because one is seeking a law of war that really does correspond with the situation that confronts all countries and all peoples. It has to have a universal legitimacy as part of its aspiration and should be sensitive to this issue of technological unevenness in the waging of war, which is becoming a more, and not a less, pronounced feature, of the way in which armed conflict is carried on.

My other point is that, in addition to the approaches that have been mentioned in the 'Elements' Document, it seems to me to be desirable and politically feasible to isolate certain kinds of warfare, that is belligerent practices which intentionally seek to damage the environment outside a battlefield context, where there is no military justification for them as military justification is ordinarily understood. I think that one thing that would be important is a careful redefinition of what it means to pursue military objectives. What are the boundaries of military objectives in relation to direct and indirect environmental harm arising out of armed conflict? I think that question creates a basis for not only isolating the kinds of tactics used by Iraq towards the oil-wells and in pumping the oil into the Gulf as distinct offences associated with specific belligerent practices, but it also creates the jurisprudential foundation, it seems to me, for specifying 'crimes against nature' as a distinct category of international crime and beginning to evolve an international criminal dimension to the law of war pertaining to the environment. This, I think, is a correlative, yet important part of the undertaking to extend the law of war so that it encompasses environmental aspects of military activity.

Rostow: I of course represent a Government (the USA) which is not Party to Protocol I and until now has made it clear that it does not intend to become a Party. I also represent a President (President Bush) who has proclaimed his commitment to the environment and who, in the course of leading the Coalition against Iraq, directed that the Armed Forces of the Coalition conduct themselves in a fashion that minimized collateral damage from military attack. I make these points, because there are some things that I would like to say and questions which I would like posed which may suggest a lesser enthusiasm for this enterprise than its sponsors and most of the speakers. This really is not so; rather, I recognize the difficulty of the enterprise.

I would like to echo what Professor Falk just said about technological disparities in warfare. Article 51 of the UN Charter, which is a bedrock principle of the Charter, recognizes and reaffirms the inherent right of self-defence. If you happen to be a small country or a poor country or a technologically deprived country which is under attack, and have no smart bombs, nothing clean with which to respond to your attacker, does it mean that you have lost your right of self-defence? This is something which the draftsmen would have to address by being precise. And I find the absence of an effort to define the environment in the 'Elements' Document to be perhaps its most severe deficiency, notwithstanding the heroism of Dr Plant in getting it out at all, given his illness.

Secondly and finally, I think we ought to look at the state of weaponry and think it through rather carefully. I notice that there are no military experts at this conference, and that is rather unfortunate. My understanding, for example, is that a smart bomb launched by an F117 Stealth fighter bomber, weighing 2,000 pounds, is a very expensive item and beyond the means of most nations. In some respects one hopes that that platform and the expertise involved in it is, indeed, beyond the means of most nations, as it is rather special and should be in the hands of responsible nations. One hesitates to think what Saddam Hussein would have done with it! But it does mean that a state having it can go after certain targets with a great deal of confidence and can take them out in such a way that collateral damage which would have been assumed to be inevitable ten years ago simply does not need to be assumed at all. Indeed, I was told by one of the US Air Force planners of the campaign that he confronted a pilot of one of these machines and said: 'Here is a hardened aircraft bunker, and if you don't hit it right there with pinpoint accuracy, don't bother showing up.' The pilot's response was: 'Don't worry.'

As I say, however, I think Professor Falk has made that point. I think that what we need to focus on here and what people need to be conscious of is that we live in a world of states, all with the right of self-defence, and that, while we all may abhor war, if we took the position of some people at this table in favour of an environmental prohibition on war, we would be, I believe, encouraging aggressors at the expense of small states. Indeed, one could argue that the logic of some of the statements made this morning would be that Kuwait should still be occupied by Iraq. We must instead advance the rule of law and respect for the law by, again following from Professor Falk's comment, being aware of and responding to the fact that, while most countries of the world are parties to the Geneva Conventions, most of those countries have no clue how to apply them and do not apply them. Even some of the countries which are parties to Protocol 1 do not apply it. The recent Liberian civil war gives us an example of a country which is party to Protocol I and, I think we all would agree, ignored its provisions.

Greenwood: I would like to pick up a point that has been made by the last two speakers and develop it a little. I think that it is terribly important, if we are trying to develop a treaty on environmental protection in time of war, not to come up with a draft that makes environmental sense but is militarily ridiculous, whether or not one takes into account disparity in technological competence between different states. I think that the key to getting it right is to have a provision that makes sense in relation to collateral environmental damage, because that is much more problematic in practice than the deliberate targeting of the environment as a means of achieving a military goal. Page 9 of the 'Elements' Document sets out the various options which are suggested in relation to which methods and means of warfare should be prohibited because of their collateral impact on the environment.[238] If one takes the more far-reaching options here, particularly option (a), they could easily produce the result that, a state engaged in a conflict against the USA, which finds that one of its naval commanders has a US nuclear-powered aircraft carrier in his sights, must let it pass by, because to sink a nuclear-powered carrier would have ecologically disastrous results. It may be that there are some people here who would like exactly that result, but let us not delude ourselves. If that is what the text is thought to mean, it will not be adopted.[239] If it were adopted, no one would take any notice of it, and it would have the ridiculous result that those states that do have nuclear-powered or nuclear-armed warships would actually enjoy a degree of protection for their military activities which states with less sophisticated weaponry would not enjoy.

Moving on from that, I would like to say a brief word about the proposals in the 'Elements' Document concerning international crimes. An environmental protection treaty must contain realistic means of enforcement. All experience suggests that the *least* realistic way of enforcing international law in times of armed conflict is anything to do with the criminal law. I am one of those who was a little disappointed that we did not end up at the end of the present Kuwait conflict with an international military tribunal of some kind. I think that, having raised that particular possibility, the governments of the USA, the UK and a number of other countries, had created an expectation which they then failed to meet. But if one cannot obtain effective criminal law enforcement in this context, where there was an almost unprecedented international consensus, I do not think it is going to be achieved in any other context either. So I would suggest that, when one is looking at methods of enforcement, international criminal jurisdiction should be placed right at the bottom in terms of its likely adoption and its likely effectiveness if adopted.

Bothe: I am afraid that we might see some wrong alliances here. The representative (Mr Rostow), because that is the way he presented himself, of a Power known for its very sophisticated means of warfare (the USA) appears to have spoken in defence of the unsophisticated warriors, if I may call them that, of the Third World.

I have a certain memory of the negotiating history of Protocol I and the provisions relating to the civilian population (Chapter III), and, as I said earlier, when drafting them, we in a sense refought the Vietnam War. It

---

238 *Supra* pp. 46–48
239 Editor's note. The commentary to this Element makes it clear that option (a) is very unlikely to be accepted.

was the technologically advanced countries who wanted to have more freedom to produce collateral damage. This is well-illustrated by the debate about the applicability (or otherwise) of the Protocol to non-conventional weapons (a matter on which most NATO countries have made declarations on the occasion of signature and/or ratification[240] as well as by the unwillingness of certain military Powers to accede to the Protocol for reasons of 'security'.[241] It was the poor countries of the Third World who insisted on further restrictions on collateral damage. That made sense. There is a very simple reason for it; in the tactical and strategic context they were considering at that time, certain armies hoped to rely rather more on manpower than on firepower, and others hoped to rely rather more on firepower than on manpower. The distinction I make here is found in a very interesting article written by the head of the US delegation at the Geneva conference,[242] and so a serious soul-search to evaluate interests is in order.

I have serious objections to an argument which links permissible means of warfare with the idea of self-defence. The delegates, and in particular the Western Power delegates, tried everything possible to dissociate the right to use force from the legality of the means and methods of warfare, to dissociate the *ius ad bellum* and *ius in bello*. The *ius in bello* should apply regardless of the just or unjust cause of war. I know that this was the ideological stance taken mainly by the Western states in the early phases of the negotiations, when there was much talk about 'wars of national liberation'. The inclusion of wars of national liberation in Protocol I was seen by them (wrongly, in my opinion) as a resurgence of the idea of 'just war', which might lead to the danger that this might be interpreted as justifying a differential treatment of the 'just' and the 'unjust' side of a conflict.

This misconception led to the insistence by Western delegations on a reference in the preamble to the Protocol to the equal application of international humanitarian law (the law of war) to both sides of the conflict. Later, however, when the diplomatic conference came to the final adoption of the Protocols (and still later when the questions of signature and ratification arose), Western states saw a link between the cause of war, namely self-defence, and the content of the Protocol.[243] France was, I think, the first country to do this. This was not entirely consistent in theoretical and ideological terms, if I may say so. It may be justified on other grounds, but I would like to state for the record that I would not follow this argument.

---

240 Gasser (in Meyer (ed.), loc. cit., *supra* n. 76, at pp. 93–94 describes the Belgian, Italian and Dutch declarations upon ratification, the French, British and American declarations upon signature and the Russian silence on the subject. Alone in the debates, India objected to this view.

241 See the declaration of the French delegation during the final debate of the Diplomatic Conference, CDDH SR. 41, para. 111.

242 G. Aldrich, 'Establishing Legal Norms Through Multilateral Negotiation: the Laws of War,' 9, *Case Western Reserve Journal of International Law*, (1977), p. 9.

243 *Cf.* CDDH SR.41 para 11. (Official Records vol. VI, p. 162): 'The French delegation . . . wished to point out . . . that certain provisions . . . were of a type which by their very complexity would seriously hamper the conduct of defensive military operations against an invader and prejudice the exercise of the inherent right of legitimate defence recognized in Article 51 of the Charter of the United Nations.'

Coming to Christopher Greenwood's argument, which is of course a very serious one, how far should we go in tying our hands for the sake of the environment? Some of the restraints contained in Protocol I are already very serious. Works and installations containing dangerous forces, for instance, may not be attacked even if they are a military objective (Article 56 of Protocol I). That is what the Article is all about. If they were a civilian object they could not be attacked anyway. If a dam is used as an essential road link for military purposes, it may nevertheless not be blown up. If a nuclear electrical generating station provides electricity for the military, it may nevertheless not be destroyed. The values threatened by the destruction of such targets are more important than the military advantage likely to be gained by a belligerent which destroys them. Now, which situations one should put into this category and which situation should he put into the other category – saying 'I won't forego an effective means of damaging the enemy; I really need that' – has to be discussed, and has to be discussed, I think, in a very concrete way. Of course a chemical factory which is used for the production of chemical weapons is a military target, but we have seriously to discuss the question whether, notwithstanding its military purpose, we do not want it to be attacked for other reasons. Oil installations were discussed when Article 56 of Protocol I was negotiated, and the Arab States were very much in favour of including oil installations among those containing dangerous forces which may not be attacked.[244] The diplomatic conference did not accept that. Perhaps today the alliances would go the other way; alliances keep shifting.

Lee: We have heard references to the right to wage war and to Article 51. I think we should not forget about Article 2(4) of the UN Charter, the prohibition against resorting to war.

Of course, I immediately hear the argument that the right to resort to war, the law on how to fight wars and the prohibition of war have nothing to do with each other, that regardless of the legality of the war, the rules of warfare apply. I wonder about that.

In the context of protecting the environment in times of warfare, I wonder whether we should ask ourselves the following questions. These limitations upon the resort to warfare and upon methods of warfare were developed in the last century when every state had the right to resort to war. It was perfectly legitimate then to resort to war. Since the premises have now changed, and a state can only resort to war under certain circumstances, should we not also ask for higher standards in relation to the *ius in bello*? If we could accept this, I think we would be provided with a philosophical basis to deal with Hague law and Geneva law in the environmental context. I put this question to you.

Pinto: I have some sympathy for what was said by Mr Rostow a moment ago and also for what Professor Falk said. My country has not been

---

244 ICRC *Commentary*, loc. cit., *supra* n. 66, at p. 687.

engaged in any international wars, but alas we have for eight years experienced an internal war; such a war can, I can assure you, have consequences as serious as any international armed conflict.

I am a little reluctant to think in terms, for example, of an environmental prohibition against certain targets or means of carrying on war which is described in over-strict and technical or technological terms. Sri Lanka's is not a well-equipped army; on the contrary. The Sri Lankan Government has suffered a tremendous amount of foreign criticism, and, as a result, the country has suffered a great deal economically, precisely because its army is not well-equipped and the weaponry it uses is said to have caused 'excessive' damage. Thus the fact that Sri Lanka does not have any weaponry that remotely approaches the category of so-called 'smart' weapons has led to the kind of criticism which has damaged it in the past and is continuing to do so. I do not want to go into the details.

What I think might be useful, however, is to consider the possibility of environmental prohibition of targets or weaponry which is couched in terms of 'significance', of 'reasonableness' or of 'proportionality'. And then, perhaps, if the experts are willing to suggest specific instances of what would be 'unreasonable', what would be 'significant', what would be 'disproportionate', we could list those also in the prohibition. But to have a prohibition couched in essentially technological terms, which is conducive to later arguments between experts on each side of a conflict saying completely different things – we all know that is what happens in an arbitration or when a case comes up for trial – I do not think will serve our purpose at all. So what I would suggest is a more general prohibition in terms of 'significance', 'reasonableness' and 'proportionality', with examples of what would be in breach of that prohibition, and then to leave it to some kind of tribunal later on to decide whether an act was in fact in breach.

Higgins: Thank you very much for those thoughts. Mr Greenwood of course thinks that there never will be a tribunal later on, that we are going to have a decentralized legal order and that we cannot afford to leave it to that. So there are two different perspectives which we will be able to discuss.

Türk: A few additional remarks. First, I would like to address a question raised by Professor Bothe in his introductory remarks. He spoke about two different regulatory areas, on the one hand the area of environmental law, on the other the area of the law of armed conflict. I think that this reflects one of the basic problems we are facing here today. We are trying to find and to elaborate legal rules, but legal rules relating to what? To the law of (international) armed conflict or to the protection of the environment in general? From a logical point of view, of course, one can ask why it should be forbidden to attack nuclear electrical generating stations during an international armed conflict, when this is legitimate in an internal conflict, or why should any kind of attack at any time be legitimate against such an installation.

It seems to me to be most realistic to focus upon the law of armed conflict in the first phase and perhaps later, in the light of experience, consider expanding those norms to situations not covered by armed conflict.

A further point I want to raise relates to remarks made by Professor Falk and Mr Rostow concerning technological unevenness between different countries. I think that this should not be a major problem because of the circumstances under which the use of force might conceivably be used. If a small country is being attacked, we may assume, I hope, that the UN Security Council will live up to its responsibilities and take or authorize the necessary actions. If so, the forces authorized to take enforcement action by the Security Council will be those of technologically advanced countries which we can expect to respect the norms laid down in the new instrument. A country which is opposing the UN collective action has no right to self-defence, and I would not feel sorry for such a country if it were not able to use certain means and would be constrained in its methods and means of warfare.

What further scenarios might we consider? A conflict between tech-nologically advanced countries which would block the Security Council's decision-making mechanism. In such a case it would be all the more essen-tial for those major military Powers to be under certain constraints as far as warfare is concerned.

Turning to the third scenario of two smaller Third World and tech-nologically less-advanced countries in conflict, one might assume a certain technological equality between those countries too.

So there is only one remaining scenario, that is of an advanced country attacking a smaller, less-developed country and the Security Council not taking action. Perhaps I am too optimistic but I hope that such a situation would never occur, notwithstanding that experience has shown that no eventuality can be completely excluded.

One last point. I want to echo the scepticism expressed by Mr Greenwood as far as international criminal jurisdiction is concerned. Experience with endeavours in that respect has not been very encouraging, and while we should not give up such an ideal as a distant aim, it will take quite a number of decades until such a jurisdiction is realized.

Higgins: Thank you very much. Perhaps I could use my position by saying that I was struck by the way you seem to have conflated collective security and self-defence. In the range of scenarios you went through there also seemed to be an assumption that never again would there be self-defence without having to rely on collective security by the Security Council. Obviously one had the curious amalgam in the recent Gulf conflict, but I don't really regard that as normative for the future in any general way. I think it was very special to those circumstances. So, while I am intrigued by the Falk/Rostow alliance, I have to say that I have sympathy for the views of both Professor Falk and Mr Rostow in this respect.

Arkin: I wish to build upon what Professor Bothe said, which is the ques-tion of what are acceptable changes. Coming from an organization that works in the public domain, Greenpeace, my analysis would be that what is acceptable is of course constantly changing; that analysis applies to the recent war as well.

Professor Sopolsky said that the modern practice of the US military shapes the effects of their targetry. I agree with him, and, indeed, our report *On Impact* generally agrees with his view of US military practice. But he uses the word 'shapes'. He does not use the word 'mitigates' or 'reduces' in relation to the effects of hitting a target. The fact is that in this conflict those effects were shaped by the nature of the weaponry used and the intensity of its use, but were not necessarily reduced in comparison with previous wars. They were perhaps *different* kinds of effect, whether these be the rather sophisticated means by which Iraq blew up Kuwait's oil infrastructure – and they *were* sophisticated – or whether they be the rather sophisticated way in which the USA and its Allies dismantled Iraq's civilian infrastructure, which was also sophisticated.

Many have a rather old-fashioned view of collateral damage in this regard. The old-fashioned view is that rubble has to fall on people or that they have to be hit by shrapnel from area bombing in order for there to be 'collateral damage'. In this war we saw something quite different. The collateral damage caused was shaped by the modes of warfare, as much by the precision-guided weapons used on the Allied side as by the sophistication with which Iraq dismantled Kuwait's resources. Thus, in reaching a new definition of collateral damage, we have to focus more effort in the future on the question of effects. I believe that the debate about who is and who is not technically advanced is not the real debate; it is a red herring. The question is not so much the 'civility' or the cleanliness of the attack. It is what the *effect* of the attack is. We did observe surgery in US and Allied attacks upon Iraq, but surgery kills too, and killing is also what we observed. So I think this notion that cleanliness or 'civility' is the standard that we should apply to the conduct of war is archaic.

Addressing more precisely this question of degrees of technological advancement, I am at a loss to know which technologically less-advanced country it was that the Coalition is supposed to have fought. Iraq had virtually all of the weapons that the USA and its Allies had; it just did not use them very well. So what are we to understand by the words 'technologically advanced'? The answer seems to lie not so much in the weapons a state possesses, but in the non-weapon attributes of the way in which it applies those weapons to various uses. Iraq had, for example, very sophisticated artillery, bombs, air-defence systems, but they were dismantled, not solely by means of the equally sophisticated weapons of the Coalition, but by virtue of the Coalition's non-weapons attributes, whether superior training, performance, electronic warfare or just the sheer intensity of a military force that overwhelmed Iraq's capacity. When we look to the future of modern warfare and its effects, therefore, we have to think about the relevance of this technological question. I think that, to some degree, it is irrelevant. Kuwait also had very technologically advanced defences, including advanced surface-to-air missiles and aircraft. It just didn't have very many of them. So this question of technology, particularly given the proliferation of weapons in the Third World, could also be a red herring.

How should we look at this war and conclude what is acceptable? To me, what is unacceptable is the precision, 'civility' and so-called 'cleanliness' by which the United States and its Allies ripped apart and took away the civil life-support systems of Iraq; this is just as unacceptable as the way in which Iraq so maliciously, viciously and vindictively destroyed Kuwait's oil infrastructure. The result for both Iraq and Kuwait has been dramatic, and in many instances on both sides the damage is not collateral but intentional.

Thus, when we look at the oil-fires and the oil-spills we are quickly able to dismiss military necessity as a justification. Saddam Hussein gave an interview on CNN Television where he said that this was his only defence, and others have argued that the destruction of Kuwait's oil installations had some military effect. Coalition pilots and ground troops complained about the smoke and its effect upon targeting. There was, indeed, some military effect, as evaluated in our report, *On Impact*,[245] but we are able quickly to dismiss the military necessity justification, because we know that, even when one can prove a military effect, there is a point at which the necessity no longer relates to the question of effect, but relates to the wantonness and the scope and intensity of the act.

On the other hand, we in the West seem to be unable to look at the dismantling of the civil infrastructure of Iraq by the bombing – and to me this is one of the most interesting intellectual issues raised by the recent war – and ask ourselves the question: 'What was its military necessity and effect?' By and large the destruction of Iraq's civil electricity and communications systems, and even, to some degree, its transportation systems, made little contribution to the defeat of the Iraqi military. Similarly the bombing of nuclear installations, chemical research and development and other industrial installations had little effect, if one accepts that the USA and its Allies were aware that it was going to be a short war, such that the impact of the military support role of those installations was minimal.

I bring this up, because I have been surprised in the discussion today by the paucity of references to the recent war and to what happened in this war that might be instructive as to what war might be like in the future. It seems to me that what we also learned from this particular war is that enforcement is achieved only through means that society will bear. I am not too impressed with Mr Greenwood's remarks about nuclear-powered ships, because I think society is dealing with that problem. First, people are abandoning investments in nuclear-powered ships, because (a) they cannot afford them, or (b) they are too controversial, or (c) the implications for the environment throughout the fuel cycle are too serious. So the question of attacking nuclear-powered ships may be with us for another 20 or 30 years, but thereafter I doubt that we will see very many of them around. That is an example of how society takes care of the problem to some degree by creating its own acceptance of what is and is not acceptable.

I conclude, therefore, that, when we look at the effects of this war and try to think about how we might want to improve the law in the future,

---

245 Loc. cit., *supra* n. 11.

we should also keep in mind that this war was fought on the US and Allied side very much with a view to what public opinion would allow and accept. I for one came out of the war with some conclusions. This is a fluid and quickly shifting world, and it may be that the law will lag behind what is acceptable to society, but the law should not use yesterday's standards to try to catch up with today's events.

Hampson: First, I would like to indicate my agreement with what Professor Falk said this morning about the danger of unrespected norms. I think that in some respects there is more danger in having a treaty on the international statute books which is ignored than in not having it in the first place.

I would also like to echo Mr Rostow's concern that there are no military men here. It is a pity, as one of our problems is to try to look at environmental concerns in some sort of framework and to tie that in with the framework of the law of armed conflict.

It seems to me there are three categories in relation to the environment that have arisen both in these discussions and in the Greenpeace report, *On Impact*.[246] First, intentional attacks upon the environment as such. I do not think any military man would have any hesitation in saying, 'Sure, ban them. It is a waste of our weaponry.' We must never forget that the British forces in the Falklands were told not to target penguins. So there is clearly not too much of a problem with this category. The problem lies rather in the environmental effect of attacks with weapons, and here, I think, one can separate two aspects of the 'effect' problem. First, there is the adverse effect of a particular weapon if it used at all; some incendiary weapons have such adverse effects. Quite separate is the effect of the cumulative use of a weapon which is not itself necessarily going to cause undue environmental damage.

Thus in environmental terms there are two issues. First, the effect of a particular weapon if used at all; second, the problem of cumulative effect. How does that fit into the framework of the law of armed conflict?

I would like to suggest a somewhat heretical and over-simplified view of what the law of armed conflict says about targeting. I would suggest that there are three categories: category one, targets prohibited *per se*; category two, targets prohibited unless 'militarily necessary' (and in this category I would place, for example, the subject-matter of the 1954 Hague Convention on Cultural Property, which provides that cultural property cannot be targeted unless it is being used for military purposes); and category three, targets 'not prohibited' at all, including, for example, soldiers of the opposing forces and their military equipment. It seems to me that, following the Gulf conflict, there might be some scope for suggesting that the description of the third category should be qualified. Perhaps that third category should be called 'targets not prohibited unless attack is militarily unnecessary'. I have in mind the attack on the convoys that were departing Kuwait. I deliberately do not specify whether in my view they were

---

246 Ibid.

'withdrawing' or were 'fleeing', but I think that, where the target is at present considered a legitimate military target, there may nevertheless be circumstances in which we would wish to change this existing position and say that an attack is not warranted.

How does this suggestion tie in with environmental targets? Take the example of installations holding dangerous forces. I have in mind oil – the oil installations in Kuwait. Under Article 56 of Protocol I, oil installations are not prohibited targets. The list of such installations is exhaustive on its face; the word used in Article 56 is 'namely', not 'including'. The list was intended to be exhaustive and, indeed, there was extensive discussion in the diplomatic conference as to whether to include oil installations; they were deliberately not included.[247] So at present, oil installations appear to be a legitimate target. Qualifying the third category, as I suggest, into 'targets not prohibited unless attack is militarily unnecessary' might, therefore, be one way forward.

Another way forward would be to reclassify oil installations as installations holding dangerous forces, but that would be much harder, given what happened in the negotiations for Article 56 of Protocol I. If one wishes to reclassify oil installations, one should put them in the same category as Article 56 (my category one) or the 1954 Convention (my category two).

It might be pointed out that my suggestion means that any attack is prohibited unless it is militarily necessary. So that raises the question whether or not an attack upon oil installations can ever serve a military purpose. Here, I am afraid, I disagree with Bill Arkin of Greenpeace. Creation of smoke may be a legitimate military purpose. There is another purpose which hasn't been discussed and is not raised in the Greenpeace report *On Impact*.[248] If I had been in Saddam Hussein's shoes, I might have believed that I was at risk of an amphibious landing. The Coalition forces were going out of their way to make me believe that there might be such a landing. Oil spillages in the Gulf might have made that landing much more difficult. Thus I think that it is quite possible that the attacks upon the oil installations *did* serve a military purpose, although this might not have been Saddam Hussein's motive. Whether it was or not is beside the point.

The question becomes, therefore, do we nevertheless wish to create a framework under which such attacks would be unlawful? This raises several questions. First, would a prohibition be respected? I have grave doubts. Second, if we think that it could be respected, then we have to approach it in one of two ways: either insert oil installations into my second category, that is to say prohibited targets 'unless militarily necessary', or requalify my third category into 'targets not prohibited unless attack is militarily

---

247 Official Records of the Diplomatic Conference on the Reaffirmation and Development of International Humanitarian Law Applicable in Armed Conflicts, vol. XV, p. 352: UN Doc. CDDH/III/264/Rev. 1, p. 449: UN Doc. CDDH/407/Rev.1, para. 12: ICRC *Commentary*, loc. cit., *supra* n. 66, at pp. 668–9; and Bothe, Partsch and Solf, ibid., at pp. 350–7.

248 Loc. cit., *supra* n. 11.

unnecessary'. Instead of saying that there are some things that are in blanket terms legitimate military targets provided one does not cause unnecessary suffering, one needs to qualify that and say that one cannot attack a legitimate military target where this is militarily unnecessary.

Goldblat: One of the basic rationales for having a new document, or one of the main reasons for it given here is the Gulf War. References were made to two occurrences: the setting on fire of the Kuwaiti oil-wells and the oil-spill in the Gulf. Bill Arkin has said that it is very difficult to find a military rationale for these acts, that there was no military necessity to resort to them. The point is arguable, but I would agree with him. Indeed, setting fire to the wells was not militarily justifiable, and Protocol 1 does apply to the facts of this case, because Article 35 (3) of the Protocol prohibits widespread, long-term and severe damage to the natural environment and this is occurring there. May I also point out that, in addition to barring the use of techniques causing widespread, long-lasting *or* severe effects, the 1977 ENMOD Convention, in the 'Understanding' relating to its Article II,[249] contains a prohibition against upsetting the ecological balance of a region. This is also occurring there.

The same arguments apply with equal force to the oil-spill.

Neither the USA nor Iraq is party to Protocol I. So why draft new treaties? Would it not be reasonable first to obtain adherence of as many nations as possible to the *existing* conventions? If the USA were to become a Party to Protocol I, the value of that document would be greatly enhanced, but there is absolutely no guarantee that it would adhere to a stronger convention.

Let me go further. Under the ENMOD Convention, to which the USA is party and Iraq is not, each Party may request the Depositary to convene a meeting of the Consultative Committee of experts. The fact that Iraq is not a fully fledged party (it has signed but not ratified the Convention) does not matter. Any country could have asked for such a meeting in order to discuss the situation in the Gulf, not necessarily to raise an accusation against Iraq, but to consider for the first time an occurrence which has the characteristics of a breach of the ENMOD Convention. Unfortunately, no state has done this. What is then the purpose of having new international documents, if those that we have are not being taken advantage of? Let us first reinforce what we have before we embark on a new venture.

Barnaby: I would like to comment on Bill Arkin's intervention and to ask him a question, because I found his argument about public acceptability persuasive. The more sophisticated a society becomes, the more likely it is to obey reasonable laws of war. On the other hand, the experience in the UK, and I am sure it was the same in the USA, during the Gulf War, was that almost any level of Iraqi casualties and damage to Iraqi society was acceptable to the public here provided that our casualties were kept low. In

---

249 Loc. cit., *supra* n. 71.

other words, given the choice between 200,000 Iraqi dead and a decimated Iraq, and 300 or so Coalition troops killed and considerably less material damage to the Coalition side, the public would overwhelmingly have gone for the first. How does this affect your argument about public acceptability?

Arkin: We could say that, of course, some things that are acceptable should be put into the category of pre-emptive public opinion, which is to say that the military will try to understand what the public will accept and to act accordingly. I think that, perhaps, this war was in this category. We didn't see area bombing, as Professor Sopolsky said. We didn't see the use of nuclear weapons. Some might think that it is absurd to make that point, but I don't think so, in some respect. We did not see the US military respond to the Amaria bunker bombing, in which 400 civilians died, by saying that the bunker was a legitimate target and that they did not care about the civilian casualties, which is what they could have said under the existing law. What they said was: 'We're sorry we killed a lot of civilians and we will look at this more closely in the future to ensure that it will not happen again.'

To my mind that response is a positive step. It shows that they are responding to a different sensitivity than the letter of the law. In our report, *On Impact*,[250] we give other examples of similar cases where they responded in like manner, and the war as a whole indicates that the basic targeting scheme and some of the intensity of the conflict reflected a similar regard for what the public would think as opposed to what was permissible in strict terms under their own laws of war manuals and their own targeting rules of engagement manuals.

Higgins: Well, thank you very much. I will ask Professor Bothe to briefly wrap it up for us.

Bothe: I think the question of collateral damage is a crucial one, and involves a very complicated equation, because the judgement on proportionality is also a value judgement. One has to compare things which are not comparable. One has to compare advances on land with civilian casualties and loss of lives, and it becomes all the more difficult when one compares advances on land with certain elements of the environment which are destroyed. There is a value judgement involved in any judgement on proportionality, and these value judgements of course change. They are constantly changing. It is the great advantage of the Marten's Clause that it takes care of that. One can say the protection of the environment is included in the Marten's Clause, because it is a dictate of public conscience. What is most important, and why I think this meeting is most timely, is to make more explicit those instances where this change has taken place, and to sum it up and write it down. That such work always lags somewhat behind events cannot be avoided.

---

250 Loc. cit., *supra* n. 11.

I think too that it is important to rethink rules which have been challenged. Why not do it in a slightly controversial mood? That makes the exercise all the more interesting.

Time does not permit me to dwell more on the question of collateral damage caused to the civilian population by attacks against the infrastructure, such as the power-supply system. This is one of the areas where I think some kind of digestive process has to take place. We have to think the matter over again, after seeing what happened in the Gulf, to decide whether or not, according to standards of proportionality, the damage done is acceptable under our current value system or not. Just as value judgements are changing, also the question of relevant impact (or 'effects') changes. There we come to a very difficult question – that is the application of the precautionary principle and integration of the question of cumulative damage into this judgement on proportionality. This is very new. Much thought has to be given to it.

A final remark on unrespected law. Of course that is a crucial point, and international law has a very simple answer to it. International law may fall into desuetude if it is no longer obeyed, and it will not come into existence if it is not acceptable to the relevant actors, because it is based on consensus. I know that this is something of an oversimplification of the present situation, but it is important to remark that it is not a very useful exercise to try to draft a document which will not be ratified. On the other hand, it is a useful exercise to find out how much public opinion may be activated in order to add to this consensus-building process. If law is to keep developing, obstacles must be removed. Power may be a very difficult obstacle, but not one which is in every case insurmountable.

9 Round-Table Session III: Weaponry and Institutions

Philippe Kirsch

Higgins (Chairman) introduced Ambassador Kirsch.

Kirsch (Special-Rapporteur): I have been asked to introduce two subjects, the 'Hague law' Part and the Institutions Part.

With respect to 'Hague law',[251a] my understanding of the general proposition underlying the Rapporteur's work is that existing instruments applicable to weapons (or to targets) in some cases are inadequate in relation to the protection of the environment. The general objective of Part 3 of the 'Elements' Document is, therefore, to afford greater protection to the environment in time of armed conflict by building on or supplementing existing instruments.

It does this in a variety of ways. One is by taking the general approach that the proposals in Part 3 of the Document of necessity have to meet standards that are higher than or at least equal to those of existing instruments. The Rapporteur then sets out three sub-Elements of a possible Convention covering different types of weapons. He deems the prohibition of some weapons to be already covered by international law, but wishes to confirm their inclusion through an express provision. In relation to others he builds upon existing instruments, notably the Inhumane Weapons Convention of 1980.

For the purposes of our discussion, I would like to raise a few questions. First, is the proposition underlying the Rapporteur's work, that the existing instruments are inadequate to protect the environment, correct? All the interventions that have been made so far seem to point in the same direction, that existing instruments relating to weapons are not adequate, but the question remains to be answered in general terms.

Second, the implications of the failure to define the term 'environment' in the 'Elements' Document should, in my view, be addressed.

The third question that I would like to raise relates to the insertion of provisions regarding weapons in this proposed Geneva Convention. I do not

---

251a *Editor's note*: the reader may, in view of the discussion *supra* at pp. 12–13, prefer to substitute the term 'weaponry' for 'Hague law' in this context. See also Prokhorov, *infra* at p. 141.

wish to prejudge the outcome of the discussion as to whether this or any other new legal instrument should be adopted, but, taking this particular format as a basis for discussion, I am a little uneasy about the coexistence in the same instrument of provisions relating to 'Geneva law' as understood in the instrument and provisions on 'Hague law'. We know, because the Rapporteur says so specifically, that these provisions cannot detract from the rest of the proposed Convention. But do they add anything? Whether or not they do in terms of protection of the environment very much depends upon the level of threshold that could be adopted in relation to environmental destruction under 'Geneva law' provisions, a question which is raised but not finally resolved in Element 2.A.

The above questions touch on the relationship between the 'Hague law' part and the rest of the Convention. Now, irrespective of whether provisions on 'Hague law' are properly placed in this instrument or could be placed in another instrument, the question also arises whether the development of a list of weapons is an adequate approach in itself. Two types of question can be raised, one from a legal and the other from a political point of view.

From a legal point of view, the first question is what we do with our list of weapons when technologies change. What if new weapons that are not specifically listed are developed but not covered in terms of their effect upon the environment? The other question that arises from the legal point of view is: what if the same negative results that are anticipated from the use of these listed weapons are attained through other means, for example, through inaction, such as the failure to maintain a system or installation, or through the use of 'acceptable' tools or means for modifying the environment?

Another general question, which is no less significant, is whether the development of a list of weapons is adequate in a political sense. Is the development of a prohibition against those specific weapons likely to be acceptable to states that may take part in a possible conference on the protection of the environment in time of armed conflict? Of course the simplest way of putting the question in this context is to ask whether the list given in Part 3 of the 'Elements' Document would be acceptable to states as it is. Here I join other colleagues who have regretted the absence here of military people who could at least address this question.

Other questions relate to the handling of traditional concepts, such as proportionality and military necessity. Some questions also depend upon the chosen definition of 'environment' for the purposes of its protection in time of armed conflict; as was once suggested to me, some definitions might mean that we have to go to cities in order to wage war because all damage to the countryside would be prohibited.

Concerning the link between these provisions under the 'Hague law' part and disarmament questions, the Rapporteur suggests that we await developments. It will be difficult, however, to deal with certain specific questions when all sorts of weapons are excluded from the proposed list, thereby leading to some complicated questions at the level of negotiation.

I think that we have to be mindful of what Professor Falk was saying earlier, that it is not enough to develop an instrument; it is necessary that

that instrument be effective. Whether it will be or not will depend upon a variety of factors which should be looked at.

Let me turn now to Part 5 of the 'Elements' Document, concerning *Institutions*, which includes a proposal to establish a 'Green Cross/Crescent'. As an introduction to this proposal, it may be useful to look at some institutional proposals that have been made outside the specific context of armed conflict. As late as a few hours ago, I felt hesitant about dealing with these proposals, which do not fall squarely within our subject. Having heard the discussion this morning, however, it is clear that the scope of the discussion has expanded considerably, and a reference to broader institutional issues might in fact be relevant. As I see it, two types of body and two general trends have developed during the past couple of years in the context of environmental emergencies.

One, triggered by the Chernobyl incident, has been advocated by the Soviet Union and Eastern European states, and is based on the idea that there should be some body to monitor, assess and anticipate environmental emergencies and to assist states that are or may be affected by them. At its 44th Session in 1989, the UN General Assembly adopted Resolution 44/224, which asked the Secretary-General to report on the possibility of a UN Centre for Environmental Emergencies; this report was to be made to UNEP and was then to go back to the General Assembly. The report was delayed, but I understand that on 31st May the UNEP Governing Council endorsed a proposal by its Executive Director to establish a United Nations 'Council for Environmental Emergencies' on an experimental basis, for 18 months beginning in 1992.[251] This body is entrusted with assessing and responding to man-made environmental emergencies, acting upon the requests of the governments concerned and maintaining a roster of experts, a list of equipment and whatever else may be useful in such emergencies. It is not permitted to duplicate work being done by other UN organs.

I raise this example because it deals with environmental emergencies in general. It is not specified whether the Council should be used in cases of peace or of armed conflict. Presumably the primary objective is to use it in times of peace, not of armed conflict, but the latter possibility is not specifically excluded.

The second general trend started with an Austrian proposal and concluded with some joint proposals made by the countries of the Pentagonale (Austria, Czechoslovakia, Hungary, Italy and Yugoslavia), plus Poland.[252] These deal with the prevention and settlement of conflicts, and perhaps our colleagues more directly involved (Professor Ferrari Bravo and Ambassador Türk) might want to say a few words about them.[253]

They are not the only proposals on the prevention of conflict in this context which have been suggested. Austria, at the 44th Session of the UN General Assembly, raised the possibility of looking at situations that might

---

251 UNEP/GC.16/L.14/Rev.1, 31 May 1991. This proposal is also mentioned in the 'Elements Document': *supra* at p. 58.
252 Loc. cit., *supra* n. 132.
253 See Ferrari Bravo, *infra* at pp. 143–44.

not only lead to conflict but also result in a threat to the global commons. This proposal may, however, have been subsumed into the Pentagonale proposal.

Yet another proposal was the one mentioned by our Chairman this morning, Sir Crispin Tickell (*supra* pp. 115–16); the United Kingdom would like to see an expansion and greater flexibility in the mandate of the UN Security Council to deal with non-conventional threats to peace and security, including, in this particular case, environmental threats.

In the context of environmental protection in wartime, in theory any of the bodies dealing with the environment from a variety of perspectives could go, so to speak, into the field, provided that they have the consent of the parties concerned. UNEP, the UN Disaster Relief Organisation (UNDRO) and IMO, for example, could all do this. This does not happen very often, however, because of concerns for the safety of the people concerned and also because a ceasefire is very difficult to obtain in many circumstances.

The Rapporteur suggests the establishment of a 'Green Cross', with a possibility of a substitute organization if this is acceptable to the parties concerned. That organization would have the right of access to and inspection of protected and damaged areas, the right to be informed of the damage taking place, the right to give advice and the right to take urgent remedial measures. The rationale of the Rapporteur is: first, that a system based on a Protecting Power is inappropriate, because the environment is the concern of mankind in general and we need an impartial organization; second, that a UN body is unlikely to be considered by certain states as sufficiently impartial to play a role equivalent to the Red Cross in the environmental field; and third, that the International Union for Conservation of Nature and Natural Resources, foremost among non-governmental organization possibilities, has some government components and might therefore also be unacceptable to some states.

I will finish with a few questions. First, what are the chances at this stage that states could consider environmental concerns on the same footing as humanitarian concerns, as under the existing Geneva Conventions? Second, what kind of functions would an organization like this be called upon to play? There is a difference if only in terms of time, between what would be required for a 'Green Cross' to successfully do something because of the scale of the problems being dealt with, and the kind of problems that the Red Cross is dealing with, which presumably necessitate shorter periods of time to be spent in the area in question. The fundamental question is, therefore, 'is the intervention of any organization in conditions that are deemed necessary for the safety and the effectiveness of that organization, likely to be acceptable to states?' Assuming that involvement of such an organization might be acceptable to states, is the proposition that a UN organization would not be perceived as impartial by some states a correct proposition? Conversely, is the proposition that a non-governmental organization would be acceptable to states also correct?

Higgins: Thank you very much, particularly for highlighting some of the key issues that we could profitably focus upon. What I would like us to do in the remaining time is to hear the views of round tablers and perhaps particularly those who have not had the opportunity or the desire to speak so far.

Caflisch: I should like to comment on the institutional side.

One can see that there are difficulties at the crossroads between the law of armed conflict and environmental law. They meet somewhere, and, if we were to take the course suggested in the 'Elements' Document, we would have to find some bodies that would be able simultaneously to fulfil the functions they are expected to perform in relation to both fields. I agree with what could be now called the 'Goldblat doctrine': namely that we should at least try, although we may not succeed, to build upon what exists already and that we should show a certain realism in doing so.

This is, in particular, the course to be followed regarding institutions. I am personally opposed to the present proliferation of institutions. There is a tendency today to form a committee whenever we have a problem on the international level, exactly as we are accustomed to do within our domestic societies. Let us try not to form a committee this time and let us use existing bodies.

Ambassador Kirsch said some very interesting things upon the question of institutions, as did the 'Elements' Document. I have found it intriguing to hear the suggestion made here that UNDRO and UNEP, for instance, cannot be used, because they are inter-governmental in nature and this means that they are not 'neutral', whatever that term means.

Can we assert, conversely, that the IUCN or, dare I say it, the International Red Cross, is always and necessarily 'neutral'? I am not sure that this question of neutrality is really central to the issue or that, if it is, the support given inter-governmental bodies by member governments is not a compensating element that should be injected into this debate.

When I read the 'Elements' Document yesterday, I wondered, for instance, who would make up the proposed 'Green Cross'. We know the composition of the International Committee of the Red Cross. It is an association established in accordance with and governed by Article 60 (*et seq.*) of the Swiss Civil Code. It is, of course, much more than a domestic association, but it is also that. Would the 'Green Cross' be conceived along the same lines?

My feeling is that we have to build upon existing inter-governmental or non-governmental institutions. I have no clear preference as to which. An example of an existing structure which might be used is the international Fact-Finding Commission provided for in Article 90 of Protocol I; this body will be set up within a few days from today.[254] It could be used for additional purposes, such as environmental protection.

In the institutional field, dispute–settlement is another matter to think about. I agree with Mr Greenwood (*supra* p. 124) that the idea of bringing

---

254 This actually occurred on 24 June 1991 when the representatives of the 19 states which have made the declaration under Article 90 bringing the Commission into existence met in Berne to elect the fifteen members of the Commission.

individual violators of environmental prescriptions before an international criminal tribunal does not sound realistic. This does not mean, however, that one should not think of a dispute-settlement mechanism between states concerning the interpretation and implementation of existing and future prescriptions for the protection of the environment in the event of armed conflict.

Prokhorov: I will try to answer the questions put by Ambassador Kirsch. I think that the course of discussion here is influenced by a kind of confusion. We mix up, for example, two branches of law, 'Geneva law' and 'Hague law'. As far as I understand it, 'Hague law' merely covers the conduct of hostilities; it is the law for the armed forces. 'Geneva law' is also the law for the armed forces, but is so, roughly speaking, only in respect of those who are not combatants. In Dr Plant's 'Elements' document, which is very interesting and deep, we see that so-called 'Geneva law' is considered to be the law of the means and methods of warfare, but *I* think that that is properly regarded as 'Hague law'.[255]

Second, there is confusion today between 'objects of attack' and 'targets'. We are saying that oil installations were the object of Iraqi 'attack' during the Gulf conflict. I do not think that is correct, because at the moment that they were set on fire those installations were controlled by occupying Iraqi forces. I think that an 'object of attack', properly speaking, is an object which is not under the control of occupying enemy forces.

Third, we mix up legal terms and perhaps the significance of the names of documents, assuming, for example, that a convention is better than a protocol. This is not necessarily so, because there are many protocols that are much more used and better implemented than many conventions. I think, moreover, that one of the most important documents in the history of international law is Protocol I. This is merely a protocol, but each of the Conventions to which it is an addition is shorter than it is.

Fourth, we are confused about another very important issue, which has been a touchy one for my country for a long time (and I stress that I am speaking in my personal capacity), weapons of mass destruction and nuclear weapons. In general, the law of armed conflict today does not explicitly cover the use of nuclear weapons, and this is the understanding between the vast majority of countries. If we want to have some progress in regard to the environment, then we should not touch this question.[256]

Fifth, we are not clear in our minds about institutions, which are very important in this field. Not only the ICRC itself, but also the national Red Cross/Crescent societies carry out useful work, not only in wartime, but also in peacetime, when a disaster occurs.

I hope that in future the Security Council will settle the problem of compensation, where there is responsibility and liability, for damage to the environment in wartime. Security Council Resolution 687 established a very

---

255 Editor's note: see *supra* n. 32.
256 Editor's note: this is, in fact, the approach taken in the 'Elements' Document.

well-developed, detailed mechanism to ensure that Iraq will pay compensation for its destruction of Kuwait's oil installations.[257] I am not sure whether this compensation is properly seen as compensation for environmental damage or for damage to the economy, but still it is compensation. Of course, we also should think of using the potential of other international bodies, and, perhaps, the Fact-Finding Commission will be of help.

Finally, I am very sceptical about including this issue on the agenda of UNCED, because armed conflict is a subject the idea of which is very unpleasant to the common man. There is a philosophical contradiction between the notions of a right to go to war and the law of war, between *ius ad bellum* and *ius in bello*. Thus, I think, it would be much better if UNCED were not to deal with armed conflict situations and were to leave them to other fora and institutions which can better deal with them.

Lee: I would like to raise two points. The first relates to the question of application of the law. I think, whether or not we are talking about having an entirely new legal instrument or about including existing law in some new additional instrument, the question one has to face is the question of application of that law. In the case of international law, when one comes to the question of application, very often the state involved is not party to the legal instrument in point, or a State Party refuses to apply the law. Whichever way we proceed, whether by agreeing a new instrument or by improving existing instruments, we have to give some thought to that question. Otherwise, even if we embark on this new enterprise of negotiating a new instrument, in ten years' time, when we have a new Convention and face a violation of it, we will have exactly the same situation: how do we apply it? I think that this is the main problem.

On the matter of liability and punishment, I think that, perhaps, we have to go one step further and adopt some additional measures, quite apart from measures on liability and responsibility, to apply to situations where the Convention is simply not applied; this would involve the States Party meeting and thinking of other measures to enforce the law. Of course, the problem with this is knowing what to do when non-Parties are involved. This is always a problem which we have to face when considering international legislation.

Many good ideas were put forward this morning concerning complementary measures which might be included in a new international instrument, but I believe that we should also think about having complementary national legislation too. In the cases of some countries, perhaps, it might be easier to achieve the intended goals through national, rather than international, legislation; in such cases one will have complementary measures filtering up from the national to the international level as well as down from the international to the national. I am quite realistic, however, and realize that we are dealing with a very specific subject, so that I would like to emphasize that we need *complementary* measures rather than 'either/or' measures.

---

257 Loc. cit., *supra* n. 126 and following text.

Turning now to the question of institutions. I think the general consensus is that there is a need for facilitation of the process of protecting the environment in time of war. My own view is that this calls for not one facilitator but many, because we are dealing with many conflicts in different geographic regions and countries of very different natures, requiring different degrees of expertise and competence. There is always room for one more facilitor, as there are countries which are more easily dealt with by non-governmental organizations than inter-governmental organizations and vice versa. We should not be too restrictive but should look at all these possibilities.

Whatever institution or institutions we are thinking about, however, I think that it is important that it or they meet four basic criteria: impartiality; the necessary capability and expertise; adequate funding; and a track record. For institutions to be acceptable to governments, it is very important that they have a track record.

Ferrari-Bravo: First of all, I wish to thank the organizers for this quite exceptional gathering of such brilliant personalities on so important a problem. The circumstances lead me to illustrate briefly the initiatives taken by the Pentagonale Group. This Group of five Central European States, including Italy, introduced, together with Poland, at the last meeting of the Preparatory Committee for UNCED, two draft resolutions which were intended to provide new patterns for the prevention and settlement of environmental disputes.[258] It is our Governments' conviction that these matters should be addressed by UNCED. As we felt that the door was about to be closed to the inclusion of these items upon the agenda, we believed that we had to introduce the proposals rapidly, leaving it to anyone who wished to contribute to do so in order to enrich their contents.

The document on the prevention of conflict speaks of an Inquiry Commission and that on settlement of disputes of Mixed Claims Commissions, the International Court of Justice (ICJ) and arbitration. Frankly these papers were intended to address the prevention and settlement of environmental disputes *in peacetime* and were not conceived specifically with a view to wartime situations. Nevertheless, several fundamental developments are proposed in the instruments, some of which might be relevant in wartime:

(1) an outline proposal for an Inquiry Commission is set out in the proposal on prevention of disputes. It is obvious that such a fact-finding commission could also operate in wartime; indeed, such a commission is established under Article 90 of Protocol I. There is some doubt, however, whether such a commission could operate properly in a rapid escalation scenario, such as the one we have recently witnessed in the Gulf; (2) each State Party may declare under the dispute-settlement proposal that it accepts as compulsory one or both of the following means for settlement of environmental disputes: submission to the ICJ; or submission to arbitration. The second of these is particularly suited to permit the

---

258 Loc. cit., *supra* n. 132.

European Communities to put forward a claim at their own behest, as they have no standing, not being a State, before the ICJ; and (3) in the event of claims being brought by nationals of a state arising from transboundary environmental pollution coming from another state, the states concerned may provide for the constitution of a Mixed Claims Commission; nationals may only have access to this Commission with the sponsorship of their state of nationality.

To give a personal remark at the end of this round table, it seems to me that we are coming ever closer to the conclusion that a proper use of existing law would be better at this stage than the creation of new law. This is related to the fact that it is extremely difficult to separate problems of environmental protection in accordance with whether they occur in times of peace or in times of war. During today's discussion, in my opinion, no convincing argument for the separation of these two situations has emerged. This leads me to think that, at least for the time being, we would better not embark upon the creation of a new instrument.

Higgins: We are inevitably against constraints of time now, so I do have the disagreeable task of asking colleagues to make their comments as concise as possible so that we may hear them all.

Sapolsky: I think that there is one thing upon which we can all agree, and that is that war is bad for the environment. Big wars are very bad for the environment and little wars are not so good either. A high-technology war is bad, but I think low-technology wars have proved to be quite bad for the environment as well. Look at Africa.

The question then is: 'How does one avoid war?', and I think that there is a way. One has to favour the growth of democracy. Democracies fight less among themselves and they respond to public opinion, placing limitations on how wars are fought. We have talked about public opinion being the really key factor here. The fact that the USA has not signed some of the agreements does not mean that it does not respond to environmental concerns. It responds to its own public opinion, which has been very much in favour of environmental limits on warfare. American forces attacked some oil installations in Iraq but, I believe, they attacked them very carefully, with the purpose of limiting environmental damage. In past wars the USA sank oil tankers without the slightest concern, but I predict that, if in the next war in which the USA fights a country which has tankers, it will not sink them; rather it will try to limit that country's production and use of oil by doing everything but sink its tankers.

The real issue arising from the Gulf War is that of proportionality, which we have already discussed and which is very much emphasized in the Greenpeace report, *On Impact*.[259] It suggests that there were 350 Coalition deaths compared with about 150,000 Iraqi deaths. This is an amazing difference. The disproportionality was supported by Coalition public opinion, but the question should be not: 'Was it supported?' It should be:

---

259 Loc. cit., *supra* n. 11.

'Was it necessary?' Perhaps, if we adopt this test, next time we can avoid some of this disproportionality. The question then will be: 'How does one coerce a dictator without a lot of killing of innocents?' We can have international laws that say we should do this or should not do that, but if one is fighting Attilla the Hun, how does he compel him to do something (like withdraw from Kuwait) without having to kill all his draftees or starve all his people, most of whom are innocent in the sense that they are against the war or the regime? We really have to worry about what it is morally right to do in this instance.

That leads, I think, to the question of institutions. Instead of creating new institutions, we should try to build on the structures of existing institutions, particularly the United Nations, because it has a quasi-democratic framework. The more we bring that institution into the process of solving international disputes, the more we will be able to reduce the role of war and perhaps its environmental effects as well.

Pinto: Just two comments on institutions. I want to emphasize again that I think it to be an absolute necessity to have some form of tribunal for the settlement of disputes. It is not possible to conclude an agreement now on an international criminal tribunal, but a tribunal to settle disputes is what is needed, particularly because of the conflict of values which someone talked of earlier. War may be seen as the ultimate result of differences in values, differences which law has been unable to reconcile or contain. The first step in restoring order should be to resolve the dispute that led to war on the basis of respect for law, and the need for an appropriate mechanism for this seems clear.

My final point concerns the difficulty of recourse to the UN Security Council. I will not bore you with the problems of small non-aligned countries which do not produce oil or some other commodity or resource generally considered to be 'vital', but it is not easy for such a country to approach the Security Council. To do so it has to go through a political process, because the Security Council is a political organ. In order to persuade the Security Council to act, there must be an external threat which the Permanent Members, in particular, are willing to characterize as a threat to international peace and security. Iraq posed such a threat in this sense, as can be seen from the recent series of resolutions.

If the Security Council is not willing, however, because of prevailing political pressures, to characterize the situation as one involving such a threat to the peace, it is impossible even to have the matter placed upon its agenda. It would be difficult, moreover, even for the government of a small country to approach the Security Council for fear that this would be taken as an unfriendly act by the state from which it seeks protection.

Gasser: May I shortly come back to the 'Elements' Document to see whether there is any necessity to make new law? I think that we can say that we should only try to make new law, first, if we have sufficiently innovative proposals to make and, second, if there is a chance of their acceptance.

If we look to what has been proposed in Part 3, I think that most of it has simply been taken over from an existing Convention, the 1980 Inhumane Weapons Convention. It is important to recall that that Convention is an open text in the sense that it is possible to negotiate new protocols within its framework. Such protocols may outlaw any type of new weapons. It should be possible to cover at least some of the concerns of the environment by means of this Convention.[260] Incidentally, one of its preambular paragraphs refers to the protection of the natural environment. Because rather few states have ratified it, moreover, I appeal for this Convention to be considered for ratification as well as Protocol I. It is better to advance existing law than to invest more than ten years in agreeing a new Convention which might not add much to existing law.

Second, I have remarks with regard to institutions. On the proposal to have a new, ICRC-type body much has been said. I would simply like to draw your attention to a few problems. If it were to be called the 'Green Cross' and to use a green cross as its emblem, there would be problems connected with the need also to use the name 'Green Crescent' and the equivalent emblem.

Third, I think that peacetime and wartime problems with regard to the environment are closely linked to each other, as Professor Ferrari Bravo has just recalled. Only by taking into account such limits can we find acceptable solutions and acceptable progress with respect to law which has to be applicable in civil war and internal strifes as well.

Finally, the ICRC would very much regret the omission of the problem of armed conflict and the environment from the UNCED agenda. We are aware, of course, that nobody likes to talk about armed conflict, but armed conflict is a reality, and UNCED might be the forum where such issues can be taken up globally.

Edmonds: I have been asked to try to fill, very inadequately, the gap in the military ranks. I am probably not the most distinguished covert military man present here, but I think I know what many military men would think.

First of all, I think that, in the eyes of lawyers and environmentalists, the military are understandably both the criminals and the potential police, and so are important to this discussion.

I think they would agree with Professor Falk that an effective control regime depends upon the right political conditions; it is up to the political leaders to take a positive interest and to sustain it. I believe the military would also agree with Ambassador Türk that the broad support of public opinion is important; this too needs encouragement by political leaders.

I am *sure* that they would also agree with Dr Goldblat that the easy answer from the military point of view is to prohibit a weapon right across the board from its development to its use. I think that that is their easiest

---

260 Editor's note: The 'Elements' document does not simply reproduce the Inhumane Weapons Convention, but improves upon its existing Protocols as well as suggesting new restrictions upon other weapons systems. It is also careful to suggest that this might be better done under that Convention's review processes rather than in a 'Fifth Geneva' Convention: *supra*, p. 40.

position: the weapon is banned; therefore they haven't got it.

Beyond that, they can readily understand rules of engagement. They also have a reasonable idea of the law of war, and, thinking of Admiral Cunningham, my own Commander-in-Chief donkeys' years ago, and of General Schwartzkopf in the Gulf War, they also, particularly at the top level, have a very considerable appreciation of international law and a humane approach to their job.

Finally, I think that they would say that it is easier to build on what you have, that is the United Nations and the various conventions we have been discussing.

Incidentally, the military played a considerable role in the negotiation of the Inhumane Weapons Convention in the late 1970s, which is another reason that it is a pity they are not here. Moreover, I am sure that they would say: 'As far as possible, keep it simple.'

Wuori: I will keep it short and simple. I agree with, among others, Mr Lee, who reminded us that we have to retain a degree of flexibility, whether in addressing ecological warfare and damage in wartime, in peacetime, or within the grey zone between. I agree that we should also have this flexibility in addressing the national and international dimensions of the situation and should not forget the complementary measures that he stressed.

International law tends to lag at least one war behind the latest developments in war, and lawyers usually lag even further behind than that. We all have to admit that. We should be reminded by the non-governmental organizations, and especially by Greenpeace, of the dramatic and tremendous impact environmental public awareness has had in the past few years and is going to have in the very near future. We are dealing with a new dimension. It is not merely a problem of man-made environmental emergencies in war. This I think should be kept in mind: we need the non-governmental organizations; we need the inter-governmental organizations too; but most of all we need the political will to utilize the existing instruments at hand, perhaps prior to creating any new measures.

We should also keep in mind, taking one of the basic requirements, as proposed in the UNEP Governing Council Decision,[261] that no armed conflict may damage the environment of a third party. We are increasingly aware of all being third parties to any conflict anywhere in the world, because of the global implications of conflict, and we have a right as third parties to request certain rules to be in place. If we do not act in a responsible manner we will become hostages to whichever conflict takes place.

Al-Khasawneh: Some very brief comments. The first regards the UN Security Council's being the institution to look at these issues. I must say that I find it disconcerting, perhaps even disturbing, that there is no system of political checks and balances at the international level, and that there is no real way of verifying, for example, whether or not the Security Council

---

261 No. 16-L.53, Part B, loc. cit., *supra* n. 6.

is acting *ultra vires*, or whether its actions are constitutional or not. This is something that has to be examined, because one can ask himself how far the Security Council is going to involve itself in this or that subject in future, including now environmental protection.

The second is that I think that it is too early in the exercise to start speaking of realism. I don't say this, because I am an incurable romantic or idealist. I think a time will come later in the discussions on possible new law when the representatives of states will take care of excess of romanticism.

Szekely: In the same vein, I want to say that, when I read the 'Elements' Document, which I think is a very welcome document, the thing that concerned me most about its level of realism was Part 5, the Institutional Part, including the question of a 'Green Cross' institution, although this is, of course, not the most substantive part. But at the same time I realized, precisely because it is here at this conference that we can still preserve some realism, that the idea of a 'Green Cross' should not die, whether it is called the 'Green Dot' or 'Green Star' or whatever. I think that it belongs in a realm which belongs mostly, as to its future possibilities, to the non-governmental organizations, who could and should build upon the idea. They should not necessarily be restricted to the framework in which it was placed in the 'Elements' Document, but should explore other possibilities.

Higgins: I have deliberately held over until last Dr Al-Awadhi. We are very pleased that Dr Al-Awadi has found, in the middle of all these difficult problems in his country (Kuwait), the time to come and join us. I thought it would be appropriate to ask him if he would care to speak last.

Al-Awadhi: I would like to say that a look at the problem of Kuwait and the huge international momentum that has gathered behind its very specific problems, following its occupation by Iraq, shows us clearly that whenever the will of the international community is properly mobilized, action can be taken to adhere to the principles of the UN Charter. For the first time I have seen this very important international organization working as it was meant to work. The United Nations was able to move.

So I would like to say that one has always to be hopeful that, as time goes on, international cooperation and international principles can be better understood and action taken to fulfil the principles of the Charter.

Regarding the proper representation of the will of the people in different affairs of the world, it is very clear that, as the situation improves and more democratic systems come to prevail in the world, that will be more properly expressed by their governments. This process will work its way through governments and will, in a very welcome manner, solve the conflicts of interest between the popular non-governmental and governmental organizations.

In the field of the environment, I think that we have an example in the terrible experience of Kuwait and the catastrophic damage that has been caused to its environment and to that of the ROPME region as a whole,[262] that should serve to provide a momentum by which the people of the world can come together to address themselves to a challenge. This challenge, I think, is going to become more urgent as long as weapons of mass destruction are going to spread more and more throughout the world.

I hope that this momentum can be further utilized and that more distinct actions can be taken to delineate the crimes that have been committed against the environment. Whether this is going to take the form of a new Convention by itself or additions or amendments to the Protocols to the existing Geneva Conventions is not the real issue. The real issue is that we should have a proper tool by which we can come to terms with ourselves and set the rules that can punish these crimes which are committed against the environment.

These crimes can truly be greater than crimes against humanity, since they impinge upon all living things on the planet. The development of a Convention, an agreement or some other kind of understanding among nations is important so that we can address such grave matters in the future in a more logical and legal way. I repeat, the time is ripe, and the international conference in Brazil is the right forum where such issues should be finalized and presented so that we can start to develop a new world in which every living thing can have a right to live and survive without being damaged or destroyed.

Higgins: May I now ask Ambassador Kirsch to sum up?

Kirsch: I am not going to venture into conclusions on the basis of what has been a rather freewheeling discussion, but I would like to give a few impressions, looking back on the whole day.

I would first note that nobody has advocated doing nothing, which seems to suggest that, indeed, existing law and existing mechanisms are felt to be not entirely adequate and to require some review, at least at the level of their application.

Second, I was struck by the number of times that speakers, both here and in private, have mentioned how difficult it is to distinguish the protection of the environment in time of war and in time of peace. This was, I think, the comment most commonly made today.

My third impression is that a number of people who have taken the floor have expressed doubts with respect to the possibility of developing one single instrument and that many of them have said that we should try to build on what already exists. I dwell on this, because very little was said about the questions that I raised in my initial intervention. On the 'Hague law' issue, apart from making a special reference to the words of caution of Mr Prokhorov, I can only repeat that I have the same impression here

---

262 The teritories of the States Party to and the relevant Gulf marine areas covered by the Regional Convention on Cooperation with a view to Protection of the Marine Environment against Pollution (ROPME), loc. cit., *supra* n. 51. Dr Al-Awadhi attended in his capacity as Executive Secretary of ROPME.

as I do in relation to other parts of the 'Elements' Document, that there is an inclination in favour of building on what already exists.

With respect to institutions, again the prevailing view seems to be that there is a need for a facilitator or facilitators, not necessarily for one single organization. In that area also participants seem to favour using one or more existing institutions, or at least using institutions that might develop within very familiar contexts, with which states can be comfortable, such as the United Nations, rather than creating entirely new organizations. It also seems clear that those who have addressed this subject would favour the development of mechanisms dealing with the settlement of disputes.

My final point on institutions is that I have some doubts about the feasibility of using the Security Council for the purpose of dealing with environmental issues. Having spent two years working in the Council, I see, potentially, a great deal of resistance to the injection of matters, such as environmental issues, that have not been traditionally linked with the maintenance of international peace and security.

C: CONCLUSION

10 An International Relations Expert's Overview

Adam Roberts

We began with the suggestion, both from the European Environment Commissioner and from Professor Falk, that we were at a legislative moment; at a moment when we might, as often happens after wars, put our minds to a convention, perhaps along the lines of Dr Plant's useful 'Elements' Document, on the issue of the environmental consequences of warfare. The question I want to pose at the end of this Conference is: are we really at a legislative moment or are we at a moment where we need to think hard about the meaning, the dissemination and the implementation of international law as it already exists (including the law of war and those many parts of international law generally that relate to the environment)?

Lawyers and those concerned with law often respond to what is seen as a new problem by wanting to invent or create new laws. This is not, however, always the best possible course to take. Sometimes it might be the case that there already is a body of law which covers the point, although it may need dusting down; or there may be some classes of problem which, although undeniably serious, do not easily lend themselves to legislative solutions; further, there is danger (alluded to by several speakers today) in rushing to legislate on the basis of one episode. It has been a particularly welcome feature of today's memorable conference that there has been extensive reference, both from Dr Leggett in his initial presentation, and from many other speakers, to the widespread and multifaceted character of threats to the environment that can emanate from warfare. It is often said that Generals spend all their time fighting the last war. It is also true that pacifists spend most of their time opposing the last war. Lawyers, of course, legislate for the last war.

At this conference at least we have got away from some of that blinkered mentality, but we have, however, I think, suffered from one defect that has been commented on several times and has been serious. That has been the absence of substantial military representation other than in the capable hands of John Edmonds. In the field of the law of war a military involvement in the process of codification is essential, if law is to be sensible and if it is to be accepted by those who have to implement it.

There is a need to consider the tone in which we have addressed, and might in future address, this problem. The environment came up in many countries in the months between August 1990 and January 1991 as an essentially anti-war issue. It was raised in Jordan, and then at a conference in London in January 1991, as a serious argument against any resort to military action by the Coalition.[263] We have had echoes today, though rather few, of the view that the environmental effects of war are so serious that they are an argument against conducting war altogether. Of course environmental effects are an argument, but I have to confess that I am on the side of Mr Rostow on this issue. As we live in a world of sovereign states, there have to be inhibitions on the use of force, one of which has to be a rule against the aggressive use of force and annexation of other states, and something must be done about it when that nevertheless takes place. So one is always balancing considerations, and I fear that on many issues concerning the environment there is inevitably a balancing of considerations which makes law-making in this area particularly difficult.

The complete abolition of war, whether on environmental or other grounds, is likely to remain as difficult a task as it has been in the past. We may all agree with Professor Sapolsky's admirable proposal that universal democracy would make war less likely, just as others have advocated enthusiastically that universal Islam would eliminate war, or that universal communism would do so. However, I fear that for the foreseeable future, Professor Sapolsky's dream is likely to be as unrealizable as the Ayatollah's or as Lenin's. We are going to live in a world where there are some wars, and the question of limiting their impact and of limiting their conduct in other ways is going to remain one which we have to address in its own right and somewhat separately from the question of the elimination of war in its entirety.

One serious question about the law of war which has come up today has to do not with its substantive content but with its enforcement. The application of the law of war in a world of sovereign states, and in an era of limited wars, presents a number of extraordinarily difficult problems, not least among which is the difficulty of bringing violators of the law of war to book if the violator's adversaries' war aims do not extend to conquest of his territory and taking over the government of his country.

In a world of over 160 sovereign states, there is also the problem of the internalization of international rules in different cultures. That was a very central problem in the Gulf War, where it was quite clear that, although Iraq was party to numerous international treaties, its cultural traditions had not fully absorbed some of the agreements to which its governments had assented in the past. This was not simply a matter of the regime of Saddam Hussein rejecting these rules but of there being rival cultural values. One can see this same problem arising in a number of other countries in the world, including some which have become party to even quite recent international agreements.

There is also the problem, which we must be frank about, that rules which relate to methods of combat have been the most difficult part of the

---

263 For reports of the symposium of scientists in London, see the *Daily Telegraph* and the *Independent*, 3 January 1991.

laws of war to implement. I am not saying that I am totally pessimistic about them and I do not go all the way with Richard Falk in his statement that the laws of war as they affect combat are pretty much a failure (*supra* chapter 5). There have been many respects in which they have contributed to the limiting of wars, even if one is bound to end up thoroughly dissatisfied with the result, but it is true that these combat rules are one of the weakest parts of the law of war, and that other parts (those that deal with protection of people in the power of the adversary, prisoners of war, civilians in occupied territory or whatever) have proved on the whole somewhat stronger and more capable of being effectively implemented.

On the question of a new Convention for the environment, one central point must be clear: environmental issues are classic issues of the types that need to be addressed by the law of war. The law of war has traditionally, since at least 1899, addressed weapons and methods of warfare which have long-lasting effects, even after the war itself is over. Hence, for example, the prohibition on such mines at sea as cannot be prevented from destroying ships long after the immediate conflict is over.[264] The law of war has always addressed methods of war which have widespread side effects, for example effects on neutral countries.[265] These are classic issues which the law of war is there to address, and they have in the past in a number of ways, however unsatisfactorily, been tackled.

Environmental issues have been addressed in various ways in the law of war. There are ancient prohibitions against the poisoning of wells, the many provisions in the Hague Conventions of 1899 and 1907;[266] the 1925 Geneva Protocol;[267] the Geneva stream of law (and especially, of course, Articles 35(3) and 55 of Protocol I); and the ENMOD Convention. All of these are evidence that the issues have been addressed and that at least clear principles have been enunciated, even if they have been lacking in detail. The question is: how serious are the omissions and how capable are they of being put right?

Richard Falk said here today that existing law is scattered, controversial, vague, uneven and of differing levels of authority (*supra* chapter 5). That is a pretty serious set of accusations to throw against existing law as it relates to damage to the environment in warfare. I have to say that, although it is true that one has to do a job of collection and collation to gather together the various provisions relating to the environment, I am not convinced that the key issue is the scattered or allegedly controversial nature or even the vagueness or unevenness of existing provisions. What Falk says does point to real problems, but I am not sure that together they amount to the key problem.

---

264 See especially the 1907 Hague Convention (VIII) on Automatic Submarine Contact Mines, which reflected widespread concern about the indiscriminate effects of mine warfare. Whatever the detailed faults of this Convention may have been, certain of its principles remain relevant.

265 See, for example, the 1907 Hague Convention (V) on Neutrality in Land War.

266 Loc. cit., *supra* n. 44.

267 Loc. cit., *supra* n. 209.

If one looks at the crisis and war over Kuwait, it seems to me that an equally grave problem was the lack of serious and consistent attention to the laws of war, including the laws relating to environmental damage, by the leaders of the Coalition and by the United Nations itself (as well as, of course, and more notably, by Saddam Hussein).

The UN Security Council, in its many resolutions on the Kuwait/Iraq issue, was extraordinarily lackadaisical in its treatment of laws of war issues. This is a reflection of the legal culture in which we live, in which the law of war is treated as a somewhat arcane issue to be raised, if at all, only when the bullets actually start flying and as in no way central to the conduct of international relations. The Security Council finally mentioned Geneva Convention IV in its Resolution No. 666, of 13 September 1990, its *sixth* resolution passed after the occupation of Kuwait by Iraq on 2 August 1990. It did so in the context of addressing the matter of third-state nationals in Kuwait. It did not at that point state clearly and unequivocally that all the inhabitants of Kuwait were protected persons under that Convention. It did belatedly and briefly urge the applicability of that Convention in its Resolution No. 670, of 25 September 1990. All this is simply an example of the rather haphazard way in which the issue was addressed. At no point in all those months when we knew that armed conflict might break out did the Security Council state clearly and unequivocally which international agreements would be unquestionably enforced in the conflict that was likely to occur. So there is a problem which relates more to our legal and political culture than to the specific provisions of actual agreements.

President Bush did give a very clear warning on environmental issues in the letter that was not delivered to Saddam Hussein, the one that was read by Foreign Minister Tariq Aziz in Geneva on 9 January 1991 and then handed back to Secretary of State James Baker. The message, although undelivered, was nonetheless publicized in the Western press.[268] In it President Bush said: 'The United States will not tolerate the use of chemical or biological weapons, support of any kind for terrorist actions, or the destruction of Kuwait's oilfields and installations. The American people would demand the strongest possible response.' So the issue of environmental damage was raised, but one may well question the extent to which it was followed through.

At the beginning of the conflict, President Bush in his 16 January 1991 speech on television, as Mr Rostow rightly noted,[269] stated clearly that there would be discrimination in targeting. Curiously, his words on this matter echoed the words of Article 48 of Protocol I. So there was some emphasis in a general way on law of war restraints, but on the environmental issue there was no very consistent follow-through by the Coalition Governments; the public record suggests that little was done on this matter. The Coalition Powers made fewer and less consistent statements on this

---

268 The text appeared in *The Sunday Times*, London, 13 January 1991.
269 *Supra* p. 122.

issue than they did, for example, on the question of the possible use of chemical weapons and poison gas.[270]

One of the central issues raised by the war is not the question whether the substantive provisions of the law itself are adequate or not, but how they are to be implemented. There were many unquestioned violations of existing law during the war, for example, over the use of hostages, looting in occupied Kuwait, the non-access of the ICRC to prisoners of war, as well as the issue of vast environmental destruction. On all of these issues, there were, in my view, clear violations of the law of war, and most of those violations were conducted on the Iraqi side. That is not to say that there were none on the Coalition side and certainly not to say that the Coalition did not commit vast destruction, but, if one is looking for clear violations of existing legal rules, they were overwhelmingly committed by Iraq.

It is thus an oddity that the Coalition Governments have maintained such a notable silence since the war ended on the issue of war crimes. I know the reasons why there has been silence, and they can be enumerated at considerable length. They include the practical difficulty of getting hold of the principal Iraqis responsible for war crimes, problems of proof and a reluctance to impose trials upon the region if local opinion does not favour them. But there is an inconsistency between what was said before the conflict broke out and what has happened since. In my view it would have been, and would still be, possible for the Coalition Powers or the UN through one of its organs as a minimum step to state clearly: (a) that war crimes occurred; (b) that there is individual responsibility for these war crimes; and (c) that, if those principally concerned should set foot in a country which is minded to put them on trial, they can still be put on trial, in accordance with the provisions of the 1949 Geneva Conventions.[271] So even if there is no intention to invade Baghdad and get hold of Saddam Hussein, the issue need not be entirely ignored.

Against this background, there is a need to think carefully about a new agreement on the protection of the environment in wartime. The dog that hasn't barked at this Conference (at least not very loudly) is the dog of the 'Fifth Geneva' Convention in the exact form in which it is proposed in the 'Elements' Document. There has been no very strong advocacy of that particular name for a possible new instrument. What there *has* been is advocacy of some kind of agreement, but not necessarily one of that name, and I think it is right that it should not be called the 'Fifth Geneva' Convention. Hans-Peter Gasser was cautious about this nomenclature (*supra* p. 112), and with his Red Cross background he spoke with considerable authority. One has to be very careful not to undermine the status of the four Red Cross (Geneva) Conventions, each of which has 165 States Parties – more than there are members of the United Nations. They

---

270 The soft-pedalling of the environmental consequence of the 1991 Gulf War extends to the 22–page official British account of the war published in July 1991 in *Statement on the Defence Estimates: Britain's Defence for the 90s*, HMSO, London, July 1991, Vol. 1, pp. 7–28.

271 See, for example, Geneva Convention IV, Article 146.

deal with issues that have succeeded in getting an astonishing degree of unanimity among states. There would be a problem if we tacked on to that a fifth Convention which tackled a much more controversial area.

It is also noteworthy that there has been no very strong advocacy of a new organization which might be called a 'Green Cross'. Mr Szekely has suggested that it might have some other name (*supra* p. 148). One might suggest that, since it is intended to deal with environmental violations in time of war, it be called 'Greenwar'. Speaking more seriously, however, its functions have to be thought about very carefully. The more one thinks about the functions, the more one realizes that it is an utterly different enterprise from that of the ICRC, and it would be quite inappropriate to model it on the ICRC. In monitoring environmental issues in war, many different kinds of technical expertise are required. Nuclear environmental issues, for example, require an entirely different body of expertise from the saving of marine birds in the Gulf. There will continue to be a need for many different types of international organization, both inter-governmental and non-governmental, each concerned with different aspects of environmental protection.

Into what category of law should any new rules be inserted? Should law to protect the environment be categorized as part of the law of war or the law of peace? In the end we are inevitably talking about development in both fields. Parallel development in both fields should help to bring about a greater degree of public awareness and official responsibility in regard to environmental issues. It is not an 'either/or' question. Interestingly, the one branch of law which does conspicuously bridge the two fields has not been much discussed today: that regarding crimes against humanity. There was some discussion during the Gulf War that, perhaps, that branch of law would be an appropriate vehicle for trials in respect of some of the Iraqi offences. 'Crimes against humanity' is a branch of law which straddles war and peace, straddles dealings with foreigners and dealings with one's own citizens. Clearly, some aspects of law relating to the environment need to be similarly broad in their scope of application. The choice of which particular branch of law is the most appropriate vehicle for restriction on environmental damage in war is, however, not a final one. All the relevant bodies of law will in fact have to develop in parallel.

If governments set out to negotiate a new Convention on the protection of the environment in war, what problems are likely to arise? No state is likely to declare itself an overt enemy of such a proposed Convention. John Edmonds was quite right to suggest that there would be formal support for the broad idea of it (*supra* pp. 146–47). It is, however, one of those issues, like disarmament, where subtle issues and difficulties would be raised at every negotiating session. Every state would have its own favourite threat to the environment and would be less interested in others; we can be quite sure that the detailed text of a Convention would be very difficult to negotiate. Françoise Hampson reminded us of the difficulties there had been on whether or not oil installations should be included in Article 56 of Protocol I (*supra* p. 132). There is no absolute answer to the question whether all attacks on oil installations should be prohibited or not. In the Second World War oil installations were a focus for targeting by the Allied

Powers, and it was only when they concentrated on them rather than on indiscriminate bombing that anything effective was achieved by their air forces. Powers with memory of that experience are, I think, not going to rush to abandon all targeting of oil installations.

In the end any approach to the limiting of environmental damage in wartime is going to have to stick to two related principles. First, the principle of simplicity. War is an exercise in deviousness, in which new practices and new threats to the environment, like new ways of waging warfare and new weapons, always emerge; one cannot expect legislators in advance to legislate for every eventuality. Second, any development in this field, I think, will have to deal more with general principles than with detail. Only by dealing essentially with general principles can one allow for technology change and changes in tactics.

There is a parallel here with national differences in philosophies for dealing with *national* environmental matters. In some countries, whether because of intellectual laziness or because of a common law tradition, we prefer having law which is very general in character. Since the nineteenth century, English law as it relates to environmental matters has been full of phrases to the effect that a factory must emit 'as little as possible' of noxious gases. In the USA, on the other hand, there is more by way of a passion for detail and specific percentages of particular gases. One can argue endlessly as to which approach is more profitable. Both have their virtues and defects, but I suspect that, in relation to the specific issue of the impact of war on the international environment, the broader approach is likely to be more effective in the long run.

There could be risks in concentrating entirely upon the introduction of a new Convention. It might let some of the governments who have a responsibility for dealing with recent infringements too easily off the hook. It might create new law that was very hard to observe with standards that were impossibly high. And, if general principles are what is needed, we already have at least a vague outline of general principles in Protocol I and we need to think carefully what precise principles we want to add to these.

What I think we virtually all agree upon, although we would disagree about the precise direction of it, is the need for better implementation of existing law, whether law of war or international law generally. There is also agreement, with what I take to be the single exception of Mr Rostow, on the need to ratify existing Conventions. Ratification is not the be-all and end-all of the observance of law. In my view some states which have not ratified Protocol I have taken it much more seriously than some which have, and on this I am with Mr Rostow. I am not sure whether the uncomfortable Rostow/Falk alliance holds up at this point or whether it is made any more comfortable by my presence in it.

At all events, even if ratification is not the only measure of an agreement's effectiveness, it is an important basis for progress, especially if we are entering an era where collective security actions are possible. It is vital that those taking part in collective security actions start from a common basis. We are now in the position within NATO, for example, that eleven Governments have ratified Protocol I and only five are not formally bound by it. These five are: France and Turkey, which have not even signed it;

the USA, which is at least very reluctant to ratify; the UK, which would ratify if the USA did; and Portugal. Thus the majority, but not all, of the NATO Allies are now committed to this Protocol. There could be a messy situation in which different legal agreements apply in different aspects or phases of a conflict, because different members of the Alliance are bound by different legal agreements. That is one thing that has to change.

Equally important, however, will be addressing the question of military manuals, rules of engagement and military training. These means by which the law of war is implemented are important. If military culture and professionalism can be associated with modes of conducting warfare which do not involve serious damage to the environment, that will be as important as having new agreements.

Finally, I am doubtful whether Sir Crispin Tickell can combine both the eminently successful parts of his career (as a writer on environmental matters and as the UK's Permanent Representative on the UN Security Council) by persuading the Security Council to have as a central concern the handling of environmental issues. I am doubtful for a serious reason. Most environmental issues are by their nature going to be ambiguous and difficult. They are going to involve not the clear-cut cases where the Security Council can act, but very complex processes which may only be capable of being dealt with over the long haul, where standard-setting is going to be important rather than decision-making by a single central international organization. Thus it may be that the Security Council will not be the central vehicle for this, although it will perhaps have its part to play in respect of the most egregious manifestations of environmental destruction, whether in peacetime or in wartime.

Overall, we need a higher level of public discussion on the issue of environmental protection in wartime, and this Conference has contributed considerably towards it. Whatever our divisions on these issues, there is no question that more rigorous thought on the environment generally, and on the law of war, and for that matter on the place of international law in international relations generally, is badly needed. The initiative in calling this Conference, and Dr Plant's admirable work in the 'Elements' Document, have all contributed considerably to this end.

In summary, my argument here has been that observance of existing law relating to the environmental impact of war, the effective handling of violations of that law, and the ratification of existing accords, is at least as important as the creation of a new Convention. I have particularly stressed the value of having a body of law in this area which expresses general principles (and this we do have, at least in rudimentary form, in the provisions of existing agreements). None of this argument is necessarily fatal to a new initiative to bring together, in a single text, important existing or, indeed, new provisions on the protection of the environment in time of armed conflict. Rather, it is a reminder that we need to be aware of the possibilities of advancing on other fronts, as well as on the path to a new Convention and that we need to continue the important debate begun here about what exactly a new Convention would add to existing law, whether by way of substantive provisions, means of enforcement or drawing public attention to the whole issue it addresses.

Part III
The Aftermath and Prospects for the Future

11 Responses to the London Conference and the Ottawa Conference of Experts on the Use of the Environment as a Tool of Conventional Warfare, 10–12 July 1991

Glen Plant

Reactions to the London Conference

Following the London Conference a number of suggestions were made as to how the debate could be carried forward, including the suggestion that the LSE initiate a Harvard Research in International Law-style project.[272]

It was clear that a number of those making these suggestions were under the impression, left by the comments of several speakers at the Conference, especially those who spoke towards the end, that the Conference had put an end to any notion of negotiating a new Convention, at least for the near future. My own initial impression, however, as stated in my letter of thanks of 20 June 1991 to participants at the Conference, was somewhat less pessimistic:

> Most round tablers agreed that existing law needed to be improved and more effectively implemented, but . . . the conference ended on perhaps an excessively pessimistic note concerning the prospects for a new instrument. It has never been pretended that the negotiation of such an instrument, however modest its aims, would be other than difficult. Notwithstanding this, a number of senior figures, not least Commissioner Ripa di Meana and Minister Vorontsov, have come out in its favour, and there has been interest in a number of national Parliaments, most recently, I believe, in Germany last week.
>
> It should be said, in addition, that in calling the conference a 'Conference on a "Fifth Geneva" Convention' the organizers did not intend to suggest that the existing Geneva Conventions be disturbed in any way. The conference was timed to coincide with a worldwide publicity campaign, and the choice of that name, carefully placed between inverted commas . . . [was] made with a view to reaching the imagination and understanding of a wider audience. It seems clear that any future proposals for a new instrument should adopt a different name (perhaps the 'First Nairobi' Convention), albeit that much of its content will be

---

272 Harvard Law School conducted a number of research projects into various areas of international law earlier this century. The results invariably took the form of a series of draft articles with detailed academic commentaries. See, for example, 26 *AJIL* (1932), Supplement.

'Geneva-style'. It should also, perhaps, seek to build on the environmental expertise of existing institutions, like UNEP, the IUCN and the Red Cross, rather than to create a new organization.

There was certainly no consensus that there was no scope for legislative improvement of the law, and Greenpeace has continued its campaign for a new instrument still using the term 'Fifth Geneva' Convention. This letter elicited, moreover, a variety of written responses from participants at the Conference,[273] and only a minority of these took the view that we should restrict ourselves to examining means of improving adherence to existing law; several others put forward views concerning possible legislative change.

The suggestion of a Harvard Research-style project was widely supported, and some considered that this might ultimately be fed into the UN Decade for International process.[274] if it were to receive the backing of a friendly Government,[275] and in that way lead to improvement in the law. It was and is clear that much benefit may be derived from detailed study of a number of issues, such as that of a definition of or enumeration of the contents of the concept of 'environment' in this context, the precise relationship between the law of war and more general international environmental law, the precise threshold of acceptable environmental harm and the possibilities of catering for differing degrees of technological sophistication. I intend to initiate such a study under the title 'LSE Research in International Law, No. 1.' On the other hand, this study is likely to take some time and is best seen as a long-term project, and the question had and has to be asked whether or not there is scope for immediate change in the shorter term. In the final chapter, I suggest a number of improvements to the law that might be achieved employing existing instruments and devices, which build upon the 'Goldblat doctrine', as expostulated at the London Conference, and which take into account the lessons learnt at the Ottawa Conference too. Nevertheless, in June the negotiation of a new Convention was still, and remains, a real possibility, and it is for this reason that I drafted a revision of the 'Elements' document for consideration at the Ottawa Conference (*infra* Appendix 5) and set out in Chapter 12 a final revision for consideration as a possible way forward, at least in the long term. My considered view after the London Conference was that the short-term response should use existing law and the long-term a new instrument, and this remains my view.

---

273 Including: Sir Crispin Tickell; Ambassador Kirsch; Lucius Caflisch; Anthony Brenton of the Foreign and Commonwealth Office (FCO); Françoise Hampson; Michael Meyer; Judge Schwebel; Adam Roberts; David Anderson, Second Legal Adviser at the FCO, on behalf of the Legal Adviser, Sir Arthur Watts; and Professor Alfred Rubin. A section of Professor Rubin's letter is reproduced in Appendix 7.

274 The Decade was established by UN General Assembly Resolution 45/40, 10 January 1991, and was discussed in this context by Ambassador Türk, *supra* p. 102.

275 The reader will recall that Ambassador Türk stated that Austria might be prepared to sponsor such an initiative: *ibid.* Other governments might also consider it, depending upon the response to discussions on the subject in the coming months. The Netherlands, for example, might be interested in such an initiative to coincide with the hundredth anniversary of the Hague Conventions of 1899.

Meanwhile in June, the Canadian Government's initiative in convening a conference of experts in Ottawa from 10 to 12 July appeared to provide the best vehicle for taking the discussion further. It appears that there had been interest in the issue in the Canadian Parliament since at least March 1991[276] and that the then Canadian Secretary of State for External Affairs, Joe Clarke, was particularly interested in the possibility of legislative change in the field.[277]

The Ottawa Conference

The Ottawa Conference of 10–12 July 1991 was a round table conference of 49 experts appearing in their personal capacities,[278] including eight who

---

276 Patrick Boyer, the MP for Etobicoke-Lakeshore, for example, had written a number of newspaper articles and helped launch a campaign to establish the framework for the establishment of a new 'Green Cross' organization by enacting Canadian domestic legislation to clothe it with a legal status similar to that of the ICRC in Switzerland: conversations of author with Patrick Boyer, 10–12 July 1991; and see the *Globe and Mail*, 6 and 11 March 1991.

277 He announced that his Ministry was sponsoring the Ottawa Conference: letter of invitation to myself from Barry MaWhinney, dated 21 June 1991. By the time of the Ottawa Conference, however, he had moved to another Portfolio. It is not clear whether or not this resulted in a diminution of interest within the Canadian Government in the possibility of legislative change in the field, although it is clear that the Canadians have continued to discuss the issue with other Western countries and that they hope that the XXVIth International Conference of the Red Cross and Red Crescent in Budapest in November and December 1991 will have a positive impact: conversation with Barry MaWhinney of 25 September 1991.

278 Apart from those who had also attended the London Conference (listed *infra* n. 279) and myself, these were: Professor Julio Barberis of the University Catolica, Buenos Aires; Brigadier W. Rolfe, Director General of the Australian Defence Force Legal Services; Georges Lamazière, Executive Coordinator of the Office of the Secretary General of the Brazilian Ministry of Foreign Affairs; Frank Berman, Deputy Legal Adviser at the Foreign and Commonwealth Office; Howard Mann, Counsel in the Constitutional and International Law Section of Justice, Canada; Dominic McAlea of the Office of the Judge Advocate General of Canadian Forces; Joseph Mrázek of the Institute of State and Law of the Czech Academy of Sciences; Dr Amin El Gamal of the Egyptian Agency of the Environment; Professor Alexandre Kiss, Directeur de recherche au Centre du Droit de l'Environnement of the Université Robert Schuman, Strasbourg; Dr Dieter Fleck, Director of International Legal Affairs at the Federal German Bundesministerium der Verteidigung; Dr Theodore Halkiopoulos, Director of the Legal Service of the Greek Ministry of Foreign Affairs; Thorir Ibsen of the Icelandic Ministry for the Environment; Professor Jung-Wook, Head of the Environmental Planning Institute of Seoul National University; Javier Riojas, Legal Adviser at the Autonomous Institute of Ecological Investigations, Mexico City; Professor Frits Kalshoven of the Netherlands; Christopher Beeby, Deputy Secretary at the New Zealand Ministry of External Relations and Trade; Judge Arne Willy Dahl, Judge Advocate General of the Norwegian Defence Forces; Morten Ruud, Director-General of the Polar Department of the Royal Norwegian Ministry of Justice; Dr Jerzy Sommer of the Institute of State and Law of the Polish Academy of Sciences; Dr Luis Caeiro Pitta, of the Legal and Treaty Service of the Portugese Ministry of Foreign Affairs; Bakary Kanté, Directeur de l'environnement, Dakar, Sénégal; Dr Ove Bring, Deputy Legal Adviser at the Swedish Ministry for Foreign Affairs; Jamal Sultan, Director of Legal Affairs, Petroleum Marketing Department, Office of the Prime Minister, Syria; Dr Huseyin Pazarci, Legal Adviser to the Turkish

had also participated in the London Conference.[279] It was chaired by Barry MaWhinney, the Legal Adviser to the Canadian Department of External Affairs and Trade (CDEAT), and Johan Nordenfelt of the Disarmament Division of the UN acted as Secretary. Jason Reiskind, Deputy Director and Head of UN Legal Affairs in the Legal Operations Division of CDEAT, acted as Rapporteur.

In the absence of the Secretary of State for External Affairs, the Honourable Mary Collins, PC, MP, the Associate Minister of National Defence, delivered an opening speech which variously referred to the aim of the Conference as that of clarifying existing law and of exploring means of strengthening international law to ensure that acts such as those committed by Iraq during the Gulf War were clearly prohibited. The letter of invitation[280] had stated that the Conference would 'allow for a review of existing international law concerning the use of the environment as a weapon of war, and a discussion on ways to improve its effectiveness and implementation'. The attached explanatory document went on to say that, 'especially in the area of customary international law, participants will want to focus on whether Iraq committed violations. One of the principal advantages of this meeting can be to help answer this question and more generally contribute to the understanding of the limits of customary international law on this delicate question.'[281] The general impression was given to arriving participants, therefore, that the discussion was intended to be concentrated upon an examination and clarification of the *existing* law relevant to conventional warfare in the light of Iraq's actions in the Gulf, but there was sufficient ambiguity in the stated aims and flexibility in the way in which the Conference was conducted to leave open the possibility of suggestions that legislative change was necessary, that Coalition actions having an impact upon the environment were also open to examination and even that the conference title itself was unduly restrictive.[282]

Following a presentation by Jim Guthrie of Gulf Resources Limited, Calgary, on the state of the post-war environment in the Gulf, and an introductory paper presented by Professor Paul Painchaud of Laval

---

Ministry of Foreign Affairs; Colonel Fred K. Green, Legal Council to the Chairman of the US Joint Chiefs-of-Staff; Alan Krezcko, Deputy Legal Advisor at the US Department of State; Professor Theodore Meron of New York University Law School; Hays Parks, Chief of International Law, International Law Division of the Office of the Judge Advocate-General of the US Army; Paul Szasz, formerly of the UN Legal Office; Y.A. Ostrovsky, Deputy Head of the Legal Bureau of the Soviet Ministry of Foreign Affairs; Professor Milan Sahovic of Yugoslavia; and Serge Sur, Director of UNIDIR.

279 Besides myself, these were: Professor George Alexandrowicz; Professor Michael Bothe; Awn Al-Khasawneh; Dr Jozef Goldblat; Dr Antoine Bouvier; Hans-Peter Gasser; and Roy Lee.

280 Op. cit., *supra* n. 277.

281 *Basis and Objectives of the Meeting of Experts on the Use of the Environment as a Tool of Conventional Warfare*, document attached to the letter, ibid.

282 It was generally felt that a title referring to the environment as a *tool* of warfare was too restrictive, as it did not comprehend deliberate or collateral damage to the environment by military actions not deliberately employing it as a tool.

University,[283] papers dealing with the relevant international law were presented by Professor Leslie Green of the University of Alberta,[284] Professor Michael Bothe,[285] and Paul Szasz, formerly a member of the UN Legal Office.[286] In addition, the Office of the Judge Advocate General of Canadian Forces (JAG Canada) distributed a note on the current relevant law[287] and copies of Paul Fauteux's excellent papers[288] were also made available.

Professor Green's paper began with a fascinating account of ancient restraints upon the causing of environmental damage in wartime, some of them dating back to classical times.[289] He continued with a review of some of the principles and rules of international environmental law and the law of war, which supported his view that no general rule of customary or treaty law can be said to exist which applies at all times in both peace and war. He then proceeded to examine the question whether Iraq would have been guilty of breach of the ENMOD Convention or Protocol I, had they been applicable to the facts of the Gulf War. He concluded that certain defences might have been available to Iraq in these circumstances,[290] subject to its ability to show that the collateral civilian damage caused by its creating the oil-slick and setting the well-heads on fire was not disproportionate to the military advantage gained (and also that they were not in truth directed at neutral or enemy civilian populations). He went on to suggest that the question of whether or not Iraq was in breach of customary law can only be determined by an impartial tribunal.[291] He argued that there is no clear law with regard to environmental war crimes

---

283 'Environmental Weapons and the Gulf War: Introductory Comments'.
284 'The Environment and the Law of Conventional Warfare', to be published.
285 'The Protection of the Environment in Time of Armed Conflict: Legal Rules, Uncertainty, Deficiencies and Possible Developments.'
286 'Study of and Proposals for Improvements to Existing Legal Instruments Relating to the Environment and Armed Conflicts.'
287 *Note on the Current Law of Armed Conflict Relevant to Protection of the Environment in Conventional Conflicts*. In addition, unofficial papers were submitted by Dr Golblat ('Protection of the Natural Environment against the Effects of Military Activities: Legal Aspects') and Josef Mrázek ('Conventional Warfare and the Protection of the Environment'), and I submitted the revised version of my 'Elements' Document.
288 Loc. cit., *supra* nn. 1 and 6.
289 He cites, for example: Deuteronomy, XX, 19 from the Bible; Josephus (see Roberts, 'Judaic Sources of and Views on the Laws of War,' 37, *Naval War Rev.* (1988), 221 at p. 231); a decree of Maximilian II of 1570; and a statement of Frederick the Great to his troops during the Seven Year's War (see *Kriegsvölkerrecht: Leitfaden für den Unterrecht*, Part 7, para. 3; German Forces Publications ZDv 15/10, 1961).
290 He suggests, for example, that Iraq might be able to justify the oil-spill as a reasonable means of frustrating the threatened Coalition amphibious landing on the coast of Kuwait. This echoes Hampson (*supra* p. 132). He also suggests that it might be able to justify the well-head fires on one of two grounds: that they were a legitimate military objective within the meaning of Article 52 of Protocol I; or that they were merely a more extensive use of smoke-cover as normally provided by traditional smoke-makers.
291 This was the general view of the Conference, which was careful not to characterize itself as a judge of Saddam Hussein.

of the *use,* as distinct from the *modification,* of the environment as a conventional weapon, but concluded that the chances of negotiating a new Convention to fill that lacuna are slim.[292] The solution, as he saw it, lay instead in a UN General Assembly, or even a Security Council, Resolution charging the ILC, as a matter of urgency, with taking up the issue in the same manner as it did the Nuremberg Principles after the Second World War,[293] followed by a binding Security Council Resolution, made under Chapter VII of the UN Charter,[294] condemning the use of weapons inimical to the environment and contrary to the Principles thus adopted by the ILC.[295]

I dwell on Professor Green's paper, because his views were given some prominence in the debate, partly by virtue of his holding a Conference office.[296] Nevertheless, the other participants were not sympathetic to his views that Saddam Hussein might have a defence to war crimes, and there was no great enthusiasm for his proposed method of proceeding.

I pass quickly over Professor Bothe's admirably clear account of the existing law and its deficiencies, as the reader is by now aware of many of his views. Suffice it to say that he emphasized that different rules apply as between belligerents on the one hand and neutrals on the other, as well as according to where the acts in question take place (in occupied or in enemy territory or in different maritime zones). Concerning institutions, he concluded that the ICRC had a vital role to play, in cooperation with other bodies expert in environmental matters, in taking the initiative to fight environmental hazards in wartime.

Dr Szasz's paper[297] surveyed most of the relevant hard- and soft-law instruments in turn and set out proposals for improvement, where he felt them to be appropriate. For the most part these take the form of proposals for inclusion in a new multilateral Convention, which he calls for convenience the Convention for the Protection of the Environment in Warfare (CPEW). He excludes nuclear weapons from his survey, in view of the title of the Ottawa Conference, and also cultural objects, in view of their

---

292 He refers to the time delays involved and the technical difficulties of securing agreement on what constitute legitimate military objectives and what effects are 'long-lasting' or 'severe'. By 'modification' it is clear that he meant the use of environmental modification techniques as contemplated by the ENMOD Convention.

293 When it formulated principles concerning war crimes, crimes against humanity and genocide. This contradicts Ambassador Türk's reservations about using the ILC: see *supra* p. 100.

294 It is difficult to see, however, how this could properly fall within the context of enforcement action carried out by the Council under that chapter of the Charter.

295 This reflects in some way the comment made by Adam Roberts concerning crimes against humanity at p. 156. The suggestion of the use of the Security Council is likewise in common with the suggestions of some of the round tablers at the London Conference *supra* p. 34.

296 He was Rapporteur of Working Group 2; for an explanation see *infra* p. 167.

297 This was a development of his paper presented to the ASIL Meeting in April (loc. cit., *supra* n. 6) and was prepared after he had seen the first version of my 'Elements' Document. There is a degree of coincidence between the two documents.

existing protection under the 1954 Hague Convention on Cultural Property.[298] Among his suggestions are the following innovations:[299] adopting, as the centrepiece of the CPEW, a provision combining the texts of Article 35(3) and 55 of Protocol I and of para. XX (and, perhaps, V) of the World Charter for Nature[300] in order to establish a lower threshold of acceptable environmental damage in war (perhaps also making the threshold criteria alternative rather than cumulative[301] and adding an additional criterion of 'irreversible');[302] requiring environmental impact assessments in relation to certain military operations, such as the design of new weapons systems; giving protection to all nuclear facilities (and certain other facilities containing dangerous substances) and characterizing attacks upon them as 'grave breaches'; and enacting provisions on state liability and individual criminal liability arising out of environmental harm. In addition, he suggests that a serious effort should be made to encourage more states to adhere to ENMOD, perhaps within the framework of UNCED.

I dwell upon Dr Szasz's paper, because it represents a possible alternative approach to the formulation of a new Convention. It must be stated, however, that the Ottawa Conference, particularly given its terms of reference and its composition, which, unlike the London Conference, was not self-consciously designed to reflect all aspects of opinion, did not embark upon a thorough examination of his proposals.

After a number of initial statements by participants in Plenary Session, the Conference divided into two Working Groups to continue discussion in less formal surroundings. These Groups reported to the Plenary at the end of each morning and afternoon. Working Group 1 was chaired by Serge April, Director-General of the Office of Legal Affairs, CDEAT; Professor Painchaud was the Rapporteur. Professor Green served as the Rapporteur of Working Group 2, which was chaired by Commander William Fenrick, Director of International Law at JAG Canada.

The Conference officers were at pains not to pressurize participants into taking any particular direction in their deliberations. The Working Groups, for example, were not given specific and separate mandates, and participants improvised their own agenda and procedures. It followed that the discussions were free-flowing and unstructured, and a wide range of views were expressed. The Conference officers did not make mention of the London Conference, and the views expressed and lessons learnt there were not taken as a starting point for the discussions. The starting point for most participants was, rather, an *ab initio* re-examination of events in the Gulf and the use of these events as a model for examination of the existing

---

298 Loc. cit., *supra* n. 90.

299 Some of his proposals involve the mere reproduction of provisions in existing instruments in the CPEW, presumably to ensure that there is a single, over-arching instrument for the environment.

300 For texts see Appendix 2 *infra*.

301 Although he considers this unlikely to be accepted. See now the final version of my 'Elements' document *infra* at pp. 192–93.

302 Ibid., at pp. 192 and 194.

applicable law of war (customary law and conventional law up to 1949),[303] to see if that law was adequate in the light of that model. In this sense, it was a valuable re-examination of the premise (or proposition) of those who were calling for a new instrument or improvements in the law that the existing law was inadequate to deal with future wars. On the other hand, while the Gulf War strongly suggested itself as the appropriate model, the danger of using it as such was that the imagination of participants was taxed in trying to predict *alternative* future wartime scenarios.[304]

The original intention of seeking a common Conference Statement was abandoned, moreover, following the early objection of one participant, and the Chairman decided to produce upon his own responsibility a set of Conclusions, which reflected his view of what had been discussed at the Conference. It is possible that these Conclusions will be published at a future date.[305]

Participants found a certain amount of common ground (which roughly coincides with my description set out *supra* at pp. 16–17). On the other hand, their views were divided on other issues, which are described immediately below. Some took the view that peacetime rules of environmental law were superseded by the law of war in wartime, whereas others considered that they still applied, subject to the application of the law of war. Some called for clarification or improvement of Articles 35 and 54–6 of Protocol I and of ENMOD and for additional ratifications by states, but others considered Protocol I to be flawed and that there was no need for or moral obligation upon states to adhere to or improve upon those instruments. Some saw a pressing need to draw the existing law together, perhaps also with some improvements, in a single instrument, whereas others stressed the need to implement existing instruments as they stood. Finally, suggestions for improvement included the creation of a 'Green Cross'-type organization and the special protection of environmentally sensitive areas.

US participation was particularly strong and influential, in the sense that several senior US Government and Armed Forces law of war experts were present in their personal capacities,[306] and were particularly eloquent in their view, which appears to coincide with that of the Bush Administration, that the existing law at the time of the Gulf war both did not include Protocol I and was adequate to cover both the events of that war and those of any foreseeable future conflict. There were relatively few voices calling for legislative change, but this was perhaps not surprising at that stage and given the composition of the round table.

As I have mentioned, early in the aftermath of the Gulf War there appeared to be positive Canadian Government interest in possible legislative change in this field and in placing the matter on the agenda of the UN

---

303 The only Parties to Protocol I involved in the conflict, it will be remembered, were Canada and Kuwait.
304 This tendency was better avoided at the London Conference.
305 Letter from Barry MaWhinney to myself, dated 12 August 1991.
306 Listed at op. cit., *supra* n. 278.

General Assembly (*supra* p. 163). By July this interest might have waned somewhat, and no Canadian proposal in relation to the UN has emerged, notwithstanding that the holding of the Ottawa Conference has created an expectation that Canada will take some sort of action. The Canadian Government appears to have greater interest at present in what will emerge from the XXVIth International Conference of the Red Cross and Red Crescent in November and December 1991 (the Budapest Red Cross Conference)[307] than in the debate at the 46th UN General Assembly.

Whatever does emerge, the chairman's conclusion that the participants' contributions to the Ottawa Conference were thoughtful and articulate can be readily agreed with, although it cannot be said that the Conference was positive in helping the case of those in favour of legislative change.

307 See *supra* n. 277.

12 Government Proposals and Future Prospects

Glen Plant

Few, if any, governments will at the time of writing have reached final positions on the issues discussed in this book. It is however, probable that their views have been influenced to a certain extent by the London and Ottawa Conferences, and it is hoped that this book will help to disseminate an account of those debates more widely.

It is clear already that no individual state or group of states has emerged or is likely to emerge calling for an immediate move to a diplomatic conference to negotiate a new Convention, whether within the context of adding to the Geneva Conventions or otherwise. Instead, the feeling appears to be that the issues need further examination and debate within international fora and that various avenues and procedures for possible further action need to be explored within those fora. This is made clear by those government proposals which have been made to date, which are described below. These indicate that some states have made choices concerning the initial fora and procedures which they consider should be used for further examination of the issues, but there is little indication in these proposals of the sponsors' views on the precise content of possible changes in the law.

Government proposals

There have been two major government initiatives touching upon environmental protection and the law of war since the London Conference, which involve proposals to place the matter on the agendas of the 46th UN General Assembly and UNCED. Only debate in the General Assembly is certain at the time of writing. In addition, the ICRC has produced a report which effectively places it on the agenda of the Budapest Red Cross Conference. I shall deal with these in turn.

First, by a note verbale dated 5 July 1991 to the UN Secretary-General, the Jordanian Mission to the UN proposed the inclusion of an item on the provisional agenda of the 46th General Assembly, to be held in the autumn of 1991, entitled, 'Exploitation of the environment as a weapon in times of armed conflict and the taking of practical measures to prevent such exploitation.'[308] As

---

308 *supra* n. 7.

required by Rule 20 of the Assembly's rules of procedure, attached to this was an explanatory memorandum, which suggested in paragraph 1 that it was common knowledge that 'the recent military conflict in the Gulf had an impact of tragic proportions on both the people of the region and the environment' and that 'closer cooperation between all nations is essential if we are to avoid further environmental destruction and conflict'.

Paragraph 2 went on to allege that the war had demonstrated ENMOD to be 'painfully inadequate', its terms being 'so broad as to be virtually impossible to enforce'. The Convention was also criticized for lacking a fact-finding and dispute-settlement mechanism and for failing to provide 'for advanced environmental data to be made available to all States at the initial stages of crisis prevention'.

In Paragraph 3, therefore, it proposed that the General Assembly establish a committee to examine these problems and to report to the next General Assembly 'proposals for an efficient mechanism to combat the exploitation of the environment in times of armed conflict'. Meanwhile, it suggested, states should be invited to make 'unilateral decisions along the lines of the treaty'.

This committee is also urged by paragraph 4 to consider the implementation of a UN Environmental Data Base as a confidence-building measure (for full text see Appendix 8).

The Jordanian Higher Council for Science and Technology, whose Director, Dr Abdullah Toukan, Scientific Adviser to King Hussein, undoubtedly played a part in the preparation of this proposal, also prepared a list of possible co-sponsors.[309]

By a letter from its UN Mission sent to the Secretary-General, dated 12 July 1991,[310] Kuwait, which had not been contemplated by Jordan as a co-sponsor, welcomed the inclusion of this item on the General Assembly agenda, albeit at the same time upbraiding the Jordanian Explanatory Memorandum by 'noticing' that it had 'overlooked the fact that this environmental calamity was not the result of military conflict (as the memorandum says), but was the product of a deliberate act that was planned in the very first days of the brutal Iraqi occupation of Kuwait'. The letter went on to request that it be distributed as both a General Assembly and a Security Council document (for full text see Appendix 8).

More recently a number of European states have proposed amendments to the drafting and methodology of the Jordanian proposal, but it remains to be seen whether or not it will gain the positive support of those states.

Second, in September 1991 Germany presented a statement to the UNCED Preparatory Committee announcing that it was preparing an initiative for the 46th General Assembly to ensure that the question of environmental crimes in war and peace time, would be further dealt with

---

309 These are: Brazil; Canada; Czechoslovakia; Indonesia; Jamaica; Japan; Kenya; Malaysia; Mexico; The Netherlands; New Zealand; Nigeria; Sweden; Tanzania; Trinidad; Turkey; and Zambia.

310 Loc. cit., *supra* n. 81.

in the UN system (for full text see Appendix 8).[311] This specifically notes that the matter has already been raised in the ILC, with the implication that it should continue to be dealt with there, as well as in the Sixth Committee of the General Assembly. In addition, it states that UNCED will have to deal with the issue. The precise form of the initiative is difficult to predict, but it seems clear that the emphasis will be on international criminal law spanning both war and peace time.[312]

Third, the ICRC has placed the issue on the agenda of the Budapest Red Cross Conference by preparing a report concerning attacks upon civilian populations, including a part on environmental protection. This suggests that states should keep the relevant issues in mind and look at existing law in the field, particularly with a view to determine whether anything can be done to improve it by setting new standards. The report does not suggest that a conference resolution will result from the debate, but there is some expectation that one will. It will be noted in this connection that Michael Meyer of the British Red Cross, who was a round tabler at the London Conference, has put forward suggestions on what a resolution of the Budapest Conference might include (see Appendix 6). This development has removed the necessity for states which, like Canada, might otherwise have done so to put in their own proposals.

Also relevant in this context are: the UNEP Governing Council Decision of May 1991, which 'recommends that governments consider identifying weapons, hostile devices and ways of using such techniques that would cause particularly serious effects on the environment and consider efforts in appropriate forums to strengthen international law prohibiting such weapons, hostile devices and ways of using such techniques' and invites 'the General Assembly to review the 1977 Convention on the Prohibition of Military or Any Other Hostile Use of Environmental Modification Techniques' with a view to strengthening and encouraging accession to it and establishing concrete means of verification of its implementation;[313] (for full text see Appendix 3); the Pentagonale proposals to UNCED on conflict-prevention and dispute-settlement which, it has been suggested, might be of some relevance in a wartime context;[314] and the UN experiment with a Council for Emergency Environmental Assistance.[315] Each of these can provide a contribution to the debate.

---

311 Statement be Professor Dr Ansgar Vogel of the Federal German Ministry for the Environment, Nature Protection and Nuclear Safety at the 3rd Session of the UNCED PrepCom, Geneva 12 August to 4 September 1991; Plenary item 2(d).
312 This is redolent of the ideas of Falk (*supra* pp. 93–94 and 122) and Türk (at p. 99).
313 No. 16/L.53; PART B, loc. cit., *supra* n. 6. This derives, it will be recalled, from a proposal made by Austria, Finland, Italy, Sweden and Switzerland.
314 Ferrari Bravo *supra* pp. 143–44.
315 See *supra* pp. 58 and 138. It will be noted, in addition, that the Economic Declaration of the London Economic Summit of the Group of Seven Most Industrialized Nations welcomed UNEP's decision to establish an experimental centre for emergency environmental assistance: para. 55.

Future prospects: fora and procedures

It follows that the question of environmental protection in the context of conventional warfare has been or is likely to be placed, in one form or another, on the agenda of perhaps the three most significant global meetings able to discuss it during the coming 12 months: the 46th UN General Assembly, UNCED and the Budapest Red Cross Conference. Its examination in these fora is likely to determine whether or not a serious reform initiative will go forward during the 1990s.

At pages 31–33 and 34–35 *supra* I examine a variety of methods and forms by which a new instrument concerning environmental protection in wartime might be developed or existing mechanisms employed or enhanced to improve the implementation of or to supplement existing law. At page 162 *supra* I explain my view that the examination of future prospects in this field should be divided into short-term and long-term approaches. I now turn to an examination along these lines of the available procedural options and of the suitability of the Government proposals to date to ensure that debate is carried forward in the best possible manner.

Whatever political choice is ultimately made (whether to convene a diplomatic conference to negotiate a new Convention or Protocol (or merely a conference or committee to draft a Code of Conduct), to seek to modify understandings concerning or to add to Articles 35, 55 and 56 of Protocol I, ENMOD or the Inhumane Weapons Convention or merely to pass non-binding hortatory and clarificatory resolutions, and whether or not new dispute-settlement mechanisms are to be established) in the absence of immediate strong governmental initiatives, the process chosen needs the strongest political endorsement possible on a global level as soon as possible.

The key forum: the UN

It is an unimpeachable proposition that a proper analysis of the issues requires their discussion in as many fora possessing a wide scope of competence as possible. The key debate must, in my view, be seen as that of the UN General Assembly, as that is where the most effective mechanisms can be initiated to allow the matter to be thoroughly examined by legal and political experts representing the vast majority of states, resulting in the best prospects for its being be taken forward fruitfully. The key proposals to analyse must, therefore, be the Jordanian proposal, which has placed the matter on the agenda of the 46th General Assembly, and now the proposed German initiative. If the UN is to make a strong contribution, however, this is likely to become apparent at the 47th General Assembly in 1992, rather than the 46th. The matter has been provisionally assigned only two days in the Sixth Committee of the Assembly this autumn. Debate is thus likely to progress little beyond an examination of what should be done next.

The Jordanian proposal   It is significant that this proposal has received the support of Kuwait, and apparently of Syria too,[316] despite Jordan's policies during the Gulf War. This augurs well for the agenda item's prospects, as it indicates interest on the part of some of the states most closely affected by the war, states which in the normal course of events would not be expected to take a high profile in this field, and a higher degree of Arab unity on the issue than might have been expected in the war's immediate aftermath. The list of suggested co-sponsors is also potentially significant, if efforts are, indeed, being made to interest those states in co-sponsorship of the item, because it includes, besides the obvious example of Canada, several countries, such as The Netherlands, New Zealand and Sweden, which generally adopt a high profile on environmental issues and, while themselves unlikely to initiate a proposal,[317] *are* likely to be very content to associate themselves with a good environmental proposal in good company. A number of Western countries have put forward proposals for amendments to the Jordanian proposal's drafting and methodology, but it is far from certain that they will ultimately support this initiative, especially given the more recent German initiative's imminent emergence.

The Jordanian proposal looks for a speedy study by a committee (to examine proposals for new mechanisms to 'combat the exploitation of the environment' in wartime), which suggests both a degree of urgency and the need to examine the matter within the UN itself. Initial discussion of the item is, therefore, likely to explore two questions. First, whether the General Assembly at its 46th or, more likely, a closely following Session should recommend to Member States the taking of certain immediate measures not requiring further debate or resolution within the UN, perhaps along the lines of the above-mentioned UNEP Governing Council Decision[318] or of Michael Meyer's suggestions (*supra* p. 172). Second, whether or not the matter should be examined further within a UN committee or programme or a UN Specialized Agency.

The Jordanian proposal was silent on the placement of the proposed committee within the General Assembly structure. The choice to be made in this respect is important to the balance between the respective political and legal and technical inputs into the examination of the issues. The item might be sent either to one of its six main political Committees or to its Legal (Sixth) Committee. Jordan favoured the Second Committee, but a number of Western countries objected, and it has been provisionally assigned to the Sixth Committee. As the matter involves highly technical and specialist legal questions, moreover, that Committee appears to be the best choice. Its being chosen will not deprive the debate of political content, especially as the Committee will be required to report on the matter to the Plenary towards the end of each Assembly as long as the item remains on

---

316 Conversation with Roy Lee on 10 August 1991.
317 For such reasons as provoking a response along the lines of: 'Oh no! They're at it again.'
318 No. 16/L.53, Part B: loc. cit., *supra* n. 6.

its agenda,[319] and will have the advantage of facilitating the application of legal expertise to the issues.[320]

Once the item is finally assigned to a Committee, the question will arise in which one of four ways it should be treated: as an item like any other, to be debated at each session of the Committee for its allotted number of days and in Plenary towards the end of the Assembly; in a working group of the Committee meeting during the period of the Assembly itself; in an *ad hoc* working group of Representatives of Member States meeting for a period of a few weeks at another time; or as a matter to be formally recommended to the General Assembly for treatment in another body, such as the ILC or a UN Specialized Agency, either alone or in combination with the Sixth Committee. The Jordanian proposal apparently contemplates only the second or third possibilities. The choice and its effect upon the success of the item very much depend upon Member States' views of the urgency of the matter, the likely practical results and how much political importance they attach to those results or to avoiding them.

If, which is unlikely, the debate were to take place within the Sixth Committee itself and not a working group (the first option) a rather sterile treatment of the topic, based largely upon the reading out of prepared statements, would probably result.[321] It is difficult to see any practical results emerging from such a procedure.

The second and third options are appropriate where it is intended to produce a draft treaty[322] or a set of principles for approval by the General Assembly and are much more likely to lead to genuine debate and concrete results. If one of these options were chosen and a draft treaty were to emerge, the likely next step would be the convocation of a diplomatic conference to finalize the text and open it for signature; in all likelihood this conference would be a short one. On the other hand, this process would be likely to take a number of years. It might also prove difficult to have the item placed within a working group in the first place. As to the second option, the Sixth Committee does not like to have more than two working groups meeting during each Assembly, and political considerations and trade-offs surround the choice of the topics for discussion; if the existing topics were not considered to be nearing completion,[323] the chances of this option being taken would be reduced. The third (*ad hoc*

---

319 It will endeavour to do so by forwarding a draft resolution or declaration.
320 The Government Representatives attending the Committee debates are invariably legally qualified diplomats, and it is also common to bring in specialist lawyers to deal with highly specialist items like this.
321 This is despite recent British attempts to inject more real debate into the proceedings of the Committee.
322 One precedent of relevance to the law of war is the *Ad Hoc* Committee on the drafting of an International Convention against the Recruitment, Use, Financing and Training of Mercenaries, which had to deal with the relationship between the proposed Convention and Protocol I: see, for example, the Report of the Committee, UN Doc. A/40/43, 30 May 1985, at paragraph 25.
323 A stage which it is difficult to predict.

working group) option, which is in any event the more likely to be adopted for matters of this importance, thus seems to be the more promising possibility of the two, although this option is subject to the additional constraints of budgetary and time-tabling considerations.

Prospects for the proper treatment of the topic might be enhanced by including it under an existing agenda item. The topic might be given greatest prominence, respectability and financial backing[324] in the Sixth Committee and Assembly debates if it were introduced under the existing agenda item, the UN Decade of International Law. The Sixth Committee established the Working Group on the United Nations Decade of International Law in 1990 to prepare generally acceptable recommendations for the Decade.[325] The General Assembly adopted the Working Group's programme for the first two years (1990–2) as an integral part of its Resolution.[326] It follows that a provision in the appropriate Resolution at the 46th Assembly is required to amend this, if it is desired immediately to include a topic on the law of war and the environment in the Working Group's programme for the period 1991–2;[327] the Jordanian proposal, of course, contemplates urgency. The danger with a 'Decade' of this kind is that it encourages a frame of mind that Representatives have a whole decade in which to debate an issue and that there is no need to hurry. It is to be hoped that the division of the Decade into five biennial programmes will obviate this tendency, and there is also further hope for dispatch, if adequate funding is made available to permit inter-sessional meetings of a committee to discuss the topic at issue.

The German Initiative   The German initiative appears to contemplate discussion in a working group of the Sixth Committee.

It also contemplates, however, bringing in the ILC. There is a clear relationship between the Commission and the Committee, as the former reports to the latter and the latter devotes at least three weeks to examining its work. What is not very clear, however, is precisely how substantive discussion of a single subject could be divided between the two, if that is, indeed, contemplated, and, if the UN Decade is involved, what the relationship between the work of the Decade and the work of the ILC is intended to be. Sending the whole matter to the ILC, perhaps as a matter of urgency, is also

---

324 Paragraph 5 of Part V of the Annex to the General Assembly Resolution establishing the Decade (loc. cit., *supra* n. 274) calls upon states to provide adequate funding and contemplates the establishment of a trust fund. It is clear that some states are prepared to spend significant sums on projects connected with the Decade, for example, the People's Republic of China in hosting the Ministerial Conference on Environment and Development and the expert Symposium on Developing Countries and International Environmental Law in June and August 1991 respectively, largely at its own expense.

325 Ibid., preamble.

326 Ibid., operative paragraph 2.

327 The existing programme could accommodate certain aspects of such an item (see, for example, operative paragraphs 2 of Part I and 3(b) and (c) of Part II), but these are not sufficient for a proper, directed debate. It will be recalled that at the London Conference both Türk (*supra* at p. 102) and Szekely (at p. 114) supported bringing the subject under the auspices of the Decade.

a possibility, although neither the Jordanian nor the German proposal contemplates this, perhaps as a result of that body's reputation for slowness.[328] Despite its reputation, however, the ILC recently succeeded in completing its work on Non-navigational Uses of International Watercourses and the Code of Offences. There is apparently, therefore, room on its agenda for a further item, and the possibility of sending the matter, or at least aspects of it, to this body (in pursuance of our fourth option) should not be dismissed, especially as it has much experience in relevant fields, such as international criminal law. What is less certain is whether the body as likely to be composed following the forthcoming elections will contain sufficient expertise on the law of war and of the environment in general to deal with more than the criminal law aspects of the matter. One disadvantage of the ILC is that its members serve in their individual capacities, and it is not possible, as it is in the Sixth Committee, to bring in additional specialists to deal with matters beyond the experience of its ordinary members.

It follows that the best option appears to be the establishment of an *ad hoc* committee of the Sixth Committee, preferably under the auspices of the Decade of International Law, to prepare a draft treaty or set of principles. In addition, the international criminal law aspects might be sent initially to the ILC. It can be said, finally, that none of the UN Specialized Agencies or Programmes, such as UNEP, recommends itself as a more appropriate forum than the Sixth Committee (or the ILC). What is needed, I suggest, is a legal body capable of straddling all the issues involved in this complex subject, rather than one with environmental law or other specialist expertise.

Other fora

None of this is, however, to deny the importance of debate in other fora.

The Budapest Red Cross Conference, for example, will be comprised of representatives from States Party to the Geneva Conventions (who are in approximately equal numbers to the Members of the UN)[329] and Protocols as well as of the ICRC, the International League of Red Cross and Red Crescent Societies and of individual national societies. Such meetings, which take place only every few years, present a significant opportunity to re-examine the workings of the humanitarian law of war. Their resolutions, though not binding, are very influential and in this instance might well be a means of encouraging states to interpret their existing obligations in the ways which are most protective of the environment.

On the other hand, the Red Cross's first loyalty must be to the existing *humanitarian* law of war, including the promotion of Protocol I, rather than to the environmental impact of war. At best we can expect a cautious approach from this Conference.

---

328 Alluded to by Türk *supra* at p. 100 and Szekely at p. 114.
329 There are 165 Parties to the Geneva Conventions and 166 UN Members at the time of writing.

UNCED is, moreover, clearly a UN Conference of major importance, marking as it does, the 20th anniversary of the Stockholm Conference on the Human Environment. It is thus an opportunity to take stock of developments in international environmental law and to provide a springboard for its future development.

On the other hand, its title also includes the topic of 'development', and the majority of Third World countries will naturally wish to emphasize the development aspects of the Conference's agenda and their peacetime concerns with attaining sustainable development.[330] They will wish to down-play any discussion of the law of war and the environment, especially bearing in mind that many so-called low-intensity wars are taking place in Third World countries.[331] More importantly, perhaps, it already has a very full agenda, and it is unlikely that much time will be able to be afforded for discussion of this topic.[332]

Whether or not the law of war and the environment will be included on the agenda remains a very controversial issue, despite Germany's initiative and the support of several Latin American States. At the time of writing no decision had been made,[333] but there appears to be a good chance that the matter will be discussed at UNCED. It is intended, in any event, to present the Rapporteur's Executive Summary of the London Conference to the relevant coordinating committee.

UN Security Council There has been no proposal to date to seek a resolution of the Council in addition to one of the Assembly to give general guidance on what is unacceptable environmental destruction.[334] This is, however, a possibility and such a resolution might give added weight to any resolutions of the General Assembly, but the Council does not strike me as the appropriate place in which to conduct a thorough debate, not least because of its composition and the fact that it is an executive body. It takes decisions in the light of concrete situations brought before it, and is not a drafter of general policy guidance; the General Assembly does this.

---

330 This was certainly the view of most Third World experts at the Beijing Symposium on Developing Countries and International Environmental Law of 12–14 August 1991: see Conclusions of the Chairman, available from Professor Sun Lin, Director of the Treaty and Law Department of the Chinese Ministry of Foreign Affairs in Beijing.

331 See also *supra* Prokhorov at p. 142.

332 The reader will have noted that, as early as March 1991, the Pentagonale and Polish Governments felt that it was rather late to add items to the agenda: see Ferrari Bravo *supra* at p. 143. It also appears that Heads of State and Government are being encouraged to attend the Conference and will be entitled to address it at whatever times they wish. This is likely to cause great time constraints to be placed upon the substantive debate.

333 The only development was the Secretariat's regrouping laws of war treaties in the list of instruments proposed for review under a new heading 'Law and the Environment'.

334 See *supra* pp. 34–35.

Future Prospects: Substance

The question arises, however, whether or not the Jordanian proposed item is drafted in adequate terms to permit the best possible debate on substance. It places emphasis, for example, upon the inadequacy of ENMOD[335] rather than Protocol I or the Inhumane Weapons Convention, although many UN Members would wish the debate to extend to those Conventions too. On the other hand it appears that this reference is superfluous to the aims of the proposal, because the proposed UN committee is not to be restricted to the examination of proposals for the modification of ENMOD. It is not clear, moreover, what the called-for unilateral decisions to conform with the requirements of the treaty are intended to comprehend in practice, as the Convention as it stands is unlikely to apply to any real potential wartime scenarios. It is to be hoped that the proposed amendments to the proposal, if accepted, will remove these superfluous references.

The meat of the proposal lies, however, in the call for a committee to examine proposals for new mechanisms to 'combat the exploitation of the environment' in wartime. This wording seems sufficiently broad to compensate to an extent for the over-restricted nature of the proposed title of the agenda item, which refers to 'exploitation of the environment *as a weapon*',[336] but, nevertheless, suffers from the implication that only deliberate, and not collateral, environmental damage is contemplated. The General Assembly debate should not be so limited. This too may be taken care of by amendments to the proposal.

The matters which it is proposed that this committee examine include the establishment of a fact-finding and dispute-settlement mechanism[337] and of a mechanism for disseminating advanced environmental data at the beginning of a conflict. But it does not seem that this is intended to be exclusive of other matters. It is also implicit that precise standards of environmental protection be established, whether through a radical amendment of ENMOD or otherwise.

In short, the Jordanian proposal appears to be sufficiently broadly worded to permit a broad debate; if and when it is amended, it is likely to permit an even broader one.

It is difficult to predict the precise substance of the forthcoming German proposal. It is possible, however, to predict that it will have the distinctive feature that it seeks to address peacetime, as well as wartime, environmental harm. The main point to note, however, is that it seems to be aimed at the creation of environmental crimes under international law and the improvement of mechanisms to deter and punish them. The proposed new legal instrument might well be useful in sending appropriate political signals to potential wrongdoers, but it is well to recall the reservations expressed at the London Conference concerning the efficacy of international criminal

---

335 The UNEP Governing Council Decision, loc. cit., *supra* n. 6, also does so.
336 It thus suffers from the same problem as the title of the Ottawa Conference: see *supra* p. 164. Again it is to be hoped that the proposed drafting amendments will resolve this.
337 This is redolent of much of the debate at the London Conference.

law as a means of enforcing the law of war[338] and on the prospects of establishing an international criminal court.[339]

It is, nevertheless possible to make recommendations concerning both short-term and long-term options on the assumption that there will be an adequate General Assembly debate.

Short-term options

The short-term options include reconfirming and encouraging additional ratifications of existing relevant instruments. This is uncontroversial. It could be done in a General Assembly (and Red Cross) Resolution. Such a UN Resolution could also, however, include recommendation of some of the more controversial possibilities: broadening the understanding of States Party to Protocol I of the meaning of the term 'natural environment' and the level of the threshold under Article 35(3); making further agreements to protect additional installations containing dangerous forces under Article 56(6) of Protocol I (and possibly removing existing exceptions to the protection of those already listed); convening a Consultative Meeting of the Parties to ENMOD in order to modify the accepted Understanding concerning the threshold and/or the environmental modification techniques covered by it; and agreeing new Protocols under the Inhumane Weapons Convention. This is much more controversial.

It is not intended to re-rehearse here all the arguments for and against these possibilities. Suffice it to say that they have the advantage of manifestly being exercises within familiar instruments rather than steps in the dark. It will be necessary, of course, to ensure that any changes take into account new weapons developments and that they are realistic, so as not to bring the law into disrepute. In particular the military and their lawyers must be intimately involved in the process. It is they who must be persuaded of the need for change more than any others.

It will, of course, be difficult to persuade the USA and other states which have not ratified Protocol I, partly out of dissatisfaction with the currently high threshold set by Article 35(3), to accept a lower threshold. Nevertheless, this is not a reason for other states not to pursue the debate and to try to persuade such countries to change their point of view. The main arguments which might be deployed are as follows.[340]

Employment of ENMOD as a model for a reduction in the threshold in Protocol I is entirely acceptable, because both instruments are in common seeking to define the *type of harm* which should be regarded as unlawful. If ENMOD contemplates outlawing environmental harm which extends over an area no greater than a few hundred square kilometers or lasts only a season, it should be possible to contemplate some movement towards this in Protocol I too.

Article 56 of Protocol I can legitimately be extended to other objects

---

338 *Supra* n. 98 and Greenwood at p. 124 and Caflisch at pp. 140–41.
339 See Pinto *supra* at p. 145.
340 I am particularly grateful to Françoise Hampson for her comments on future prospects.

containing dangerous forces which bear similar *risks* to the presently listed objects, and in particular to those which bear similar risks to nuclear electrical generating installations, which will generally pose the greatest risks of the three. In addition, it should extend to those objects which have similar *functions* to such installations: that is, the production of power by use of means involving the holding back of dangerous forces (or frequently in the case of dams and dykes merely the holding back). There is no logical reason why nuclear electrical generating plants should be singled out from other nuclear installations, from which the escape of radioactive substances would be equally disastrous. In addition, there are close parallels between the effects of Chernobyl and the firing of the Kuwaiti oil-wells. It is difficult to resist the conclusion that oil-fields should also be protected, apart from the military's attachment to the belief that denying the enemy access to oil-fields was the key to victory in the Second World War.

Supplementary to this is the possibility that the qualifying term 'severe losses among the civilian population' in Article 56 of Protocol I should be interpreted to be also satisfied when 'widespread, long-term and[/or] severe damage to the *natural environment*' occurs. Given the existence of Articles 35(3) and 55 and the extension of environmental considerations into the customary law of war, this proposition is difficult to resist.

Finally, there is no reason why fuel-air explosives weapons should be excluded from the scope of the Inhumane Weapons Convention when incendiary weapons are included. If anything, they are the more horrendous of the two, both from the human and the environmental point of view.

An *additional possible course of action*, suggested by Professor Alfred Rubin after the London Conference involves expressly empowering states to intervene to protect the environment as a 'neutral' right, for example, by making efforts to amend Article 1 of the International Convention relating to Intervention on the High Seas in Cases of Oil Pollution Casualties[341] so as to extend its application (and that of its Protocols extending its application to other noxious substances besides oil) to warships and other government vessels (for full text see Appendix 7). This would have the effect that neutral warships and military aircraft would be entitled to intervene to destroy or remove a stricken and unsalvageable belligerent warship or support vessel causing a severe threat of pollution to the neutral state's coast. It deserves further thought, but, quite apart from the question of the danger that such acts might be seen as unfriendly acts by the belligerent, it is difficult to see how this would be of great importance in practice. Only stricken naval auxiliary oil-tankers are likely to pose such a threat in normal circumstances.

Long-term options

These options are to seek the adoption by a diplomatic conference of: a Fifth Geneva Convention; a Third Additional Protocol to the Geneva

---

341 Done at Brussels, 29 November 1969: UKTS No. 77 (1975).

Conventions; or a Convention which is not a Geneva Convention as such but is sufficiently closely related to it to be counted, nevertheless, as a law of war instrument, perhaps along the lines of the 1954 Hague Convention on the Protection of Cultural Property.[342] I set out some of the reasons for considering these options in the 'Elements' Document (see *infra* pp. 184–88) and the respective advantages of each (*supra* pp. 31–32). Many other reasons emerge from the proceedings of the London Conference (chapters 3–10 above). My own present preference is for the latter alternative, but the relative advantages of each will, I hope, be clarified by the LSE Research in International Law project on this topic.

The arguments set out above in favour of the short-term options apply with equal force here, except that it is difficult to resist the conclusion that this would be a new adventure, and so one which government lawyers and the military will be less willing to contemplate. They might also be unwilling to contemplate it, because of the problems surrounding and work involved in amending existing legislation and military manuals to take into account the new Convention and the dissemination of knowledge of the new rules. The other reasons for caution are, of course, amply expressed in the record of round table sessions at the London Conference set out in chapters 7 to 9.

Nevertheless, I commend the following final revised version of my 'Elements' document to readers for their consideration in the same spirit as I presented the first version; it is not a monolithic whole. Please note that references in it are unchanged and correspond to the brief bibliography set out *supra* at p. 62.

---

342 Loc. cit., *supra* n. 90.

Elements of a New Convention on the Protection of the Environment in Time of Armed Conflict

Second Revision

Introduction

Summary

The document is divided into several Parts, each consisting of an 'Element' and a commentary on that Element. It does not purport to be comprehensive of all that might appear in a new instrument. In the Annex is set out a short bibliography of texts referred to in the main document.

The deliberate, massive environmental damage in the recent Gulf conflict is considered by many to call for a distinct instrument on environmental destruction in the context of conventional war. Many think that this is equally true of the collateral damage caused by the Coalition forces.

The timing of the negotiation of such an instrument should take into account the closeness in time of the recent conflict and the possibilities of taking advantage of provisions in existing instruments which permit immediate improvement of those instruments.

It seems desirable to include in such an instrument clear statements on the relevant rules of customary law concerning, *inter alia*, state and personal criminal responsibility.

It seems desirable in this connection to bring the laws of war up to date to reflect major developments in international environmental law as it applies in time of peace. This might be best achieved by means of a general instrument concerning protection of the environment in time of peace as well as war, but this document prefers to apply rules primarily to wartime and to continue them beyond the end of hostilities except where the context dictates otherwise.

It also seems desirable to build upon existing Geneva and Hague law as far as possible. It will be necessary to establish a specific threshold of protection for the environment which has practical meaning.

This all calls for a new Convention, rather than another Protocol to the existing Geneva Conventions, because it essentially marks a new departure within Geneva and Hague law. This Convention need not necessarily be called a 'Geneva' or 'Hague' Convention, and certainly should not be allowed to jeopardize the widespread adherence to the existing Geneva Conventions and Protocols, but it should have some sort of relationship with the corpus of existing law.

It is appropriate at this initial juncture to await developments in disarmament fora and elsewhere before seeking to regulate in such a new instrument the use or first use of nuclear weapons.

Consideration should be given to the possibility of the establishment of a new organization or the enhancement of the role of an existing suitable international organization to act as a monitoring and rapid response body which could carry out in the environmental field functions similar to those of the Red Cross/Crescent in the humanitarian field, including acting as a Protecting Organization for the Environment.

It will be difficult to define 'environment' for these purposes. The main problem is to distinguish attacks upon humans and their environment from attacks upon the environment as such, in so far as this is a meaningful distinction. It might thus be felt appropriate to employ the term 'natural environment' instead of 'environment'. Similarly it will be difficult to determine the degree of damage to the environment warranting regulation or prohibition.

Introduction

1 This document is not intended to be an exhaustive introduction to the many issues surrounding the possible adoption of a new Convention on the Protection of the Environment in Time of Armed Conflict, nor is it necessarily comprehensive of all matters which might be included in such a Convention. It is designed to serve merely as an aid to governmental and non-governmental experts' deliberations. It is divided into several Parts, each consisting of an 'Element' and a commentary on that Element. In the annex is set out a short bibliography of texts referred to in the document. No attempt is made to draft specific texts of articles nor is the order suggested by the way in which the Elements are set out intended to be compelling. It is assumed, however, that any such Convention would possess a preamble, substantive clauses and final clauses. It uses throughout the term the 'environment', although others might prefer 'natural environment' or another term.

2 The obvious reason for the drafting of this document is the widespread concern about the deliberate harm to the environment wreaked by Iraq at the time of the recent conflict in the Gulf region, when it created a major oil-spill in the Gulf and set fire to large numbers of Kuwaiti oil-wells to little or no apparent military advantage. Nevertheless, the less well-publicized occurrence of 'collateral' environmental damage as a result of the Coalition's military activities, in particular its intensive aerial campaign, should also be considered in this context. Its drafting at this time is not intended to prejudice judgements as to the correct timing of any possible negotiations.

3 That timing should, of course, take into account the closeness in time of the recent conflict and the possibilities of taking advantage of provisions in existing instruments which permit immediate improvement of the law through the instrumentality of those instruments. That said, the present outrage over Iraq's actions alone arguably makes it desirable for the international community to mark as soon as possible in a new instrument the concern that in future the need to give protection to the *environment* as such in time of armed conflict should be *explicitly* catered for, if only in relation to deliberate environmental damage. This is so even if it is agreed that Iraq's

actions were already proscribed by existing customary norms of the law of war, since those do not address themselves to the environmental impact of the destruction so much as to the indiscriminate and excessive nature of damage to enemy *property*. Their application to environmental harm is implicit at best. Even if one accepts that the Martens Clause now implicitly requires belligerents to take environmental damage into account, it is desirable to make this explicit. They also leave the protection of the environment subject to judgements on proportionality and military necessity.

It is also arguably no longer sufficient to rely on the fact that the environment as such *is* expressly protected in the odd treaty provision in the law of war, such as Article 35(3) of Additional Protocol I to the Geneva Conventions (Protocol I), especially when major Powers are not party to that Protocol and the practical efficacy of those provisions is seriously in doubt anyway.

Third, there is growing evidence that the prohibition of deliberate massive destruction of the environment is developing or has developed into a norm of international criminal law. It seems desirable to state this clearly in an international instrument.

The Gulf war was not the first time that the environment had been blatantly abused in time of armed conflict, but it was perhaps the first time that the facts had been broadcast on such a wide scale. An unscrupulous leader is, moreover, likely to have increasing destructive possibilities for causing such harm at his disposal as the world moves to more and more intensive exploitation of natural resources and energy sources.

4 As regards collateral damage to the environment, two matters might suggest the need, at the very least, to update existing Geneva and Hague law to improve the protection afforded to the environment, notwithstanding that many areas of this body of law were re-examined and improved upon during the decade commencing in 1970. Those improvements were, after all, made largely for humanitarian rather than environment-protection purposes. Firstly, the 1980s and early 1990s have seen the development of new generations of weapons systems, which are available in varying degrees to military establishments worldwide; many of these pose an enhanced threat to the environment either by their very nature or in circumstances where they are used intensively or indiscriminately. Secondly, those years have also seen an environmentally significant diversification of military options in relation to possible targets, in two senses: that new weapons systems might be taken to make possible (and 'legitimize') precision (or other) attacks against targets which it would formerly have been impracticable, or even unlawful, to attack in such a way as to increase risk of damage to the environment; and that the number and variety of targets containing dangerous forces, besides nuclear electricity generating stations, dykes and dams (which are the only ones given enhanced protection in Article 56 of Protocol I), the destruction of which might result in environmental disaster, has grown greatly. The Chernobyl disaster is a sobering indication of the potential effects of a strike against the core of a nuclear reactor in time of armed conflict, when evacuation and other response measures will be even more difficult than they are in peacetime.

5 Long-term improvement in the law might be best achieved by means of

a general instrument concerning protection of the environment in time of peace as well as war, but this document prefers to follow the examples of the existing Geneva Conventions and to apply rules primarily to wartime and to continue them beyond the end of hostilities except where the context dictates otherwise.

It therefore suggests improvements mainly to the Geneva law, but also to the Hague law, which cannot be entirely separated from Geneva law, as is illustrated by Protocol I itself. It calls for a new Convention, rather than a Protocol to the existing Geneva Conventions, because it essentially marks a new departure within Geneva and Hague law, rather than an improvement upon an existing corpus of law. It follows that the new Convention need not be negotiated necessarily as a 'Fifth Geneva' Convention, and certainly it does not seem necessary to seek to incorporate it into the integrated system established by the existing four Geneva Conventions, or even to place it beside them in such a way that the widespread adherence to those Conventions were threatened by what would be a much more controversial instrument. Nevertheless some formal relationship ought to be created with that corpus of law, perhaps along the lines of the Hague Convention on the Protection of Cultural Property in the Event of Armed Conflict of 1954.

The author is conscious, moreover, of the many fora in which the laws of war are dealt with. If it is felt that this document contains too much law concerning restrictions upon types of weaponry and that the correct domain for restrictions upon conventional weaponry is the Inhumane Weapons Convention, it is suggested that to that extent the regulation of weapons systems might be pursued with a view to environmental protection within the review processes set upon under that treaty.

6 It is a trite proposition, too, that both Geneva law and Hague law are in practice closely connected with the law of disarmament. It is, for example, much easier to regulate attacks upon targets or the use of certain weapons in armed conflicts, if those weapons are not being developed, tested or stockpiled or have not already been used in practice by armed forces. While the author is aware that improvement of the law of war is frequently the first step in movements towards disarmament measures, he is also aware that disarmament negotiations are proceeding in various fora on various types of weapon, and considers that negotiation of a new Geneva-style instrument should not be allowed to prejudice those negotiations.

It follows that, while nuclear and other weapons of mass destruction should properly be regulated by any such new instrument, being obvious examples of weapons which, if used, seriously threaten the environment, it is, in the author's view, appropriate at this initial juncture to await developments elsewhere before seeking to regulate or further regulate in such a new instrument the use or first use of such weapons. This may also be true of certain other weapons. It is certainly true of nuclear weapons, which form part of the deterrent forces of a number of states and are stockpiled in vast numbers; disarmament measures are likely to be far more important than law of war measures in their case. It might be, however, that a provision or provisions concerning chemical, biological and other toxin weapons, the stockpiling of which is much less acceptable among the vast majority of states, should be included in a new instrument.

In this context, too, it is recognized that over-strict attempts to regulate weaponry and targetry in an indirect attempt to induce disarmament raises the danger of bringing the law into disregard, given the capacities of modern weaponry, and to weaken its legal and moral force. It is, therefore, necessary to seek a realistic threshold of regulation. What is clear is that this threshold should be expressed in specific, and not general, terms; it must have a real impact, at least sufficient to cover the excesses in the Gulf conflict and any forseeable future conflict, and not merely seek to prohibit or regulate weaponry or targetry which in practical terms is unlikely to be used.

7 A third reason for the consideration of a new instrument governing the laws of war and the environment is the desirability of updating the law of war to reflect major developments in international environmental law as it applies in time of peace. Changes in state practice and the adoption of a large number of international environmental law instruments since the 1970s have reinforced the establishment or imminent emergence of a number of principles of customary international law.

Few of the international instruments refer expressly to their application in times of armed conflict, and the precise applicability of these and of the customary law principles as between belligerents is not clear. (They continue to apply as between a belligerent and a neutral state, subject to exceptions under the law of neutrality.) The principle of *lex specialis* suggests that a case must be made for their continued application as between belligerents. Nevertheless, a number, if not all, of the principles have potential applications here too. They include: the principle that states are responsible for ensuring that activities within their jurisdiction or control do not cause damage to the environment of other states or of areas beyond the limits of national jurisdiction; a duty to cooperate with other states by notifying and consulting with them in cases of risk of transboundary harm affecting their territory; (possibly) a duty of 'risk avoidance' in relation to the global commons; (possibly) a duty to monitor and carry out an environmental impact assessment prior to carrying out activities carrying a risk of transboundary harm; and (possibly) the application of the precautionary principle to such activities.

A new convention could be used to clarify their application in wartime. Even taking into account the difficulties surrounding the practical application of several of these principles and norms in peacetime, their application in time of armed conflict might have useful consequences, especially upon the geographical limitation of the effects of such conflict.

As has been mentioned, given the artificiality of the distinction between times of peace and times of war in this context, it might even be felt that an instrument covering deliberate environmental destruction and the use of weapons and devices which might be expected to produce environmental harm *at all times* is more appropriate. After all, it is possible to describe Iraq's destruction of the Kuwaiti oil-wells as acts of revenge rather than as acts of war having any military value at all. In any event, this document makes it clear that the obligations mooted should continue to apply after the cessation of hostilities, except where the context requires otherwise.

8 A number of states, inter-governmental and non-governmental organizations have been involved in trying to put out the burning oil-wells and clean up the pollution in the Gulf region following the recent conflict. With all due respect to their valiant efforts and cooperation through existing coordinating structures, the response has been both improvised and delayed by the absence of a neutral body expert in environmental protection with access to the war zone during the conflict. The possibility of establishing a rapid response body which could also be accepted as a sort of Protecting Power for the Environment and could perhaps carry out other functions parallel to those of the ICRC and/or League of the Red Cross and Red Crescent Societies in the humanitarian field ought to be considered. This could either be a new organization or be based upon an existing one.

9 Finally, the author makes no attempt to define the term 'environment'. Many have failed in this difficult venture. A definition is not, however, a unique problem in this context; it has not always been easy to find a workable distinction between civilians and combatants. A new Convention would clearly be concerned with: damage to the marine environment as a whole and marine wildlife and habitats in particular; pollution of the atmosphere, destructive climate modification, enhanced global warming and degradation of the ozone layer; and the destruction or degradation of terrestrial fauna and flora and their habitats. It should take an ecosystems approach.

Difficulties will be encountered in defining what amounts to destruction or degradation and what degrees of destruction or degradation warrant regulation or prohibition under a new Convention. Strict protection would be justified, for example, of particularly threatened species and of areas of special vulnerability or importance in aesthetic, evolutionary (biodiversity) or other similar terms.

Perhaps the greatest difficulty, however, is posed by the fact that man and many of his works form part of the environment. It is accordingly very difficult to determine whether or not, for example, attacks upon the means of survival of human populations themselves, such as attacks upon agricultural land or harvested forest or attacks which result in the spread of malnutrition or disease among humans as well as animals or plants, should always be considered also as attacks upon the environment. If all attacks which cause human suffering were treated as attacks upon the environment for these purposes, the result would be absurdity; a dividing line must be found. The author notes once more that many might prefer to adopt the term 'natural environment'. Similar considerations might also be applied to attacks upon culturally important sites and monuments. No provision is included concerning these, because they are already protected by the Hague Convention for the Protection of Cultural Property in the Event of Armed Conflict 1954 and by provisions in Protocol I. If such a provision were added to a new Convention, it would only make sense if it were intended to remove the exception to the prohibition of attacks on such objects on grounds of military necessity.

PART 1
GENERAL PRINCIPLES
ELEMENT 1

UNDER A CHAPTER HEADING:
'CHAPTER I: GENERAL PROVISIONS'

UNDER A SECTION HEADING:
'SECTION I: GENERAL PRINCIPLES AND SCOPE OF
APPLICATION'

A. A provision that, in cases not covered by the Convention, the environment remains under the protection of principles derived from established custom and the dictates of public conscience.

Commentary

This is derived from, *inter alios*, the Martens Clause as reformulated in Article 1(2) of Protocol I, and recognizes that much of the law of war remains customary law, despite the many steps taken to codify and progressively develop it. In this context, the 'dictates of public conscience' relate in particular to concepts of humane treatment of fauna and protection of the natural environment, and may possibly extend to inter-generational equity and sustainable development.

*****

B. A provision that the Convention applies at all times, except where the context requires that it apply only during hostilities, and to all situations of armed conflict, wherever occurring.

Commentary

This is derived from Protocols I and II. The period of application of obligations which need not be applied in time of peace too can be defined along the lines set out in Article 3 of Protocol I. The Convention should apply to all situations of armed conflict covered by both Geneva Protocols.

*****

C. A restatement of the principles that the right of the Parties to a conflict to choose methods and means of warfare is not unlimited and that the only legitimate objective of states in time of armed conflict is to weaken the enemy forces.

Commentary

These are well-known principles stated, for example, in the Declaration of St Petersburg of 1868 and Article 22 of the Regulations attached to Hague Convention (IV) of 1907, and restated in *inter alios* Article 35(1) Protocol I.

*****

D. A provision that states shall be liable to pay compensation in respect of and shall bear responsibility for breaches of the Convention.

Commentary

This derives from equivalent provisions in Article 3 of the Hague Convention (IV) of 1907 and Article 91 of Protocol I, which represent the customary law of war. It might in addition or alternatively be placed in Element 4.

*****

E. A provision that:

(a) **a Party has the responsibility to ensure that military activities under its jurisdiction or control do not cause damage to the environment of neutral states or of areas beyond national jurisdiction;**

(b) **a party wishing to conduct such military activities should notify any neutral state the environment of which is likely to be damaged by them of its intention to carry them out and should consult and, where appropriate, cooperate with it in minimizing the danger and effects of such damage, at least to the extent that this does not compromise the security of the military operation in question;**

(c) **where applicable, the precautionary principle and environmental impact assessments should be applied; and**

(d) **if such damage in fact occurs, the Party conducting the military activities should monitor this and fully inform the neutral states affected and/or, where damage to the global commons occurs, appropriate international organizations of the existence of the damage and of its findings.**

Commentary

This provision reflects established and emerging principles of international law. They are reflected in various formulations in various places, such as: international judgements, for example the *Trail Smelter, Corfu Channel* and *Lac Lanoux* cases; Principle 21 of the Stockholm Declaration of Principles on the Human Environment of 1972; the International Law Commission's (ILC's) draft articles on *inter alia* Non-Navigational Uses of

International Watercourses and International Liability for Transboundary Injurious Consequences Arising from Acts not Prohibited by International Law ('Injurious Consequences'); and in various international treaties.

*****

F. A provision or provisions expressly stating that the principles of state necessity and military necessity do not automatically prevail over the principle of environmental protection.

Commentary

This provision might be regarded as unnecessary, as it can be readily implied from the provisions concerning targetry in Part 2 below. No equivalent occurs in Protocol I. Nevertheless, the concept of state necessity has been discussed within the ILC since the 1970s (see, for example, 1982 Yearbook II (Pt. II), para. 28 *et seq*.), and a statement of general principle might well be considered to be useful, at least on the subject of state necessity in view of recent perceptions that national sovereignty must have effective limits.

*****

UNDER A SECTION HEADING:
'SECTION II: LEGAL STATUS OF THE PARTIES TO THE CONFLICT'

G. A provision reproducing with minor amendment Article 4 of Protocol I, that the legal status of the Parties shall not be affected by the Convention.

*****

UNDER A SECTION HEADING:
'SECTION II: DEFINITIONS'

H. A provision defining 'environment' for the purpose of the Convention and other matters which it will be necessary to define.

PART 2
TARGETRY
ELEMENT 2

UNDER A CHAPTER HEADING:
'CHAPTER I: METHODS AND MEANS OF WARFARE'

UNDER A SECTION HEADING:
'SECTION I: METHODS AND MEANS OF WARFARE'

A. A provision establishing the threshold at which methods and means of warfare are prohibited because of their intended or expected impact upon the environment. There appear to be approximately four options for change:

Option (a): **prohibiting the employment of methods or means of warfare which are intended, or may be expected, to cause** *any* **(except** *de minimis*, **or 'insignificant', or 'unappreciable') damage to the environment;**

Option (b): **prohibiting it at least where the damage is widespread, long-lasting** *or* **severe;**

Option (c): **prohibiting it as under alternative (b), but adding a fourth alternative criterion, 'significant (or 'appreciable') and irreversible'.**

Option (d): **choosing some mid-way position between alternative (b) and the existing high threshold as it appears in Article 35(3) of Protocol I.**

Commentary

The prohibition should arguably apply to protect the environment *in general* and not merely (like the equivalent provisions of the Convention on the Prohibition of Military or any Other Hostile Use of Environmental Modification Techniques of 1977 (ENMOD Convention), explained *infra*) the environment of the enemy state or the global commons. Similarly, like Article 35(3), it should be aimed to protect the environment *per se*, and not merely (like Article 55 of Protocol I) the environment because of the ultimate impact of the damage upon humans.

As a minimum, just as Article 35(3) was in large part intended in 1977 to respond to some of the worst environmental excesses of the Vietnam conflict, *this provision should be aimed to provide a specific prohibition of a repetition of the worst environmental excesses of the Gulf conflict*. Only options (a), (b) or (c) are likely to do this.

Option (a): is the least likely option to be chosen. Some slight support for a total prohibition might be derived from state practice as reflected in unilateral statements, such as those made by certain states during the Vietnam conflict that weapons damaging the environment, such as defoliants and herbicides, were unlawful. It might also be derived from such soft law instruments as the World Charter for Nature of 1972, which provides that 'Nature shall be secured against degradation caused by warfare or other hostile activities' (Article V) and that 'Military activities damaging to nature shall be avoided' (Article XX). On the other hand, this support is very slight. The only *negotiated* response to the outcry raised over the Vietnam War which was supported by the majority of states was the very high threshold in Article 35(3) of Protocol I, and, while the Charter for Nature is drafted in treaty language, it is still a soft law instrument and of limited significance.

Option (b) is derived from Article I of the ENMOD Convention. The threshold there is lower than that established by Article 35(3) of Protocol I in two senses. First the three criteria to be applied are *alternative* and not cumulative, as in Protocol I. Second, although no definition of any of these three criteria appears in the ENMOD Convention itself, the Conference of the Committee of Disarmament (CCD), which drafted the Convention, drafted an 'Understanding relating to Article I', which, while not forming part of the Convention, is frequently taken to reflect the intention of its drafters, and this is clearly to establish a lower threshold than under Protocol I. It is set out below:

> It is the understanding of the Committee that . . . the terms 'widespread', 'long-lasting' and 'severe' shall be interpreted as follows:
> (a) **'widespread'**: encompassing an area on the scale of several hundred square kilometres;
> (b) **'long-lasting'**: lasting for a period of months, or approximately a season;
> (c) **'severe'**: involving serious or significant disruption or harm to human life, natural and economic resources or other assets.

In contrast the criteria in Article 35(3) of Protocol I, 'widespread', 'long-term' and 'severe' seem to be 'primarily *directed to high-level policy decision-makers* and would affect such unconventional means of warfare as the *massive use of herbicides or chemical agents* which could produce widespread, long-term and severe damage to the natural environment' (Bothe, Partsch and Solf at p. 348 – emphasis added), and the 'Conference Reports indicate that collateral damage from conventional warfare, even very severe damage such as that which occurred in France in the First World War, was not intended to be covered and that *"long-term" should be understood in terms of decades.*' (Aldrich at p. 711 – emphasis added).

*This existing high threshold in Protocol I certainly does **not** encompass the deliberate creation of a major oil slick and the setting light to extensive oil fields.* Indeed, it is difficult to think of many realistic situations in which it would apply (apart from the destruction of dams, dykes and nuclear electricity generating stations in the circumstances which are in any event given additional protection in the circumstances described in Article 56 of Protocol I – see *infra*). Perhaps one example is the bombing of a chemical tanker containing a very noxious and easily spread chemical or a liquified petroleum or natural gas (LPG/LNG) tanker near a coast.

The ENMOD Understanding is expressed to be for the purpose of the ENMOD Convention alone, and thus the threshold at present applies only to such matters as the artificial creation of earthquakes or tidal waves, the artificial depletion of the ozone layer and the artificial modification of ocean currents or climate. It is difficult to envisage the successful use of any of these techniques by a belligerent, and this leads ineluctably to the conclusion that the negotiators were aware of this in 1977. It might be difficult, therefore, to achieve the extension of the lower threshold to more meaningful armed conflict scenarios. Nevertheless, the Understanding set out above might be usefully employed as a guide in drafting a new Convention. *This lower threshold so applied would certainly encompass the deliberate creation of an oil slick and the setting light to extensive oil fields.*

There remain problems with this option. One problem with the term 'widespread' as defined in the ENMOD Understanding is that spatial criteria are not always relevant to the seriousness of an impact in overall environmental terms. The greatest problem with this option however, is that in practice it might be little different from option (a), because the criteria will be alternative. Arguably many, if not most, military activities have a 'long-lasting' environmental effect in the sense of its lasting for several months or a season.

Option (c): The same considerations apply as in the case of Option (b), except that the threshold is set still lower. The criterion of '*irreversibility*' relates primarily to the loss of ecosystems, species or genetic material or the diversity thereof in a given area, which can have a serious impact upon the ecology of a region or of the world as a whole, even if the damage in other terms is limited. The addition of this criterion thus recommends itself. Guidance as to the choice of the qualifying term, whether '*significant*' or '*appreciable*', might be derived from the debates of the ILC on the topics of State Responsibility, Injurious Consequences and International Watercourses mentioned above in Part I.

Option (d): is perhaps the most realistic but also the most difficult to define. One possibility is the adoption of both cumulative and alternative criteria. Thus, for example, it might comprehend damage which is either 'severe and widespread' or 'long-lasting and irreversible' or 'severe and long-lasting' or 'widespread and irreversible'. Of course, more sophisticated alternatives might profitably be explored, including taking into account different sorts of military activity and different types of ecosystem.

*****

B. A provision that a state is obligated, in the study, development, acquisition or adoption of a new weapon, means or method of warfare, to determine whether or not its employment would, in all the circumstances, be prohibited by the Convention.

Commentary

This is derived from Article 36 of Protocol I. It aims to discourage the development of weapons systems on the ground that, although their use would be prohibited by Element 2.A, they might nevertheless be employed in disregard of the prohibition, if they existed, in the heat of war.

UNDER A CHAPTER HEADING:
'CHAPTER II: GENERAL PROTECTION AGAINST EFFECTS OF
HOSTILITIES'

UNDER A SECTION HEADING:
'SECTION I: BASIC RULE AND FIELD OF APPLICATION'

C. A provision or provisions reproducing Articles 48 and 49 of Protocol I substituting the term 'environment' or suitable variations for 'civilian' and its variants, where appropriate.

Commentary

This would preserve the narrow definition of military objectives and the broad definition of attack which are progressive elements of the Protocol. It would also move away from reliance on the implicit inclusion of the environment among civilian objects for its protection and towards explicit protection for it.

*****

UNDER A SECTION HEADING:
'SECTION II: PROTECTION OF THE ENVIRONMENT'

D. A provision that, in case of doubt whether or not an object or area is part of the environment, it is to be presumed that it is.

Commentary

This reflects Articles 50(1) and 52(3) of Protocol I. which are progressive elements of the Protocol. It should, of course, be interpreted in the light of the definition clause to be agreed.

*****

E. A provision reproducing the prohibition of acts against the environment by way of reprisal in Article 55(2) of Protocol I. This is to clearly comprehend all acts of reprisal and not merely those which result in ultimate loss to or injury of humans.

Commentary

Article 55(2) of Protocol I, which this essentially reproduces, was adopted by consensus, albeit in the light of a high threshold of what constitutes prohibited harm to the environment.

*****

F. A provision that attacks upon works and installations containing dangerous forces is prohibited in all circumstances which carry an 'appreciable' (or 'significant') risk of the release of dangerous forces and consequent severe environmental damage (regardless of losses among the civilian population). It might also prohibit all attacks upon nuclear electricity generating stations in all circumstances. It should reproduce, with necessary modifications, Article 56(3)–(7) of Protocol I.

Commentary

This provision would follow the spirit of Article 56(6) of Protocol I. It is particularly important to enhance the protection afforded to nuclear electricity generating plants, which at present have less protection under existing Geneva Law in certain circumstances than dams or dykes, notwithstanding the fact that, with few exceptions, their destruction is likely to have far more harmful results for mankind and his environment than a dam or dyke-burst. The consequences of a full-scale attack upon such a station is well illustrated by the Chernobyl disaster.

Article 56(2)(b), for example, has the effect that such a station may be attacked, even if it is being used for its normal purpose of generating electricity, if it is doing so in regular, significant and direct support of military operations and the attack is the only feasible way to terminate this support. This appears to include attacks merely because the station is supplying the national grid and the operating armed forces of the state are drawing power from the grid, at least when other means of cutting off the power, such as attacking power lines, are proving inefficacious.

The criterion of 'appreciable' or 'significant' risk of causing an escape of dangerous forces with a high risk of severe environmental damage is loosely derived from the work of the ILC on Injurious Consequences.

*****

UNDER A SECTION HEADING:
'SECTION III: PRECAUTIONARY MEASURES'

G. A provision or provisions reproducing the relevant parts of Articles 57 and 58, substituting the term 'environment' and variants thereon as appropriate.

Commentary

This would mean that Parties could not carry out an attack which would cause excessive damage to the environment; in view of the intricacy of the provision in question, the judgement whether or not an attack should be carried out should be made at as a high a level of command as possible and in the light of all of the information which is available or should be available upon making reasonable inquiry (see Kalshoven at pp. 98–100).

*****

UNDER A SECTION HEADING:
'SECTION IV: LOCALITIES AND ZONES UNDER SPECIAL
PROTECTION'

H. A provision that localities and zones containing ecosystems, species or genetic material of vital international importance shall not be subject to attack and shall be demilitarised zones.

Commentary

Guidance as to the precise content of this provision can be derived from Articles 59 and 60 of Protocol I. The protection of the areas and localities will be absolute. The areas and localities in question will not be subject to identification by agreement between the parties, but should be *identified by general international agreement* on a continuing basis. The World Heritage Convention might be modified to provide a suitable forum for this. A new sign might be adopted for their identification and demarcation, notwithstanding the practical difficulties encountered in using such signs.

PART 3
WEAPONRY
ELEMENT 3

UNDER A CHAPTER HEADING:
'CHAPTER I: PROHIBITIONS OR RESTRICTIONS ON THE USE OF
CERTAIN WEAPONS WHICH MAY BE CONSIDERED TO BE
EXCESSIVELY INJURIOUS TO THE ENVIRONMENT'

UNDER A SECTION HEADING:
SECTION I 'GENERAL PROVISIONS'

A. A provision that nothing in Part 3 of the Convention should be interpreted to detract from other provisions in the Convention, nor from obligations imposed upon Parties by international humanitarian law, nor from the Convention on Prohibitions or Restrictions on the Use of Certain Conventional Weapons which may be Deemed to be Excessively Injurious or to Have Indiscriminate Effects 1980 (the Inhumane Weapons Convention).

*****

UNDER A SECTION HEADING:
SECTION II: 'DEFOLIANTS, HERBICIDES, *DAISY CUTTER* BOMBS,
MASSIVE CONVENTIONAL BOMBING OR CRATERING AND
FOREST PLOWS'

B. A provision prohibiting the massive use of defoliants, herbicides, '*daisy cutter*' bombs, massive conventional bombing and cratering and large plows to remove forest and other kinds of plant cover, except on a small scale to assist in the preparation of air strips, harbours or military camps and of reasonable cleared perimeters around these and roads or tracks bordered by cover which can facilitate an ambush.

Commentary

State practice seems to support the view that the massive use of defoliants and herbicides is already prohibited. They may well be prohibited by both Article 35(3) Protocol I and the ENMOD Convention. A US Government spokesman has accepted that this is true of the ENMOD Convention; see also *supra* commentary to Element 2.A, option (a).

It is far more difficult to argue that the other methods are unlawful under existing law. Objections to their use on environmental grounds can only be voiced where they are used intensively or indiscriminately. It will be very difficult in practice to set a threshold of acceptability.

'Daisy cutter'-type bombs are high explosive devices which burst at a height designed to ensure clearance of a forest area of a size sufficient to clear an air strip.

Forest plows were used extensively in Vietnam after 1969 largely to replace the use of defoliants and herbicides; as they uproot fragile forest earth and root systems, they tend, if anything to be even more destructive than defoliants and herbicides.

*****

UNDER A SECTION HEADING:

SECTION III 'MINES, BOOBY TRAPS AND OTHER DEVICES'

C. A provision or provisions that provide that:

(a) the direction of mines, booby traps and other devices (as defined in Article I of Protocol II to the Inhumane Weapons Convention 1980, with the addition of sea mines) against the environment is prohibited;

(b) all precautions which are practicable or practically possible, taking into account all of the circumstances, should be taken to protect the environment from pollution caused by or other injurious effects of these weapons;

(c) these weapons are to be designed so as to minimize damage to the environment;

(d) the location of minefields, mines, booby traps and other devices is to be recorded;

(e) Parties are to cooperate to ensure their removal after their military purpose has been served.

Commentary

This provision builds upon the provisions of Protocol II to the Inhumane Weapons Convention.

Certain varieties of persistent mine can secrete noxious chemicals which might have significant environmental impact if the mines are present in large numbers. Anti-personnel land mines present in large numbers can endanger significant numbers of large animals.

*****

UNDER A SECTION HEADING:

SECTION IV 'INCENDIARY AND BLAST EFFECT WEAPONS'

D. A provision or provisions that provide that:

(a) it is prohibited to make the environment, including forests and other kinds of plant cover, the object of attack by incendiary or blast effect weapons,

even when plant cover is used to cover, conceal or camouflage combatants or other military objectives *and* the incendiary or blast effect is not specifically designed to cause burn injury or blast injury, respectively, to persons, but to be used against military objectives, such as armoured vehicles, aircraft and installations or facilities. In so far as this prohibition conflicts with Article 2(4) of Protocol III to the Inhumane Weapons Convention 1980, this provision is to prevail.

(b) Incendiary weapons may as an exception to this prohibition be used to set fire to military obstacles such as oil-filled ditches, where this does not cause widespread, long-lasting or severe damage to the environment (or perhaps exceed another threshold to be chosen).

(c) Blast-effect weapons may as an exception to this prohibition be used to clear minefields.

Commentary

This provision builds upon the provisions of Protocol III to the Inhumane Weapons Convention. The definitions in Article 1 of that Protocol might be used, with suitable modification, to include, for example, blast-effect weapons, which are at present excluded from its scope. It is necessary to overrule the exceptions in Article 2(4) of the Protocol, which make a mockery of that provision, since virtually the only time that plant cover is likely to be attacked is when it is being used as cover or camouflage (Kalshoven at p. 157).

Blast-effect weapons, which disperse and then ignite an explosive fuel/air mixture, were originally developed as anti-mine weapons. The USA has announced that it will restrict their use to this purpose. Second, third and fourth generations may, however, be being considered by some states for anti-personnel use. They kill everything within the range of the mixture, humans and lung-breathing animals by internal asphyxiation and bleeding caused by explosion and burning within their lungs. If used in large numbers, they are likely to seriously effect the stability of wildlife in the area.

PART 4
EXECUTION OF THE CONVENTION
ELEMENT 4

UNDER A CHAPTER HEADING:
'CHAPTER I: EXECUTION OF THE CONVENTION'

UNDER A SECTION HEADING:
'SECTION I: GENERAL PROVISIONS'

A. A provision reproducing with minor modifications Articles 80 and 82 to 84 of Protocol I.

*****

UNDER A SECTION HEADING:
'SECTION II: REPRESSION OF BREACHES OF THE CONVENTION'

B. A provision that a deliberate breach of the prohibition on causing environmental damage under Element 2.A, F or H is a 'grave breach' of the Convention, justifying criminal prosecution of responsible individuals.

Commentary

Article 85(3)(c) and (4)(d) of Protocol I already give some limited protection to the environment in this manner. To make such provision in the Convention would, moreover, reflect certain trends in the work of the ILC on state responsibility and international criminal law (including the Draft Code of Offences).

Article 19(3) of its Provisional Draft Articles on State Responsibility (Report of 33rd Session of ILC, 1981, in 1982 Yearbook II (Pt. II)) provides, moreover, in relevant part:

> Subject to paragraph 2, and on the basis of the rules of international law in force, an international crime may result, *inter alia*, from . . .

> (d) a serious breach of an international obligation of essential importance for the safeguarding and preservation of the human environment, such as those prohibiting massive pollution of the atmosphere and of the seas.

Paragraph 2 goes on to provide: 'An internationally wrongful act which results from the breach by a State of an international obligation so essential for the protection of fundamental interests of the international community that its breach is recognized as a crime by that community as a whole, constitutes an international crime.' It is, however, perhaps a little early to include a provision concerning the possible criminal liability of *states* in a new instrument, since the ILC has not yet had a proper opportunity to examine the full consequences of this new concept.

More recently the ILC has added a provision concerning the protection of the environment *per se* to its draft Articles on Injurious Consequences.

*****

C. A provision or provisions reproducing with minor amendments Articles 86, 87, 89 and 90 of Protocol I.

*****

D. There are two possible options:

Option (a): **A provision that a Party in whose territory an offender or alleged offender under Element 2.A, F or H is present and which does not submit his case for possible prosecution to its own prosecuting authorities shall detain him at the request of a state requesting it to do so and deliver him up to that state for prosecution. This obligation should also extend to the making available of evidence in the required state's possession and should not depend upon the existence of extradition arrangements between the states in question. It should also reproduce Article 88(3) Protocol I;**

Option (b): **A provision reproducing with minor amendments Article 88 Protocol I.**

Commentary

The intention of Element 4.B above is to create universal jurisdiction in relation to the international crime in question, permitting any state to detain and prosecute an alleged offender. Nevertheless, one weakness of war crimes provisions to which this principle applies has arguably been the absence of effective means to ensure that alleged offenders are brought to justice. This is because, unless he is captured by enemy forces, he can only be brought to justice if he is present in a state which is willing to prosecute him or to (deport or) extradite him to a requesting state. But extradition is only possible where extradition arrangements are in place between the two countries. Option (a) would avoid this reliance upon existing bilateral arrangements. Guidance as to its precise drafting could be sought from any of the existing *aut dedere, aut iudicare* Conventions (on terrorism).

*****

E. A restatement of the general principle of state responsibility stated in Element 1.D.

PART 5
INSTITUTIONS
ELEMENT 5

UNDER A CHAPTER HEADING:
'CHAPTER I: EXECUTION OF THE CONVENTION'

UNDER A SECTION HEADING:
'SECTION I: PROTECTING ORGANIZATION'

A. A provision:

(a) requiring Parties to a conflict to accept a new organization or an existing organization (the 'Organization') to be determined as a Protecting Organization for the purpose of applying the Convention and safeguarding the environment;

(b) permitting a substitute organization or organizations, which offer(s) all guarantees of impartiality and efficacy in the environmental protection field, to be appointed instead but only with the consent of all Parties to the conflict and following and taking into account the results of consultations between it and the Parties;

(c) permitting the Organization to operate under a distinctive emblem, and providing that its personnel operating under it should be immune from attack;

(d) referring to an *Annex I* setting out the structure and functions of the Organization (see *infra*).

B. A provision reproducing Article 81, with necessary modifications, requiring Parties to provide the Organization with all necessary facilities within their power.

Commentary to 5.A and B

Further discussion of the possible structure of a new Organization appears in the Commentary to 5.C below. These provisions are derived from Articles 5(4) and 81 of Protocol I.

It is inappropriate to adopt a system of Protecting *Powers* in relation to the environment, as no one state is in a position to protect the environment, which is a concern of mankind in general and not merely one or other of the belligerent parties; an impartial international organization is necessary. This Organization could, like the ICRC in relation to existing Geneva law, be a co-guarantor of the treaty and could produce an annual report on the environmental impact of armed conflict.

*****

UNDER A SECTION HEADING:
'SECTION II: RELIEF IN FAVOUR OF THE ENVIRONMENT'

C. A provision:

(a) authorizing the Organization to carry out actions which are impartial and remedial of environmental damage caused by a Party in breach of its obligations under the Convention and stipulating that these actions shall not be regarded as interference in the conflict nor as unfriendly acts; and

(b) reproducing, with necessary amendments, Articles 70(2)–(5) of Protocol I.

Commentary

If the Organization were given a Relief role, like the Red Cross/Crescent, it would need, besides immunity, guaranteed rights of access to and inspection of protected and damaged areas, the right to be informed of damage and the rights to give advice and to take urgent remedial measures. Like the Red Cross/Crescent, it would need a right of initiative and would not merely be a passive organ.

This provision echoes in most respects the Soviet call, which was debated at the UN's 44th session and resulted in a General Assembly Resolution, for a new 'Council for Emergency Environmental Assistance'[343] 'to send international groups of experts without delay to areas with a badly deteriorating environment' and 'to organize international cooperation in critical environmental situations' on the basis of the experts' recommendations concerning the limitation and elimination of the consequences of the environmental disaster (statement of President Gorbachev before the UN General Assembly, 7 December 1988: UN Doc. A/43/PV.72, p. 19; and letter from Edvard Sheverdnadze, then Soviet Foreign Minister, to the UN Secretary-General, dated 30 April 1989: Annex to UN Doc. A/44/264 E/1989/73, 2 May 1989). Although they had in mind a peacetime disaster, Chernobyl, nothing in their proposal suggests that such an organization could not also operate in time of armed conflict. A report on the possibility was prepared as the Resolution requested and UNEP's Governing Council recently reported to the General Assembly on the matter.

The Soviet suggestion is, however, for the formation of such a Centre within the UN Secretariat, along the lines of UNDRO and UNEP. It is possible, however, that certain states will consider such a UN body to be insufficiently impartial to carry out the counterparts to the relief activities of the Red Cross/Crescent in the environmental field. It might, nevertheless, be appropriate to establish such a body within the UN but to seek alternative solutions in relation to states unwilling to accept its auspices.

One existing *non-governmental* international organization commends

---

343 No. 44/224, December 1989. See also *supra* text at p. 138.

itself at first sight as an ideal alternative, the International Union for the Conservation of Nature and Natural Resources (IUCN). Founded in 1948, this is the largest and perhaps most representative alliance of conservation agencies and interest groups, with over 500 member organizations and a permanent Secretariat, operating in three specialist Centres with the support of over 3,000 experts. Indeed, Professor Nicholas Robinson of Pace University, New York, has prepared for the IUCN's Commission on Environmental Law a set of Draft Articles for Inclusion in a 'Convention Securing Nature from Warfare or Other Hostile Activities'. This would give the IUCN powers of inspection in zones protected in time of conflict for environmental purposes, the right to give advice and the right to be informed of damage to natural areas. It would also give (unidentified) 'environmental workers' rights of access to such zones to permit their 'maintenance and operation'.

The one drawback, however, is that the IUCN's membership includes governments and government agencies, so that this organization might also be perceived by some states to be insufficiently impartial. Nevertheless, this body does commend itself as one possibility.

Thirdly the ICRC, the International League of Red Cross and Red Crescent Societies and many national Red Cross societies have first-hand experience of dealing with certain environmental consequences of war. It might well be that the Red Cross's role could be expanded in this area. One of the main fears, however, would be that this would detract from its primarily humanitarian orientation.

Despite these possibilities, a new Organization, possessing many of the characteristics which guarantee the impartiality of the Red Cross/Crescent, might commend itself to many. If created, such an Organization would, of course, need to liaise very closely with the Red Cross/Crescent, the UN Organization, UNEP and the IUCN. It might be organized along a number of lines (for one suggestion see Annex I).

ELEMENT 5 continued
ANNEX 1
ORGANIZATION OF A NEW ORGANIZATION

The most sensible model to follow for the organization of the new Organization might be the Red Cross/Crescent model. An organizational chart which assumes a single internationally-oriented Organization and is based on the ICRC since 1980 is set out below.

If the Organization were to have both a Protecting and a Relief role, the choice of President would be crucial. As well as having expertise in environmental science and administration, he would need to be capable of filling a high-profile diplomatic role. He would need an efficient permanent Secretariat.

The Organization would need a properly financed regular budget, as well as an Extraordinary Budget. It might be wished to copy the dual structure of the Red Cross/Crescent, the ICRC and the League of (national) Red Cross and Red Crescent Societies. This might ensure the 'Green Cross' grass roots support and might result in the equivalent of the League contributing to the finances of the ICRC equivalent, as occurs with the Red Cross/Crescent. If such an Organization were established, however, it is likely that it would rely relatively little on government contributions and would need to rely less on any national societies' contributions. Environmentalist NGOs are likely to wish to contribute a large proportion of the budget. It might follow that a single stream-lined structure could be adopted.

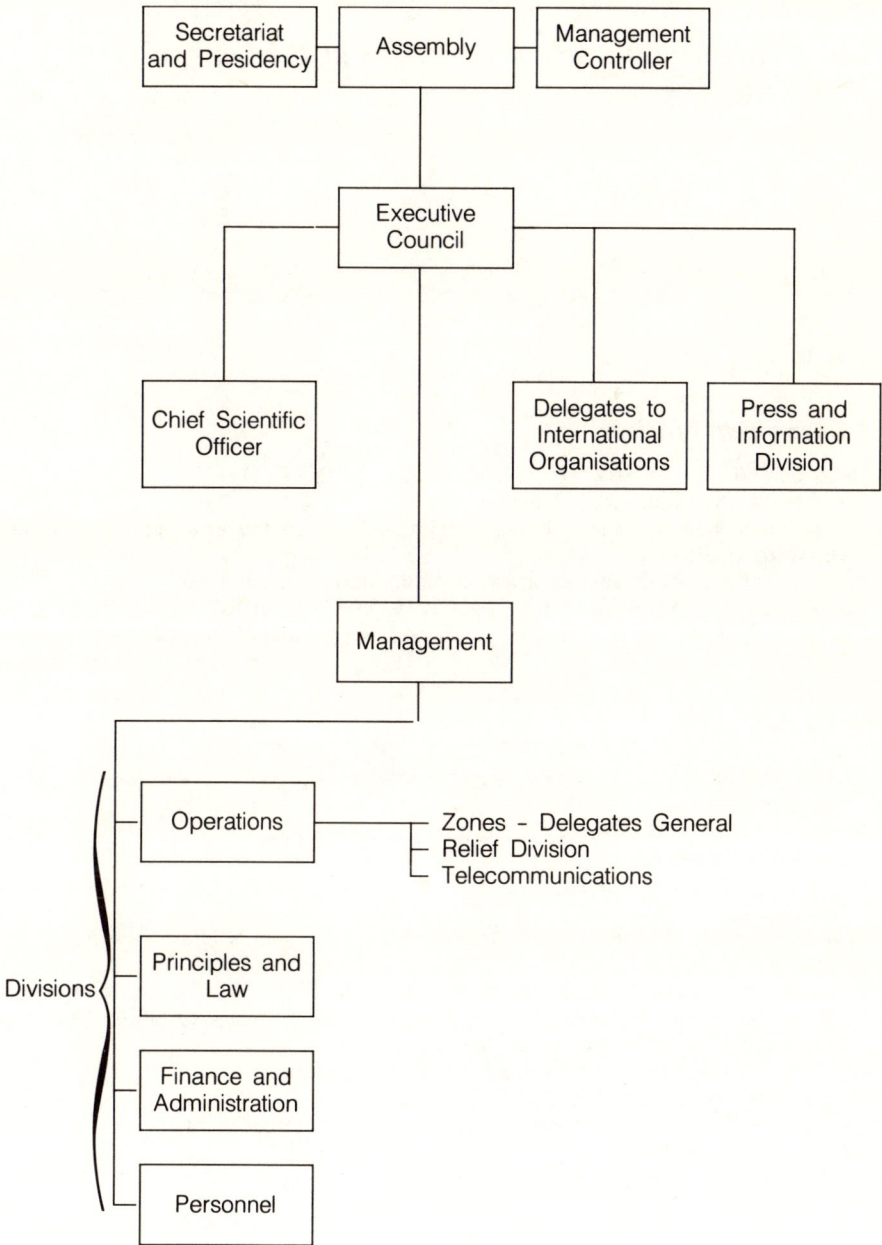

APPENDIX 1

List of Invited Guests and Observers at the London Conference

Guests

1 Government officials:

Sir Arthur Watts, KCMG, QC, Legal Adviser to the FCO.
Gill Barrett, Assistant Legal Adviser, FCO.
Marita Landaveri Porturas, Peruvian Representative to the Food and Agriculture Organization, Rome.
Alexandra York, Assistant Attorney-General, State of New York.
Antoine Bouvier, Member of the Legal Division of the ICRC.
Kaj Mannheimer, Office of the Legal Adviser, Swedish Ministry of Foreign Affairs.

2 Academics:

Alan Boyle, Senior Lecturer in Law, Queen Mary and Westfield College, London University.
Professor Maurice Mendelson, Professor of International Law, University College, London University.
Professor Nicholas Robinson, Professor of Environmental Law, Pace University, New York.
Professor George Alexandrowicz, Professor of Law, Queen's University, Kingston, Ontario.
Professor T. Waelde, Director of the Petroleum Law Institute, Dundee University.
Professor Al Rubin, Professor of International Law, Fletcher School of Law and Diplomacy, Tufts University, USA.
Eduardo Marino, Director, International Alert, London.
Lisa Wilder, Temporary Lecturer in Law, LSE.
Miss Lynne Jurgielewicz, M.Phil Student, LSE Law Department.
Henry Krupa, Canadian Barrister; LL.M. Student at LSE.
Christine Elwell, Research Student at LSE.
Professor Neville Brown, Birmingham University.

3 International and non-governmental organizations:

Stephen Sawyer, Director of Greenpeace International.

David B. Pascoe, Adviser on Marine Pollution, Marine Environment Division, International Maritime Organization.
Lord Melchett, Director of Greenpeace UK.
Damian Durrant, Greenpeace USA.
Marianne Cherney, Greenpeace USA.
Regina Monticone, Greenpeace International.
Roger Wilson, Greenpeace International.
Dr Rosalind Reeve, Environmental Investigation Agency.
Lena Ag, Greenpeace Sweden.

4 Practising lawyers

Jeremy Carver, Partner, Clifford Chance.
Anthony Hallgarten, QC, Head of Chambers, 3 Essex Court.
Daniel Bethlehem, Barrister, 3 Essex Court.
Owen Davies, Barrister, 2 Garden Court.
Dr Kamal Hossein, Attorney and Former Government Minister, Bangladesh.

Observers

1 Governments and Embassies

Ms Cecilia MacKenna, Chilean Embassy.
Mr G. O. Asaolu, Nigerian High Commission.
Mr Renan Barreto, Brazilian Embassy.
Representative of the German MFA or Embassy.
Ms Norma Dumont, Counsellor, Embassy of Argentina.
Dr David Walker, Second Secretary, New Zealand High Commission.
J. K. Kandie, Kenyan High Commission.
Mrs K. Geelan, First Secretary, Danish Embassy.
Bahaa Mowafi, Egyptian Embassy.
Augustin Garcia-Lopez, Secretary for Foreign Affairs, Mexican Embassy.
Li Jing Guang, First Secretary, Embassy of the People's Republic of China.
Per Westerberg, Legal Adviser to the Swedish Armed Forces; Research Student at the LSE.

2 Academics and students

Benedict Kingsbury, Lecturer in Law, Oxford University.
Professor Mary Ellen O'Connell, Indiana University.
Paula Casey-Vine, University College, Galway.
Dr Ian Scobbie, Lecturer on International Law, Dundee University.
David Tolbert, Lecturer in Law, Hull University.
Andrew Cunningham, Lecturer in Law, Reading University.
Heike Spieker, Senior Research Assistant, International Law Department, Ruhr University.
Michael Chapman, US Attorney attached to Geography Department, University College, London; Visiting Fellow, Policy Studies Institute.
Molina Hernandez, Spanish Attorney; M.Sc. Student at LSE.
Cleta Brown, LL.M. Student at LSE.
Jeremy Grose, Falkland Islands Government; M.Sc. Student at LSE.

Lewis Clifton, M.Sc. Student at LSE.
Anne-Charlotte de Fontaulent, M.Sc. Student at LSE.
Alke Schmidt, LL.M. Student at LSE.
Husna Ahmad, LL.M. Student at LSE.
Loide Lungameni, LL.M. Student at LSE.
Khalid M. Sofi, LL.M. Student at University College, London.
Haseena Mayat, LL.M. Student at LSE.
Simon Curran, LL.B. Student at LSE.
Mehmet Kilig, M.Sc. Student at LSE.
Azhar Khan, LL.M. Student at LSE.
Caroline Dommen, LL.M. Student at LSE.
Greg Maggio, US Attorney with Citicorp, London; LL.M. Student at LSE.
Chanaka Wickremasinghe, LL.M. Student at LSE.

3 Inter-governmental and non-governmental organizations

Sarah Lee, Greenpeace UK.
Susan Adams, Greenpeace UK.
Junior Bridge, Greenpeace USA.
Sebia Hawkins, Greenpeace USA.
Marc Pallemaerts, Free University of Brussels; Greenpeace Belgium.
Duncan Curie, Greenpeace International.
Vivienne Simon, Greenpeace International.
Elizabeth Mealey, Greenpeace International.
Richard Miller, Mankind in Media.

4 Practising lawyers

Arthur Marriott, Wilmer Cutler and Pickering.
Malcolm Forster, Freshfields.
David Bulman, Taylor Joynson Garrett.
Glen McLeod, Denton, Hall, Burgin and Warrens.
James Cameron, Barrister, 3 Gray's Inn Place.

APPENDIX 2*

Relevant Treaty Texts and Soft Law Instruments

Hague Convention on Land Warfare (IV) 1907

Article 23: In addition to the prohibition provided by special Conventions, it is forbidden:
> (g) to destroy or seize the enemy's property, unless such destruction or seizure be imperatively demanded by the necessities of war.

Geneva Convention (IV) 1949

Article 15: Any Party to the conflict may . . . propose to the adverse Party to establish, in the regions where fighting is taking place, neutralised zones intended to shelter from the effects of war the following persons:
> (b) civilian persons who take no part in hostilities, and who, while they reside in the zones, perform no work of a military character.

Article 53: Any destruction by the Occupying Power of real or personal property belonging individually or collectively to private persons, or to the State, or to other public authorities, or to social or cooperative organisations, is prohibited, except where such destruction is rendered absolutely necessary by military operations.

Article 147: Grave breaches . . . shall be those involving any of the following acts, if committed against persons or property protected by the present Convention: . . . extensive destruction and appropriation of property, not justified by military necessity and carried out unlawfully and wantonly.

---

* Texts of Geneva Conventions and Protocols reprinted by kind permission of the International Committee of the Red Cross, Geneva.

Additional Protocol I to the 1949 Geneva Conventions Relating to the Protection of International Armed Conflicts

MAIN PROVISIONS

Article 35: *Basic rules*:
3. It is prohibited to employ methods or means of warfare which are intended, or may be expected, to cause widespread, long-term and severe damage to the natural environment.

Article 55: *Protection of the natural environment*:
1. Care shall be taken in warfare to protect the natural environment against widespread, long-term and severe damage. This protection includes a prohibition of the use of methods or means of warfare which are intended or may be expected to cause such damage to the natural environment and thereby to prejudice the health or survival of the population.
2. Attacks against the natural environment by way of reprisals are prohibited.

Article 56: *Protection of works and installations containing dangerous forces*:
1. Works or installations containing dangerous forces, namely . . . nuclear electrical generating stations, shall not be made the object of attack, even where these objects are military objectives, if such attack may cause the release of dangerous forces and consequent severe losses among the civilian population.
2. The special protection against attack provided by paragraph 1 shall cease:

   (a) for a dam or dyke only if it is used for other than its normal function and in a regular, significant and direct support of military operations and if such attack is the only feasible way to terminate such support;

   (b) for a nuclear electrical generating station only if it provides electrical power in regular, significant and direct support of military operations and if such attack is the only feasible way to terminate such support;

PART I

GENERAL PROVISIONS

Article I – General principles and scope of application

1. The High Contracting Parties undertake to respect and to ensure respect for the Protocol in all circumstances.

2. In cases not covered by this Protocol or by other international agreements, civilians and combatants remain under the protection and authority of the principles of international law derived from established custom, from the principles of humanity and from the dictates of public conscience.

3. This Protocol, which supplements the Geneva Conventions of 12 August 1949 for the protection of war victims, shall apply in the situations referred to in Article 2 common to those Conventions.

4. The situations referred to in the preceding paragraph include armed conflicts in which peoples are fighting against colonial domination and alien occupation and against racist regimes in the exercise of their right of self-determination, as enshrined in the Charter of the United Nations and the Declaration on Principles of International Law concerning Friendly Relations and Co-operation among States in accordance with the Charter of the United Nations.

Article 3 – Beginning and end of application

Without prejudice to the provisions which are applicable at all times:

(a) the Conventions and this Protocol shall apply from the beginning of any situation referred to in Article 1 of this Protocol;

(b) the application of the Conventions and of the Protocol shall cease, in the territory of Parties to the conflict, on the general close of military operations and, in the case of occupied territories, on the termination of the occupation, except, in either circumstance, for those persons whose final release, repatriation or re-establishment takes place thereafter. These persons shall continue to benefit from the relevant provisions of the Conventions and of this Protocol until their final release, repatriation or re-establishment.

Article 4 – Legal status of the Parties to the conflict

The application of the Conventions and of this Protocol, as well as the conclusion of the agreement provided for therein, shall not affect the legal status of the Parties to the conflict. Neither the occupation of a territory nor the application of the Conventions and this Protocol shall affect the legal status of the territory in question.

Article 5 – Appointment of Protecting Powers and of their substitute

1. It is the duty of the Parties to a conflict from the beginning of that conflict to secure the supervision and implementation of the Conventions and of this Protocol by the application of the system of Protecting Powers, including *inter alia* the designation and acceptance of those Powers, in accordance with the following paragraphs. Protecting Powers shall have the duty of safeguarding the interests of the Parties to the conflict.

2. From the beginning of a situation referred to in Article 1, each Party to the conflict shall without delay designate a Protecting Power for the purpose of applying the Conventions and this Protocol and shall, likewise without delay and for the same purpose, permit the activities of a Protecting Power which has been accepted by it as such after designation by the adverse Party.

3. If a Protecting Power has not been designated or accepted from the beginning of a situation referred to in Article 1, the International Committee of the Red Cross, without prejudice to the right of any other impartial humanitarian organization to do likewise, shall offer its good offices to the Parties to the conflict with a view to the designation without delay of a Protecting Power to which the Parties to the conflict consent. For that purpose it may, *inter alia*, ask each Party to provide it with a list of at least five States which that Party considers acceptable to act as Protecting Power on its behalf in relation to an adverse Party, and ask each adverse Party to provide a list of at least five States which it would accept as the Protecting Power of the first Party; these lists shall be communicated to the Committee within two weeks after the receipt of the request; it shall compare them and seek the agreement of any proposed State named on both lists.

4. If, despite the foregoing, there is no Protecting Power, the Parties to the conflict shall accept without delay an offer which may be made by the International Committee of the Red Cross or by any other organization which offers all guarantees of impartiality and efficacy, after due consultations with the said Parties and taking into account the result of these consultations, to act as a substitute. The functioning of such a substitute is subject to the consent of the Parties to the conflict; every effort shall be made by the Parties to the conflict to facilitate the operations of the substitute in the performance of its tasks under the Conventions and this Protocol.

5. In accordance with Article 4, the designation and acceptance of Protecting Powers for the purpose of applying the Conventions and this Protocol shall not affect the legal status of the Parties to the conflict or of any territory, including occupied territory.

6. The maintenance of diplomatic relations between Parties to the conflict or the entrusting of the protection of a Party's interests and those of its nationals to a third State in accordance with the rules of international law relating to diplomatic relations is no obstacle to the designation of

Protecting Powers for the purpose of applying the Conventions and the Protocol.

7. Any subsequent mention in the Protocol of a Protecting Power includes also a substitute.

PART III

METHODS AND MEANS OF WARFARE COMBATANT AND PRISONER-OF-WAR STATUS

SECTION I – METHODS AND MEANS OF WARFARE

Article 35 – Basic rules

1. In any armed conflict, the right of the Parties to the conflict to choose methods or means of warfare is not unlimited.

2. It is prohibited to employ weapons, projectiles and material and methods of warfare of a nature to cause superfluous injury or unnecessary suffering.

3. It is prohibited to employ methods or means of warfare which are intended, or may be expected, to cause widespread, long-term and severe damage to the natural environment.

Article 36 – New weapons

In the study, development, acquisition or adoption of a new weapon, means or method of warfare, a High Contracting Party is under an obligation to determine whether its employment would, in some or all circumstances, be prohibited by this Protocol or by any other rule of international law applicable to the High Contracting Party.

PART IV

CIVILIAN POPULATION

SECTION I – GENERAL PROTECTION AGAINST EFFECTS OF HOSTILITIES

CHAPTER I – BASIC RULE AND FIELD OF APPLICATION

Article 48 – Basic rule

In order to ensure respect for the protection of the civilian population and civilian objects, the Parties to the conflict shall at all times distinguish between the civilian population and combatants and between civilian objects and military objectives and accordingly shall direct their operations only against military objectives.

Article 49 – Definition of attacks and scope of application

1. 'Attacks' means acts of violence against the adversary, whether in offence or in defence.

2. The provisions of this Protocol with respect to attacks apply to all attacks in whatever territory conducted, including the national territory belonging to a Party to the conflict but under the control of an adverse Party.

3. The provisions of this Section apply to any land, air or sea warfare which may affect the civilian population, individual civilians or civilian objects on land. They further apply to all attacks from the sea or from the air against objectives on land but do not otherwise affect the rules of international law applicable in armed conflict at sea or in the air.

4. The provisions of this Section are additional to the rules concerning humanitarian protection contained in the Fourth Convention, particularly in Part II thereof, and in other international agreements binding upon the High Contracting Parties, as well as to other rules of international law relating to the protection of civilians and civilian objects on land, at sea or in the air against the effects of hostilities.

CHAPTER II – CIVILIANS AND CIVILIAN POPULATION

Article 50 – Definition of civilians and civilian population

1. A civilian is any person who does not belong to one of the categories of persons referred to in Article 4 A (1), (2), (3) and (6) of the Third Convention and in Article 43 of this Protocol. In case of doubt whether a person is a civilian, that person shall be considered to be a civilian.

2. The civilian population comprises all persons who are civilians.

3. The presence within the civilian population of individuals who do not come within the definition of civilians does not deprive the population of its civilian character.

Article 51 – Protection of the civilian population

1. The civilian population and individual civilians shall enjoy general protection against dangers arising from military operations. To give effect to this protection, the following rules, which are additional to other applicable rules of international law, shall be observed in all circumstances.

2. The civilian population as such, as well as individual civilians, shall not be the object of attack. Acts or threats of violence the primary purpose of which is to spread terror among the civilian population are prohibited.

3. Civilians shall enjoy the protection afforded by this Section, unless and for such time as they take a direct part in hostilities.

4. Indiscriminate attacks are prohibited. Indiscriminate attacks are:

   (a) those which are not directed at a specific military objective;

   (b) those which employ a method or means of combat which cannot be directed at a specific military objective; or

   (c) those which employ a method or means of combat the effects of which cannot be limited as required by this Protocol;

   and consequently, in each such case, are of a nature to strike military objectives and civilians or civilian objects without distinction.

5. Among others, the following types of attacks are to be considered as indiscriminate:

   (a) an attack by bombardment by any methods or means which treats as a single military objective a number of clearly separated and distinct military objectives located in a city, town, village or other area containing a similar concentration of civilians or civilian objects; and

   (b) an attack which may be expected to cause incidental loss of civilian life, injury to civilians, damage to civilian objects, or a combination thereof, which would be excessive in relation to the concrete and direct military advantage anticipated.

6. Attacks against the civilian population or civilians by way of reprisals are prohibited.

7. The presence or movements of the civilian population or individual civilians shall not be used to render certain points or areas immune from military operations, in particular in attempts to shield military objectives from attack or to shield, favour or impede military operations. The Parties to the conflict shall not direct the movement of the civilian population or individual civilians in order to attempt to shield military objectives from attacks or to shield military operations.

8. Any violation of these prohibitions shall not release the Parties to the conflict from their legal obligations with respect to the civilian population and civilians, including the obligation to take the precautionary measures provided for in Article 57.

CHAPTER III – CIVILIAN OBJECTS

Article 52 – General protection of civilian objects

1. Civilian objects shall not be the object of attack or of reprisals. Civilian objects are all objects which are not military objectives as defined in paragraph 2.

2. Attacks shall be limited strictly to military objectives. In so far as objects are concerned, military objectives are limited to those objects which by their nature, location, purpose or use make an effective

contribution to military action and whose total or partial destruction, capture or neutralization, in the circumstances ruling at the time, offers a definite military advantage.

3. In case of doubt whether an object which is normally dedicated to civilian purposes, such as a place of worship, a house or other dwelling or a school, is being used to make an effective contribution to military action, it shall be presumed not to be so used.

Article 53 – Protection of cultural objects and of places of worship

Without prejudice to the provisions of the Hague Convention for the Protection of Cultural Property in the Event of Armed Conflict of 14 May 1954, and of other relevant international instruments, it is prohibited:

(a) to commit any acts of hostility directed against the historic monuments, works of art or places of worship which constitute the cultural or spiritual heritage of peoples;

(b) to use such objects in support of the military effort;

(c) to make such objects the object of reprisals.

Article 54 – Protection of objects indispensable to the survival of the civilian population

1. Starvation of civilians as a method of warfare is prohibited.

2. It is prohibited to attack, destroy, remove or render useless objects indispensable to the survival of the civilian population, such as foodstuffs, agricultural areas for the production of foodstuffs, crops, livestock, drinking water installations and supplies and irrigation works, for the specific purpose of denying them for their sustenance value to the civilian population or to the adverse Party, whatever the motive, whether in order to starve out civilians, to cause them to move away, or for any other motive.

3. The prohibitions in paragraph 2 shall not apply to such of the objects covered by it as are used by an adverse Party:

(a) as sustenance solely for the members of its armed forces; or

(b) if not as sustenance, then in direct support of military action, provided, however, that in no event shall actions against these objects be taken which may be expected to leave the civilian population with such inadequate food or water as to cause its starvation or force its movement.

4. These objects shall not be made the object of reprisals.

5. In recognition of the vital requirements of any Party to the conflict in the defence of its national territory against invasion, derogation from the prohibitions contained in paragraph 2 may be made by a Party to the

conflict within such territory under its own control where required by imperative military necessity.

Article 55 – Protection of the natural environment

1. Care shall be taken in warfare to protect the natural environment against widespread, long-term and severe damage. This protection includes a prohibition of the use of methods or means of warfare which are intended or may be expected to cause such damage to the natural environment and thereby to prejudice the health or survival of the population.

2. Attacks against the natural environment by way of reprisals are prohibited.

Article 56 – Protection of works and installations containing dangerous forces

1. Works or installations containing dangerous forces, namely dams, dykes and nuclear electrical generating stations, shall not be made the object of attack, even where these objects are military objectives, if such attack may cause the release of dangerous forces and consequent severe losses among the civilian population. Other military objectives located at or in the vicinity of these works or installations shall not be made the object of attack if such attack may cause the release of dangerous forces from the works or installations and consequent severe losses among the civilian population.

2. The special protection against attack provided by paragraph 1 shall cease:

   (a) for a dam or dyke only if it is used for other than its normal function and in regular, significant and direct support of military operations and if such attack is the only feasible way to terminate such support;

   (b) for a nuclear electrical-generating station only if it provides electrical power in regular, significant and direct support of military operations and if such attack is the only feasible way to terminate such support;

   (c) for other military objectives located at or in the vicinity of these works or installations only if they are used in regular, significant and direct support of military operations and if such attack is the only feasible way to terminate such support.

3. In all cases, the civilian population and individual civilians shall remain entitled to all the protection accorded them by international law, including the protection of the precautionary measures provided for in Article 57. If the protection ceases and any of the works, installations or military objectives mentioned in paragraph 1 is attacked, all practical precautions shall be taken to avoid the release of the dangerous forces.

4. It is prohibited to make any of the works, installations or military objectives mentioned in paragraph 1 the object of reprisals.

5. The Parties to the conflict shall endeavour to avoid locating any military objectives in the vicinity of the works or installations mentioned in paragraph 1. Nevertheless, installations erected for the sole purpose of defending the protected works or installations from attack are permissible and shall not themselves be made the object of attack, provided that they are not used in hostilities except for defensive actions necessary to respond to attacks against the protected works or installations and that their armament is limited to weapons capable only of repelling hostile action against the protected works or installations.

6. The High Contracting Parties and the Parties to the conflict are urged to conclude further agreements among themselves to provide additional protection for objects containing dangerous forces.

7. In order to facilitate the identification of the objects protected by this article, the Parties to the conflict may mark them with a special sign consisting of a group of three bright orange circles placed on the same axis, as specified in Article 16 of Annex I to this Protocol. The absence of such marking in no way relieves any Party to the conflict of its obligations under this Article.

CHAPTER IV – PRECAUTIONARY MEASURES

Article 57 – Precautions in attack

1. In the conduct of military operations, constant care shall be taken to spare the civilian population, civilians and civilian objects.

2. With respect to attacks, the following precautions shall be taken:

   (a) those who plan or decide upon an attack shall:

   (i) do everything feasible to verify that the objectives to be attacked are neither civilians nor civilian objects and are not subject to special protection but are military objectives within the meaning of paragraph 2 of Article 52 and that it is not prohibited by the provision of this Protocol to attack them;

   (ii) take all feasible precautions in the choice of means and methods of attack with a view to avoiding, and in any event to minimizing, incidental loss of civilian life, injury to civilians and damage to civilian objects;

   (iii) refrain from deciding to launch any attack which may be expected to cause incidental loss of civilian life, injury to civilians, damage to civilian objects, or a combination thereof, which would be excessive in relation to the concrete and direct military advantage anticipated;

   (b) an attack shall be cancelled or suspended if it becomes apparent that the objective is not a military one or is subject to special protection or that the attack may be expected to cause incidental loss of civilian life, injury to civilians, damage to civilian objects, or a combination thereof, which would be excessive in relation to the concrete and direct military advantage anticipated;

(c) effective advance warning shall be given of attacks which may affect the civilian population, unless circumstances do not permit.

3. When a choice is possible between several military objectives for obtaining a similar military advantage, the objective to be selected shall be that the attack on which may be expected to cause the least danger to civilian lives and to civilian objects.

4. In the conduct of military operations at sea or in the air, each Party to the conflict shall, in conformity with its rights and duties under the rules of international law applicable in armed conflict, take all reasonable precautions to avoid losses of civilian lives and damage to civilian objects.

5. No provision of this Article may be construed as authorizing any attacks against the civilian population, civilians or civilian objects.

Article 58 – Precautions against the effects of attack

The Parties to the conflict shall, to the maximum extent feasible:

(a) without prejudice to Article 49 of the Fourth Convention, endeavour to remove the civilian population, individual civilians and civilian objects under their control from the vicinity of military objectives;

(b) avoid locating military objectives within or near densely populated areas;

(c) take the other necessary precautions to protect the civilian population, individual civilians and civilian objects under their control against the dangers resulting from military operations.

CHAPTER V – LOCALITIES AND ZONES UNDER SPECIAL PROTECTION

Article 59 – Non-defended localities

1. It is prohibited for the Parties to the conflict to attack, by any means whatsoever, non-defended localities.

2. The appropriate authorities of a Party to the conflict may declare as a non-defended locality any inhabited place near or in a zone where armed forces are in contact which is open for occupation by an adverse Party. Such a locality shall fulfil the following conditions:

(a) all combatants, as well as mobile weapons and mobile military equipment must have been evacuated;

(b) no hostile use shall be made of fixed military installations or establishments;

(c) no acts of hostility shall be committed by the authorities or by the population; and

(d) no activities in support of military operations shall be undertaken.

3. The presence, in this locality, of persons specially protected under the Conventions and this Protocol, and of police forces retained for the sole purpose of maintaining law and order, is not contrary to the conditions laid down in paragraph 2.

4. The declaration made under paragraph 2 shall be addressed to the adverse Party and shall define and describe, as precisely as possible, the limits of the non-defended locality. The Party to the conflict to which the declaration is addressed shall acknowledge its receipt and shall treat the locality as a non-defended locality unless the conditions laid down in paragraph 2 are not in fact fulfilled, in which event it shall immediately so inform the Party making the declaration. Even if the conditions laid down in paragraph 2 are not fulfilled, the locality shall continue to enjoy the protection provided by the other provisions of this Protocol and the other rules of international law applicable in armed conflict.

5. The Parties to the conflict may agree on the establishment of non-defended localities even if such localities do not fulfil the conditions laid down in paragraph 2. The agreement should define and describe, as precisely as possible, the limits of the non-defended locality; if necessary, it may lay down the methods of supervision.

6. The Party which is in control of a locality governed by such an agreement shall mark it, so far as possible, by such signs as may be agreed upon with the other Party, which shall be displayed where they are clearly visible, especially on its perimeter and limits and on highways.

7. A locality loses its status as a non-defended locality when it ceases to fulfil the conditions laid down in paragraph 2 or in the agreement referred to in paragraph 5. In such an eventuality, the locality shall continue to enjoy the protection provided by the other provisions of this Protocol and the other rules of international law applicable in armed conflict.

Article 60 – Demilitarized zones

1. It is prohibited for the Parties to the conflict to extend their military operations to zones on which they have conferred by agreement the status of demilitarized zone, if such extension is contrary to the terms of this agreement.

2. The agreement shall be an express agreement, may be concluded verbally or in writing, either directly or through a Protecting Power or any impartial humanitarian organization, and may consist of reciprocal and concordant declarations. The agreement may be concluded in peacetime, as well as after the outbreak of hostilities, and should define and describe, as precisely as possible, the limits of the demilitarized zone

and, if necessary, lay down the methods of supervision.

3. The subject of such an agreement shall normally be any zone which fulfils the following conditions:

   (a) all combatants, as well as mobile weapons and mobile military equipment, must have been evacuated;

   (b) no hostile use shall be made of fixed military installations or establishments;

   (c) no acts of hostility shall be committed by the authorities or by the population; and

   (d) any activity linked to the military effort must have ceased.

   The Parties to the conflict shall agree upon the interpretation to be given to the condition laid down in sub-paragraph (d) and upon persons to be admitted to the demilitarized zone other than those mentioned in paragraph 4.

4. The presence, in this zone, of persons specially protected under the Conventions and this Protocol, and of police forces retained for the sole purpose of maintaining law and order, is not contrary to the conditions laid down in paragraph 3.

5. The Party which is in control of such a zone shall mark it, so far as possible, by such signs as may be agreed upon with the other Party, which shall be displayed where they are clearly visible, especially on its perimeter and limits and on highways.

6. If the fighting draws near to a demilitarized zone, and if the Parties to the conflict have so agreed, none of them may use the zone for purposes related to the conduct of military operations or unilaterally revoke its status.

7. If one of the Parties to the conflict commits a material breach of the provisions of paragraphs 3 or 6, the other Party shall be released from its obligations under the agreement conferring upon the zone the status of demilitarized zone. In such an eventuality, the zone loses its status but shall continue to enjoy the protection provided by the other provisions of this Protocol and the other rules of international law applicable in armed conflict.

Article 69 – Basic needs in occupied territories

1. In addition to the duties specified in Article 55 of the Fourth Convention concerning food and medical supplies, the Occupying Power shall, to the fullest extent of the means available to it and without any adverse distinction, also ensure the provision of clothing, bedding, means of shelter, other supplies essential to the survival of the civilian population of the occupied territory and objects necessary for religious worship.

2. Relief actions for the benefit of the civilian population of occupied

territories are governed by Articles 59, 60, 61, 62, 108, 109, 110 and 111 of the Fourth Convention, and by Article 71 of this Protocol, and shall be implemented without delay.

Article 70 – Relief actions

1. If the civilian population of any territory under the control of a Party to the conflict, other than occupied territory, is not adequately provided with the supplies mentioned in Article 69, relief actions which are humanitarian and impartial in character and conducted without any adverse distinction shall be undertaken, subject to the agreement of the Parties concerned in such relief actions. Offers of such relief shall not be regarded as interference in the armed conflict or as unfriendly acts. In the distribution of relief consignments, priority shall be given to those persons, such as children, expectant mothers, maternity cases and nursing mothers, who, under the Fourth Convention or under this Protocol, are to be accorded privileged treatment or special protection.

2. The Parties to the conflict and each High Contracting Party shall allow and facilitate rapid and unimpeded passage of all relief consignments, equipment and personnel provided in accordance with this Section, even if such assistance is destined for the civilian population of the adverse Party.

3. The Parties to the conflict and each High Contracting Party which allow the passage of relief consignments, equipment and personnel in accordance with paragraph 2:

   (a) shall have the right to prescribe the technical arrangements, including search, under which such passage is permitted;

   (b) may make such permission conditional on the distribution of this assistance being made under the local supervision of a Protecting Power;

   (c) shall, in no way whatsoever, divert relief consignments from the purpose for which they are intended nor delay their forwarding, except in cases of urgent necessity in the interest of the civilian population concerned.

4. The Parties to the conflict shall protect relief consignments and facilitate their rapid distribution.

5. The Parties to the conflict and each High Contracting Party concerned shall encourage and facilitate effective international co-ordination of the relief actions referred to in paragraph 1.

Article 71 – Personnel participating in relief actions

1. Where necessary, relief personnel may form part of the assistance provided in any relief action, in particular for the transportation and

distribution of relief consignments; the participation of such personnel shall be subject to the approval of the Party in whose territory they will carry out their duties.

2. Such personnel shall be respected and protected.

3. Each Party in receipt of relief consignments shall, to the fullest extent practicable, assist the relief personnel referred to in paragraph 1 in carrying our their relief mission. Only in case of imperative military necessity may the activities of the relief personnel be limited or their movements temporarily restricted.

4. Under no circumstances may relief personnel exceed the terms of their mission under this Protocol. In particular they shall take account of the security requirements of the Party in whose territory they are carrying out their duties. The mission of any of the personnel who do not respect these conditions may be terminated.

Article 90 – International Fact-Finding Commission

1. (a) An International Fact-Finding Commission (hereinafter referred to as 'the Commission' consisting of fifteen members of high moral standing and acknowledged impartiality shall be established.

   (b) When not less than twenty High Contracting Parties have agreed to accept the competence of the Commission pursuant to paragraph 2, the depositary shall then, and at intervals of five years thereafter, convene a meeting of representatives of those High Contracting Parties for the purpose of electing the members of the Commission. At the meeting, the representatives shall elect the members of the Commission by secret ballot from a list of persons to which each of those High Contracting Parties may nominate one person.

   (c) The members of the Commission shall serve in their personal capacity and shall hold office until the election of new members at the ensuing meeting.

   (d) At the election, the High Contracting Parties shall ensure that the persons to be elected to the Commission individually possess the qualifications required and that, in the Commission as a whole, equitable geographical representation is assured.

   (e) In the case of a casual vacancy, the Commission itself shall fill the vacancy, having due regard to the provisions of the preceding sub-paragraphs.

   (f) The depositary shall make available to the Commission the necessary administrative facilities for the performance of its functions.

2. (a) The High Contracting Parties may at the time of signing, ratifying or acceding to the Protocol, or at any other subsequent time, declare that they recognize *ipso facto* and without special agreement, in relation to any other High Contracting Party accepting the same

obligation, the competence of the Commission to enquire into allegations by such other Party, as authorized by this Article.

(b) The declarations referred to above shall be deposited with the depositary, which shall transmit copies thereof to the High Contracting Parties.

(c) The Commission shall be competent to:

    (i) enquire into any facts alleged to be a grave breach as defined in the Conventions and this Protocol or other serious violation of the Conventions or of this Protocol;

    (ii) facilitate, through its good office, the restoration of an attitude of respect for the Conventions and this Protocol.

(d) In other situations, the Commission shall institute an enquiry at the request of a Party to the conflict only with the consent of the other Party or Parties concerned.

(e) Subject to the foregoing provisions of this paragraph, the provisions of Article 52 of the First Convention, Article 53 of the Second Convention, Article 132 of the Third Convention and Article 149 of the Fourth Convention shall continue to apply to any alleged violation of the Conventions and shall extend to any alleged violation of this Protocol.

3. (a) Unless otherwise agreed by the Parties concerned, all enquiries shall be undertaken by a Chamber consisting of seven members appointed as follows:

    (i) five members of the Commission, not nationals of any Party to the conflict, appointed by the President of the Commission on the basis of equitable representation of the geographical areas, after consultation with the Parties to the conflict;

    (ii) two *ad hoc* members, not nationals of any Party to the conflict, one to be appointed by each side.

(b) Upon receipt of the request for an enquiry, the President of the Commission shall specify an appropriate time limit for setting up a Chamber. If any *ad hoc* member has not been appointed within the time limit, the President shall immediately appoint such additional member or members of the Commission as may be necessary to complete the membership of the Chamber.

4. (a) The Chamber set up under paragraph 3 to undertake an enquiry shall invite the Parties to the conflict to assist it and to present evidence. The Chamber may also seek such other evidence as it deems appropriate and may carry out an investigation of the situation *in loco*.

(b) All evidence shall be fully disclosed to the Parties, which shall have the right to comment on it to the Commission.

(c) Each Party shall have the right to challenge such evidence.

5. (a) The Commission shall submit to the Parties a report on the findings of fact of the Chamber, with such recommendations as it may deem appropriate.

(b) If the Chamber is unable to secure sufficient evidence for factual and impartial findings, the Commission shall state the reasons for that inability.

(c) The Commission shall not report its findings publicly, unless all the Parties to the conflict have requested the Commission to do so.

6. The Commission shall establish its own rules, including rules for the presidency of the Commission and the presidency of the Chamber. Those rules shall ensure that the functions of the President of the Commission are exercised at all times and that, in the case of an enquiry, they are exercised by a person who is not a national of a Party to the conflict.

7. The administrative expenses of the Commission shall be met by contributions from the High Contracting Parties which made declarations under paragraph 2, and by voluntary contributions. The Party or Parties to the conflict requesting an enquiry shall advance the necessary funds for expenses incurred by a Chamber and shall be reimbursed by the Party or Parties against which the allegations are made to the extent of fifty per cent of the costs of the Chamber. Where there are counter-allegations before the Chamber each side shall advance fifty per cent of the necessary funds.

Article 91 – Responsibility

A Party to the conflict which violates the provisions of the Conventions or of this Protocol shall, if the case demands, be liable to pay compensation. It shall be responsible for all acts committed by persons forming part of its armed forces.

Convention on the Prohibition of Military or Any Other Hostile Use of Environmental Modification Techniques (ENMOD)

Article I

1. Each State Party to this Convention undertakes not to engage in military or any other hostile use of environmental modification techniques having widespread, long-lasting or severe effects as the means of destruction, damage or injury to any other State Party.

Article II

As used in article I, the term 'environmental modification techniques' refers to any technique for changing – through the deliberate manipulation of natural processes – the dynamics, composition or structure of the Earth, including its biota, lithosphere, hydrosphere and atmosphere, or of outer space.

Convention on Prohibitions or Restrictions on the Use of Certain Conventional Weapons which may be Deemed to be Excessively Injurious or to have Indiscriminate effects

The High Contracting Parties

Recalling that it is prohibited to employ methods or means of warfare which are intended, or may be expected, to cause widespread, long-term and severe damage to the natural environment.

PROTOCOL III

Article II.4

It is prohibited to make forests or other kinds of plant cover the object of attack by incendiary weapons except when such natural elements are used to cover, conceal or camouflage combatants or other military objectives, or are themselves military objectives.

Hague Convention for the Protection of Cultural Property in the Event of Armed Conflict

Article 4: Respect for Cultural Property

1. The High Contracting Parties undertake to respect cultural property . . . by refraining from any use of the property and its immediate surroundings or of the appliances in use for its protection for purposes which are likely to expose it to destruction or damage in the event of armed conflict; and by refraining from any act of hostility directed against such property.

Article 9: Immunity of Cultural Property under Special Protection

The High Contracting Parties undertake to ensure the immunity of cultural property under special protection by refraining, from the time of entry in the International Register, from any act of hostility directed against such property and, except for the cases provided for in paragraph 5 of Article 8, from any use of such property or its surroundings for military purposes.

IAEA RESOLUTIONS

IAEA GC (XXVII)/RES/407 (14 October 1983)

Protection of Nuclear Installations Devoted to Peaceful Purposes Against Armed Attack

The General Conference

(e) *Recalling* that additional Protocol I to the Geneva Convention of 1949 prohibits attacks on peaceful nuclear electricity generating stations while other nuclear installations also devoted to peaceful uses are not covered by that prohibition, and

(f) *Believing* that it would further the cause of peace to extend the prohibition of armed attack so as to protect all nuclear installations devoted to peaceful purposes,

1. *Declares* that all armed attacks against nuclear installations devoted to peaceful purposes should be explicitly prohibited;

2. *Urges* all Member States to make, individually and collectively and through competent international organs, every possible effort for the adoption of binding international rules prohibiting armed attack against any nuclear installation devoted to peaceful purposes; and

IAEA GC(XXVIII)/RES/425 (28 September 1984)

Consequences of the Israeli military attack on the Iraqi nuclear research reactor and the standing threat to repeat this attack for: (a) the development of nuclear energy for peaceful purposes; and (b) the role and activities of the International Atomic Energy Agency

The General Conference

2. *Further considers* that any threat to attack and destroy nuclear facilities in Iraq and in other countries constitutes a violation of the Charter of the United Nations and of the Statute of the Agency;

IAEA GC(XXIX)/RES/444 (27 September 1985)

Protection of nuclear installations devoted to peaceful purposes against armed attacks

The General Conference

2. *Considers* that any armed attack on and threat against nuclear facilities devoted to peaceful purposes constitutes a violation of the principles of the United Nations Charter, international law and the Statute of the Agency;

IAEA GC(XXXI)/RES/475 (25 September 1987)

Protection of nuclear installations against armed attacks

The General Conference

> (b) *Aware of* the fact that an armed attack on a nuclear installation could result in radioactive releases with grave consequences, within and beyond the boundaries of the State which has been attacked, and

IAEA GC(XXXIV)/RES/533 (21 September 1990)

Prohibition of all armed attacks against nuclear installations devoted to peaceful purposes whether under construction or in operation

The General Conference

> (b) *Recalling* resolution GC(XXIX)/RES/444 . . .,

> (c) *Recalling* also resolution GC(XXXI)/RES/475 . . .,

1. *Recognizes* that attacks or threats of attack on nuclear facilities devoted to peaceful purposes could jeopradize the development of nuclear energy;

2. *Considers* that the safeguards system of the Agency is a reliable means of verifying the peaceful use of nuclear energy;

3. *Recognizes* that an armed attack or a threat of armed attack on a safeguarded nuclear facility, in operation or under construction, would create a situation in which the United Nations Security Council would have to act immediately in accordance with the provisions of the United Nations Charter;

UN GENERAL ASSEMBLY RESOLUTIONS

UNGA Resolution 45/58J (4 December 1990)

Prohibition of attacks on nuclear facilities

The General Assembly

Recalling [IAEA] resolution GC(XXIX)/RES/444 . . .

Recalling also [IAEA] resolution GC(XXXI)/475 of 25 September 1987, in which the General Conference states, *inter alia*, that it is:

> *Aware* of the fact that an armed attack on a nuclear installation could result in radioactive releases with grave consequences within and beyond the boundaries of the State which has been attacked, and

> *Convinced* of the need to prohibit armed attacks on nuclear installations from which such releases could occur and of the urgency of concluding an international agreement in this respect,

3. *Appeals* to all States that participate in the Conference on Disarmament to overcome their differences, and urges the cooperation of all States for the successful resolution of this issue in the near future;

4. *Calls upon* all States that have not done so to become parties to Additional Protocol I of 1977 to the Geneva Conventions of 12 August 1949 and upon all States parties to that Protocol to consider, in the context of a possible diplomatic conference, how to improve the present regime with regard to the protection of nuclear facilities;

6. *Appeals* to all States to take into account, when reviewing their military policies, the danger of radioactive releases potentially resulting from an attack on a nuclear facility;

SECURITY COUNCIL RESOLUTIONS

Security Council Resolution 686(1991) (2 March 1991)

The Security Council

3. *Further demands* that Iraq:

(d) Provide all information and assistance in identifying Iraqi mines, booby traps and other explosives as well as any chemical and biological weapons and material in Kuwait, in areas of Iraq where forces of Member States cooperating with Kuwait pursuant to resolution 678 (1990) are present temporarily, and in adjacent waters;

Security Council Resolution 687 (1991) (3 April 1991)

The Security Council

16. *Reaffirms* that Iraq, without prejudice to the debts and obligations of Iraq arising prior to 2 August 1990, which will be addressed through the normal mechanisms, is liable under international law for any direct loss, damage, including environmental damage and the depletion of natural resources, or injury to foreign Governments, nationals and corporations, as a result of Iraq's unlawful invasion and occupation of Kuwait;

APPENDIX 3

Developments in May 1991: UNEP Governing Council Decision and Pentagonale Proposals to UNCED

UNEP Governing Council Decision 16/L.53; Part B: May 1991:

'ENVIRONMENTAL EFFECTS OF WARFARE'

ANNEX I

SECTION III. LEGAL ASPECTS

19 Environmental disruption is an inevitable concomitant of war. In many instances, this combat-associated disruption of the environment is an incidental outcome of hostile military actions. In other instances, it is an intentional component of a belligerent's strategy. The salient legal constraints on environmental disruption in time of war are summarised here, especially those that might apply to the Iraq/Kuwait conflict, together with an indication of their level of formal acceptance.

(a) The Hague Conventions II of 1899 and IV of 1907 on the Laws and Customs of War on Land

20 Both of these treaties commit their Parties – when in the role of occupying state – to safeguard the public buildings, real property, forests, and agricultural works of the occupied state, administering them according to the rules of usufruct. To date, approximately 31 per cent of all nations are parties to one or both of these treaties (including four of the five permanent members of the United Nations Security Council), although not Iraq.

(b) Berne Protocol I of 1977 (additional to the Geneva Conventions of 1949) on the Protection of Victims of International Armed Conflicts

21 This treaty commits its Parties to take care in warfare to protect the natural environment against widespread, long-lasting, and severe damage. Prohibited, therefore, are methods or means of warfare that are intended, or may be expected, to destroy, remove, or render

useless – for any motive – objects indispensable to installations, foodstuffs, crops, livestock, agricultural areas, and irrigation works. The Parties also agree not to attack dams, dykes, and nuclear electrical generating stations, if such attack may cause the release of dangerous forces and consequent severe losses among the civilian population. To date, approximately 37 per cent of all nations are Parties to this treaty (including two of the five permanent members of the United Nations Security Council), although not Iraq.

(c) World Cultural and Natural Heritage Convention of 1972

22 The Parties to this treaty recognise that certain cultural and natural heritage sites and monuments are of outstanding universal value and constitute a world-wide heritage whose protection is the duty of the international community as a whole. The parties undertake not to take any deliberate measures that might damage, directly or indirectly, any cultural or natural heritage situated on the territory of other parties. To date, approximately 67 per cent of all nations are Parties to this treaty (including all five permanent members of the United Nations Security Council), and including Iraq, which at present has registered one such historic monument.

(d) Geneva Protocol of 1925 on Chemical and Bacteriological Warfare

23 The parties to this treaty accept a prohibition of the use in war of all chemical agents, and also of the use of bacteriological methods of warfare.

(e) Convention of 1977 on the Prohibition of Military or Any Other Hostile Use of Environmental Modification Techniques

24 The parties to this treaty undertake not to engage in military or any other hostile use of environmental modification techniques (i.e., deliberate manipulations of natural processes) having widespread, long-lasting, or severe effects as the means of destruction, damage, or injury to other parties. To date, approximately 32 per cent of all nations are parties to this treaty (including three of the five permanent members of the United Nations Security Council), although not Iraq.

(f) Proposed action by the Governing Council of UNEP

25 It is obvious that all these treaties need to be thoroughly reviewed, particularly (e). The Governing Council may wish to recommend to the General Assembly that it review this treaty and consider strengthening it.

ANNEX II

2. With regard to these issues, the Governing Council may wish to adopt a policy decision along the following lines:

The Governing Council . . .

3. *Invites* Governments in a position to do so to contribute generously to the technical cooperation trust fund established within the United Nations Environment Programme to develop and coordinate the implementation of the plan for the survey, assessment and dealing with the consequences of the environmental damage caused by conflict between Kuwait and Iraq;

4. *Invites* the General Assembly to review the 1977 Convention on the Prohibition of Military or Any Other Hostile Use of Environmental Modification Techniques with a view to:

(a) Strengthening the Convention;

(b) Encouraging accession to the Convention;

(c) Establishing concrete means of verification of the implementation of the provisions of the Convention.

Recommends that governments consider identifying weapons, hostile devices and ways of using such techniques that would cause particularly serious effects on the environment and consider efforts in appropriate forums to strengthen international law prohibiting such weapons, hostile devices and ways of using such techniques.

Pentagonale proposals to UNCED

PREPARATIONS FOR THE UNITED NATIONS CONFERENCE ON ENVIRONMENT AND DEVELOPMENT ON THE BASIS OF GENERAL ASSEMBLY RESOLUTION 44/228 AND TAKING INTO ACCOUNT OTHER RELEVANT GENERAL ASSEMBLY RESOLUTIONS: A/CONF. 151/PC/L.29

Letter dated 19 March 1991 from the Head of the delegation of Austria to the Preparatory Committee for the United Nations Conference on Environment and Development at its second session addressed to the Deputy Secretary-General of the United Nations Conference on Environment and Development

Please find attached a proposal 'Resolution on prevention of international disputes concerning the environment' submitted by PENTAGONALE countries (Austria, the Czech and Slovak Federal Republic, Hungary, Italy and Yugoslavia) and Poland. I would greatly appreciate if this proposal could be distributed as a Conference Room Paper, i.e. in the same manner as the proposal 'Code (fundamental principles) of environmental ethics' submitted during the first session of the Preparatory Committee.

(Signed)   George Calice
              Head of the Delegation of Austria to the Preparatory
              Committee for the United Nations Conference on Environ-
              ment and Development at its second session.

ANNEX

Proposal submitted by the PENTAGONALE countries (Austria, the Czech and Slovak Federal Republic, Hungary, Italy and Yugoslavia) and Poland (tentative draft)

Resolution on Prevention of international disputes concerning the environment

The States participating in the United Nations Conference on Environment and Development,

Recalling General Assembly resolution 44/228 on the United Nations Conference on Environment and Development and in particular paragraph 15 (w),

Bearing in mind the importance of the environment for peaceful cooperation and development,

Recalling Principle 21 of the Declaration of the United Nations Conference on the Human Environment, held in Stockholm in June 1972,

Bearing in mind that situations in which States assume that their territory might be impaired by the transboundary effects of activities or omissions on the territories of other States could lead to disputes between the States concerned,

Convinced that mechanisms to deal with such situations will promote peaceful and friendly relations between States and thus contribute to sustainable development,

1. *Urge* all States where situations originating on their territory might lead to disputes with other States concerning the environment to provide adequate information to those other States, which on their part should be entitled to request and to receive such information; this information should be treated as confidential if so demanded by the State providing it,

2. *Recommend* that States whose territory is likely to be impaired by transboundary environmental effects of activities or omissions on the territory of other States – after having received this information or in the case no information is provided – request at any time the establishment of an inquiry commission to clarify and establish the factual issues of the situation,

3. *Call* on the Executive Director of the United Nations Environment Programme to initiate negotiations on a legal instrument providing for a mechanism for dispute prevention concerning the environment between

States containing, *inter alia*, the following elements:

(a) The request to establish an inquiry commission should be conveyed by the State which originally requested information on a given situation to the State on the territory of which the situation originates. It should also be notified to the Executive Director of the United Nations Environment Programme. The members of the inquiry commission should be drawn from a list of experts on environmental issues to be established and maintained by the Executive Director of the United Nations Environment Programme on the basis of nominations received from States.

(b) Unless the States concerned agree otherwise, the inquiry commission should consist of three members and be established as follows:

   (i)   The State which originally requested information should appoint a member to be chosen from the above-mentioned list of experts on environmental issues.

   (ii) The other State should within 30 days of receipt of the notification appoint its own member to be chosen from the list. If appointment is not made within that period, the State instituting the proceedings may request the Executive Director of the United Nations Environment Programme to make the appointment.

   (iii) The two initial members should agree on a third member, chosen from the list of experts, who should be the Chair. If agreement on the Chair is not reached within 30 days he/she shall be appointed by the Executive Director of the United Nations Environment Programme.

(c) The inquiry commission should clarify and establish the factual issues of the situation. It should scrutinize the activity or omission which gives rise to the situation and hear the States involved as well as any person or entity capable to provide pertinent information. The States involved should give every support to the enquiry commission so as to enable it to fulfil its task. In particular, the enquiry commission should be given access to any relevant document as well as to the site of any activity which gives rise to the situation.

(d) The inquiry commission should submit a report within six months after its establishment. The report should be deposited with the Executive Director of the United Nations Environment Programme and transmitted to the States involved.

(e) The Executive Director of the United Nations Environment Programme should provide the inquiry commission with such assistance and facilities as it may require. The expenses of the proceedings should be borne by the interested parties. In order to facilitate the use of such a mechanism by Least Developed Countries, they should be entitled to financial assistance by the Environment Fund.

(f) In case a State conducts administrative proceedings concerning the environmental effects of certain activities on its territory and nationals of other States have access to these proceedings, due consideration should be given to these proceedings by a State requesting the establishment of an inquiry commission.

OTHER LEGAL, INSTITUTIONAL AND RELATED MATTERS: A/CONF. 151/PC/WG.III/L.1

Letter dated 26 March 1991 from the Head of the delegation of Austria to the Preparatory Committee for the United Nations Conference on Environment and Development at its second session addressed to the Secretary-General of the United Nations Conference on Environment and Development

Please find attached elements for a 'Resolution on settlement of international disputes concerning the environment' submitted by PENTAGONALE countries (Austria, the Czech and Slovak Federal Republic, Hungary, Italy and Yugoslavia) and Poland. In this context I would like to refer you to the Austrian working paper presented to the Preparatory Committee at its first session at Nairobi. I would greatly appreciate if these elements could be distributed as a Conference Room Paper for further consideration in Working Group III.

(*Signed*) George Calice
            Head of the Delegation of Austria to the Preparatory
            Committee for the United Nations Conference on Environ-
            ment and Development at its second session.

Proposal submitted by the PENTAGONALE countries (Austria, the Czech and Slovak Federal Republic, Hungary, Italy and Yugoslavia) and Poland (tentative draft)

Elements for a resolution on settlement of international disputes concerning the environment

The States participating in the United Nations Conference on Environment and Development,

Recalling General Assembly resolution 44/228 on the United Nations Conference on Environment and Development and in particular paragraph 15 (w), under which the UNCED should assess the capacity of the United Nations system to assist in the settlement of disputes in the environmental sphere and to recommend measures in this field, while respecting existing bilateral and multilateral agreements that provide for the settlement of such disputes,

Bearing in mind the importance of the environment for peaceful cooperation and development,

Recalling Principle 21 of the Declaration of the United Nations Conference on the Human Environment, held in Stockholm in June 1972,

Recognizing that situations in which States assume that their territory might be impaired by the transboundary effects of activities or omissions on the territories of other States could lead to disputes between the States concerned,

Recognizing also that situations in which States assume that the global or regional environment might be damaged by the transboundary effects of activities or omissions having occurred in areas not under national jurisdiction could lead to international disputes,

Convinced that a mechanism to deal with such situations will promote peaceful and friendly relations between States and thus contribute to sustainable development,

Stressing that all States shall settle their disputes by peaceful means in such a manner that international peace and justice are not endangered,

1. *Affirms* that international disputes concerning transboundary environmental effects which activities or omissions occurring on the territory of one State have or may have on the territory of other States or on areas not under national jurisdiction, shall be settled by peaceful means in accordance with Article 2, paragraph 3, of the Charter of the United Nations. To this end, States shall seek a solution by the means indicated in Article 33, paragraph 1, of the Charter and shall establish on bi- or multilateral treaties international procedures for the peaceful settlement of such environmental disputes, recognizing that recourse to, or acceptance of, a settlement procedure freely agreed to by them with regard to existing or future environmental disputes is not incompatible with their sovereign equality;

2. *Recommends* that States take appropriate steps to manage their international environmental disputes pending their settlement. To that end, States will address disputes at an early stage, refrain throughout the course of a dispute from any action which may aggravate the situation and make more difficult or impede the peaceful settlement of the dispute and seek by all appropriate means to make arrangements enabling the adoption of interim measures to prevent serious harm to the environment, without prejudice to their legal positions in the dispute;

3. *Recommends* that States strengthen their international commitments relating to the settlement of environmental disputes. To that end, they will in particular: (a) include, in their future treaties relating to environment, clauses providing for the settlement of disputes arising from the interpretation or application of those treaties; (b) apply in good faith the settlement procedures that they have agreed through general, regional or bilateral agreements or otherwise, when such disputes shall, at the request of any party to the disputes, be submitted to a procedure that entails a binding decision; (c) consider recognizing the compulsory jurisdiction of the International Court of Justice, either by treaty or by unilateral declaration under Article 36, paragraph 2, of the Statute of the Court, in all legal disputes concerning the environment;

4. *Recommends* that in the event of disputes concerning the claims of nationals of one State against another State for compensation of losses or damages suffered by those nationals or their properties for transboundary environmental effects of activities or omissions on the territory of that State, the States concerned provide for Mixed Claims Commissions following, *inter alia*, the elements set forth in annex 1 to the present resolution;

5. *Recommends* that international disputes concerning transboundary environmental effects which activities or omissions occurring on the territory of one State have or may have on the territory of other States or in areas not under national jurisdiction be settled by the States concerned in accordance with international procedures established on bi- or multilateral treaties containing, *inter alia*, the elements set forth in annex 2 to the present resolution;

6. *Believes* appropriate that the International Court of Justice form a permanent chamber, composed of three or more judges, for dealing with environmental disputes in accordance with Article 26, paragraph 1, of its own Statute.

ANNEX 1

1. In the event of claims of nationals of one State against another State for compensation of losses or damage suffered by those nationals or by their properties originating from transboundary environmental effects of activities or omissions on the territory of that State, the States concerned may provide for Mixed Claims Commissions for the purpose of deciding such claims.

2. To that end, a 'national' of a State means:

    (a) a natural person who is citizen of one of the States concerned;

    (b) a corporation or other legal entity which is organized under the laws of one of the States concerned.

3. 'Claims of nationals' of a State means claims espoused by nationals of that State against another State or jointly against such State and any person subject to the jurisdiction thereof.

4. Nationals shall have access to the Mixed Claims Commissions through the sponsorship of their national State.

5. Presentation of a claim for compensation shall not require prior exhaustion of local remedies which may be available to a claimant national; the Mixed Claim Commission may, however, decide that local jurisdiction be resorted to before the case is pleaded before the Commission.

6. Claims referred to the Mixed Claims Commissions shall, as of the date of filing of such claims with the Commission, be considered excluded

from the jurisdiction of the courts of either of the States concerned or of any other court.

7. The Mixed Claims Commissions shall decide the merits of the claim for compensation and determine the amount of compensation payable, if any.

8. When deciding a claim the Mixed Claims Commissions shall strive to achieve an equitable solution.

9. The Mixed Claim Commission shall not condemn a non-State party, for an activity which was legal according to the law of the place where it was accomplished.

10. The States concerned shall assist the Mixed Claims Commissions in performing investigations in order to clarify the factual situation of the case.

11. All decisions of the Mixed Claims Commissions shall be final and binding. The decision of the Mixed Claims Commissions shall, upon being presented for enforcement in accordance with the formalities required by the law of the State where enforcement is sought, be enforceable against non-State parties as if it were a judgement of a court of that State.

ANNEX 2

1. In the event of a dispute between States concerning transboundary environmental effects which activities or omissions occurring on the territory of one State have or may have on the territory of another State, the parties concerned shall, without undue delay and in good faith, consult among themselves with a view to settle the dispute through negotiation or any other means of their own choice. When the dispute arises for damages to the global or regional environment caused by activities or omissions having occurred under the responsibility of one State in areas not under national jurisdictions, any State party of the relevant treaties shall be entitled to initiate consultation for the settlement of the dispute and, where appropriate, to institute proceedings against the aforementioned State even if its own territory is not directly affected by the damage.

2. If the States parties to the dispute cannot reach agreement by negotiation, they may jointly seek the good offices of, or request mediation by, a third party.

3. If the States parties to the dispute cannot reach agreement following the third party good offices or mediation, the dispute shall be submitted to conciliation or to any other means of settlement freely agreed on by the States concerned.

4. Each State, when signing, ratifying, accepting, approving or acceding to bi- or multilateral treaties establishing the aforementioned procedures,

or at any time thereafter, may declare that it accepts as compulsory one or both of the following means for the settlement of environmental disputes:

(a) submission of the dispute to the International Court of Justice;

(b) submission of the dispute to arbitration.

5. The Arbitral Tribunal and the International Court of Justice shall decide the dispute on the basis of international law, as referred to in Article 38 of the Statute of the International Court of Justice.

6. The Arbitral Tribunal may prescribe any provisional measures which it considers appropriate under the circumstances to preserve the respective rights of the parties to the dispute or to prevent serious harm to the environment, pending the final decision. Provisional measures may be modified or revoked as soon as the circumstances justifying them have changed or ceased to exist. The States parties to the dispute shall comply promptly with any provisional measures prescribed by the Arbitral Tribunal. In case of submission of environmental disputes to the International Court of Justice those provisional measures shall be adopted by the Court in accordance with Article 41 of its own Statute.

7. Any decision rendered by the Arbitral Tribunal shall be final and shall be complied with by all the parties to the dispute. Any such decision shall have no binding force except between the parties and in respect of that particular dispute, as in the case of decisions of the International Court of Justice in accordance with Article 59 of the Statute of the Court.

APPENDIX 4

Letter from Professor Nikolai Vorontsov, Soviet Environment Minister to Dr Gerd Leipold, dated 24th May 1991

Dear Dr Leipold,

I would like to thank you for your kind letter of 13th April, 1991 and the invitation to take part in the round table conference on 'A Fifth Geneva' Convention on the Protection of the Environment in Time of Armed Conflict, in London, on 3rd June 1991.

Unfortunately, my schedule has already been set and at that time I am to host Mr Klaus Topfer, the German Minister of Environmental Protection and Nuclear Reactors Safety. Although I don't have a possibility to participate in the conference, I still cannot neglect the moral obligation to announce my attitude towards the problem to be discussed in London.

1. I consider the initiative put forward by Greenpeace International to convene the round table as very important.

2. There was no sound scientific examination of the destruction caused to the environment during the war in Vietnam, no lessons were learned. After the war, no measures on environmental protection in case of armed conflicts were worked out.

3. There was another tragic lesson during the Gulf war. It was the first time when ecological war appeared as a form of combat operations: the discharge of oil into the Gulf, etc.

4. I would like to stress that not only were the confronting parties involved in ecological warfare in the Gulf, not only were the ground and marine ecosystems of neutral countries (like Iran) destroyed, but this war caused great damage to countries distant from the Gulf too.

January to March in the Gulf is the wintering period of waterfowl and coastal migratory birds from Iran, Turkey, Syria, Iraq, the USSR and a number of other European countries, Pakistan and India. Their wintering grounds (including species contained in the World Red Book and the USSR Red Book) were greatly damaged. Besides this, in February to March a lot of birds species that winter on the territory of the African Horn passed through the Gulf region towards the North (the Caspian Sea, Volga, etc.)

They also suffered the consequences of ecological war. The fall-out of soot, acid rains caused by burning of the oil-wells not only affects the climate but can also speed up the growth rate of cancer.

5. The sad experience of the environmental aspects of the Gulf war has clearly shown the lack of an adequate legal structure to combat 'environmental crimes'. Moreover, there is no such definition of 'environmental crimes' in international Law.

6. In this connection I consider the working out of an internationally acceptable notion of 'Environmental Crime' to be a priority task and would appreciate any Greenpeace International action aimed at achieving this objective.

7. I have spoken in Nairobi during the informal Ministerial meeting in March about the necessity of the development of this notion of 'Environmental Crimes'.

I have authorized my deputy Mr S. Tsurikov to put forward an official proposal on this matter during the UNEP Governing Council Session in Nairobi (21–30 May, 1991).

8. President Gorbachev made a proposal on the development of an International Environmental Ethics Charter. This proposal corresponds to the idea of defining the concept of 'Environmental Crimes'.

9. It would be desirable for the notion of 'Environmental Crimes' to find a reflection in the final document of UNCED in Brazil in 1992.

I ask you to inform the participants of the London Conference about my letter and wish you success in your important activity.

APPENDIX 5

First Revision of the Elements of a New Convention on the Protection of the Environment in Time of Armed Conflict (Revised Parts)

Glen Plant, June 1991

Introduction

Summary of introduction

The document is divided into several Parts, each consisting of an 'Element' and a Commentary on that Element. It does not purport to be comprehensive of all that might appear in a new instrument. In an appendix is set out a short bibliography of texts referred to in the main document.

The deliberate, massive environmental damage in the recent Gulf conflict is considered by many to call for a distinct instrument on environmental destruction in the context of conventional war. Many think that this is equally true of the collateral damage caused by the Coalition forces.

The timing of the negotiation of such an instrument should take into account the closeness in time of the recent conflict and the possibilities of taking advantage of provisions in existing instruments which permit immediate improvement of those instruments.

It seems desirable to include in such an instrument clear statements on the relevant rules of customary law concerning, *inter alia*, state responsibility and international criminal law.

It seems desirable in this connection to bring the laws of war up to date to reflect major developments in international environmental law as it applies in time of peace. This might be best achieved by means of a general instrument concerning protection of the environment in time of peace as well as war, but this document prefers to apply rules primarily to wartime and to continue them beyond the end of hostilities except where the context dictates otherwise.

It seems desirable also to build upon existing Geneva and Hague law as far as possible. It will be necessary to establish a specific threshold of protection.

This all calls for a new Convention, rather than another Protocol to the existing Geneva Conventions, because it essentially marks a new departure within Geneva and Hague law. This Convention need not necessarily be called a 'Geneva' or 'Hague' Convention, and certainly should not be allowed to jeopardize the widespread adherence to the existing Geneva Conventions and Protocols, but it should have some sort of relationship with the corpus of existing law.

It is appropriate at this initial juncture to await developments in disarmament fora and elsewhere before seeking to regulate in such a new instrument the use or first use of nuclear weapons (and possibly also other weapons of mass destruction).

Consideration should be given to the possibility of the establishment of a new organization or the enhancement of the role of an existing suitable international organization to act as a monitoring and rapid response body which could carry out in the environmental field functions similar to those of the Red Cross/Crescent in the humanitarian field, including acting as a Protecting Organization for the Environment.

It will be difficult to define 'environment' for these purposes. The main problem is to distinguish attacks upon humans and their environment from attacks upon the environment as such, in so far as this is a meaningful distinction. Similarly it will be difficult to determine the degree of damage to the environment warranting regulation or prohibition.

1. This document is not intended to be an exhaustive introduction to the many issues surrounding the possible adoption of a new Convention on the Protection of the Environment in Time of Armed Conflict, nor is it necessarily comprehensive of all matters which might be included in such a Convention. It is designed to serve merely as an aid to governmental and non-governmental experts' deliberations. It is divided into several Parts, each consisting of an 'Element' and a Commentary on the Element. In an appendix is set out a short bibliography of texts referred to in the document. No attempt is made to draft specific texts of articles nor to suggest a particular form and ordering of a possible draft Convention, although it is assumed that its form will be conventional in the sense of having a preamble, substantive clauses and final clauses. It uses throughout the term the 'environment', although others might prefer 'natural environment' or another term.

2. The obvious reason for the drafting of this document is the widespread concern about the deliberate harm to the environment wreaked by Iraq at the time of the recent conflict in the Gulf region, when it created a major oil-spill in the Gulf and set fire to large numbers of Kuwaiti oil-wells to little apparent military advantage. Nevertheless, the less well-publicized occurrence of 'collateral' environmental damage as a result of the Coalition's military activities, in particular its intensive aerial campaign, should also be considered in this context. Its drafting at this time is not intended to prejudice judgements as to the correct timing of any possible negotiations.

3. That timing should, or course, take into account the closeness in time of the recent conflict and the possibilities of taking advantage of provisions in existing instruments which permit immediate improvement of those instruments. That said, the present outrage over Iraq's actions alone arguably makes it desirable for the international community to mark as soon as possible in a new instrument the concern that in future the need to give protection to the *environment* as such in time of armed conflict should be *explicitly* catered for, if only in relation to deliberate environmental damage. This is so even if it is agreed that Iraq's actions were already proscribed by customary or treaty norms, since the existing relevant norms do not address themselves to the environmental impact of the destruction so much as to the indiscriminate and excessive nature of damage to enemy *property*. Most existing norms which might be construed to apply to environmental damage do not expressly mention the environment.

It is also arguably no longer sufficient to rely on the fact that the environment as such *is* expressly protected in the odd provision in one or two instruments, such as Article 35(3) of Additional Protocol I to the Geneva Conventions (Protocol I), especially when the efficacy of those provisions is seriously in doubt.

Third, there is growing evidence that the prohibition of actions like those in question either is or is developing into a norm of international criminal law. It seems desirable to state this clearly in an international instrument.

This is not the first time that the environment has been blatantly abused in time of armed conflict, but it is perhaps the first time that the facts have been broadcast on such a wide scale. An unscrupulous leader is, moreover, likely to have increasing destructive possibilities for causing such harm at his disposal as the World moves to more and more intensive exploitation of natural resources and energy sources.

4. As regards collateral damage to the environment, two matters might suggest the need, at the very least, to update existing Geneva and Hague law to improve the protection afforded to the environment, notwithstanding that many areas of this body of law were re-examined and improved upon during the decade commencing in 1970. Those improvements were, after all, made largely for humanitarian rather than environment-protection purposes. Firstly, the 1980s and early 1990s have seen the development of new generations of weapons systems, which are available in varying degrees to military establishments worldwide; many of these pose an enhanced threat to the environment either by their very nature or in circumstances where they are used intensively or indiscriminately. Secondly, those years have also seen an environmentally significant diversification of military options in relation to possible targets, in two senses: that new weapons systems might be taken to make possible (and 'legitimize') precision (or other) attacks against targets which it would formerly have been impracticable, or even unlawful, to attack in such a way as to increase risk of damage to the environment; and that the number of targets, such as nuclear power stations, chemical

facilities and high dams, the destruction of which might result in environmental disaster, has grown greatly. The Chernobyl disaster is a sobering indication of the potential effects of a strike against the core of a nuclear reactor in time of armed conflict, when evacuation and other response measures will be even more difficult than they are in peacetime.

5. Long-term improvement in the law might be best achieved by means of a general instrument concerning protection of the environment in time of peace as well as war, but this document prefers to follow the examples of the existing Geneva Conventions and to apply rules primarily to wartime and to continue them beyond the end of hostilities except where the context dictates otherwise.

It, therefore, suggests improvements mainly to the Geneva law, but also to the Hague law, which cannot be entirely separated from Geneva law, as is illustrated by Protocol I itself. It calls for a new Convention, rather than a Protocol to the existing Geneva Conventions, because it essentially marks a new departure within Geneva and Hague law, rather than an improvement upon an existing corpus of law. It follows that the new Convention need not be negotiated necessarily as a 'Fifth Geneva' Convention, and certainly it does not seem necessary to seek to integrate it into the self-contained system established by the existing four Geneva Conventions or even to place it beside them in such a way that the widespread adherence to those Conventions were to be threatened by what would be a much more controversial instrument. Nevertheless some relationship ought to be created with that corpus of law, perhaps along the lines of the Hague Convention on the Protection of Cultural Property in the Event of Armed Conflict of 1954.

The author is conscious, moreover, of the many fora in which the laws of war are dealt with. If it is felt that this document contains too much law concerning restrictions upon types of weaponry, it is suggested that to that extent the regulation of weapons systems might be pursued with a view to environmental protection within the review processes set upon under the various relevant conventions.

6. It is a trite proposition, too, that both Geneva law and Hague law are in practice closely connected with the law of disarmament. It is, for example, much easier to regulate attacks upon targets or the use of certain weapons in armed conflicts, if those weapons are not being developed, tested or stockpiled or have not already been used in practice by armed forces. Improvement of the Geneva law is, moreover, frequently the first step in movements towards disarmament measures. The author is aware that disarmament negotiations are proceeding in various fora on various types of weapon, and negotiation of a new Geneva-style instrument should not be allowed to prejudice those negotiations.

It follows that, while nuclear and other weapons of mass destruction should properly be regulated by any such new instrument, being obvious examples of weapons which, if used, seriously threaten the environment, it is, in the author's view, appropriate at this initial juncture to await developments elsewhere before seeking to regulate or further regulate in such a new instrument the use or first use of such weapons. This may also be true of certain other weapons. It is certainly true of nuclear weapons, which form part of the deterrent forces of a number of states and are stockpiled in vast numbers; disarmament measures are likely to be far more important than Geneva law measures in their case. It might be, however, that a provision or provisions concerning chemical, biological and other toxin weapons, the stockpiling of which is much less acceptable among the vast majority of states, should be included in a new instrument.

In this context, too, it is recognized that over-strict attempts to regulate weaponry and targetry in an indirect attempt to induce disarmament raises the danger of bringing the law into disregard, given the capacities of modern weaponry, and to weaken its legal and moral force. It is, therefore, necessary to seek a realistic threshold of regulation. What is clear is that this threshold should be expressed in specific, and not general, terms; it must have a real impact, at least sufficient to cover the excesses in the Gulf conflict, and not merely seek to prohibit or regulate weaponry or targetry which in practical terms is unlikely to be used.

7. A third reason for the consideration of a new instrument governing the laws of war and the environment is the desirability of updating the laws of war to reflect major developments in international environmental law as it applies in time of peace. Changes in state practice and the adoption of a large number of international environmental law instruments since the 1970s have reinforced the establishment or imminent emergence of a number of principles and norms of international law. Few of the international instruments refer expressly to their application in time of armed conflict, and the precise applicability of the norms and principles at such times is not clear. Nevertheless, a number, if not all, of them have potential applications at such time, too. They include: the principle that states are responsible for ensuring that activities within their jurisdiction or control do not cause damage to the environment of other states or of areas beyond the limits of national jurisdiction; (possibly) a duty to carry out an environmental impact assessment prior to such activities; requirements of notification of such activities and (possibly) of consultation with affected states; (possibly) the application of the precautionary principle to such activities; and requirements to warn neighbouring states when an injurious transboundary escape in fact takes place. A new convention could be used to clarify their application in wartime. Even taking into account the difficulties surrounding the practical application of several of these principles and norms in peacetime, their application in time of armed conflict might have useful consequences, especially upon the geographical limitation of the effects of such conflict.

As has been mentioned, given the artificiality of the distinction between times of peace and times of war in this context, it might even be felt that an instrument covering deliberate environmental destruction and the use of weapons and devices which might be expected to produce environmental harm *at all times* is more appropriate. After all, it is possible to describe Iraq's destruction of the Kuwaiti oil-wells as acts of revenge rather than acts of war. In any event, this document makes it clear that the obligations mooted should continue to apply after the cessation of hostilities, except where the context requires otherwise.

8. A number of states, inter-governmental and non-governmental organizations have been involved in trying to put out the burning oil-wells and clean up the pollution in the Gulf following the recent conflict. With all due respect to their valiant efforts and cooperation through existing coordinating structures, the response has been both improvised and delayed by the absence of a neutral body expert in environmental protection with access to the war zone during the conflict. The possibility of establishing a rapid response body which could also be accepted as a sort of Protecting Power for the Environment and could perhaps carry out other functions parallel to those of the ICRC and/or League of the Red Cross and Red Crescent Societies in the humanitarian field ought to be considered. This could either be a new organization or be based upon an existing one.

9. Finally, the author makes no attempt to define the term 'environment'. Many have failed in this difficult venture. A definition is not, however, a unique problem in this context; it has not always been easy to find a workable distinction between civilians and combatants. A new Convention would clearly be concerned with: damage to the marine environment as a whole and marine wildlife and habitats in particular; pollution of the atmosphere, destructive climate modification, enhanced global warming and degradation of the ozone layer; and the destruction or degradation of terrestrial fauna and flora and their habitats. It should take an ecosystems approach.

Difficulties will be encountered in defining what amounts to destruction or degradation and what degrees of destruction or degradation warrant regulation or prohibition under a new Convention. Particularly strict protection would be justified, for example, of particularly threatened species and of areas of special vulnerability or importance in aesthetic, evolutionary (biodiversity) or other similar terms.

Perhaps the greatest difficulty, however, is posed by the fact that man and many of his works form part of the environment. It is accordingly very difficult to determine whether or not, for example, attacks on the means of survival of human populations themselves, such as attacks upon agricultural land or harvested forest or attacks which result in the spread of malnutrition or disease among humans as well as animals or plants, should always be considered also as attacks upon the environment. If all attacks which cause human suffering were treated as attacks upon the environment for these purposes, the result would be absurdity; a dividing line must be found.

Similar considerations might also be applied to attacks upon culturally important sites and monuments. No provision is included concerning these, because they are already protected by the Hague Convention for the Protection of Cultural Property in the Event of Armed Conflict 1954 and by provisions in Protocol I. If such a provision were added to a new Convention, it would only make sense if it were intended to remove the exception to the prohibition of attacks on such objects on the grounds of military necessity.

PART 5
INSTITUTIONS
ELEMENT 5

UNDER A CHAPTER HEADING:
'CHAPTER I: EXECUTION OF THE CONVENTION'

UNDER A SECTION HEADING:
'SECTION I: PROTECTING ORGANIZATION'

A. A provision:

(a) requiring Parties to a conflict to accept a new organization or an existing organization (the 'Organization') to be determined as a Protecting Organization for the purpose of applying the Convention and safeguarding the environment;

(b) permitting a substitute organization or organizations, which offer(s) all guarantees of impartiality and efficacy in the environmental protection field, to be appointed instead but only with the consent of all Parties to the conflict and following and taking into account the results of consultations between it and the Parties;

(c) permitting the Organization to operate under a distinctive emblem, and providing that its personnel operating under it should be immune from attack;

(d) referring to an *Annex I* setting out the structure and functions of the Organization (see *infra*).

B. A provision reproducing Article 81 of Protocol I, with necessary modifications, requiring Parties to provide the Organization with all necessary facilities within their power.

Commentary to 5.A and B

Further discussion of the organization of the Organization appears in the Commentary to 5.C below. These provisions are derived from Articles 5(4) and 81 of Protocol I.

It is inappropriate to adopt a system of Protecting *Powers* in relation to the environment, as no one state is in a position to protect the environment, which is a concern of mankind in general and not merely one or other of the belligerent parties; an impartial international organization is necessary. This Organization could, like the ICRC in relation to existing Geneva law, be a co-guarantor of the treaty and could produce an annual report on the environmental impact of armed conflict.

*****

UNDER A SECTION HEADING:
'SECTION II: RELIEF IN FAVOUR OF THE ENVIRONMENT'

C. A provision:

(a) authorizing the Organization to carry out actions which are impartial and remedial of environmental damage caused by a Party in breach of its obligations under the Convention and stipulating that these actions shall not be regarded as interference in the conflict nor as unfriendly acts; and

(b) reproducing, with necessary amendments, Articles 70(2)–(5) of Protocol I.

Commentary

If the Organization were given a Relief role, like the Red Cross/Crescent, it would need, besides immunity, guaranteed rights of access to and inspection of protected and damaged areas, the right to be informed of damage and the rights to give advice and to take urgent remedial measures. Like the Red Cross/Crescent, it would need a right of initiative and would not merely be a passive organ.

This provision echoes in most respects the Soviet call, which was debated at the UN's 44th session and resulted in a General Assembly Resolution, for a new 'Council for Emergency Environmental Assistance', 'to send international groups of experts without delay to areas with a badly deteriorating environment' and 'to organize international cooperation in critical environmental situations' on the basis of the experts' recommendations concerning the limitation and elimination of the consequences of the environmental disaster (statement of President Gorbachev before the UN General Assembly, 7 December 1988: UN Doc. A/43/PV.72, p. 19; and letter from Edvard Sheverdnadze, then Soviet Foreign Minister, to the UN Secretary-General, dated 30 April 1989: Annex to UN Doc. A/44/264 E/1989/73, 2 May 1989). Although they had in mind a peacetime disaster, Chernobyl, nothing in their proposal suggests that such an organization could not also operate in time of armed conflict. A report on the possibility was prepared as the Resolution requested and UNEP's Governing Council recently reported to the General Assembly on the matter.

The Soviet suggestion is, however, for the formation of such a Centre within the UN Secretariat, along the lines of UNDRO and UNEP. It is possible, however, that certain states will consider such a UN body to be insufficiently impartial to carry out the counterparts to the relief activities of the Red Cross/Crescent in the environmental field. It might, nevertheless, be appropriate to establish such a body within the UN but to seek alternative solutions in relation to states unwilling to accept its auspices.

One existing *non-governmental* international organization commends itself at first sight as an ideal alternative: the International Union for the Conservation of Nature and Natural Resources (IUCN). Founded in 1948, this is the largest and perhaps most representative alliance of conservation agencies and interest groups, with over 500 member organizations and a permanent Secretariat, operating in three specialist Centres with the support of over 3,000 experts. Indeed, Professor Nicholas Robinson of Pace University, New York, has prepared for the IUCN's Commission on Environmental Law a set of Draft Articles for Inclusion in a 'Convention Securing Nature from Warfare or Other Hostile Activities'. This would give the IUCN powers of inspection in zones protected in time of conflict for environmental purposes, the right to give advice and the right to be informed of damage to natural areas. It would also give (unidentified) 'environmental workers' rights of access to such zones to permit their 'maintenance and operation'.

The one drawback, however, is that the IUCN's membership includes governments and government agencies, so that this organization might also be perceived by some states to be insufficiently impartial. Nevertheless, this body does commend itself as one possibility.

Third, the ICRC, the International League of Red Cross and Red Crescent Societies and many national Red Cross societies have first-hand experience of dealing with certain environmental consequences of war. It might well be that the Red Cross's role could be expanded in this area. One of the main fears, however, would be that this would detract from its primarily humanitarian orientation.

Despite these possibilities, a new Organization, possessing many of the characteristics which guarantee the impartiality of the Red Cross/Crescent, might commend itself to many. If created, such an Organization would, of course, need to liaise very closely with the Red Cross/Crescent, the UN Organization, UNEP and the IUCN. It might be organized along a number of lines (for one suggestion see Annex I).

ANNEX I

Organization of a New Organization

The most sensible model to follow for the organization of the new Organization might be the Red Cross/Crescent model. An organizational chart which assumes a single internationally-oriented Organization and is based on the ICRC since 1980 is set out below.

If the Organization were to have both a protecting and a relief role, the choice of president would be crucial. As well as having expertise in environmental science and administration, he would need to be capable of filling a high-profile diplomatic role. He would need an efficient permanent secretariat.

The Organization would need a properly financed regular budget, as well as an extraordinary budget. It might be wished to copy the dual structure of the Red Cross/Crescent, the ICRC and the League of (national) Red Cross and Red Crescent Societies. This might ensure the 'Green Cross' grass-roots support and might result in the equivalent of the League contributing to the finances of the ICRC equivalent, as occurs with the Red

Cross/Crescent. If such an Organization were established, however, it is likely that it would rely relatively little on government contributions. Environmentalist NGO's are likely to wish to contribute a large proportion of the budget. It might follow that a single streamlined structure could be adopted.

APPENDIX 6

A Definition of the 'Environment'

Michael A. Meyer, British Red Cross

The definition of 'environment' in any new instrument on the protection of the environment in time of armed conflict must be realistic. This means, *inter alia*, that the definition must take into account military considerations as well as environmental concerns, and, of course, the likelihood of its acceptance by states.

Definitions or the use of the term 'environment' in existing agreements, perhaps particularly those related to armed conflict such as the 1977 United Nations Convention on Environmental Modification Techniques ('ENMOD') and 1977 Additional Protocol I to the Geneva Conventions 1949, will also be relevant to formulations of the term in any new instrument. For example, the term 'natural environment' is used in Protocol I without definition, perhaps because it was felt by the drafters that the meaning of the words was sufficiently plain, and this approach may suffice in future agreements. Indeed it might be in the interest of environmental protection not to seek to define the term 'environment' but rather to rely on the general understanding of that word.

During the consideration of the two relevant articles at the Diplomatic Conference which led to the adoption of Protocol I, the term 'ecosystem' was used, although it does not appear in the final texts of the provisions. If it is necessary to devise a definition of 'environment' for any new instrument, the concept of the ecosystem may be helpful.

The ICRC *Commentary* to Additional Protocol I advises that the term 'natural environment' used in Articles 35(3) and 55 should be understood in the widest sense to cover not merely objects indispensable to the survival of the human population, such as foodstuffs, drinking water and livestock, but also forests and other vegetation mentioned in Protocol III (on incendiary weapons) to the 1980 UN Conventional Weapons Convention, as well as flora, fauna and other biological and climatic elements.[344] The 1977 ENMOD Convention has an even broader definition, covering 'the dynamics, composition or structure of the Earth, including its biota, lithosphere, hydrosphere and atmosphere, or of outer space' (Article II).

---

344 At p. 662.

States are unlikely to agree to a new instrument which prohibits acts of warfare which cause short-term damage to the natural environment; as others have noted, warfare cannot fail to damage the natural environment. Methods or means of warfare which cause widespread, long-term and severe damage to the environment, such as the heavy use of herbicides, are prohibited by Additional Protocol I. In the light of events since 1977, States may be more willing to consider some protection of natural resources, albeit with qualifications. For example, referring to a proposal rejected during the Diplomatic Conference which led to Protocol I, states may now be more receptive to a treaty provision to the effect that: 'Publicly recognized nature reserves with adequate markings and boundaries declared as such to the adversary shall be protected and respected except when such reserves are used specifically for military purposes.'

It must be recognized that during armed conflict a number of delicate judgements may need to be made, balancing military, humanitarian and/or environmental considerations. As others have observed, given the choice between saving the lives of combatants or of saving important environmental assets, military commanders and government policy-makers are likely to choose the former. However, most would agree that gratuitous environmental damage during armed conflict must be prevented.

As already indicated, the principle of environmental protection in time of armed conflict is found in Additional Protocol I 1977, and it may be that the most practical way forward at this point is to concentrate upon disseminating knowledge of and implementing the two relevant provisions rather than seeking to develop a new single-issue agreement, containing a number of detailed articles. In this connection, it might be useful for the XXVIth International Conference of the Red Cross and Red Crescent, which will meet in Budapest in December 1991, to consider adopting a resolution on the matter. Such a resolution might: note the widespread concern for the protection of the natural environment during armed conflict; also note the efforts being made to examine the matter; reaffirm the existing rules contained in Protocol I; appeal to states to interpret these provisions in the way which is most favourable to the protection of the natural environment; and urge states both to take the necessary measures to implement these rules and to encourage and if requested, to help, other states to do so.

United Nations organs and regional bodies also might consider adopting similar resolutions.

If a new convention is desired, then it might be most useful to have a short and clearly worded agreement enunciating general principles, with a system of optional protocols covering different aspects of the protection of the environment in time of armed conflict.

Defining the 'Environment'

David Tolbert[345]

The task of defining a term as ever-present as the 'environment' is no doubt a 'poisoned chalice'.[346] One is tempted to throw one's hands in the air and declaim, with the American judge attempting to define 'pornography', 'I know it when I see it.' Unfortunately, it is in fact in response to what we have recently seen in the Gulf that protecting the environment in time of armed conflict has become a burning issue, literally as well as metaphorically. Although any method of defining the environment is open to criticism, this paper will first examine some concepts of the environment which have emerged in the field of international environmental law, on the grounds that this overview will provide scope for understanding what the term has come to mean in international law. Thereafter, an attempt will be made to delimit the meaning of the term within the context of armed conflict.

International law has done little specifically to define what the term the 'environment' means. It is impossible to identify any international agreement or source which adequately defines either 'environment' or 'environmental protection'.[347] Although reference can be made to other sources such as McDougal and Beesley's literal dictionary definition[348] or the slightly more helpful US Council on Environmental Quality statement – 'the natural and physical environment and the relationship of people with

---

345 Lecturer in Law, University of Hull. I would like to express my gratitude to David Freestone, Senior Lecturer, University of Hull, for his helpful comments and suggestions in the preparation of this paper.

346 As the Conference's 'Elements' document put it: 'Many have failed in this difficult venture' (*supra* p. 41).

347 See L. Gündling, 'Environment, International Protection', 9 *Encyclopedia of Public International Law*, The Hague: North Holland, (1986), pp. 119–27.

348 J. Beesley and M. McDougal, 'Preface', in J. Schneider, *World Public Order of the Environment: Towards an International Ecological Law and Organization*, London: Stevens and Sons, (1979), p. xi. They refer to Webster's definition: 'All the conditions, circumstances, and influences surrounding and affecting the development of an organism or group of organisms'.

that environment',[349] – these definitions, despite having some value,[350] are too broad to have much substantive legal significance. Thus, as Gündling recognizes, we are left with 'consideration of various measures which have been taken to control pollution . . . [where] there is at least some common understanding'.[351] A number of international agreements and materials have sought to define 'pollution' and/or 'environmental damage', and such definitions, by addressing what is being polluted or damaged, implicitly give some indication of what constitutes the environment and, more critically, what constitutes the environment for purposes of international legal protection.

Although there can be no definitive definition of pollution,[352] there are a number of multilateral conventions and other authoritative sources which contain broad definitions of the term. These definitions emanate from and track the Organization for Economic Cooperation and Development's (OECD) definition which defines pollution as follows:

'Pollution' means any introduction by man, directly or indirectly, of substance or energy into the environment resulting in deleterious effects of such a nature as to endanger human health, harm living resources and ecosystems, impair amenities or interfere with other legitimate uses of the environment.[353]

This definition is, *mutatis mutandis*, adopted with respect to marine pollution,[354] with regard to air pollution in the 1979 Convention on Long-Range Transboundary Air Pollution[355] and has wide-spread acceptance.[356] This definition of pollution raises a number of key points in considering how a definition of the environment could be approached as well as giving some indication as to what might be acceptable to the international

---

349 American Law Institute, Restatement of the Foreign Relations Law of the United States, St Paul, Minn.: American Law Institute Publishers, (1987), Sec. 601, Reporter's Comments, p. 110.
350 See M. Hardy, 'The United Nations Environment Program', in L. Teclaff and A. Utton (eds), *International Environmental Law*, New York: Praeger, (1974), pp. 57–77. ('The fact the word "environment" may be interpreted to include the entire relationship between man and his surroundings lent support to calls for resolute, universal action. Rigorously pursued, however, all-embracing interpretations of this character, while serving to rally support, led naturally to the question of whether there were any human activities and organizations which did not need to be examined and recast.')
351 Gündling, *op. cit., supra* n. 347, at pp. 120–1.
352 J. Barros and D. Johnston, *The International Law of Pollution*, New York: Free Press, (1974). ([A] comprehensive definition of pollution is impossible . . .').
353 OECD Council Recommendation on the Implementation of a Regime for Equal Rights of Access and Non-Discrimination in Relation to Transfrontier Pollution, 17 May 1977, reprinted in 16, *ILM* (1977) p. 977. This recommendation is on all fours with previous recommendations of the OECD Council. See, e.g., Council Recommendation of 14 November 1974, reprinted in 14, *ILM* (1975) p. 242.
354 Principle 7, Declaration of the United Nations Conference on the Human Environment, loc. cit., *supra* n. 51.
355 Article I.
356 See, e.g., International Law Association, Montreal Rules of International Law Applicable to Transfrontier Pollution, 4 September 1982, reprinted in Sands, *Chernobyl: Law and Communications*, (1988), pp. 180–1. See also Barros, *op. cit., supra* n. 352, p. 6.

community. The OECD definition takes a bifurcated approach to determining when pollution occurs: one prong is measured in terms of how humans are affected – 'endanger human health', 'reduction of amenities', 'interfere with other legitimate uses'; the other prong identifies aspects of the natural environment which are notionally separate and independent from humans – ecosystems and perhaps flora and fauna.[357] Although there clearly is a wide overlap between environmental damage which has deleterious effects on humans and that which has such effects on nature, one test of environmental harm is essentially 'human-centric' while the other test describes pollution in terms of harm to the environment *qua* nature and is not dependent on showing actual injury to humans or the interests of humans.

This tension in defining environmental damage stems from an underlying conceptual problem which arises from what the 'environment' is and how we define it. If the 'environment' is defined in terms of human relationships to the resources of nature, then the 'environment' becomes a term that simply describes a type of economic resource and environmental damage is simply a calculation of resultant economic and/or social loss arising out of injury to that economic resource. Although there is an undoubted economic dimension to the environment, which is critical to the idea of 'sustainable utilization' upon which much of present environmental law depends,[358] such a 'human-centric' approach puts a single aspect of the environment and its protection into the anomalous position of being the central focus in defining the environment. Furthermore, such a 'human-centric' definition equates one consequence of environmental damage – damage to humans and their interests – as the sole or major determinant of environmental damage. Therefore, it is submitted that for the 'environment' to have any real meaning it must be defined in terms that do not principally rely on humans; thus, the definition must be 'nature-centric' rather than 'human-centric'.

Although both the 'human-centric' and the 'nature-centric' elements can be seen in the Stockholm Declaration and the other quasi-constitutional documents which form the basis of international environmental law,[359] there is one particularly good example in the area of armed conflict which takes a 'nature-centric' approach, the Environmental Modification Convention of 1977 (ENMOD)[360] which seeks to prohibit 'environmental

---

357 The term 'natural resources' is somewhat ambiguous in that it can be viewed either as referencing parts of nature as resources for human use or as a more generic term for e.g. plants and animals. For a discussion of the term 'natural resources' as a human-dependent concept, see L. Caldwell, 'Concepts in Development of International Environmental Policies', in Teclaff, *op. cit., supra* n. 350, pp. 12–24, at pp. 18–19.

358 See, e.g., 'World Conservation Strategy', *IUCN*, 1980; World Council on Environment and Development, *Our Common Future*, Oxford: Oxford University Press, 1987.

359 See, e.g., *ibid.*; Stockholm Declaration; World Charter for Nature, UNGA A/RES/37/7, 1982.

360 16, *ILM* (1977) p. 88. See also Article 55 of Protocol I, which calls for the protection of the natural environment, but does not define the natural environment and states that it includes environmental damage which will cause 'prejudice [to] the health or survival of the population'. This latter point is reinforced by the ICRC *Commentary*: 'The concept of the natural environment should be understood in the widest sense to cover the biological environment in which a population is living.'

modification techniques' of the 'natural processes – the dynamics, composition or structure of the earth, including its biota, lithosphere, hydrosphere and atmosphere, or of outer space'.[361] Thus this approach does not measure environmental degradation in terms of impact on human beings (although humans would clearly benefit from the enforcement of the treaty provisions), but in terms of the elements of the natural environment – water, air, space, seas and living matter, etc. If this approach is married to the special emphasis on biodiversity implicit in the above-discussed pollution definitions and in the Stockholm Declaration and its progeny, we would have a broad definition of the environment with scope to provide special status to biodiversity via a strict approach to ecosystems, habitats and endangered species. Thus, the definition would be constructed along these lines:

> The environment includes the earth and its natural processes, including its biosphere, lithosphere, hydrosphere, atmosphere, outer space and particularly those aspects of its processes which preserve its biodiversity such as its ecosystems and habitats.

What then are the consequences of taking such a 'nature-centric' view of the environment in terms of a convention seeking to protect the environment in armed conflict? Although much will depend on the approach taken on other issues, such as the level at which environmental damage is sufficient to trigger the provisions of the convention, the proposed definition would give scope to address a number of important issues such as global climate change, ozone depletion, endangered species, the effects of defoliants and deliberate oil-spills, as these matters all affect the environment within the ambit of the definition. The definition would also provide the basis for providing special protection for certain ecosystems and habitats. Consideration could be given to absolute protection of certain areas which could be separately designated, e.g. Antarctica. On the other hand, other natural processes could be subject to less demanding standards, through modulation of the level of harm permissible.

Although the definition is undoubtedly broad, there are a number of matters which are excluded by the definition. Since the emphasis is on the natural processes of the earth, there is no scope for protecting aspects of the environment which result from human efforts. For example, culturally important sites and buildings would not come within the purview of the definition; these are protected elsewhere.[362] Furthermore, this definition does not provide protection to the works of humans *per se* such as agriculture works, except coincidentally. Thus, damage to the environment is not predicated on damage to humans or triggered by effects on human health or suffering, nor does damage to other human works or interests

---

361 ENMOD, Article II.
362 See Hague Convention for the Protection of Cultural Property in the Event of Armed Conflict, 1954; Article 53 of Protocol I; and World Heritage Convention, Article 6(3).

necessarily qualify. This is not the result of failure to recognize the link between humans and the environment, but the convention is aimed at a limited target and that target must be kept firmly in focus.

It has been the intention of this paper to forge a definition that is broad enough to include the target of the convention but to exclude those matters which are better dealt with elsewhere. It is submitted that a 'nature-centric' approach will best meet these objectives; it is hoped that the above definition provides a basis for discussion.

APPENDIX 7

Written Comment by Professor Alfred Rubin

Taking environmental threats as equally serious whether in war or peacetime, whether perpetrated by persons acting with a soldier's privileges or for personal gain or even arbitrarily, I suggest that efforts be made to amend article I of the Brussels Convention of 29th November 1969 on Intervention on the High Seas in Case of Oil Pollution Casualties and to delete paragraph 2, that makes the Convention inapplicable to warships and to other ships used for the time on government non-commercial service. The effect would be to authorize intervention on the high seas necessary to prevent, mitigate or eliminate grave and imminent dangers to a coastline or related interests from pollution or threat of pollution of the sea by oil.

If this basic approach were acceptable, then many further steps could be considered to extend the right of intervention to threats from other noxious substances than oil, perhaps based on the terms of the London Protocols to the Convention of 2 November 1973[363] and the International Convention on Oil Pollution Preparedness, Response and Cooperation of 30 November 1990, and threats to other parts of the commons than the seas.

In any event, in order to preserve the basic notion that protection of the environment in the interest of all humanity is consistent with the structure of law designed to confine military action to the parties directly concerned and to minimize its impact on third countries and their interests, I suggest that the right of intervention be overtly labelled a 'neutral' right, to be enjoyed by neutrals regardless of how its enjoyment affects the balance of forces in an armed conflict. Recognizing that such a grant of neutral rights to act in ways that would affect the outcome of an armed conflict could be abused, I argue that all rights can be abused, including the belligerent right to destroy property in ways that impact on neutral third parties. The possibility of abuse of rights I regard as no excuse for inaction along the only lines I see at present as feasible and consistent with the structure of the current world legal order.

---

363 The Protocol Relating to Intervention on the High Seas in Cases of Marine Pollution by Substances other than Oil: IMCO Doc. MP/CONF/WP.35.

APPENDIX 8

Text of Government Proposals made after the Conference:
Jordanian Proposal and Kuwaiti Response; German Proposal

REQUEST FOR THE INCLUSION OF AN ADDITIONAL ITEM IN
THE PROVISIONAL AGENDA OF THE FORTY-SIXTH SESSION

EXPLOITATION OF THE ENVIRONMENT AS A WEAPON IN TIMES
OF ARMED CONFLICT AND THE TAKING OF PRACTICAL
MEASURES TO PREVENT SUCH EXPLOITATION

**Note verbale dated 5 July 1991 from the Chargé d'affaires a.i. of the
Permanent Mission of Jordan to the United Nations addressed to the
Secretary-General**

The Chargé d'affaires a.i. of the Hashemite Kingdom of Jordan to the
United Nations presents his compliments to the Secretary-General of the
United Nations and has the honour to inform him that the Jordanian
Government, in accordance with rule 13 of the rules of procedure of the
General Assembly, would like to propose the inclusion of an item in the
provisional agenda of the forty-sixth General Assembly entitled 'Exploitation of the environment as a weapon in times of armed conflict and the
taking of practical measures to prevent such exploitation'. In accordance
with rule 20 of the rules of procedure, an explanatory memorandum is
annexed to this request.

Annex

Explanatory memorandum

1. In a world where all humanity is ecologically vulnerable, it has become
   evident that warfare is no longer a tenable policy option for civilized
   nations. It is common knowledge that the recent military conflict in the
   Gulf had an impact of tragic proportions on both the people of the
   region and the environment. Scientists have calculated that it will take
   decades to recover from the environmental damage resultant from the
   confrontation. This emphasizes the urgent necessity to prevent any
   further exploitation of the environment as a means of indiscriminate

destruction. The environment must be taken into consideration from the initial stages of conflict decision-making by both politicians and military decision makers. In our approach to the next millennium, it is evident that closer cooperation between all nations is essential if we are to avoid further environmental destruction and conflict. All should realize that environmental degradation is not limited to the confines of any one nation State.

2. The existing 1977 United Nations Convention on the Prohibition of Military or Any Other Hostile Use of Environmental Modification Techniques was revealed as being painfully inadequate during the Gulf conflict. We find that the terms of the existing convention are so broad and vague as to be virtually impossible to enforce. We also find no provision for a mechanism capable of the investigation and settlement of any future disputes under the Convention. Furthermore, the Convention does not provide for advanced environmental scientific data to be made available to all States at the initial stages of crisis prevention.

3. We therefore propose that the General Assembly establish a committee to examine the above-mentioned problems, the committee to submit to the General Assembly, if possible by the forty-seventh session in 1992, proposals for an efficient mechanism to combat the exploitation of the environment in times of armed conflict. We believe that this may lead to the drafting of a new treaty and we trust that any such treaty would give all humanity the confidence to face a more peaceful future. Pending the finalization of any such treaty, we would suggest that all nations should be invited to make unilateral decisions along the lines of the treaty.

4. In recognition of the importance of the free flow of information, we urge the committee to consider the implementation of a United Nations Environmental Data Base as a confidence-building measure and another step towards the international protection of the environment. This would further the precedent recommendations of the Independent Commission on International Humanitarian Issues on the international and institutional framework for disaster management as detailed in their report, first published in 1988, under the apt title of 'Winning the Human Race'.

IRAQI AGGRESSION AND THE CONTINUED OCCUPATION OF KUWAIT IN FLAGRANT VIOLATIONS OF THE CHARTER OF THE UNITED NATIONS

Letter dated 12 July 1991 from the Chargé d'affaires a.i. of the Permanent Mission of Kuwait to the United Nations addressed to the Secretary-General

Upon instructions from my Government, and with reference to the request from the Hashemite Kingdom of Jordan, contained in document A/46/141, to include in the provisional agenda of the forty-sixth session of the General Assembly an item entitled 'Exploitation of the environment as a weapon in times of armed conflict and the taking of practical measures to prevent such exploitation', and the explanatory memorandum annexed to that request, I should like to state that my country welcomes the inclusion of the said item out of our substantial concern and interest in protecting the environment and natural resources, which are the property of the entire mankind, and preventing their use as a weapon of terrorism as we witnessed during the war of Kuwait's liberation.

However, we regrettably notice that in citing the environmental devastation suffered by Kuwait and the region the explanatory memorandum annexed to the request has overlooked the fact that this environmental calamity was not the result of military conflict (as the memorandum says), but was the product of a deliberate act that was planned in the very first days of the brutal Iraqi occupation of Kuwait. Our delegation has already asserted that in its memorandum addressed to Your Excellency on 20 August 1990 (S/21572) when the invading Iraqi forces set out then to mine all the vital Kuwaiti institutions and installations, including the oil facilities, thereby setting the stage to destroy them when the operation of liberating Kuwait begins. That is exactly what occurred, as the vanquished Iraqi forces applied the scorched-land policy by burning more than 700 oil wells, and they also destroyed all the oil refineries and gathering stations as well as the power and water desalinization plants, not to mention the other industrial and civil installations. All that was preceded by flooding several millions of oil barrels into the waters of the Arab Gulf, an act that constituted the most extensive pollution of the marine environment in history.

I should be grateful if you would have this letter circulated as a document of the General Assembly, under agenda item 153, and of the Security Council.

(*Signed*) Mohammad AL SALLAL
Chargé d'affaires a.i.

Statement by Prof. Dr Ansgar O. Vogel, Federal Ministry for the Environment, Nature Protection and Nuclear Safety Germany at the 3rd Session of the UNCED PrepCom, Geneva, 12 August – 4 September 1991: Plenary item 2 (d)

Mr. Chairman,

I would like to draw the attention of the Preparatory Committee to an issue which has already been raised within the United Nations system, especially within the Sixth Committee of the General Assembly and the International Law Commission: the problem of environmental crimes.

As the protection of the environment is of outstanding importance for the earth's ecological balance, we hold the view that massive damage to the environment which may lastingly impair the basis of life on earth must be prevented by all appropriate political and legal means. We are convinced that any wilfully caused massive ecological damage which cannot be justified under international law has to be banned at the international level. The environment must not be used as a weapon or taken hostage, for whatever purpose. This applies not only to times of war, but also to times of peace.

In June 1991, the Soviet and German ministers for environment agreed that this issue should be addressed at the international level and should also be raised in the UNCED process. Subsequently, the ministers presented this idea at the Ministerial Conference 'Environment for Europe' at Dobris Castle, Czech and Slovac Federal Republic (CSFR), this summer.

The German government is preparing an initiative for the forthcoming General Assembly, with the aim that this issue should be dealt with further in the UN System. As you might know, there are other states pursuing similar ideas.

We believe, that the United Nations Conference on Environment and Development with its comprehensive mandate on the issue of Environment and Development will have to express itself on this important question, too.

APPENDIX 9

Bibliography

American Law Institute, *Restatement of the Foreign Relations Law of the United States*, American Law Institute Publishers, St Paul, Minnesota, 1987.

Arkin, W., Durrant, D., Cherni, M., *On Impact: Modern Warfare and the Environment – A Case Study of the Gulf War*, Greenpeace, London, 1991.

Barros, J., Johnston, D., *The International Law of Pollution*, Free Press, New York, 1974.

Bomb and the Law, The, A summary Report of the London Nuclear Warfare Tribunal, Stockholm, Myrdel Foundation, 1989.

Bothe M., Partsch, K., Solf, W. (eds), *New Rules for Victims of Armed Conflicts*, Martinus Nijhoff, Boston, The Hague, London, 1982.

Butler W.E. (ed.) *Control over Compliance with International Law*, Martinus Nijhoff, Dordrecht, Boston, London, 1991.

Falk, R., *Revitalizing International Law*, Ames: Iowa State University Press, 1989.

Falk, R., Kolko, G., Lifton, R., (eds), *Crimes of War*, Random House, New York, 1971.

Golblat, J., Bernauer, T., *The Third Review of the Biological Weapons Convention: Issues and Proposals*, UNIDIR Research Paper No. 9, UNIDIR, Geneva, 1991.

Grob, F., *The Relativity of War and Peace*, New Haven, 1949.

Gündling, L., 'Environment, International Protection', 9 *Encyclopedia of Public International Law*, North-Holland, The Hague, 1986.

Kalshoven, F., *Constraints on the Waging of War*, ICRC, Martinus Nijhoff, Geneva and Leiden, 1987.

McKinnon, M., *Arabia: Sand, Sea, Sky*, BBC Books, London, 1990.

Meyer, M., (ed.), *Armed Conflict and the New Law: Aspects of the 1977 Geneva Protocols and the 1981 Weapons Convention*, British Institute of International and Comparative Law, London 1989.

Miller, A., Feinrider, M., (eds), *Nuclear Weapons and Law*, Greenwood Press, Westport, CT, 1984.

Oppenheim, L., *International Law*, H. Lauterpacht (ed.), 1952.

Roberts, A., Guelff, G., *Documents on the Law of War*, Clarendon Press, Oxford, 2nd edn. 1989.

Sandoz, Y., et al. (eds), ICRC *Commentary on the Additional Protocols of 8 June 1977 to the Geneva Conventions of 12 August 1949*, Martinus Nijhoff, Geneva, 1987.

Sands, P., *Chernobyl: Law and Communications*, Grotius, Cambridge, 1988.

Schneider, J., *World Public Order of the Environment: Towards an International Ecological Law and Organization*, Stevens, London, 1979.

Statement on the Defence Estimates: Britain's Defence for the 90s, HMSO, London, July 1991.

Teclaff, L., Utton, A., (eds), *International Environmental Law*, Praeger, New York, 1974.

UN War Crimes Commission, *History of the United Nations War Crimes Commission and the Development of the Laws of War*, HMSO, London, 1948.

US Department of the Navy, *Annotated Supplement to the Commander's Handbook on the Law of Naval Operations*, NWP 9 (Rev. A), 1989.

US Government Printing Office, *11 Trials of War Criminals before the Nuremberg Military Tribunals under International Law*, No. 10, 1947.

Westing, A., (ed.), *Ecological Consequences of the Second Indochina War*, Stockholm, Almquist & Wiksell, 1976.

Westing, A., (ed.), *Explosive Remnants of War: Mitigating the Environmental Effects*, Taylor & Francis, London and Philadelphia, 1985.

Westing, A., (ed.), *Environmental Hazards of War*, Sage Publications, London, New Delhi, 1990.

World Council on Environment and Development, *Our Common Future*, Oxford University Press, Oxford, 1987.

Yergin, D., *The Prize*, Simon and Schuster, 1991.

APPENDIX 10

Stop Press: Jordanian Draft Resolution and Legal Argument

Request to the Secretary General of the United Nations that the General Assembly of the United Nations should investigate the means to protect the human and natural environment from exploitation as a weapon in times of war, in accordance with the following draft resolution.

The General Assembly,

Alarmed by the extent of damages inflicted upon the human and natural environment, due to the Gulf War of 1991;

Determining that it is therefore in the interests of humanity to be protected from any repetition of such destruction;

Recalling the United Nations 1977 Convention on the Prohibition of Military or Any Other Hostile Use of Environmental Modification Techniques (ENMOD) Convention;

Recalling also the Geneva Protocol I of 1977 on the Protection of Victims of International Armed Conflicts (with particular reference to Articles 35.1, 35.3, 54.2, 55, and 56.1);

Recognizing that the ENMOD Convention was revealed as painfully inadequate during the Gulf Conflict of 1991;

Recognizing also that the restrictions within Protocol I rendered it ineffective during the Gulf Conflict of 1991;

Desiring that the ultimate purpose is to protect the natural environment – specifically in times of war – from both deliberate environmental modification techniques and the detrimental impact on the environment due to any use of conventional and non-conventional arms during hostilities;

1. *Decides*, that ENMOD should be made more comprehensive. Comprehensiveness could be achieved by removing the threshold established, as limited by the terms of 'widespread, long-lasting or severe', and extending its applications to any hostile use of the techniques in question.

2. *Urges*, that all nations should undertake to abstain, not only from environmental modification techniques, but also from the preparations for their use against any state or people; an environmental weapon

knows no boundaries and could strike both combatants and non-combatants in an indiscriminate way. This contravenes the basic rule of international law that requires the protection of the civilian population.

3. *Decides*, that a definitive treaty should encompass all the precedent legislation for environmental protection imbedded in the disparate texts of the various legal treatises.

4. *Resolves*, that the implementation of such an environmental protection treaty should be signed and ratified under the auspices of the United Nations and enacted as other related international conventions are covering the use of nuclear, biological and chemical weapons.

5. *Advises*, that while such issues are under consideration, it would be preferable for all nation states to agree to make a unilateral declaration of their resolve not to exploit the natural environment as a weapon in times of conflict.

6. *Requests* that the Secretary General recommend that a committee be established to examine the above proposals; the Committee to submit their final recommendations to the General Assembly, if possible by the 47th session in 1992.

The Legal Argument for the Initiative Against the Exploitation of the Environment as a Weapon in Times of Armed Conflict as placed before the United Nations General Assembly by the Hashemite Kingdom of Jordan, October 1991

The act of placing an initiative against the exploitation of the environment as a weapon in times of armed conflict before the Assembly of the United Nations for consideration is indicative of two basic truths: (a) the preservation of humanity necessitates the formulation of effective legislative provisions for environmental protection. The legislative process towards safeguarding life can be said to have begun with the Regulations attached to the Hague Convention of 1899 which stated that *'the right of belligerents to adopt means of injuring the enemy is not unlimited'* (Annex to Article XXII); (b) the preservation of humanity necessitates the support of nations for the international bodies that were established to safeguard human rights and world peace in the aftermath of the, formerly, unprecedented scale of human suffering during the two world wars – i.e. the United Nations.

The legal rationale

History has proven that the greatest global efforts for the protection of humanity usually arise in the aftermath of conflict. The 1972 Stockholm Declaration on the Human Environment stated that 'both aspects of man's environment, the natural and the man-made, are essential to his well-being and to the enjoyment of basic human rights, even the right to life itself' (*Preamble Paragraph 1*), specifying that 'Man and his environment must be spared the effects of . . . all . . means of mass destruction. States must strive to reach prompt agreement, in the relevant international organs, on the elimination and complete destruction of such weapons' (*Principle 26*). The 1982 World Charter for Nature gave us another opening with 'every form of life is unique, warranting respect regardless of its worth to man' as a preamble to providing that 'nature shall be secured against degradation caused by warfare or other hostile activities' (*Article V*) and stipulating that 'military activities damaging to nature shall be avoided' (*Article XX*).

Any tracing of the history of environmental legislation leads us to the one conclusion that has grown into human consciousness in the awakened aftermath of every war: humanity and the environment are one and the same; survival is an interdependent issue. In the interest of all humanity the Gulf war of 1991 must provide us with yet another, and perhaps the strongest, incentive for protecting the human and natural environment from the ill effects of future conflict. It may well go down in history as the war that most vividly brought the dangers of environmental devastation to life. Before the Gulf war it was a matter of disastrous incidents like Chernobyl, Three Mile Island, the Exxon Valdez, Bhopal, Seveso and our historic memories of the atom bomb over Hiroshima and Nagasaki, which all rank in ecological as well as human loss and destruction. The environmental damages wrought by the Gulf war – which are of tragic proportions – may take decades to recover from and the degradation is not limited to any single state's boundaries. Any future repetition of the exploitation of the environment as a weapon in times of war could signify economic, demographic and ecological catastrophes of an unprecedented global dimension.

It took 78 years after the Hague Convention of 1899 for the Convention on the Prohibition of Military or any other Hostile Use of Environmental Modification Techniques (ENMOD) to provide us with the following more definitive legal provision for environmental protection: 'Each State Party to this Convention undertakes not to engage in military or any other use of environmental modification techniques having *widespread, long-lasting or severe* effects as the means of destruction, damage or injury to any other State Party' (*Article 1.1*) as signed at Geneva on 18 May 1977. The ENMOD Convention entered into force on 5 October 1978 as a result of several years of bilateral Soviet–US talks and multilateral talks convened at the Geneva Conference of the Committee on Disarmament (CCD) which lead to the Four Understandings of the 1976 Conference of the Committee on Disarmament by which 'widespread, long-lasting or severe' were interpreted as follows:

(a) 'widespread': encompassing an area on the scale of several hundred square kilometres;
(b) 'long-lasting': lasting for a period of months, or approximately a season;
(c) 'severe': involving serious or significant disruption or harm to human life, natural and economic resources or other assets.

While ENMOD has many basic flaws, the Geneva Protocol I is bound by restrictions: in either case they have proved unacceptable to one or the other of the major powers – and therefore are equally unrestrictive of any new power groupings that may arise with time in one of the world's many developing trouble spots. Therefore, it is unfortunate that ENMOD never acquired sufficient status to be binding under international law, specifically among states that have not ratified it – and though it dealt with changes in the environment brought about by 'deliberate human manipulation of natural processes', it left many gaps in the definition of what could be termed 'deliberate'. Covert hostile operations, using environmental modification techniques – releasing an insect or disease against the crops or population of another state – would be almost impossible to verify as 'deliberate' manipulation of natural processes.

ENMOD thus remains indefinite as it could ironically be interpreted to condone 'benign' means of manipulating the environment. This ambiguity is dangerously open to interpretation. While ENMOD applies to 'hostile' uses (by military or non-military personnel) that cause destruction, damage or injury at the described thresholds (*widespread, long-lasting or severe*), non-hostile uses of modification techniques, even if destructive, and/or hostile uses with a destructive impact below the stated thresholds are still unprovided for. Even though the destruction of oil wells and/or deliberate oil spills are not explicitly covered, they should qualify as '*widespread, long-lasting or severe*' damages.

ENMOD does not address conventional acts of warfare that could result in adverse effects on the environment as covered in the Geneva Protocol I of 1977 (*opened for signature at Berne on 12 December 1977 and entered into force on 7 December 1978*) that provided for the protection of victims of international armed conflicts. This more comprehensive protection for civilians provided a necessary development of the original, open-ended, 1949 Geneva Convention IV Relative to the Protection of Civilian Persons in Time of War that left the issue of what could constitute '*military necessity*' open.

The interpretations of the legislative restrictions on '*military necessity*' have been the major bone of contention between nations in time of armed conflict since then. To date, the laws governing armed conflict have been, somewhat ineffectually, used to ensure some degree of humanitarian conduct during war rather than to prevent warfare in itself. The fact remains that there are very few outright or unconditional prohibitions on the conduct of armed conflict. The St. Petersburg Declaration of 1868, stated that 'the only legitimate object which states should endeavour to accomplish during war is to weaken the military force of the enemy' and has often been used in statements designed to allay fears of the impact of large-scale military intervention on the civilian population of any given country.

Environmental protection is treated, at least in part, by a number of legislative texts. It may be claimed that all the related protective principles, including article 35 of the Geneva Protocol I that gave us 'in any armed conflict, the right . . . to choose methods or means of warfare is not unlimited' (Article 35.1) and 'it is prohibited to employ methods or means of warfare which are intended, or may be expected, to cause widespread, long term and severe damage to the natural environment' (Article 35.3) are subject to the principle of military necessity. Furthermore, while Article 55 provided that 'care shall be taken in warfare to protect the natural environment against widespread, long-term and severe damage . . .' (Article 55.1), this gives no absolute protection and still leaves us open to the quandary of evasions on the interpretation of the declared thresholds.

Experts acknowledge that international law provides scant protection at present, leaving all that is open to interpretation as militarily permissible with great leeway. While the Hague and Geneva Conventions and Protocols do regulate the conduct of war and protect the natural environment to some extent, many major countries, such as some of those that formed the coalition during the Gulf war are not a party to the Additional Protocol I to the Geneva Conventions, but subscribe to the concept of military necessity. Furthermore, while some of the major powers do accept the prohibition of the deliberate starvation of civilians and the intentional destruction of crops, livestock and other objects indispensable to civilian survival and accept the protection of 'drinking water installations' this does not extend to the destruction of support installations that could result in the secondary effect, allowing for the destruction of power grids, transport and telecommunications networks. Attacks on facilities that could be said to contain 'dangerous forces' are also open to being interpreted as military targets.

The Gulf war has elevated environmental destruction into a weapon for acts of war or retaliation. The inadequacy of the traditional and conventional laws of war which focus on humanitarian conduct without restricting war in itself highlighted the whole question of relative force. Such gaps should be used to create more comprehensive prohibitions on environmental damage and the protection of civilian support systems. Wartime destruction of civil installations for the generation of electricity, oil supply, roads and bridges and industrial research and production has had a severe impact on the civilian capacity to sustain modern life. All that was essential to survival and therefore restricted from attack – including medical care, safe water and food – was disabled by military attack, as inseparable from the facilities supporting the military establishment. The intense media coverage of the Gulf war also brought public opinion into play on what could be termed as acceptable behaviour in times of war as never before. It has now became an inescapable fact that non-combatants are no longer safeguarded in modern warfare, regardless of the niceties of the standard laws on armed conflict. There are no boundaries to state-of-the-art destruction.

In future, regional bodies to control monitoring and verification activities should be created, giving priority to the array of confidence-building measures, that would include information exchange, crisis management/prevention. The threat of future developments in or possession of modification techniques must be covered, and applied to any hostile uses, or preparations for the same, against any state or people (ENMOD confines itself to injuries to given state parties – leaving the whole issue of intra-national damages open while Protocol II of 1977 only deals with 'objects necessary for the survival of the civilian population' in Article 14, and attacks that 'may cause the release of dangerous forces and consquent severe losses among the civilian population' in Article 15). Verification measures should also be made to cover all research and development activities related to environmental or geophysical modification, including those affecting weather, climate, earthquake and the ocean.

No scope for subjective judgements can be allowed. There are many discrepancies in the perceptions of rational behavior among states – in both covert or overt operations against the population and resources of another – and the finer legal points of treaties will not protect us from the differing perceptions of the varying interests of national survival. The rational environment that would be the best safeguard can only be approached through continuous verification measures. Universal and equitable verification measures are a principal tool in allaying the fears and suspicions of states that could otherwise escalate into conflict. Any new Convention protecting the environment in times of war should include the right to inspect all research, development, production and possession of environmental modification techniques and related fields. The issue here is in the greater threat of *ad hoc* aberrations, as opposed to continuous compliance. Under the current provisions, a complaint has to be filed prior to any monitoring or inspection. This has proved inadequate.

Recommendations:

1. Establish an International Environmental Data Base The initial studies undertaken on the environmental damages of the Gulf war clearly indicated a wide discrepancy in global perception. Particular reference is made to the studies that predicted that damage to the Kuwait oil fields would be negligible and the consequences of any such damage dismissible. Diverse assessments of the long-term environmental consequences of the Gulf war have also been very contradictory and not much clarified by highly conflicting press reports. The establishment of the proposed international environmental data base would create a repository for the accumulation and dissemination of the relevant – and scientifically accurate – data that can provide the key to responsible global decision making in times of crisis.

2. Establish an Environmental Crisis Management System The rapid supply of the correct environmental data is essential in mobilizing global efforts to rectify any future environmental disaster, particularly of this scale.

One only has to review the number of contradictory views on the amount of damage caused by the oil fires to realize the extent of discrepancy, even among the reports of the teams that actually undertook field surveys of post-war Kuwait. This failure emphasizes the need for the establishment of an independent system that can provide rapid assessments of global environmental crises and mobilize international resources to combat them efficiently.

Within this system, a committee of international experts may be formed upon request (under the Additional Protocol I to the Geneva Conventions, Article 90; and under the four Geneva Conventions of 1949: No. I, Article 52; No. II, Article 53; No. III, Article 132; No. IV, Article 149 as well as under Articles IV and V and the Annex of ENMOD) for the purposes of:

(i) fact-finding towards the formation of expert views on problems raised by the Party requesting the service.

(ii) the consultative committee, as a body *would not be entitled to pass judgement on whether a violation has occurred* or on who has committed it, or to formulate recommendations.

(iii) the *political decision* that a party has been harmed or 'is likely to be harmed' as a result of a violation of the ENMOD Convention, including the determination of culpability, will be *the prerogative of the UN Security Council.*

3. The recognition of environmental consequences at the initial stages of decision making in times of crisis The scientific assessment of the potential environmental consequences of any given act in times of conflict should be introduced at the initial stages of relevant decision making – as expressed by His Majesty King Hussein, before the Gulf War of 1991, in his address to the Second World Climate Conference held in Geneva in November 1990. While such issues are under consideration, it would be advisable for all nation states to agree to make a unilateral declaration of their resolve not to exploit the natural environment as a weapon in times of conflict.

Although all international conflicts are best resolved by pacific means, humanity and nation-states have, regrettably, not arrived at this level of civilization as yet. Therefore, at least some contingency plans to deal with any of the environmental aftermath of disasters as rapidly as possible should be drawn up in advance.

4. The prohibition of environmental modification techniques should be made more comprehensive. This could be achieved by removing the thresholds established by the ENMOD Convention, as limited by the terms of 'widespread, long-lasting or severe'. The Convention should be made applicable to any hostile use of the techniques in question.

5. Parties should undertake to abstain, not only from environmental modification techniques, but also from preparations for such use.

6. It would be desirable to prohibit the hostile use of modification techniques against any state or people, instead of confining the ban, as ENMOD does, to injuries to parties; an environmental weapon knows no boundaries and could strike both combatants and non-combatants in an indiscriminate way. This contravenes the basic rule of international law that requires the protection of the civilian population.

7. To ensure the survival of humanity, we hope for the implementation of a definitive environmental protection treaty to be signed and ratified under the auspices of the United Nations and enacted as other related international conventions are – covering the use of nuclear, biological and chemical weapons. Such a treaty should encompass all the precedent legislation for environmental protection imbedded in the disparate texts of the

various legal treatises that dealt with the issue of environmental protection
from 1899 to date, once and for all. The ultimate purpose is to protect the
global environment, specifically in times of war, from both deliberate
environmental manipulation techniques and the detrimental impact on the
environment due to any use of conventional and non-conventional arms
during hostilities.

Conclusion

Jordan has always tried to span the expanse between the interests of rapid
and equitable global development and the humanitarian ideals that could
ensure human survival. This initiative for environmental protection is put
forth to this assembly of nations in that vein. We consider it to be crucial
to take action now as it has become universally evident that the Gulf
conflict of 1991 has had a tragic impact on the environment of that region
as well as grave and wide-ranging, and yet, unacknowledged global implications.

It must also be increasingly obvious to all nations that the exploitation
of the environment in times of conflict is a matter of intensified urgency
due to the alarming improvement of the technical and logistical abilities
available to armed forces matched by a dangerous accumulation of the
environmental stress due to rapid and often unregulated industrialization
worldwide – along with the related socio-economic strains of such forced
development trends. To this scenario must be added the environmental
stresses of the growing numerical mass of often deprived humanity.

The lasting heritage of the 1991 Gulf War must be reaped in the form
of strengthened and more comprehensive legal restraints on the disruption
of the environment, particularly in times of armed hostilities. Public
opinion, fuelled by the intensive media coverage of this landmark war, can
also be put to work in support of such restraints – in all cases of man
against man and man against nature that they may be more widely adopted
and respected by all Nation-States.

Commentary Glen Plant

Since the time of writing Chapter 12 I have been supplied with a copy of
the Jordanian draft UN resolution and accompanying 'Legal Argument'
dated October 1991. These have been prepared in the light of the Kuwaiti
letter of 12 July and of a more recent Iraqi response to the proposal, as
well as informal consultations with other states. A statement introducing
these will be made at the start of a two day debate in the UN Sixth
Committee by the Jordanian Representative on 22 October. Since the draft
resolution and legal argument introduce several matters significantly
different from the content of the original Jordanian Note Verbale of 5 July,
discussed in Chapter 12, it seems appropriate to reproduce them here and
to discuss them briefly in this additional, 'stop press' appendix.

It is important to stress that, while several of the recommendations made
in the Legal Argument are reflected in the draft resolution, four are not.

These are Recommendations 1 to 3 and the additional, rather broad recommendation on p. 274 that '[a]ny new Convention protecting the environment in times of war should include the right to inspect all research, development, production and possession of environmental modification techniques and related fields.' Recommendation 1 repeats and elaborates upon the Note Verbale's call for an international environmental data base, and Recommendations 2 and 3 call for an environmental crisis management system and the recognition of the potential environmental consequences of war at the initial stage of decision-making on the eve of war. This failure to reflect them in the text of the draft resolution is not, however, intended to diminish their importance, but is the result of a recognition, derived from the informal consultations with other states, that they raise important additional financial and institutional questions.[364]

The Draft Resolution

The draft resolution is best seen as a procedural resolution. Its sponsor wishes to avoid a resolution condemning Iraq for its actions in the Gulf War and wishes to look to the future by reexamining ENMOD and Protocol I during the coming year to see what improvements can be made, first in a Red Cross committee of experts established at the XXVIth Congress in Budapest and then back in the UN itself.[365]

Nevertheless, there appear to be several substantive proposals, the most significant of which is the call for a 'definitive treaty' concerning environmental protection in wartime, which places the Jordanian Government squarely in Camp 3 of my putative four Camps.

The text of the draft resolution is most clearly understood if it is read with the Legal Argument, and in particular with Recommendations 4 to 7.

The effect of operative paragraph 1 of the draft resolution, when read with the Legal Argument, would appear to be to prohibit uses of environmental modification techniques for any hostile purpose, including intra-, as well as inter-, state uses, however small their impacts.

Since such techniques as presently defined are rarely likely to be used in practice, it is difficult to see how this would have much practical impact. A clue to the real intention of this paragraph is perhaps, however, derived from the Legal Argument, which states: 'the destruction of oil wells . . . should qualify as "*widespread, long-lasting or severe*' damages (sic)'. If ENMOD is thus qualified, it is likely to have real applications in future conflicts.

---

364 Telephone conversation with Dr. Abdullah Toukan, 22 October 1991.
365 Ibid.

The following paragraph can also be criticised on the ground that it is unlikely to have significant practical impact; if adopted, it would also seem to necessitate the adoption of the means of verification mentioned above (at p. 274).

Operative paragraphs 3 and 4 call for a new UN treaty which would draw together all the relevant 'precedent legislation'. This seems to imply consolidation in a single instrument of not merely all generally accepted treaty provisions but also of those relevant provisions in treaties, such as Protocol I, which are not generally accepted as customary law. In addition, it seeks to extend the application of those provisions to non-conventional weapons. This is thus a radical proposal unlikely to succeed as it stands.

The Legal Argument

It is not possible in the space available to give a detailed commentary upon this lengthy document. I will concentrate, therefore, on Recommendations 1 to 3.

The establishment of an international environmental data base, which would apparently be accessible to major decision makers is a laudable aim. Nevertheless, Recommendation 1 is short on the detail of who would establish and maintain the data base, what existing sources of data might be called upon and how this ambitious and expensive task would be likely to be financed. It would require the collection and dissemination of environmental data on an unprecedented scale and would, nevertheless, supply no guarantee of scientific consensus on the environmental impact of a given military action.

Recommendation 2 seems essentially to be a call to use the recently established Fact-Finding Commission under Article 90 of Protocol I for environmental fact-finding purposes. In addition, it seeks to reserve the determination whether or not a Party to ENMOD has been or is likely to be harmed by a violation of that Convention to the UN Security Council, calling this a 'political', rather than a judicial, decision. This would appear to involve authorising the Council to give authoritative interpretations of the Convention, even where a breach of it does not constitute a threat to international peace and security. It would thus increase the competence of the Council in relation to environmental matters, albeit that in practice few instances, if any, are likely to arise. The reference to 'culpability' might well be suggestive of a repetition of the responsibility-fixing and compensation-determining exercise carried out in pursuance of Article 678 following the Gulf War.

Finally, Recommendation 3 is unimpeachable, although it is unlikely that agreement could be reached on the placing of any constraints upon existing rights to resort to force merely on the grounds of the potential environmental consequences arising from the commencement of the outbreak of hostilities, which was the concern of many anti-Gulf War campaigners following King Hussein's speech at the Second World Climate Conference in November 1990, which is referred to in the Recommendation.

21 October 1991

Index

Note: Numbers in bold indicate entries most significant to provisions and resolutions.